The Irish-American
Athletic Club
of New York

ALSO BY PATRICK R. REDMOND

*The Irish and the Making of American Sport,
1835–1920* (McFarland, 2014)

The Irish-American Athletic Club of New York

The Rise and Fall of the Winged Fists, 1898–1917

PATRICK R. REDMOND

McFarland & Company, Inc., Publishers
Jefferson, North Carolina

ISBN (print) 978-1-4766-7239-7
ISBN (ebook) 978-1-4766-3162-2

LIBRARY OF CONGRESS CATALOGUING DATA ARE AVAILABLE

BRITISH LIBRARY CATALOGUING DATA ARE AVAILABLE

© 2018 Patrick R. Redmond. All rights reserved

No part of this book may be reproduced or transmitted in any form or by any means, electronic or mechanical, including photocopying or recording, or by any information storage and retrieval system, without permission in writing from the publisher.

Front cover: John Jacob Eller wins the 120-yard high hurdles at the Met Championships at Celtic Park in Queens, New York, on September 16, 1911 (Library of Congress)

Printed in the United States of America

McFarland & Company, Inc., Publishers
Box 611, Jefferson, North Carolina 28640
www.mcfarlandpub.com

To my wife
Claudia Redmond

Table of Contents

Acknowledgments ix

Preface 1

1. The "staid" and the "poor man's" Athletic Clubs 7
2. "For the encouragement of manly sports and exercises … of the Irish-American Athlete": The First and Second I-AAC 15
3. "The 'Mecca' of attraction for every proud son and fair daughter of Erin": The Building of Celtic Park 21
4. "Our name is the Irish-American Athletic Club": The I-AAC and Other Ethnicities 36
5. "An overwhelming success numerically and financially": Establishing the GNYIAA Between 1898 and 1904 51
6. "A roistering carefree set of hellions": The Irish Immigrant Athlete and the I-AAC 64
7. "The banner organization of the United States": St. Louis and Onwards, 1904–1906 74
8. "The social element in Clubs is like 'dry rot'": Snobbery and the American Athletic Club 88
9. "The first, if not the foremost, athletic club in the world": The I-AAC Between 1906 and 1908 100
10. "If you see an Irish head, hit it": The I-AAC and Accusations of Professionalism 118
11. "You carry the Stars and Stripes proudly!" The I-AAC Athletes at the 1908 Olympics 137

12. "Blood stirred by its games and sports": The I-AAC
    and Promoting Irish Sport and Identity in America   158
13. "Condemned for wholesale proselyting": The I-AAC
    Growth Between 1908 and 1912   168
14. "Such shameful spectacles would never be permitted in
    pious New York": The I-AAC: Policemen, Politicians
    and Sabbatarians   187
15. "In spite of depressing conditions": The Beginning of
    the End of the I-AAC (1912–1916)   206
16. "Service first, athletics afterward": The I-AAC
    Finally Closes   230
17. "Perhaps we shall again see the day"   244

Glossary of Athletic Events   253
Appendix: Irish-American Athletic Club Team Honors   257
Chapter Notes   258
Bibliography   279
Index   283

Acknowledgments

Writing any book requires the help of a number of sources, organizations and individuals, and this book is no different. Therefore I would like to thank firstly the vast numbers of online resources on the internet that make any such project easier to create than it would have been 20 to 30 years ago. As in my previous book, my first thanks goes to the internet creator, Timothy Berners Lee. Cyberspace is criticized by many for propagating "fake news" and conspiracy theories, but it is also a force for good and education.

In connection to this, I'd like to thank the excellent resources of information that were invaluable to researching this book: the *New York Times* online news archive; the ProQuest Archiver stable of newspaper archives; LA84foundation.org, which hosts most of the editions of *Sporting Life* and *Outing*; the British Newspaper Archive; the Library of Congress' Chronicling America (*New York Herald, Tribune, The Sun, The Evening World*) and its online photographic archive, Genealogy Bank; the *Sports Illustrated* vault; and Google News. Other web-sources on this subject include the Winged Fist Organization (www.wingedfist.org), the only online website dedicated to the memory of the Irish-American Athletic Club.

Elsewhere, I would like to thank the British Newspaper Library of Colindale, London, which is no longer with us, and which has moved to the British Library at St. Pancras in central London. I didn't think that the facilities or the staff would be as good as they were in Colindale, but I've been gladdened by what I've seen and that the new library's research equipment is indeed better, while the staff are equally as charming. I would also like to say thanks to my *alma mater*, the University of North London (now Metropolitan University of London). Sadly no longer a center of Irish studies, its library is a shadow of what it was. It still has a substantial section on Irish history, literature and social studies, and to this I would also thank them for their help.

Once again I would like to thank Peter Carbery, the former editor of the *Daily Star on Sunday* (London) whom I first met many years ago while he was working for the newspaper *London Irish News* and who got my first way into writing articles while he was with *The Irish Post* [London]. Also I would like to thank former editors of the *Irish Post*, Martin Doyle, now books editor with *The Irish Times*, and the late Donal Mooney. I would also like to thank all the staff at McFarland & Company, Inc., Publishers, for their assistance in getting this work printed.

Finally I would like to thank my fantastic family. Without his pride and knowledge of his country and its history, especially during the "troubles" of the 1970s and 1980s living in England, I would never have been interested in Irish history and therefore Irish-American sport without my father, John. I'd also like to thank my mother, Maria, for all the help that she gave me to allow me the time to research and write this book. I would also like to thank my children, Sean, Shannen and Eléna, for their support. Finally, I could never have written one let alone two books and these acknowledgments without the help and support from my wonderfully charming, intelligent and beautiful wife, Claudia. As I have said before, it was her perseverance and encouragement in getting me to get the best out of my brain that pushed me into university and eventually onto writing. I am eternally thankful for her support in creating this book. It is therefore fitting that as we met each other in New York just over 30 years ago, and that I am writing about an Irish athletic club from the Big Apple, I dedicate this book to her.

I hope this work will bring entertainment, amusement, education and interest to all that read it. As usual, any mistakes found are all mine, and I would be pleased to hear any feedback.

Preface

I can't exactly remember the day that I first read anything about the Irish-American Athletic Club, but I believe it was somewhere around the mid-'90s when I was preparing an idea for my BA dissertation at university. I wanted to do my thesis on the history of the Irish in American sport, but such was the scale and complexity of the subject, in the end I could only concentrate on one aspect of it, settling on their role in prizefighting instead. However, while reading one of the books I had picked up, *City Games*, by Steven A. Riess, I saw that Riess writes of this hitherto unheard-of club. I had heard of the Fightin' Irish (complete with its trademark missing "g") of Notre Dame, and I had even written an article for the London-based Irish community newspaper, *The Irish Post*, on the Boston Celtics. But who were the "Greater New York Irish Athletic Club" Riess mentions?

After many years of research for my book *The Irish and the Making of American Sport: 1835–1920*, I found that this club was no mere local outfit serving the young Irish males of a portion of New York City. It was instead one of greatest athletic clubs either America or indeed the world had ever seen. Indeed, this club was special in other ways: Riess claims in *City Games* that it had granted two Jewish athletes, Meyer Prinstein and Abel Kiviat, who had been previously barred from joining the New York Athletic Club (Kiviat never bothered applying), membership. As I delved more, this club became unique in that the number of non–Irish athletes, Irish or American-born, were almost outnumbered by those from other ethnicities, including the odd African American.

Riess' misnamed "Greater New York Irish Athletic Club" was an amalgamation of two names. From 1898 to 1905, this Irish athletic organization operated under the name of the Greater New York Irish Athletic Association. Then it took the name of two nineteenth-century New York athletic clubs with the identical title, changing to the snappier Irish-American Athletic Club. By then the club was already the champions of American athletics, and would within three years "conquer the world" with 11 gold medals at the 1908 Olympic Games in London.

This book is not only a history of the club's existence, both its "Rise" and its "Fall." It aims to bring in a number of elements that forged the club's identity—immigration, ethnic nationalism, discrimination, class and education—and other matters that infected American society in general during its life—amateurism, politics, and "Sabbatarianism." The book covers the athletic achievements of the club and its athletes, but also wants to highlight the challenges that faced any American athletic club—especially one run for the benefit of a single ethnic minority, with a majority of athletes and members of limited education and means of financial support—as the nineteenth century turned into the twentieth.

Chapter 1 is an introduction to the book. It begins at the New York Athletic Club in 2012, when the club was hit by scandal, and argues that the NYAC is defined as a "staid" club, a snooty home for the wealthy and privileged who can afford their high fees and have the connections to gain membership. I bring the I-AAC into the chapter, describing what kind of club the I-AAC was and how it contrasted sharply with what we know of the NYAC. Chapter 2 speaks about the Irish athletic scene in New York City before the GNYIAA/I-AAC was formed in 1898. Here I chronicle the role of the two brief "Irish-American Athletic Clubs." When the third I-AAC was founded, the club initially operated under the title of the Greater New York Irish Athletic Association, changing its name to the Irish-American Athletic Club in February 1905, in what I argue was an attempt to capitalize on this previous heritage. Chapter 3 covers the construction of the I-AAC's home, Celtic Park, located in then-rural Queens in 1898. The I-AAC's stadium provided not only the main center for the club's activities and events, but a home for most Irish sporting activities and major events and gatherings in the city. Here I outline the resentment that this perceived monopoly had within the rival Irish Counties Athletic Union (ICAU). I also list other properties owned by the I-AAC, mainly its midtown Manhattan homes. Although purchased ostensibly for indoor recreational purposes, these were also declarations of intent, as the club tried to compete with the NYAC for prestige, rather than just membership numbers.

Chapter 4 describes how the club made the decision to seek athletes and members from outside New York's Irish community. It lists many of its "non-Irish" competitors, including "big-name" foreign athletes who would compete for the I-AAC while on sabbatical to the U.S., mostly following the 1908 Olympics. Particular coverage is given to the club's Jewish and African American sportsmen, who were crucial to cementing a club reputation that stated clearly that it welcomed all the city's sportsmen regardless of race, religion or ethnic origin (women weren't allowed to compete as athletes, as the AAU did not recognize them until shortly after the death of its long-serving head, James E. Sullivan, in 1914). Chapter 5 chronicles the first five years of the club as it tried to establish itself amongst the nation's major clubs. Initially the I-AAC supplied few athletes to its meetings, making money instead from hiring out Celtic Park to other clubs and Irish societies hosting "picnics" and other assorted events. Later the GNYIAA/I-AAC also took a chance on resurrecting indoor athletics in the city at Madison Square Garden, successfully bringing in crowds and convincing the Amateur Athletic Union to introduce regional and national Indoor Championships at the same venue. Chapter 6 looks at the Irish athletes who migrated to America and eventually joined the club. Particular emphasis is placed on the renowned "Irish Whales" group of field athletes who were the backbone of the club for many years.

Chapter 7 begins with the first of ten national championships that the club won over a 12-year period. It covers the period between 1904—including that year's Olympics in St. Louis—to the eve of the Intercalated Olympic Games in Athens two years later. While declining to defend its first National title in 1905, the I-AAC finally consolidated its place as New York City's, and the country's top athletic club during these two years. Chapter 8 deals with the club's significant rivalry with the New York Athletic Club. It illustrates how athletic clubs—not just the NYAC, but also the Knickerbocker and Manhattan Athletic Clubs and numerous elitist clubs in the country's other major cities—had morphed from a group of similarly-minded men seeking sporting distraction into organizations hell-bent on exclusion and snobbery, where athletics was little more than a side-show. I also write here about how the "upstarts" of the I-AAC's dismantling of the NYAC's supremacy of national amateur athletics led to their rivals beginning a campaign of accusations against the club of underhand practices to win events. Chapter 9 covers the club's athletes at the 1906 Olympics and the period between Athens and the 1908 Olympics in London. This includes the growing accusations of "professionalism" at the club, principally by the NYAC, which led to one of the club's major stars, Mel Sheppard, being denied a place on the U.S. athletic team that traveled to Greece.

Chapter 10 discusses the subject of amateurism and the impact that accusations of professionalism, excessive expenses, "stock watches" and other forms—alleged or real—of rule-breaking had on the club's reputation. Coverage is also given to how this impacted the I-AAC's other sports, principally ice hockey. Chapter 11 covers the events surrounding the 1908 Olympics in London. Here I define the role that I-AAC athletes and officials played in what became an acrimonious two weeks that were infamous for the battles the U.S. Olympic team had with British officials, referees and umpires over a number of decisions. It also highlights how the I-AAC's relations were strained from the start when the NYAC official—and scourge of the I-AAC regarding accusations of professionalism—Matt Halpin was originally announced as coach. I detail how club pressure finally forced his removal from the role of U.S. coach at the Olympics in favor of Mike C. Murphy. Chapter 12 covers the club's involvement in promoting and defending Irish identity in New York City. This ranged from picketing theatres performing plays deemed detrimental to the Irish to the resurrection of the so-called "Irish Olympics," the Tailteann Games, at Celtic Park on Labor Day. It also covers the club's relations with "Old-World" political groups such as Clan na Gael and the Ancient Order of Hibernians and how the club helped in aiding fund-raising for nationalist militaristic causes in Ireland.

Chapter 13 depicts the club's life between 1908 and 1912, including the success in attracting to the club a number of foreign athletes who had traveled to America after competing in London. In Chapter 14, I recount the close connections between the I-AAC and the NYPD, local judiciary and politicians. I also talk about the I-AAC's battle against "Sabbatarianism" that was impeding on the club's sporting business. As Sunday was the only day of the week that the club could make optimum use of crowd attendance, with Gaelic sports traditionally having been played on the Sabbath, I chronicle the lengths the club went to in the battle against the "Blue Laws" that harassed its activities.

Chapter 15 details the period from 1912 to 1917, the beginning of the end of the Irish-American Athletic Club. 1912 was the last time that its athletes would compete at an Olympic Games and the years following witnessed the club begin to lose various crucial members either to retirement or rivals. Chapter 16 delves into the circumstances that led to the club eventually folding. America's entry into World War I was seen only as a temporary measure, but a lack of clarity from the club's hierarchy to almost everyone entailed that the club would lose its athletes not only to the U.S. Army but to other clubs. Also the I-AAC was hit in March 1918 by the devastating news that its most prominent athlete, Martin Sheridan, had been killed by "Spanish 'flu." Celtic Park would also eventually become tainted by various problems associated with the illegal sale of alcohol following Prohibition, including riots and shootings. It would lose its place as the home for the city's Gaelic games before the end of the '20s and briefly survived only on the profits from greyhound racing. With a rapidly expanding city, the club came under fierce pressure to sell Celtic Park to developers and eventually to dissolve itself. Chapter 17 is the concluding chapter or epilogue, and summarizes what happened in the years to New York athletics following the death of the I-AAC. Particular emphasis is placed on how the NYAC, regaining its ascendancy in the city if not the country, becoming known as an "Irish" club, but not one that gave a hundred—let alone a thousand—welcomes to its neighbors in the Big Apple, but a club which was seen as continuing to keep out not just ethnic minority members, but also its own working-class constituency.

Notes on Times, Distances and Abbreviations

With regards to the abbreviations for the Greater New York Athletic Club (GNYIAA) and its name change in 1905 to the Irish-American Athletic Club (I-AAC), I have used the GNYIAA when talking about specific events about the club between the GNYIAA's founding in 1898 and name-change in 1905. In contrast, I have either used the abbreviation GNYIAA/I-AAC or just I-AAC when relating to anything concerning the club in general from 1898 through to the present day.

For record distances I have used a system that lists feet, inches and fractions of inches in distance. Thus 100.1.375 translates to 100 feet, 1⅜ inches. Record times are presented in hours, minutes, seconds and fractions of seconds. A complicating factor when it comes to time is that a century ago, races were measured in fifths of seconds, while today it is in tenths.

When mentioning record times and distances, I have used a system that lists feet, inches and fractions of inches in distance, and hours, minutes, seconds and fractions of seconds as times. Thus 100.1.05 translates as 100 feet, one and a half inches. A similar distance in meters would be 101.1.05, which is one hundred and one meters, one and a half centimeters. Similarly, a reading of 1:10:10:04 means one hour, ten minutes, ten and two fifths seconds.

For athletic categories, yards are listed as "Yds," so the 220-yard dash becomes the 220Yds. Quarter and Half-Mile runs are listed as 440Yds and 880Yds unless in quotes, while meters are listed as "m," hence 200m, 400m, 800m, 1500m. Miles are written as 1Mile for the one-mile run, 2Mile for the two-mile run, etc. Abbreviations are also used for athletic categories. LB indicates the weight in "pounds," so the 56LB Weight means the 56-pound weight. Also, BJ means Broad Jump or the modern-day Long Jump. HSJ is short for Hop, Step and Jump, or the modern-day Triple Jump.

Team points in Championships (Metropolitan and National) ran by the AAU, and indeed in most meetings, would carry five points for first place, three for second place and one for third place: The club accumulating the most points won the team title. However, in events such as the 10-Mile and Cross-Country Championships, it is the team with the fewest points that wins. This system is based on points accumulated by the team—often a five-man side—on the places they secure in the race. For instance if team "A" comes in the first five places it will accumulate one point for first, two for second and so on, accumulating fifteen points altogether. If team "B" takes places six to ten, it will get six points for sixth place, seven for seventh, and so on, and will acquire 40 points in total. Therefore team A beats team B by 15 points to 40.

The I-AAC in its three different guises also played a number of team sports unrelated to track and field events. The main ones were soccer, lacrosse, ice hockey, hurling and Gaelic football. With the first three sports, the numbering system of the final score registers the number of "goals," all of which are scored by the ball going into a framed net called a "goal." With Gaelic football and hurling, goals are also counted, but the scoring system has two numbers for each team: The first figure counts the number of goals scored, as in soccer or ice hockey, while the second figure is the amount of times the ball is kicked over the crossbar but between the posts, similar to a "PAT" dropkick in a Football game. Scores, while written in such a manner, are still counted by adding the number goals, which count as three points, to the number of kicks over the crossbar, which count as one point: The winning team is therefore the one with the most combined points, no matter how many, or few, "goals" are scored. If the final score between team "A" and team "B" were 3–1 to 0–11, we see team A has scored three goals and one ball over the bar which culminates in ten points. However it loses to team B, who despite not scoring any goals, is victorious as it has accumulated eleven points solely through kicks over the crossbar, thus beating team A by one point.

Finally, there is the issue of event records, of which there were three types: Those that were universally recognized events that would be run at Metropolitan or National AAU championships, and would be both U.S. and World records and reported as such. Then there were those events that were part-distance or weights, and again would be noted as American or global records. Then there were the plain quirky records, for example a "World record" for the three-legged race. Records that would lead cynics like one man, quoted in Chapter 13, to remark: "Perhaps the next time they want a world's record for a set of games they will have a four-and-a-half-pound shot or perhaps a sixteen-and-three-quarter-pound hammer."

Indeed, the gathering of evidence for records was often badly organized. It required a number of things to be recognized by the AAU; "normal" conditions for a start, meaning that a strong tailwind or steep slope would rule any record out. It also required confirmation that the weights thrown or track distance covered was actually the same as the weight or distance of the record. Finally, it needed a minimum number of officials to validate the record. As many of the events where records were allegedly broken were small-run affairs, with "amateurism" taken to the max, was it any wonder that so many of these records were never officially compiled? It also begs the question about how these records had a bearing on an athlete's reputation. To a certain extent they did, but winning a national championship or, even better, an Olympic gold medal, were equally significant.

1

The "staid" and the "poor man's" Athletic Clubs

The year 2012 was hardly a great year for the then 144-year-old New York Athletic Club. The Big Apple's most prestigious sporting institution was hit by two major scandals, as the *New York Post's* Dareh Gregorian wrote sardonically of employees at the "staid" club, describing it as "a real animal house behind the scenes."[1]

It started with an unseemly brawl in the "Tap Room" late on Thursday, April 12, eventually leading to a high-profile lawsuit two years later. The *New York Times'* Michael Wilson reported how responding cops "did a double take" when told of the address: "We arrive in the club," explained Sergeant Kenneth Monahan. "In the rear of the lobby, we are able to observe maybe five males, fighting. Wrestling. Everybody, for the most part, was dressed in a suit. They had their hands on each other. Immediately, the officers started separating everyone. We restrained everybody." Three men were arrested. Andrew Haesler would later sue Peter Doran and Colin Drowica for the medical bills for treating a fractured eye socket suffered while trying to break up the brawl.[2]

The club's grand poo-bah was hardly amused: "I cannot state forcefully enough how abhorrent this event is to me," the NYAC president, S. Colin Neill, wrote to members, before demanding the incident be kept hushed:

> Distribution via the various social media ... detrimental to the club and its reputation, will not be tolerated. It is the responsibility of ... member[s] to protect and embellish the standing of the N.Y.A.C. ... The club's constitution does not permit publicizing internal matters ... or otherwise undermining the private nature of the club.

Those who failed to comply "will be subject to disciplinary action."[3]

This was like putting a plaster over a crack in the Hoover Dam. One blogger, WallStreetJackass, quoted a "third-hand" account of the Donnybrook: "It was the best fight I've ever seen. Young people, old people, girls, members, non members, it was a nondiscriminatory ragematch."[4]

Wilson meanwhile mocked the club, citing the reason for the fight—"a woman" who wouldn't have been allowed in the tap-room if the club hadn't lost a 1989 sexual discrimination battle:

> Across the city, in cemeteries marked with fancy mausoleums, former members of the ... club began spinning. This was not good. The police were coming! This was not a civilized start to the weekend, which begins at the club every Friday at 5 p.m., when the dress code relaxes from a mandatory jacket to an optional jacket. What in heaven's name had happened to prompt a 911 call from inside the building?[5]

Then in November, the club that the *New York Times* was quick to point out charged an $8,500 joining fee and three further grand a year in subs, got hit by a discrimination case. Gregorian noted that the NYAC was a " hotbed of sexual harassment, racist remarks and wild behavior in recent years ... [where] members and managers would often make racial cracks, including using the N-word, and no action would be taken by the club."[6]

* * *

It's easy to see how the NYAC doesn't fit in with New Yorkers' self-view as a melting pot of equality. And the club has history: It routinely denied access to Jews, blacks and other minorities until in 1968 the Olympic Committee for Human Rights (OCHR) organized a boycott of its centenary meeting. Indeed, one of the OCHR's most famous faces, John Carlos, recalls as a confused 12-year-old the moment his father told him to forget about becoming an Olympic swimmer, as he needed to join a "private club," like the NYAC, that was "connected to the Olympic people in order to train." "'Well what is it?' I demanded. And [his father] said, 'The color of your skin.' He explained that they train three times a day in the finest of pools with the best coaches, and that just wasn't a place where I'd be welcome—because of the color of my skin."[7]

Jews suffered similarly. In 2003, a *New York Times* article about the City Athletic Club—founded in 1907 by Jews who were "excluded from established city clubs"—noted that the NYAC was "the king of athletics in New York.... Its typical member, it was widely acknowledged, was Roman Catholic and of Irish extraction."[8]

The trouble with this story is that in 1907 the NYAC wasn't the city's major athletic club, let alone the first place any top Irish-Catholic athlete would stop at. Indeed, Jews were not excluded from New York's leading athletic club that year, one the *Evening World* then acknowledged "now lead the world," following an impressive 1,696 points for that year. "This is the greatest number of points ever scored by an athletic club and stamps [its] stars as real world beaters." No greater a figure than "the best authority on amateur

1. The "staid" and the "poor man's" Athletic Clubs

The New York Athletic Club headquarters on West 59th Street, viewed from Central Park, circa 1901. The NYAC was seen in later year as a "crusty old Irish-dominated club" (Library of Congress).

sporting matters now living," James Edward Sullivan, claimed that it had "the right to the title of the foremost athletic club in the world." By 1911, the *Evening World* noted that 59 American and World records had been broken by its athletes.[9]

This was the Irish-American Athletic Club, an institution not a decade old, but described with perhaps some hyperbole and bias by the *Gaelic American* as "being the leader and controlling factor in amateur athletics in the United States." Its feats would be recorded not just in America, but in British newspapers like the (Birmingham) *Evening Despatch*, the *Dundee Courier* and the *Manchester Courier and Lancashire General Advertiser*. And yet it would effectively be dead in a decade.[10]

Rebecca Jenkins, in her 1908 London Olympics history, highlights the animosity the Irish encountered in the United States: "At the turn of the century the Irish-American immigrant still suffered considerable prejudice in the American community at large." Pointing to comic strips in the Pulitzer and Hearst newspapers, like the tramp "Happy Hooligan" or the "Yellow Kid" called Mickey Duggan, these "endearing rogues ... were never expected to amount to anything."[11]

The road to racial acceptance, the so-called transformation to being white argued by Noel Ignatiev, had indeed been progressing since the American Civil War. John Kuo Wei Tchen argues:

> Irish men were able to become Americanized by actively participating in racial masquerades of the established political culture. And by so doing that became increasingly viewed as "white."..Being an Irish American, even within the highly negative view created by elite, radical, Republicans, constituted the primary means for a positive identity formation and a chance of making life better.[12]

In New York City, excellence in both politics and sport helped the Irish become the city's foremost ethnic group. By the time of the I-AAC's birth, they controlled much of its social, political and popular culture, and there had been calls for a unique Irish athletic club over the decades. As early as 1879, the *Irish American Weekly* justified this need: "[Here] in New York and vicinity, where so many Irish and Irish-Americans have settled, no opportunity was afforded to develop their superior qualities as athletes, except in clubs where their identity as a nationality was entirely lost sight of, and some other nationality carried off the credit of their prowess."[13]

* * *

There was not just one "Irish-American Athletic Club" in New York but three, founded in 1879, 1890 and 1898 respectively. Of course, the notion of an Irish sporting club in a foreign city was nothing new in 1898, when the third club, initially called the Greater New York Irish Athletic Association, was organized. The London Irish Rugby Football Club was founded by the city's leading Irish—men like the MPs Edward Carson and William Redmond—in the same year, while 12 years earlier, a less ecumenical set-up was initiated by the County Sligo, Marist Brother Walfrid, when he set up the Celtic Football and Athletic Club in Glasgow. Even earlier, in 1875 the Hibernian Football Club was founded by members of the Edinburgh Irish community. The GNYIAA's success would in time inspire the formation of other "Irish-American Athletic Clubs"—less franchise and more imitation—across America.[14]

It was on Sunday, January 30, 1898, that a group of one hundred Irish New-Yorkers, many of them well-heeled members of the city's Irish community, gathered to create the third athletic club. As Alan S. Katchen—probably the only biographer of any I-AAC athlete—surmised, the club was "far more than some Broadway stereotype of wild Irish characters, with their 'tremendous, earthy humor,' or worse, the incarnation of the Victorians' Celtophobic images" of the drunken Irish:

> No track club in American history has had a more colorful governing body....
> [Mostly] native New Yorkers, the acculturated children of immigrants who owed their success to the political machine ... their involvement in the Winged Fist was

an expression of their Irish nationalism, their pride in the role of athletic prowess in Irish culture, and their belief in achieving equality of opportunity through sport.[15]

Jenkins notes that Patrick J. Conway, the club president for 27 years, was a man detached from contemporary stereotypes. Full of unbridled energy, he "epitomized the increasing prosperity and respectability of the established Irish-American community in turn-of-the-century New York ... [who] had worked his way up to become a man of property who owned his own business, a stable and blacksmith's servicing the city's dray horses." In a 1908 article titled "IRISH-AMERICAN ATHLETIC CLUB: Its Rise to Influence and Sporting Prominence," the *Irish American Weekly* described Conway's organization of the club's Indoor Carnival at Madison Square Garden: "As soon as the plans for the games are laid, 'PJ' is on the job day and night, hustling here and there collecting features. Even now he is busy working on what he hopes will be the greatest indoor meeting New York has ever seen."[16]

Undoubtedly the lion's share for the club's formation goes to "Pay Jay," or "Chief," as everyone called Conway. The *Evening World* in 1905 described him as being "the head of that small band of founders with the blood of the Gael in them." The *Irish American Weekly* would later say: "The rise of the [I-AAC] ... from the position of an obscure organization, possessing but a handful of athletics, to that of the strongest athletic club in the world has been deftly steered by a master hand—that of Patrick J. Conway, President of the 'Winged Fist' organization since its beginning." Conway would try many times to give up "the reins" to someone else, "but the mere mention of such intention raises such a storm of protest among his friends that his resolution to retire has been broken time and time again." In January 1906, the *Gaelic American* reported that Conway was unanimously re-elected president "despite his wish to be retired so as to give some other man a chance," unsuccessfully urging club members to vote for another "hustler."[17]

Patrick "Pay Jay" Conway, the long-time president of the GNYIAA/I-AAC, pictured in 1908 (Library of Congress).

One question to ask is why an athletic club? Why not baseball or even soccer? Part of that was because athletics was one of the most popular activities at the time in the city, while the Irish provided some of its best participants. But there was also a belief that specific Irish athletics—the throwing of heavy weights, Gaelic football and hurling—were not getting enough recognition. As the *Gaelic American* observed in 1903, no one else "has done more for the popularizing of Irish pastimes in this country" than the GNYIAA:

> That Irishmen occupy a foremost place in the athletic world is a recognized fact, and it is strange that those games, which are particularly Irish, such as hurling, Gaelic football, handball, etc., are not popular in the United States, where so many millions of our race dwell and where the Irish athlete has long shown his superiority.[18]

Amateur athletics was not compromised by professional "franchises" limiting sporting bodies to a single business per city, and for Irish-American New Yorkers, the club became a unique source of pride. The *Gaelic American*, in an attack on the AAU head, James E. Sullivan, and his war on professionalism that disproportionately targeted the I-AAC, accused others of jealousy: "A galaxy of athletic stars, the like of which the autocrat of the AAU never before saw gathered in one club, have been representing the 'Winged Hand,' and from St. Louis to Buffalo and Montreal have shown the 'pets' of 'His Emminence [*sic*]' the road." When the club started attracting top athletes, critics dismissed the success as temporary: "'Oh this is only a flash in the pan,' quoth the wise ones. 'They'll soon blow up,'" said the *Irish American Weekly*. 'We will never blow up as long as Pat Conway is our leader!' cried the athletes, and history has proven that they were right."[19]

In two articles in January 1905, the *Evening World* hailed this "Gaelic association" as "the banner organization of the United States and never has there been one since amateur athletics reached their present plane, which has been able to emblazon on its colors" in a short space of time:

> The handful of Irishmen and Irishmen's sons who seven years ago saw the need of such an organization in this city as the Greater New York Irish Athletic Association has become and who had the initiative to effect it little dreamed that with the opening of 1905 such a record as that would be theirs.... [It] has enrolled under its banners the most famous athletes in the world and surpasses all other organizations in the number of champions.... The advancement of this Gaelic association in the ranks of amateur athletics in the past seven years is marvelous. It has made rapid strides, and at the present time is the greatest organization of its kind in the country. It has won in seven years five world's championships, nine national championships, five metropolitan championships and eight junior championships ... under the emblem of the shamrock wreath and the winged fist.[20]

However, organizing meetings were only one aim of the club. Irish athletic cranks wanted a club where they were in charge, not one where they were only welcome if they were of a suitable caliber. The club collaborated closely with other interested parties, such as Irish societies, the Gaelic Athletic Association, or U.S. Army regiments and trade unions with high Irish membership. The club also included other sports: Lacrosse, cycling, ice skating, ice hockey and swimming, while there were also plans to build a handball court. George Cameron was a member when he reached the semi-final of four cycling events at the 1908 Olympics, while Allen Taylor was regarded as one of the country's top distance skaters. Their trump card was the magnificent Celtic Park stadium in Queens, which would be home for all things Irish and athletic for over a quarter of a century, a place the *Gaelic American* later noted would show that "the Irish abroad and their descendants, like their kindred in the Old Land, are lovers of all kinds of athletic sports and pastimes."[21]

Eventually it broke the stronghold of the New York Athletic Club. Between their win in Milwaukee in 1903 and their next in Philadelphia in 1919, the Mercury Foot Club didn't win a single national championship. Of the championships they sent athletes to, the Irish-Americans won every competition between 1904 and 1914, while they took all Metropolitan Championships during the same period except for 1910. A rivalry was born that would agitate not only domestic athletics but also U.S. Olympic teams. "The old time rivalry between the Irish-American Athletic Club and the New York Athletic Club will be brought out in all its intensity," the *New York Times* forecast on the eve of the Mercury Foot's Indoor Games in 1908. When the Oregonian Dan Kelly arrived in the city after leaving the University of Michigan, he pondered for weeks which of these clubs he should join.[22]

However, despite being avowedly Irish in name and identity, the I-AAC played a pivotal role in integrating athletics. Influential in constructing an American identity at the Olympics and being at the vanguard of removing restrictions on Sunday sport, the club made its name with its own athletic "galacticos," snapping up the foreign runners—even English ones—who had come to America. The I-AAC could only be successful by welcoming all peoples, but this mission to collect the nation's best athletic talent contributed to its demise. The reliance on its stars would ultimately raise the question of how far the athletes were swaying from amateurism, inviting numerous suspensions by the AAU, often instigated by the NYAC.

* * *

Despite its place in American athletics, revitalizing the sport in the Big Apple, integrating club athletics almost 40 years before it would be done in baseball, plus the number of athletes it supplied to the London Olympics, there is little written on the club. There's no mention in *Encyclopedia of the Irish in America*, edited by Michael Glazier. Despite "the IAAC's important role in the early history of American track and field," wrote Gregory Bond, "this institution has received little scholarly attention." Only a small section of the NYU's Bobst Library and Ian McGowan's excellent Winged Fist Organization website are notable research sources. McGowan himself wrote of how he got interested in the club:

> [W]hen I moved into an apartment complex called Celtic Park, in Sunnyside/Woodside, Queens. I was curious as to where the complex got its name.... I soon discovered that Celtic Park had an incredibly rich and almost completely forgotten history, and that it was once the home of a world-renown group of athletes called the Irish-American Athletic Club, also known as the Winged Fists of Celtic Park.[23]

The Irish-American Athletic Club's journey was one that would ultimately reach the highs and lows in a very short time. It would climb to be National Champions 11 times and would have 27 American Olympic medal winners, with a total of 56 different metals. But it would fall apart virtually overnight, through a combination of war, Prohibition, competing attractions, and ultimately poor management.

This book, therefore, is the story of what the Tammany politician and lawyer Daniel F. Cohalan hailed as "a poor man's" athletic club. This is the story of the rise and fall of the Irish-American Athletic Club of New York, once the greatest athletic club in the whole world.[24]

2

"For the encouragement of manly sports and exercises ... of the Irish-American Athlete"
The First and Second I-AAC

The Greater New York Irish Athletic Association, founded in 1898, was not the first "Irish-American" athletic club in New York. Two previous bodies were set up as a home to Irish sports, and both suddenly disappeared without any mention in the press. Back in April 1879, the first of these clubs was founded. One hundred and fifty—Irish, one must presume—members of the Kings County Athletic Club decided to change its name "to the more comprehensive one," the *Irish American Weekly* opined, of the "Irish-American Athletic Club." With a piece of ground on 32nd Street, Brooklyn, the same newspaper reported excitedly that

> the club is now started on a firm basis, and in a short time will most probably have enrolled among its members most of the Irish-American element in this city and Brooklyn, when, it is to be expected, after the necessary training, they will be able to contend against any athletic club in the country in those exercises for which their ancestors were once famous.[1]

In May 1879, H. Alsheimer was the first recorded I-AAC athlete, competing in the 56LB Weight at NYAC's Spring Games at Mott Haven, and with a non–Irish name, perhaps proving an early tradition of an open club. Soon other notable athletes joined, including the middle distance American champions, James H. Gifford and Patrick Joseph McDonald, the latter winning the three-mile race at a meeting of the American Athletic Club in October 1879. One club member was "Captain" James Daly (or Daley), one of the great all-round athletes of the 1870s. A stone-cutter and professional athlete born in Shanballymore, County Cork, in 1852, he had arrived in the U.S. by the mid–'70s, and by the end of the decade was described as "Champion Athlete of the World." A member of the Kings County AC when it reorganized, he also performed as a low-level prize-fighter, gaining a disqualification against "Joe" Prendergarst on Staten Island in 1883, before fighting E. Stoddard in February 1884.[2]

The I-AAC held its first annual picnic at Jones' Wood Coliseum on Monday June 23, 1879. Attended not only by a large Irish crowd, but also by what the *Irish American Weekly* described as "large numbers of various nationalities of which the community [is] composed," the program included ten athletic events concluded by a tug-of-war match, where the married men beat the bachelors. The *Irish American Weekly* couldn't heap enough praise on the young club:

> The great ordeal through which the "Irish-American Athletic Club" had to undergo is now passed. They have made their bow to the public as a chartered club and have come off with flying colors. The picnic has been a success financially and socially, and their games have commanded the commendation of rival athletic clubs.... Everything looks favorable in the direction we have indicated, and great things will be expected at their hands in keeping up the traditions of their ancestors, whose exploits were the theme of bard and historian.[3]

In September, the I-AAC sent a group of athletes to Mott Haven for the fourth NAAAA Amateur Championships of America. McDonald won the 3Mile run, beating the Montreal Lacrosse Club's George Maclaine in 15:38:6 minutes, while also breaking E.C. Stimson's American record. The following

Print of the Caledonian Games at Jones Wood, 1867. The Manhattan venue was the site for the I-AAC's first event on June 23, 1879 (Library of Congress).

month, the club hosted its own Fall Games on the grounds of the Manhattan Athletic Club. Amongst those present was one Mr. Price, a visiting competitor from England, and another Irish "World Champion," the future "Strong Man" of the U.S. Army, Thomas F. Lynch. While attendance was dampened by the rival O'Leary Belt "pedestrian" contest at Madison Square Garden, the numbers were still respectable, although the *Irish American Weekly* was scathing that more Irish attended the rival event: "[The] Irish-American element in this community should make it their duty to lend their aid in advancing the material progress of the club by attending their games in large numbers, and thus give it the prestige it deserves, and the encouragement that is necessary for its further development."[4]

On May 24, 1880, at Jones Wood, the I-AAC attracted upwards of 2,000 patrons to its second "Annual Picnic." Here the event made the city's press pages, which commented on the hot weather competitors endured. The *New York Tribune* reported at least one athlete fainting, while *Wilkes Spirit of the Times* claimed the track was "in poor condition, rough, dry and dusty." The *New York Times* noted:

> The heat was intense, and the seconds and backers of the contestants were fully occupied in sponging and rubbing down their charges, feeding them with lemonade, soda, pieces of ice, &c., in order to supply the waste of perspiration. In the long runs and walks men followed at the heels of the pedestrians, flinging water from sponges upon their backs and limbs.

Wilkes added that the three-hour, "go-as-you-please" Challenge Belt race was "in itself a whole sermon on the remarkable benefits" of training: "The most oppressively hot day of the year, and ordinary people were gasping in the shade or reluctantly attending to their business, yet, between 1 and 4 p.m., five young men ran steadily for three hours under the blazing sin, and half an hour afterwards, were all dancing an Irish jig and ready for another contest."[5]

The Irish-Americans J.J. Clark and W.T. Bailey won the One Mile and Two Mile Runs respectively, but an incident occurring around ten minutes to three overshadowed the day. Thomas Gallagher, the 17-year-old son of a Circuit Court clerk, tried to climb over the dancing pavilion's wall bordering the East River when suddenly it gave way. Gallagher fell "amid the shrieks of the spectators" upon the rocks below, breaking his nose, ribs, and knee cap, while also cutting his face and scalp: "From the rocks the stunned and senseless lad bounded off into the swiftly-running current, where he would have assuredly been drowned but for the exertions of two passing boatmen who fished him out and bore him, bleeding profusely to the shore." The club would hold four further annual meets before disappearing sometime between 1885 and 1888, although in January 1889, a boxing match between the I-AAC's

James Maher and Oscar Finn of the Union Bicycle Club was mentioned in the *New York Times*.[6]

* * *

The 1888 GAA "Invasion" of America, led by Maurice Davin, seemed to provide the impetus to revive the I-AAC. It also brought one man who would play a key role in the third I-AAC, William F. Prendergast, who along with James S. Mitchell and four other athletes decided to remain in America. On April 18, 1890, it was announced that a group of men from the city's Fifth Ward, which included much of the historic Irish-dominated Five Points, led by Michael O'Sullivan—"the well known Pastime Athletic Club athlete"— James Fitzgibbon, Thomas Curran and Richard Mahoney, were now, according to the *New York Times*, "foremost in a movement to form an Irish-American athletic club in this city. All Irishmen living in this vicinity are invited to join." The *Evening World* added that they had called "upon others of their nationality to meet them at Berrigan's Hall, Desbrosses and Hudson Streets, next Sunday at 3 PM." The *Irish American Weekly* gleefully reported:

> It will not be denied that the Turn Verein has done much for the Germans, and in our native land the [GAA] is developing successfully the athletic prowess of our race much to the benefit of the individual and the credit of our people ... for the encouragement of manly sports and exercises, and the advancement of the standard of the Irish-American Athlete, the Irish Athletic Club has been organized.[7]

The club's first meeting was on April 20, 1890. *The Sun* reported, "There is a significance attending the birth of this club, that is possessed by probably no other club in this country, from the fact that it will affiliate with the Gaelic Athletic Association of Ireland." Around 100 "young men, athletically disposed," attended, mostly between 20 and 30 years old and "well developed physically as any like body of men that could possibly be gotten together." Thomas Lonergan was elected president and Joseph Bradley vice-president, with Michael O'Sullivan granted the post of "corresponding secretary." Patrick Curtis became the club treasurer. Edward Condon, Richard Mahoney, Marshall Hazel, William J. Knoud, and Thomas J. O'Sullivan took up other positions.[8]

However, the meeting was not without controversy, with a heated debate over the sale of alcohol on club premises. The *New York Times* reported, "There had been an announcement that liquor dealers were to be excluded ... and in consequence the Irishmen of the ward turned out in large numbers, among them being many saloon keepers." One John Pursell opened proceedings with a speech that called for a ban on booze-peddlers, suggesting that "their connection with the club meant its ruination." This was met by protests from the "liquor element" that dominated the meeting, causing "a scene of confusion." A row erupted which included one "anti-saloon" man claiming there were

700 saloons in the Fifth Ward alone and "that they were attempting to take the club by storm in order to use it for political purposes." Lonergan agreed, causing more uproar by suggesting that some had paid simply to vote "for the admission of the saloon." The whole matter was put to the vote, with "the saloon men" triumphing with a majority of 20.[9]

Despite this, the club was upbeat. It had affiliated with the AAU beforehand and was set to host athletic meetings and enter other clubs' events. The *Irish World* noted that membership by the first week of July was up to 200, "all of who are among the sturdiest and most active of the young Irish and Irish-American element in the city." The *Evening World* commented, "The management of this newly organized Club report that there is an assured, brilliant, future.... They claim that their coming meeting will bring to light some athletes of the first rank." With headquarters acquired at Halcyon Hall, 597 Third Avenue, the club was further boosted by 300 entries—including the top Irish middle-distance runner, Tom Conneff—for its first meeting at Jones Wood on July 29.[10]

Unlike the first I-AAC, this club diversified into other sports, including baseball, soccer and Gaelic sports. In August 1890, the club became a founding member of the New York State Football League, providing the league its Vice-President, Patrick E. Powers. On September 22, they took on and lost to the talented Nonpareil FC, 5–1, in the first game under the NYSFL auspices, in "one of the roughest games ever played in New York," according to *Sporting Life*. Before long the I-AAC were languishing bottom of the five-team league, and *Sporting Life*, in the lexicon of the day that relied on science for sporting success, muttered: "The Irish AA ... have good men, but they lack science in the playing of the game."[11]

Gaelic team sports also featured more prominently than with the other two clubs. One newspaper report claimed that "the object of the Irish-American Club ... is to gain a foothold in this country for a typical Irish game." On Thanksgiving Day 1890, it hosted the first game of football played in New York under the new GAA rules. Three thousand spectators traveled to the newly opened second Polo Grounds on 155th Street and Eighth Avenue to watch a "Championship of the United States" between the I-AAC, wearing blue jerseys, caps and "maroon-colored knee pants ... [presenting] an extremely natty appearance," and the Sarsfield Club of Portchester, Westchester County. The Irish-Americans won, 2–7 to 0–1 or 2–6 to 0–2, depending on which report you believe (for how these scores are calculated, see "Notes on times, distances, abbreviations and scoring").[12]

Enthusiasm for local Gaelic football was transformed by the second I-AAC, the *Evening World* observing that "interest in Gaelic football has wonderfully increased" since the above game. By the following May, the *Sun* commented that the "several hundred enthusiastic spectators assembled" at

Homeyer's Park, Ridgewood, to watch the Emmetts defeat the I-AAC, proving that "the lover of the Gaelic Football game is legion in name." An extensive article in the *Sun* in March 1893 about hurling still suggested that the club claimed "the best team of hurlers hereabouts," with the team's captain Patrick Dee from Tipperary "one of the best-known wielders of the hurley in this country."[13]

The future initially looked good. Two hundred members celebrated the club's first anniversary at the Military Hall, Bowery, on April 20, 1891: "Songs, recitations, and refreshments made up the evening's entertainment, which was heartily enjoyed," reported the *Sun*. "Heretofore the club has confined its efforts to football, hurling, and weight throwing, but from now on the organization will go in for general track athletics." *Sporting Life* would report the club returning new officers, and in October 1892 the I-AAC finally secured the Polo Grounds for Gaelic Football and hurling. But the failure to grab a permanent home near to the Irish strongholds proved a major setback, the club acquiring grounds instead far away at Erastina on Staten Island, with the clubhouse at 24 North Moore Street.[14]

The club's blue-collar members were also finding it hard to compete against the city's bigger clubs. Handicapped by the journey to Staten Island, the *Evening World* reported, the I-AAC had 250 men, "many of whom are fine athletes, whose chief trouble is that they have no time to practice." The newspaper added that the I-AAC had rejected further AAU membership, confining themselves to Irish sports, which increased its isolation from mainstream athletics, as any AAU athlete competing at I-AAC games risked being banned for life.[15]

By the time the club celebrated its third anniversary, the cracks were showing that would break the club apart the following year. A meeting in April to consider "the advisability" of the club remaining within the GAA was postponed when a quorum couldn't be gathered. Despite assurances that they intended to elect officers, by September it was announced that the club was suspended by the city's GAA Central Council for "unbecoming conduct."[16]

In the space of 15 years, two athletic clubs in the largest Irish city in the United States had been formed and collapsed. Top Irish sportsmen preferred to make money in baseball or the prize ring, and those who could cope with remaining an amateur athlete were snapped up by better resourced clubs. A radical approach was needed. Firstly was how to attract Irish athletes and keep them, which would involve the subject of "compensation" and "expenses." Secondly, should such a club remain exclusively Irish? But before that, any new club needed a home that was within easy reach of the city's Irish.

3

"The 'Mecca' of attraction for every proud son and fair daughter of Erin"
The Building of Celtic Park

Following the 1908 Olympics, Joe Fitzgerald, a reporter for Joseph Pulitzer's *The World*, interviewed Pat Conway. Born in Limerick on St. Patrick's Day in either 1859 or 1861, there's little doubt that Conway's unbridled vision was crucial to establishing the Greater New York Irish Athletic Association. He had migrated around the end of the '70s and had set up his own "equine shoe parlor on East Sixtieth Street … one of the finest in the city" that had a contract with the city's fire department. Despite being a businessman, Conway was keen to enhance the lot of the Irish working man, being listed by the *New York Times* in April 1897 as speaking at a blacksmiths' trade union mass meeting fighting for better conditions. He was also a member of numerous Irish societies in the city: Clan na Gael, the Owen Roe Club, the Knights of Columbus, and the American Historical Society, and was even a director of the Gaelic American Publishing Company.[1]

In the interview reprinted later in the *Gaelic American*, Fitzgerald asked about the club's founding. Conway replied with "a chuckle that bumped the bumps over his half dozen chins": "You'll laugh when I tell you about its birth. I was always a crank on the subject, and one Sunday afternoon while half a dozen of us were discussing athletics in a back kitchen on East Sixty-Sixth Street, someone suggested that we organize a club. That was the start of the I-AAC." From that "back kitchen," known as "The Annex," which Conway later disclosed as Doris's Restaurant, "which was so small that a man was not permitted to bring more than one idea with him," a charter was obtained on October 7, 1897: "The history of the I-AAC from its organization ten years ago is the life story of 'P.J.' for a like period," Fitzgerald offered. "No man ever worked harder for the success of a project and no man has reason to feel prouder over the good news that is crowding the cables these days."[2]

His enormous girth and personality hid the fact that Conway was not alone. Crucial to success was the club's first treasurer, William Prendergast, whose ability to acquire Celtic Park pointed to a man more adroit than the ordinary "beat cop" he was. Not to be confused—as I had done—with William A. Prendergast, the American-born New York City comptroller and Progressive Party nominee for governor in 1912 who often attended I-AAC events, this Prendergast was a native of Clonmel, Tipperary. Previously a weight athlete before being elected as GAA general secretary in his early 20s in 1888, he first visited the United States with the "Gaelic Invasion" tour later that year, returning to live in the U.S. in 1892.[3]

Other colleagues had experience in law, accounting, and local politics, such as C.M. Breen, William Dunne, F. Campbell, M. Quinilin, J. Dovis, Thomas Fenton, James J. Frawley and M.J. Jennings. Dunne was made secretary and Frawley vice-president. John Murtha, Thomas Breen, C.M. Breen and Thomas Dunne were added to the committee. With the initial meeting proving popular, a further session at "The Annex" was arranged where new members would be admitted, while the intention "to secure a place within the territory of the greater city in which athletic sports of all kinds, and Irish pastimes in particular, can be indulged" was also debated.[4]

* * *

Whatever Conway's dreams and ambitions, 1898 was not the ideal year to start a sporting venture. Athletics' popularity had been fluctuating over the past 30 years, from the "Pedestrian Craze" to indifference, and it would swing back within a decade. The *New York Times* had commented on the decline at the 1895 AAU National Championships, blaming the Manhattan AC's demise that left the NYAC with no rival:

> Time was when a contest like that of yesterday would have brought out an enormous crowd of enthusiasts. That was when the hot rivalry existed between the New York and Manhattan Athletic Clubs. With the death of the latter club and the absorption of about all the best athletes in the country into the ranks of the former, interest in field and track athletics seems to have materially lessened. The interscholastic and the intercollegiate games seem now about the ones in which alone the general public seems to take any great interest.[5]

The year 1898 also saw war with Spain, which had a severe impact on all American sport. That year's Metropolitan Athletic Association Championships—held at Celtic Park—made just 80 bucks on the gate. An article in August in the *Sun*, called "Athletics Lack Interest," denied that this was due to the war: "The lack of public interest in track and field athletics is a matter of deep concern, not only to those who have spent their lives in attempting

3. "The 'Mecca' of attraction"   23

to further the competitive feature, but to those who regard the universal practice of athletics as a means to increase the strength and usefulness of the population." Athletics had "arisen at times to general favor, [but] ... the tide of popularity has been followed by a period of depression" since the Manhattan AC folded. Event entries had fallen sharply, and while the war took away many young men, the writer pointed the finger instead at exorbitant membership fees. This last comment was a challenge the GNYIAA had to meet. Conway later disclosed to Fitzgerald that financial problems were the club's greatest threat in its early years: "It was a hard struggle ... and the club was always in debt. But there was a game lot of men behind it. They gave their time and money to keep it afloat."[6]

Much of the "debt" went to obtaining "a large piece of land," revealed at the initial meeting, at Laurel Hill, Long Island—in what is today's Woodside/Sunnyside neighborhoods in Queens—that would eventually become Celtic Park. The size of two blocks and built on a high ground, making it rarely waterlogged, it would include athletic grounds with a third-of-a-mile track, a 5,000-spectator grandstand, and a summer clubhouse. The *New York Times'* Robert F. Kelley would years later exaggerate that the plot was more inaccessible than Montauk Point: "All these [athletes] worked for a living somewhere

A typical scene from an athletic meeting at Celtic Park. The 3,000M steeplechase handicap of the Post Office Clerks Association on May 26, 1912, was eventually won by John J. Daly (Library of Congress).

in New York City, and after an arduous day on the job, took this tiresome trip in order to engage in training."[7]

The *New York Times* claimed that the area covered no more than three-quarters of an acre, while *The Sun* suggested that it stretched to nine. Both agreed that the plot—previously owned by the major landowner in the area, George Thomson—had been bought for the sum of $9,000. $2,000 had already been paid, while another $5,000 was raised by selling shares at $50 each. It was further disclosed that an engineer was drawing plans for "a mammoth grand stand and routes for a bicycle track," with enough room within the running track for football and baseball. Trams to the Catholic Calvary cemetery ran near the ground, while others would later be built. A new "Irish" regiment would also use it as an armory. Ready for opening by May 1, 1899, it met one setback: $2,000 of outstanding debt due to unsold shares.[8]

In an effort to prevent power falling to one person, the club blocked members obtaining more than five shares each, the minimum needed to vote at meetings. In 1905, rules were relaxed and directors were allowed to hold positions for three years instead of the previous one, but this met resistance: "According to a man well versed in club politics this new clause may create some trouble," commented the *Sun*. "He said: 'Suppose any political party or clique should at any time gain control of the club and that they wished to run things their own way, they could by a sort of rotatory policy remain in power all the time. In my opinion the old clause was the fairer and the yearly election the safer.'"[9]

By late February, things were moving quickly, as a civil engineer named C.E. Smith pledged that construction would begin immediately. The *Sun* reported: "Irish athletes are taking a deep interest in Celtic Park, which is now being fitted up." The main stand itself would cost an additional $9,000 and eventually seat 2,500 patrons, with the "bleacheries" accommodating a further 6,000, while the club announced it had bought a strip of adjoining land for "an amphitheater" seating 3,000 to watch "boxing, vaudeville, gymnastics, dancing and other forms of indoor amusements."[10]

On April 12, 1898, the *Brooklyn Daily Eagle* announced that the grandstand would cover 50 feet by 200 feet, while the stadium cost was now $25,000—corresponding to nearly three-quarters of $1,000,000 in 2014. Inexpensive by modern standards, partly due to its rural location, kickbacks or graft were either absent or carefully hidden, with little evidence either of local government grants. From the plans being commissioned in January, the stadium was all but ready to open on Tuesday, May 30, for the club's Memorial Day meeting.[11]

Celtic Park could have ended as a classic "White Elephant" had it not been for the ready-made market to fill it. New York-Brooklyn's Irish-born populace in 1890 was listed at 275,156, or 12 percent of the city population.

Between 1890 and 1900, New York City contained the largest Irish-born community in the world, over 30,000 more than the entire—native and foreign-born—population of Dublin. Soon Irish bodies were enticed to use the ground to host annual picnics, with attendances boosted if a football or hurling match concluded it. In time, as P.J. McInerney of the Clare Mens Association would claim, Celtic Park became "the 'Mecca' of attraction for every proud son and fair daughter of Erin, who revel in the deeds of daring, and glory in the heroic supremacy which have made the men of Erin famous."[12]

When completed, it was hardly an architectural masterpiece. This was no Soldier Field, a piece of grandeur to the doughboy fallen, or the Los Angeles Coliseum, America's retort to the Great Depression. In 1898 there was very little given over to making stadiums the palaces or cathedrals that came later. Functionality trumped aesthetics, with the priority to form a boundary so people could be charged to enter. Seats were given to the rich or connected, while the rabble was left with the "bleachers": Surviving photos portray Celtic Park as a basic oval with a small grandstand.

It wasn't just cost that determined Celtic Park's ordinariness. As seen from the brief lives of I-AAC I and II, sport was an unpredictable business. The *Evening World* in January 1905 noted that when the stadium had finally been free of a mortgage for a year,

> the association acquired a dreary plot of ground at Laurel Hill.... Conway said it was just the spot for a track and athletic field. The association said "Go ahead and build. We're behind you," while the scoffers said surely now is the time the Shamrocks will go "down and out." That "dreary waste of sand" at Laurel Hill is now Celtic Park within whose precincts is to be found the most complete outdoor athletic plant in the country.[13]

Indeed when the ground of Celtic Park was broken, baseball parks were still being built on the cheap. Due to instability from poor gates and failing leagues, franchises moved or folded at short notice. As Robert C. Trumpbour observes, "[The stadium] was not generally a symbol of civic pride, but rather a Spartan, utilitarian setting." In this turbulent period of sport's growth, stadiums morphed from wooden fire hazards that collapsed easily, to safer, concrete and steel constructions, epitomized by Philadelphia's Baker Bowl, destroyed by fire in 1894 and replaced by a concrete grandstand the following year. Decent athletic stadiums were also hard to find. The *New York Times* shrugged at the news of Celtic Park being chosen to host the 1903 AAU All Around Championships: "Perhaps the union could not select a better or more picturesque place for holding its contests. The track is about as good as could be obtained near here for running races, but, as it is a dirt track when the sun is shining brightly it is extremely hot."[14]

The *Irish American Weekly*, on the eve of opening, described the stadium as "the first park or pleasure ground ever owned by Irishmen and Irish-Americans" in New York City:

> Celtic Park is conveniently located ... and can be reached from all parts of Brooklyn and Queens for one car fare, and from the Boroughs of Manhattan and Bronx by way of Thirty-fourth Street Ferry, then by trolley car direct to the grounds, or the distance from the ferry to Celtic Park can be walked at an easy pace in twenty minutes.

Later in 1913, the Manhattan and Queens Traction Company began running directly to Celtic Park from downtown Manhattan without transfer and on a single fare.[15]

Situated in a desolate part of central Queens, it was surrounded by "dirt hills" that caused havoc when windy, with one such "blinding sandstorm" lasting ten minutes, disrupting the Brooklyn and Long Island Clan na Gael's Annual Picnic in July 1913: "So violent was the storm that persons caught in it had difficulty in finding their way to the shelter of the park pavilions," reported the *New York Times*. "[It] first appeared in thin clouds of yellow dust ... [then] grew rapidly thicker and heavier and in a few minutes the players on the field were enveloped in them completely." Despite the intensity and its success in ruining a fair few female spectators' dress, it failed "to discourage the stout hearts of the Irishmen, who decided they would enjoy their annual picnic, rain or shine."[16]

The weather's effect on the cinder track was a persistent nuisance. 1902 proved a particularly bad summer, and overnight rain forced the abandonment of most of the Knights of Columbus Annual Games on July 21. When they returned two weeks later, more heavy rain damaged the track. Running conditions at the Red Men Games the following month were made almost impossible, "The runners had to take the outside of the track in sprints and long races, and, consequently, the time made in each event was slow, but was considered very fair because of the conditions." Even dry weather caused problems: The 1903 Memorial Day Games track was described by the *New York Times* as "thick with dust, the upper surface of which had been caked by the morning's sprinkle of rain."[17]

Nobody illustrated the importance of Celtic Park in early twentieth-century Irish New York life more than the author Charles J. Rosebault. In a 1921 *New York Times* article, he wrote of his intrigue when a Clare-born acquaintance, "Delia," had spoken about the stadium after her fellow countryman, "Mike," had become "stretched"—or killed—there: "From what she said I gathered that it was an oasis in the desert, a refuge for the real Irish from would-bes—make believes and utter barbarians.... One met there people of real color. Color, of course means character. That, no doubt, explained the fact that the buildings had been set on fire three times. The enemies of Ireland are everywhere—and capable of anything."

To get there, Rosebault departed Bliss Street subway station and followed "a long line of stalwart sons and daughters of Erin across the long stretch of dust road" to a fenced arena where the American flag "floated" beside the yellow, white and green of Sinn Fein. "It was not an attractive setting, this waste of flat, weed-grown land, and many a moon has been born and waned since the fence and buildings have seen a paint brush, but there could be no question about the high spirits of the crowd. However old they may be, the boy and girl are never extinguished in the Irish." Passing through a gate where publications, like "Sinn Fein," were sold alongside "East Indians" with pamphlets "to prove the similarity of the Indian and Irish causes and giving reasons why America should support the revolutionaries of India against the Sassenach," Rosebault saw inside two bars selling what seemed was "innocuous" beer but "a whiff from the breath of a wabbly [sic] young man whom I passed presently demonstrated the possibility of the private flask being not altogether surpassed." All members were well-behaved, but patrons were clearly divided into two groups:

> [T]hose who were fully broken into American customs and those who were still under the influence of their native habits. Among the former, the men smoked cigars and cigarettes and the women and girls would have passed unnoticed in any city throng. Of the newcomers the men clung to their pipes and the girls still wore their home-made finery, mostly simple frocks of cheap materials, with here and there a startling costume of ancient vintage, one doubtless which had created a sensation at a county meet of foxhunters or at some smart races when it may have seemed appropriate to the original owner.[18]

* * *

Within its first three years it became clear that the GNYIAA was beginning to outgrow Celtic Park, entailing either a suitable upgrade of facilities or new premises. Yet the *New York Tribune* heaped praise on it, arguing that top-class New York athletic stadiums were rare:

> Athletics, both amateur and professional, have grown to such importance that athletic grounds in this city large enough for the most important affairs have been hard to obtain. The [GNYIAA] is now in possession of grounds where athletic tournaments can be held, no matter how big the crowd or what games or sports are demanded....

A proposed revamp of Celtic Park would bring "piazzas," bowling alleys, "fitting rooms for those desiring to watch the games," a restaurant for 1,000 patrons, a cafe, and dressing rooms, with reception rooms amid private dining rooms to each side. "The track is a circular quarter mile one, and constructed for all kinds of races. There are fields for baseball, cricket, polo, football—in fact, accommodations for all manner of sports. On the east side of the track will be a rifle range 300 feet long, with four ranges, for match shoots." To pay for this, the club "executed" a five-year mortgage in early 1901 for $19,000 at a rate of six percent. "The proceeds are to be applied toward the erection of a club building, for the giving of exhibitions by the association and for athletic games and exercise."[19]

A new "clubhouse" was opened at the rescheduled 1901 Memorial Day Games, where Conway handed over the keys to Frawley. The *New York Tribune* reported: "The new quarter-mile cinder track, which is banked on the turns for cycle racing, is in fair condition, notwithstanding the storms, and as the athletic field is on elevated ground it will dry quickly with a few hours of fine weather." Meanwhile the *Brooklyn Daily Eagle* anticipated a great day:

> Thousands of invitations have been liberally distributed by the Celts and an enormous gathering is expected to take part in the festivities. For many years the erection of an Irish athletic club house in this vicinity has been spoken of, and now ... the wish had become a reality, and the structure just erected on the spacious athletic field, on which there is a quarter mile cinder track, is one of the prettiest and best appointed athletic club houses in the country.

The *Irish American Weekly* added with equal enthusiasm, "Our people have ever been famed for their athletic accomplishments. At the present time, men of Irish birth and blood hold the records in many specialties. The opening of the new club-house ... ought to meet with the immediate favor of popular approbation." The ceremony was augmented by military events, with the 69th Regiment, commanded by Colonel Edward Duffy, performing a sham battle between two battalions.[20]

Maintaining such facilities entailed balancing the stadium expenditure and paying the mortgage, with the membership relied on to help out with an extra $25,000 paid through 400 members' subscriptions. At the club's annual meeting in February 1902, 170 unsold capital stock shares were eagerly snapped up by members, with the *New York Times* observer writing: "More than half of these were immediately subscribed for, with promises that the remainder would be purchased during the coming week." Money raised would now go towards "the erection of a gymnasium, additional training quarters and dressing rooms adjoining the club-house."[21]

A year later, the *Sun*'s headline hailed forthcoming "Improvements to Be Made at Celtic Park" and spelled out the club's "active plans ... laid out for this years [sic] athletic season." Conway explained:

> The athletic committee has a large proportion for this year and the club proposes to foster amateur athletics in every way possible. Many improvements are to be made to the grounds.... The track is to be leveled and enlarged. Marble tablets will in future indicate the start and finish of all races. This will include tablets at the start and finish of the mile, half and quarter. There will also be stone tablets at the start of the 100, 120, 220 and 300 yard marks. Many other improvements will be made ... for the benefit of athletes, larger dressing rooms will be built and altogether the track

will be thoroughly renovated. Nearly all the important fixtures this year will be held at Celtic Park.

Complaints about a seating shortage for the more affluent patron were to be addressed: "It was found last year on certain occasions that the seating capacity was not equal to the emergency, and it is contemplated to erect a new field stand; the playground for the children is to be enlarged and many new attractive features will be added." The elevated corners for cycle racing were now deemed redundant in a stadium that would be booked almost every summer weekend for athletics, Gaelic football or hurling matches.[22]

The success of the stadium was fully assured as the club passed its fifth anniversary. The *Gaelic American* noted that since foundation, "a magnificent clubhouse containing bowling alleys, commodious quarters for athletes and many other improvements have been added to it." The *Evening World* cooed that Celtic Park "has during the past few years become the Mecca for athletes and lovers of athletic sports."[23]

* * *

What made Celtic Park popular for the city's Irish was not just its athletics, but as the venue for the city's Gaelic football and hurling matches. It was no mistake that so many athletic meetings at Laurel Hill were concluded by a Gaelic football or hurling game. The Big Apple's Irish organizations sought to bolster "picnics" with high-profile sporting attractions. The Corkmen's Patriotic, Protective and Benevolent Association's picnic at Forest View

Mel Sheppard crosses the line at Celtic Park on September 16, 1911, to win the Met AA Championships 880 yard race (Library of Congress).

Grove up the Hudson River in 1905 attracted 7,000 exiles from the Rebel County, but the huge crowd prevented a football match between New York and Boston being played because the organizers underestimated the attendance that could have been accommodated at Celtic Park.[24]

The GNYIAA wanted Celtic Park funded by the city's Irish-dominated organizations where groups like Clan Na Gael, the Ancient Order of Hibernians, and the Gaelic League would be encouraged to see Celtic Park as much theirs as the I-AAC's. This would lead to accusations that the club was an organization that John T. Ridge would sneeringly mock as mixing "patriotism and profit in varying degrees." The GAA itself was of course caught in a Catch-22 situation: They had already found out, to the cost of its own track and field events, that team games were far more appealing to the public, but they also needed a stadium. Was it better to go to the expense of building their own grounds or pay to use a stadium—and an Irish one at that? As Brendan Behan noted in his "the first item on the agenda is the split" regarding Irish political associations, this conundrum would inevitably tear the city's Gaelic games' fraternity apart.[25]

What was unique about New York was that from 1900 the city's GAA teams were taken over or replaced by Irish county societies. In 1902 Conway, Victor J. Dowling and Michael Sullivan tried to bring some order to America's GAA by calling the nation's clubs to organize themselves into a "National Association of Gaelic clubs" similar to what had happened to baseball 30 years previously. The move was in vain; as New York sides came under the umbrella of the Irish Counties Athletic Union in 1904, by 1909 it counted 24 county teams. Strong independent clubs with players drawn from one particular county, such as the overwhelmingly Tipperary Kickhams, were amalgamated or closed down. While the GNYIAA could still announce in October 1903 the opening of the Gaelic football season at Celtic Park with the New York championship being battled between a club side—the Irish Volunteers—and a county team—the Kerry Men's Association—this would be the last time that clubs would compete in the New York championship.[26]

The success of this coup was put down to the GAA's inability to form a strong national body. The 1914 enactment of the Gaelic Athletic Association of the United States was one example: When the so-called New York "Big Four"—Cork, Kerry, Kildare and Kilkenny—were asked to restrict their match income to $50 of expenses, they set up a rival "Gaelic League of New York." The GAAUS relented, and the "Four" returned for the 1916 season with their Celtic Park attendances often reaching five figures.[27]

Immediately the ICAU, despite clearly having a large cross-over of directors and members with the GNYIAA, envisioned itself as a sporting rival to the club, leading eventually to a turf war for the heart—and pockets—of the Irish sporting enthusiast. A letter to the *Irish World* in October 1904 from the Unions' Luke Finn and M.F. Dowling set out its aims to "propagate and develop ... all Irish athletics" and "to promote and cherish a brotherly feeling among all County organizations and in fact all Irishman, and banish from our midst any trifling grievances which may heretofore have existed among us." But soon it resented what it saw as the GNYIAA's exorbitant charging and sought a better deal, which received short thrift. Martin J. Hurley, writing in the *Irish American Advocate* under the pseudonym of Liam O'Shea in 1913, described the club as "some ungrateful scoundrels who, years ago, played the dastardly part of the grabber ... [with] the most open-faced robbery ever rubbed into a decent race."[28]

The "split within a split" of New York's Gaelic football between the "Big Four" and the rest, mirrored the twenty-first-century battle for TV sporting revenue. They sought financial distance against the smaller, less attractive counties, and this being the land of unrestrained capitalism, they wanted to keep the bulk of their games' gate money for themselves. In turn, the smaller counties vowed to smash simultaneously both the "Big Four's" power and their own dependence on the I-AAC. Their solution was to purchase their own grounds, Irish Park. Opened in 1907 on 12 acres in Wakefield, just south of Mount Vernon, Yonkers, it proved an unmitigated disaster that almost finished the ICAU.[29]

The "Big Four" saw any move to Yonkers as an unnecessary risk that made no economic sense. Wakefield was 12½ miles from Grand Central Sta-

Leitrim county Gaelic football team, one of New York City's many county associations that played at the Celtic Park, before and after of the ICAU's move to Irish Park, Yonkers, between 1907 and 1910 (Library of Congress).

tion, and more importantly was the sort of semi-rural outpost that detested sport, Sunday business and anything smacking of Roman Catholicism in almost equal measures. They were proved right: the other counties failed to find even half of the $70,000 asking price—almost three times the price of building Celtic Park—and were immediately lumbered with a huge mortgage. With none of this outlay, Celtic Park proved adequate for the needs of the "Big Four." The *Irish Advocate* noted Kerry's dissent:

> Kerrymen never stood aside when called upon to a charitable, manly, or national act.... The society will march on as it has done in the past and will not be bulldozed by any threats that may emanate from a few irresponsible men who claim all the virtues and find fault with men who differ from them, whether it be in the journalistic or football field.

The ICAU responded by preventing their members going to Celtic Park for the 1909 season. Paul Darby claims the "Big Four" were unmoved, "unwilling to play at a venue where they would receive lower gate receipts."[30]

As feared, the Yonkers authorities began invoking Blue Laws, with local Police Chief Daniel Wolff the man doing the most to shut down Irish Park. He was later slammed for his aggressive attitude during the 1909 Yonkers Marathon, where the *New York Tribune* claimed his "principal work during the afternoon consisted in driving a horse up and down the track" while his men jostled officials and reporters. When they complained to Wolff, he "merely smiled and drove his horse at the officials, scattering them right and left." Eventually, threatened by angry fans, they abandoned the race before the last competitors had even passed the finish line.[31]

Irish Park closed in 1910. The counties lost every dime invested, leading to the ICAU effectively splitting in two. It was taken over by new management, which included the New York GAA, in May 1911 a new "Irish Park" opened, with optimism that it and Celtic Park would both operate successfully: "With these two parks going full blast there should be plenty of opportunity for the young Irish athletes of this city to indulge their love of their national pastimes to their heart's content, and to do their part toward pushing them to the front," stated the *Irish American Weekly*. However, Irish Park barely lasted the year. As Darby concludes, the union had been fatally undermined and was "unable to oversee the longer-term health of Gaelic games in New York." Celtic Park would remain the home for Gaelic games for another 17 years.[32]

Indeed, by 1907 the club's financial report showed "a most gratifying condition," as after old debts were cleared, a net profit of $3,100 was returned. Shareholders swiftly approved $20,000 worth of previously proposed improvements, including a grandstand, a new pavilion, "new quarters" for athletes, and "a general overhauling of the grounds and track." All this despite protests over high admission charges: In July 1906, patrons refused to pay to watch the Irish Counties Athletic Games. The *New York Times* reported, "The reason for the drop in the box office receipts was the determination of the management to raise the regular admission to 50 cents, and the determination of the patrons who had planned to take in the carnival, not to pay it." Fans pressed against entrance gates and as "the portals gave way under strain ... the crowd quickly settled the question of price by paying nothing." Just $50 was collected from 5,000 spectators.[33]

* * *

Throughout its history, Celtic Park was only one-half of the I-AAC's property portfolio. While it suited its summer needs, it wasn't going to satisfy the club's winter athletic program. While its membership—mostly blue-collar—weren't interested in a yachting club, the club still needed training facilities, a gymnasium, offices, and an indoor venue in which to host boxing, "smokers," and other such events too small for Madison Square Garden. Neither did Celtic Park satisfy the club's desire to equal the NYAC in status: The I-AAC craved a Manhattan address, eventually settling for one on the same street as its rivals.

The GNYIAA/I-AAC first "club-house" at 207 East 58th Street, was opened on Saturday January 23, 1899. Formerly occupied by the "Wyandotee Club," it was re-decorated throughout, with upper floors used as committee and "card rooms" with a gymnasium promised. The club would remain there until May 23, 1905, when the *Evening World* wrote, "the latch was taken off the door" and "streams of the young men who run a mile in less than ten and men who throw the side of a house a mile when they feel like it" flowed into the "new commodious clubhouse" at 163 East 60th Street. The club would justify the move by citing growing harassment of athletes over accusations of professionalism: "The intensity of our feelings upon beholding our men struggling against the most adverse circumstances, impelled us also to secure for them the best facilities possible, even if somewhat expensive." Katchen writes that while the club eschewed elitism, this "three-story brownstone, across the street from today's Bloomingdale's" with a bar on each floor, a dining room and ballroom for functions and meetings, oozed middle-class respectability.[34]

By 1910, with membership outgrowing this building, the I-AAC moved to 110–112, East 59th Street. "It is a handsome brick building, 50 feet wide, 100 feet deep and 4 stories high," recorded the *New York Tribune*. Originally constructed for the Progress Club, it was fully equipped for the club's athletic needs. The first floor contained bowling alleys along with "facilities for serving dinners to a great number of persons," and included, according to the *New York Times*, "an extensive kitchen and refrigeration plant." The floor above housed the club's offices, two large meeting rooms and a billiard hall accommodating up to seven billiard or pool tables. The third floor had a "smoking or lounging room," a card room, a library and a "grill and cafe." The top floor was to be housed completely by a gymnasium with "hot and cold shower baths." Both the *Tribune* and *Times* chimed in unison from what appears to be a club press statement: "These rooms will be comfortably furnished and attractively decorated and will contain the many championship banners and the scores of cups and other trophies won by the athletes of this club." The *New York Times* added that the premises "when furnished will contain one of the most complete outfits in this country." On April 10, 1910, 400 members inspected the building for the first time, while Conway revealed that the club had received 300 applications in the past month, with the target being 1,000.[35]

The I-AAC celebrated the opening on May 28 with a "stag" for its members, bringing together, according to the *New York Times*, "one of the largest gathering of athletic and pugilistic stars ever assembled under one roof." The *New York Tribune* described "characters famous on the stage, track and squared circle ... on hand to help in the evening's entertainment" and to give the new clubhouse a well-heeled start in life. In attendance were the pugs Stanley Ketchel, Terry McGovern and Young Corbett, while Melvin Sheppard, Martin Sheridan and other athletes attended. Conway made a brief speech summarizing the club's stellar progress and what he predicted the future would bring, while an exhibition boxing match was arranged between "Kid" Griffo and Joe Bernstein, with Tommy Murphy—"the pride of Harlem"—refereeing. The light-hearted nature of this scrap was noted by the *Tribune*, when in the third round Griffo knocked down Bernstein. Murphy began to count: "1, 2, 3—aw! Get up and box. You go to our corner—4, 5— Will you get up? I'll count you out in a minute." Other bums and contenders on the night included Ketchel's opponent, Young Snowball, who was "an English importation" according to the *Times*, Badger O'Brien, Boyo Driscoll, Knockout Brown and his brother, the boringly named Adam, Sammy Keller, Mat Wells, Johnny Murphy, Johnny McAvoy, Young Melat and Young Burns.[36]

Further events were hosted: A "Formal Opening/Housewarming" on June 25, of boxing and wrestling, entertained more than 1,500 guests. "The new clubhouse came in for much admiration. It has been renovated and dressed up with new furnishings," noted the *New York Times*. "From the top to the bottom it is well appointed and has all the attractions a clubman looks for." Terry McGovern acted as official referee and Joe Dunn the timekeeper for the main event, a ten-round bout between Irish Paddy and Kid Rose. A pie-eating contest "between six negroes, each weighting more than 200 pounds," entertained the crowd, reported the *Times*. "There were twenty-five large huckleberry, cocoanut, and pumpkin pies," with the winner finishing off five and a half of them.[37]

By September, the club was hosting a city-wide amateur tournament: "Not since the palmy days of amateur boxing, when conducted by the [NYAC] and the old Knickerbocker and Manhattan organizations, has such a crowd attended one of these events," claimed the *New York Times*. The success of the night meant that the club would organize more. It also widened its audience with a "Ladies Night," primarily, cooed the *New York Times*, to "entertain the mothers, sisters and sweethearts of their members." After a theatrical vaudeville performance had concluded, "the dancing part of the program will proceed to give the athletes and their friends an opportunity to dance the light fantastic to their hearts' content." Top athletes seen at these functions "sat modestly in the audience ... with their lady friends, enjoy[ing] heartily the vaudeville bill" the committee had organized.[38]

There was no doubt that the GNYIAA/I-AAC sought to have facilities that matched its aspirations to be the best athletic club in the country. The challenge for the GNYIAA/I-AAC now was whether it could match the top clubs on the athletic field. It was a big call, and it needed crucially top-class athletes. The question was: Could—or even should—this be achieved through exclusively ethnically Irish representatives?

4

"Our name is the Irish-American Athletic Club"
The I-AAC and Other Ethnicities

Back in the mid–1960s, shortly after being appointed manager of Celtic Football Club, Glasgow, Scotland, Jock Stein was interviewed on television and asked a simple yet precarious question. "Given two [soccer players], of equal ability, but one Catholic and another Protestant, which one would you, Jock, sign?"

Scottish soccer was then dominated by two clubs: Celtic—like the I-AAC, a club founded by Irish immigrants—and Rangers, which had been hijacked by much of the city's indigenous non–Catholic community to fight a proxy civil war against the Irish community. However, one major difference was that while Rangers refused then to sign Catholics, Celtic had accepted Protestants for decades, of whom Stein was one example. Responding to the question, Stein sat back and let out two words: "The Protestant." The reporter, slightly wrong-footed, countered: "Why?" Stein's reply was simple and legendary: "Because I know that Rangers would never sign the Catholic."[1]

Some 60 years earlier, Pat Conway thought along similar lines. He knew that his club couldn't be successful with just Irish athletes. For one thing, there were not enough of them. For another, unlike Rangers, its rival, the NYAC, would welcome top Irish athletes. Also, as the *Irish American* would castigate them, New York's snobby "lace-curtain" Irish failed to support the I-AAC sufficiently:

> Pat Conway, the good-natured but unrivalled manager and maintainer of the IAAC, has kept such a string of world-beaters in hand that no other athletic organization in existence can approach him. Yet he is not supported as he should be. The wealthy Irish of this city take little or no interest in the truly wonderful exhibition of physi-

cal prowess which the race has been giving, and contribute little to the upkeep of this unrivalled institute of physical culture. In this, as in many other matters of high Irish import, an ignorance, a misappreciation of essential values, prevails among our well-to-do folk. They are glad enough to participate in Irish glory in the abstract, but when a concrete proposition is before them which deserves and should have their support, they cannot see it, they do not support it.

Conway had no choice but to seek out athletes that the NYAC wouldn't admit: Jews, Southern and Eastern Europeans, and African Americans. While the club remained Irish in name, from its coaching staff to its most lowly runner, non–Irish athletes would prove pivotal to success.[2]

There was therefore a certain contradiction in the title of "Irish-American" that welcomed other communities. It could be argued that given the period the club operated, the I-AAC was one of the earliest promoters of sporting integration. Indeed, between 1900 and 1908, two of the U.S. Olympic team's five non–White Christians were also members of the I-AAC.[3]

How the club coped with this contradiction mirrors how Tammany Hall's Democratic machine conceded that they also couldn't rely solely on the Irish vote. It is easy to oversimplify the battle between both the I-AAC and the NYAC down to ethnicity. The Irish Olympic historian Kevin McCarthy claims that the "difficulties for the Irish in gaining acceptance among the elite of such as the [NYAC] had led the immigrants to effectively set up their own club." But class played a far greater factor, because the NYAC always recruited Irish athletes.[4]

* * *

Admitting "outsiders" wasn't at the top of the list of the new club's priorities, but there were plenty of good reasons why it should embrace its "humble" origins. At the Astor in 1906, Daniel F. Cohalan's speech welcoming back the Irish-American athletes from Athens played on this, hailing his "poor man's club" while sidestepping the uncomfortable discrepancy of hosting a banquet in one of New York's top hotels. The *Irish American Weekly* as early as 1901 expressed an opinion that the club belonged to more than just Irish-Americans: "It is an excellent thing to encourage this Irish-American Athletic Association. Not Irishmen alone, but all who are interested in the development of the human race, should watch the records and the relative achievements of this association."[5]

The Jewish runner Abel Kiviat recalled the disparity between both New York clubs, claiming that "the wealthier boys" tended to join the NYAC. In contrast, the I-AAC had "very few college men," having instead "guys out of grammar school or from high school or kids who worked. If you could run or jump, you could try out." Yet this lack of exclusivity proved an asset, not a hindrance. Kiviat was clearly impressed when he joined in 1909, not just

Abel Kiviat (*center*) flanked by John J. Eller (*left*) and John Reynolds before departing for the Stockholm Olympics, 1912. Kiviat was a Jewish schoolboy sensation when he joined the club in 1909 (Library of Congress).

because of the I-AAC's reputation as an "athletic powerhouse," but because he felt at ease with what Katchen describes as the club's administrators' "democratic approach ... [that] stood in stark contrast to that of its great rival, the NYAC." Clearly he saw this as not just giving an opportunity for every ethnic Irish athletic protégé in the New York, regardless of job or wealth, but to *every* male athlete in New York.[6]

Outside of Irish-Americans, athletes of British or Northern European ancestry made up the largest group of members. There were the Finns Hannes Kolehmainen, Frans Johansson and Bruno Brodd, the Swede John Eke and the Italian Emilio Lunghi. Even English runners Harold A. Wilson, "Baldy" Jack Monument, a 24-year-old, follicly-challenged middle-distance runner, and Anthony Higgins joined. The *Evening World* noted that for the latter in 1911, "the climate here is better for him than that of his native country, and he expects to walk in even better time than he did on the other side of the ocean." Coaches were also foreign: Ernie Hjertberg was a Swedish-born former Columbia University manager, while his successor, Lawson Robertson, was a sprinter from Aberdeen, Scotland.[7]

However, it was Jewish and black athletes who established I-AAC as the club for all. Of New York's 4,669,162 inhabitants in 1910, the African American population of 91,709 was dwarfed by the mostly newly disembarked 1,252,000 Jews, the biggest immigrant group to arrive since the Irish, making up almost half the nation's Jewish population. This was a community, Peter Levine claims, similar to the Irish in their desire to both assimilate and enjoy sports:

> Aspiring immigrants eagerly embraced obvious and accessible avenues that permitted immediate identification as Americans, even as they tackled more formidable barriers of language, livelihood, and prejudice. Indeed, central to our concerns is the importance of appreciating that, like other outsiders—the Irish before them, Italian immigrants who arrived in the United States when they did, and American blacks who followed—enthusiasm for sport, both as participants and spectators, provided one such route for Jewish immigrants.[8]

Altogether three Jewish I-AAC members won Olympic medals. While not a huge number, it still forced one reporter for the *American Hebrew*, New York's principal English-language weekly, to remark in 1915 that it's "more common to find the names of the star Jewish performers on the roster of the Irish-American athletic Club" before wondering whether it brought "joy to thousands of Irishmen when they [saw] the colors of the IAAC brought to the fore by such loyal sons of Erin" with Jewish and other non–Irish surnames.[9]

The first of these "exotic" members was Myer Prinstein. Born in the then-Russian (now Polish) town of Szczuczyn, his parents migrated in 1883 to upstate New York, where Prinstein later studied law at Syracuse University. Captaining its athletics team at Philadelphia's Franklin Field in 1900, he broke A.C. Kraenzlein's world record in the long jump. And while Peter O'Connor broke it a month later, it stood as an American record for 20 years.[10]

After winning a gold and silver at the 1900 Olympics, Prinstein moved to New York to open a law practice, but like many top Jewish athletes, he found the doors of the NYAC closed. The superintendent of the Young Men's Hebrew Association, William Mitchell, would later echo this at a meeting of the Atlas (Athletic) Club in 1907, that Jews "at present are barred from other clubs, partly on account of their religion and partly because they find themselves in an environment which is not congenial."[11]

It was at the AAU All-Around Championships at Celtic Park in July 1902 that Prinstein, representing the Syracuse YMCA, was probably first approached by GNYIAA officials. Prinstein was unlike most other Jews who would join the Irish: A varsity champion, an Olympic gold medalist, and a brief world record holder, who should've been able into walk into any club. While there is nothing written about Prinstein's reasons for joining the I-AAC, it seems likely that the NYAC were sufficiently confident in their strength to decline his services.[12]

Turn of the century Hiberno-Jewish relations in New York often cement the reputation of the Irish as a community who, once up the ladder, would swiftly pull it up behind them. But despite the undoubted antagonism between both communities at low levels, where the Irish viewed Jews as Christ-killers and the Jews looked on the Irish as drunks, Gil Rabak observes what the young Jewish male also saw:

> The Irish represented an Americanization model: they spoke the language and displayed toughness, and serving as police officers, firefighters, politicians, and pugilists, they emanated authority and self-confidence. Irish males exemplified a type of manliness that attracted some Jewish boys and young men—Jewish prizefighters and ballplayers frequently assumed Irish names.[13]

During this period of large-scale immigration, there were no major disturbances like the Orange Day riots of the 1870s. Local Irish politicians courted Jewish votes and offered job opportunities, lucre and graft previously reserved for their own, to get them. While there was still only one Jewish district leader by 1907, Tammany made appeals in Yiddish, employed young, ambitious Jews, and would come down hard on anti–Semitism. One story claims that notorious Tammany leader "Big Tim" Sullivan got the NYPD to throw out a group of Irish toughs who were harassing orthodox Jews at their clubhouse, which was subsequently turned into a synagogue. Indeed Sullivan's most famous protégé was the man who organized one of sport's biggest frauds—the 1919 World Series—Arnold Rothstein.[14]

Whatever his reasons, by the end of August 1902, Prinstein wore the Winged Fist vest at the Metropolitan Association Championships at Celtic Park. While the Knickerbocker AC took the points competition, Prinstein managed to beat the Knicks' champion, W.S. Edwards, in the running broad jump by over four feet, making Prinstein the first-ever champion of the GNYIAA at a major event.[15]

Prinstein won two further national championships in the long jump and three Olympic golds with the club in 1904 and 1906, although in May 1905, the *Sun* claimed that he was leaving the club, running unattached until he decided his next stop. He reconsidered and remained an "Irish-American" athlete for a further five years.[16]

On his retirement from competition, his legal career took a turn for the worse. In 1910, proceedings commenced for disbarment following accusations that he had refused to return a client's mortgage deposit in 1907, claiming it as his fee. The following February, Prinstein was disbarred by the Appellate division of the Supreme Court for "misappropriating" the deposit. The finding claimed that his explanation was "evidently an afterthought for the purpose of excusing what was clearly a breach of trust and serious professional misconduct." He moved from his Broadway home out to Jamaica, Queens, where he opened a stationery and real-estate business, while being the financial secretary of his local synagogue. He died young in 1925 at 45 from heart disease.[17]

In contrast, Abel Kiviat, the I-AAC's second-most successful Jewish athlete, with two medals at the 1912 Olympics, was not an established athlete. Snapped up after a successful year in the Public School's Athletic League with Curtis High School, Staten Island, Katchen illustrates the complexities and contradictions of amateur athletics in the early twentieth century. Much of the club's success was due to its two top coaches, Ernie Hjertberg and Lawson Robertson. Hjertberg's innovative techniques in training, expounded in his 1914 thesis, *Athletics in Theory and Practice*, were ahead of his time, while Robertson advocated a novel approach to a healthy diet and preparation. But it was their collective, "aggressive" recruitment policy that aided the I-AAC's success.[18]

Kiviat moved seamlessly from a schoolboy runner to unofficial world record holder to Metropolitan champion in less than four months. On May 29, 1909, he won the half-mile and mile titles at the PSAL annual Outdoor Championships. Watching on was Robertson, who was so impressed that he encouraged Kiviat to write to the I-AAC's secretary, David Keane, to plead for a trial: "I'm 18 years old and very strong for my age. I want to become a fast runner and think I can succeed if you will give me a trial."[19]

Katchen argues that Robertson, who had taken over from Hjertberg in 1907, was under great pressure to maintain standards. To entice Kiviat, he resorted to one of the oldest tricks in recruiting athletes: The offer of a job. This was nothing new. The NYAC was reported in 1897 as luring John Flanagan with work and paying his registration fee. The I-AAC had done likewise with Johnny Hayes before the 1908 Olympics. Now Robertson was forced to do this again by getting Kiviat a Wall Street summer job that Kiviat recalled was "little higher than a runner," and the cab fare to Celtic Park to seal the deal.[20]

Kiviat entered his first athletic meeting with the Winged Fist singlet at the American Athletic Club's Annual Games on July 11, where he won the

Cigarette card featuring Lawson Robertson. The Scottish-born sprinter and high jumper was, along with his predecessor, Ernie Hjertberg, an innovative club coach of the I-AAC (Mecca Cigarettes card).

660Yds race. The *New York Times* enthused, "In yesterday's event [Kiviat] went to the front almost from the flash of the pistol, and ran the other contestants … off their feet." The following month, Kiviat entered the ⅔ mile handicap of the Asbury Park Athletic Club. Despite losing to the YMCA's William F. Fawley, who had a handicap of 60 yards, Kiviat came within two yards of reaching him and also broke William G. George's 1882 world record by three-fifths of a second.[21]

With the I-AAC refusing to attend the national championships in Seattle, Kiviat had to wait for the Met Championships to grab a major title. With his "boy wonder" reputation, he breezed past his rivals in the final lap of the 1Mile race, beating club-mate Joseph Bromilow into second place. The *New York Tribune* concluded he had won the race "just about as he had pleased," while the *Times* enthused that "the phenomenal schoolboy" had ran "one of the best races" of his short career: "He hung back for the greater part of the way, being content to let the others do the pacemaking."[22]

Another notable Jewish runner was Alvah Meyer, the 1912 Olympics 100m silver medalist, and a double world record holder over 60 and 330 yards.

Meyer appeared from nowhere in June 1911; representing the Irish-Americans, he came in third behind the Mercury Foot's W.G. Packard and F.J. Reynolds in the 100yds handicap dash at the NYAC's Spring Games. That same month, he came in second in both the Met and National Juniors' 110Yds and 220Yds races. Of the latter competition in Pittsburgh, the *New York Times* wrote, "The day was conducive to the making of good performances, and crack-a-jack work began with the 'hundred,' won by the New England sprinting champion, H.P. Drew, a colored lad, who scampered away with the event from A.T. Meyer, a much improved lad, from the Irish-American's [sic] of New York." At the Mets, he beat clubmates James Rosenberger and J.J. Archer in both the 100 and 220Yds events.[23]

There was also Harry Hymen, a minor runner who was apparently the man Ernie Hjertberg recruited to get Mel Sheppard to join the Winged Fist. According to Katchen, Hyman, a fellow alumnus of Pennsylvania, accompanied Sheppard back to the city of Brotherly Love after he'd won an invitation race in New York in December 1905. By the following morning, Hjertberg had managed to get Sheppard's address and was knocking on the front door with a membership form before a rival could dispatch their coaches. Finally, the 1904 Olympic long jump silver medalist, Dan Frank, joined the club around 1906 from the New West Side AC.[24]

* * *

Unlike Jews, there were no obstacles to men like Melvin Sheppard joining the NYAC. Sheppard was neither Irish nor from New York, originally from a working class American Protestant family in Almonesson, South New Jersey, who after years of moving around finally settled in Philadelphia when he was 15. Attending an Ivy League University meant that he would have been a shoe-in for the NYAC. Another athlete whose ethnic group wouldn't have barred him joining the Mercury Foot club was German-born William Gottlieb Frank. Originally from today's Baden-Württemberg state, he started out as a cyclist in the early '90s before a serious accident around 1892 made him switch to middle-distance running with the New West Side AC, before joining the Irish-Americans sometime around the turn of the century.[25]

In the wake of the 1908 Olympics, this aggressive recruitment was drawing the envy of other clubs, as Harvey Cohn, a young, Methodist middle-distance runner was joined by Ralph Young, Edward Cook and John Eller, the son of German immigrants from New Jersey, whose brother Bob also joined the club. The *Sun* would later sardonically remark about the diversity of the club when comparing it to other pastimes unrecognized by the AAU, "such as butting through the shopping district, tug of warring on a subway station platform during the rush hour or figuring out the nationality of a given athlete who runs under the colors of the Irish American Athletic Club."[26]

The athlete whom Sheppard beat narrowly in London for his 1500m gold was Lincolnshire-born Harold Allan Wilson. He had entered the White City games as the favorite, not only running on home ground but as the first man to cover the distance in under four minutes. He made up for the disappointment of silver in the 1500m with a gold in the 3Mile Team race. The following year, Wilson decided to try his luck across the pond, arriving in late May aboard the appropriately named White Star Line's liner, *Celtic*. Within an hour of setting foot in the United States, the former Hallamshire Harriers runner was taken to Celtic Park, where he filled out an application form. The *Sun* reported, "It is not known whether or not Wilson was a member of the Irish American AC before landing, but at any rate [they] made an attempt a couple of weeks ago to register Wilson with the AAU." The club secretary, John J. Dolan, had already asked the AAU "registry clerk" to grant Wilson a permit; thinking Wilson was a local resident, he promptly issued one. However, when the AAU realized that Wilson was somewhere over the Atlantic at the time, they quickly cancelled his card, claiming that he needed a special permit from the AAU national registration committee, and was meanwhile ineligible for any championship.[27]

Wilson was cleared in time to race at the New York Press Club Games on June 26, along with the Irish-American's other top-ranked international "signing," Emilio Lunghi, another silver medalist to Sheppard (800m) in London, and the first Italian to win an Olympic medal, who it seemed had been persuaded by the I-AAC to travel to America. The *New York Times* noted, with not a little exaggeration, the international attractiveness of this event: "While the track events will bring together the greatest runners in the world, the path events have nothing on the field con-

Cigarette card featuring Harold Wilson. An Englishman, he was one of the many foreign athletes who joined the club when visiting the U.S. (Mecca Cigarettes card).

tests. The greatest galaxy of weight men that ever competed either here or abroad will battle for the laurels."[28]

Born in Genoa the day before St. Patrick's Day, 1886, Lunghi was later advertised as the star of the Labor Day Tailteann Games, breaking Lon Myers' 26-year world record in the 700Yds. Later that month, he broke the world half-mile record in Montreal, before finally, at the I-AAC's Fall Games on October 10, smashing the ⅔Mile record that had stood since 1883. He remained with the Irish-Americans for a year, receiving Honorary Life Membership in 1911, before returning to Italy, dying young at 38 from typhoid fever.[29]

Questions were asked concerning what the foreign athletes got out of it all: Who paid their passage or organized accommodation and work for them when they arrived? Wilson—who was not wealthy, yet living off unearned income and who turned professional within a year—was being registered before he walked onto the quay. How was a self-proclaimed ethnic club able to attract these foreigners?

The flow continued. The Olympics multi-medalist and original "Flying Finn," Juho "Hannes" Kolehmainen, was snapped up shortly after passing the Statue of Liberty, irking more people outside America than within. A few British newspapers made the false allegation that he was detained at Ellis Island after arriving from Glasgow and was likely to be deported: "Numerous powerful athletic organizations are interesting themselves on the Finn's behalf, and a big effort is being made to secure his release," the *Yorkshire Post* concluded its report. Another observer, in the *Dundee Evening Telegraph*, sarcastically observed:

> The reason why this world-famous athlete bearing the Celtic name Kolehmainen should join the Irish-American organization as a member is that it was the club which was first at the pier when the ship came in.... Otherwise he might conceivably have become affiliated to the Greek-American Club, the Chinese-American Club or the Hebrew-American club.[30]

Kolehmainen's brother, Willie, denied any inducement to go to the United States, and Hannes added that he aimed to work there as a stonemason. However, later in the month the *New York Times* reported an angry article by Georges Rozet in *L'Information* titled "Club Spirit and Crimping," saying that the "bitterness felt by the French Nation over the defeat in the Olympic games by the Americans still rankles deep." Rozet claimed that American sporting circles had largely rejected Kolehmainen, "disgusted at his lack of sporting loyalty, or, rather, fearing that one of their clubs would enlist him to the detriment of others." That club was the I-AAC, and Rozet sneered that it was "the first whose representative was able to reach him and argue with him in the proper way." He suspected underhand machinations while also conceding that this "custom" had also "taken root" in his homeland: "In the United States, the clubs have been for a long time past given over to a fierce contest of professionalism among themselves, taking each other's men away by open bids of dollars, or, perhaps by the bait of disguised advantages."[31]

Kolehmainen could have chosen the I-AAC not just because of its success. He may have been impressed that the I-AAC was a club that operated with many ethnicities. Also, his disgust at the Russian flag being raised for his victories was such that he wished he hadn't won his medals; therefore he could freely discuss national grievances with Irish clubmates.[32]

The I-AAC signed other foreign athletes like the Swede John Eke, although Nikolaos Georgantas, the 1906 Stone Throwing Olympic gold medalist, was just a passing interest when he visited America. The "wonder athlete ... who was so sensationally vanquished at the discus free style by Martin Sheridan" was announced as a feature at the I-AAC's Labor Day Games, and the *Evening World* noted that Georgantas' failure to keep the Discus championship in Greece entailed exile: "He is limbering up here in New York, and when he gets into good shape he will try it out with Sheridan with the hope that if he wins he can return in triumph to his classic native land."[33]

The *New York Times* complained that Greeks and Americans loved a cheerful loser, and Georgantas was an "uncheerful" one. "When Sheridan beat him, and beat him fairly ... he declined to hear his name when he was called up by the Crown Prince of Greece to receive some lesser prizes. He was extruded from his official position, cut, ostracized, forced to leave. And now he has come to New York to 'make candy.'" Georgantas gave an exhibition in front of 10,000 spectators, with at least 1,000 Greeks turning up to give him "a tremendous ovation." Also passing through that day was the Australian double bronze Olympian, Nigel Barker, who ran in a special 300yds run with the I-AAC's J.W. Colliton and J.H. Teeven, finishing behind both runners.[34]

A year later, more news of a "sensation in world of sport" reached the United States. Minoru Fuji, a Japanese student from the Imperial University, Tokyo, had reportedly broken two world records—one with a 100Yds time of nine and two-fifths second, the other pole-vaulting 12 feet and six inches. While Robert Edgren in the *Evening Word* wisecracked that "athletic experts here pointed out the fact that the average Japanese runs like a duck," he conceded there was "a great desire" for athletic-loving New Yorkers to see Fuji perform in the Big Apple. Who else but the Irish-Americans, always looking out "for athletic features with which to make its meets more interesting," could bring over Fuji? Dolan invited him to compete for the Irish in the national championships, but he replied:

> I duly received your favor of the 21st of April by which you kindly invited me to enter in you Athletic Games of this year. Very very sorry to inform you that, having entered to the Department of Foreign Affairs in Tokyo after my university studies, it

became for me my formerly [sic] intention to visit your athletic fields must be changed for a time.[35]

* * *

There was, however, one ethnic group that was harder to accommodate in early twentieth century American society than any other. It's hard to imagine any form of sport today without black athletes, but the initial two Olympics were almost devoid of them. Not until St. Louis, 1904, was there a black medalist—George Coleman Poage—ironic given that this was the venue for one of the greatest Olympic stains, James E. Sullivan's "Anthropological Games," a circus-style offshoot of the main event, that Kevin McCarthy records "saw African pygmies and other tribes brought half way around the world for little more than fairground sideshow entertainment."

John B. Taylor during his University of Pennsylvania days. He was the I-AAC's first black athlete and the first African American to win a gold medal at the Olympics (University of Pennsylvania Archives Digital Image Collection).

Top-class black athletes at the time were a rarity. As John Carlos noted later, much to the exclusion of myths about heel bones and genetics, black athletes needed training as much as any white to succeed. Excluded from baseball outside the "Negro Leagues," there were some good black athletic clubs, like the Salem Crescent AC and the hip-sounding Smart Set AC of Brooklyn, who were making their mark on local junior championships, and eventually in the AAU Championships. Instead, African American athletes initially emerged through Northeastern universities. The first of these promising athlete-students was a Philadelphia resident, John Baxter Taylor, an athlete the *Evening World* described upon his sudden early death as "the greatest negro athlete America ever produced."[36]

Taylor was born in Washington, D.C., but had moved north at seven. Educated at

Brown Preparatory School, he was first noticed in 1903 at New Haven when he beat Yale's interscholastic record, held by J.F. Doyle, for the quarter-mile. He entered the University of Pennsylvania, eventually studying veterinary medicine, and was coached by Mike Murphy, the Irish-American trainer who would overcome deafness to lead the American team at London and Stockholm.[37]

By 1905, the New York Irish had one of their first glimpses of Taylor when he ran in the I-AAC Winter Games. The *New York Tribune* wrote: "[T]he negro runner, said to be the fastest one-quarter mile runner in America, and who made himself famous on the Penn track team, was hailed with great applause when ... he won handily by twenty yards." Two years later, as he completed his studies, the Irish-Americans took the decision to remove "the color line" and approach him. He had caught their eye at the recent Pastime AC meeting at Madison Square Garden, where he equaled the 600Yds record. The *New York Tribune* reported that "Taylor was regarded as more or less of an unknown quantity before the race ... but demonstrated his ability to break into the middle distance game a week ago, when he ran a fast mile in the college relay race."[38]

As with others, the intricate details, inducements or promises were never disclosed. The *New York Times* even reported with "surprise" that Taylor's membership had been cleared in time for the summer, adding that he had tried to join the Pastime AC but had been refused membership, with the proposal or the refusal leading to "the withdrawal of some influential members from the club." The Irish denied this: "In explaining their action the Irish-American advocates declared that Taylor had applied to no other club than the Irish American, and that in view of his ability and favorable reputation they considered it proper not to draw the color line and exclude him from membership."[39]

Unlike other non–Irish invitations to join the I-AAC, this move was clearly far from uncontroversial, with the implication being that Taylor's ability swung his membership. Issues of race are complex, with many people more "prejudiced," often ignorant prisoners of their own upbringings. At the I-AAC, Matt McGrath, who having no children adopted a Chinese orphan that he and his wife had met while holidaying in upstate New York, with "the little 3½-year-old Chinese and the burly Irishman from Tipperary had taken such a liking to each other that McGrath decided they must not be parted."[40]

What was perhaps more telling of contemporary attitudes, and how to combat them, was the meeting to allow Taylor membership. Despite the *Evening World* describing it as a multi-racial club "which despite its name, includes the greatest athletes in the country and of every race and creed," Taylor wasn't just another non–Irish runner causing a little disquiet at what some thought should remain an "Irish" club. Central to all things was skin color. While signing Taylor was to have huge ramifications for the club's reputation and identity, it wasn't going to be painless.[41]

One report, if accurate, describes the polemic of accepting Taylor, one which the *New York Mail* described as "a fine burst of eloquence on the part of several members" of the club's hierarchy. "'We don't want a naygur in oor club' said one. 'We have enrolled on our lists the foam of the Irish aristocracy and it behaves us to draw the color line in self-respect.'" The *Mail* feared that there were as many members present keen to keep Taylor out as to let him in, "and it sure did look bad for the speedy smoke until President Conway, liberal minded, genial and democratic in the extreme, took the floor." Conway wasted no time; despite reaching for the "n" word, he argued how his club's relations to prospective African American members should be

> gintlemin, the greatest runner we have in our club ... is a Dootchmin [Bonhag]. The greatest broad jumper in the wurruld ... is a member of our club, and a Jew [Prinstein].... Now if our name was the Irish AC, these names might look inconglomerinous (whatever that is), but it is not. Our name is the Irish-American Athletic Club, and under that wurrud, American, comes our justificableness in having these Dootchmin and Jews as our fellow-members, an' where there's room for Dootchmin and Jews, there's no excuse in this wurruld for keeping out a man like this excellent naygur, more power to his lungs and speed to his legs.

After this forceful speech, Taylor was unanimously elected amid "tremendous applause," with the members exiting to the bar "still cheering."[42]

To put this decision in context, it was four further years before the NYPD would employ its first black cop, Samuel J. Battle. Taylor's recruitment therefore suggested that the I-AAC now had an "anyone welcome" policy. Indeed, countering any suggestion of a color line, one "high AAU authority" announced, following Southern "reservations" at Taylor's 1907 National 440Yds victory: "There has never been any such [racial] discrimination in our sports, nor will there be—a good amateur, whether he be black or white, will have always have the same footing in the AAU." Certainly if you were a top African American athlete, you would be welcomed. The truth was that few others joined. W. Randolph Granger, Roy Morse, and Irving Tecumseh Howe were all listed at one point or another as I-AAC members, while in 1910, Lawson Robertson eyed up Jimmie Ravenall, a 17-year-old "negro sprinter of the High School of Commerce," who he predicted would be a future champion. But none can be found competing for the club.[43]

What would have happened if Taylor were just an average athlete trying to join the club is a valid question. Perhaps in view of the times, he wouldn't have even bothered asking. But Taylor's admittance was something that other Irish athletic clubs saw as positive. Boston's Irish aims at re-establishing an Irish athletic club in 1911 were to be "modeled" on the I-AAC. Led by a desire to form an egalitarian rival to the exclusive Boston AA, open to all Bostonians,

Dr. John McDonnell, a former weight thrower with the by-now crumbling South Boston AC, told the *Boston Journal*:

> I have always been interested in the organization of an Irish-American athletic club in Greater Boston and believe in developing athletes who will stick to a club that has brought them from the novice state into the championship class.... I will always be ready to add my mite [sic] in furthering the interests of a local club that will have among its prime objects the development of athletes who are not born with gold spoons in their mouths.

The *Journal* added that the New York I-AAC "numbers Hebrew and gentile in its ranks ... and J.B. Taylor, deceased ... also wore the winged fist."[44]

Despite what could be seen as half the club's members initially wanting Taylor barred from admission, I-AAC cranks came to adore Taylor. The sprinter became an instant hit, although, being a student, his initial appearances were limited. He competed at the NYAC Games at Travers Island on June 29, with the *New York Tribune* noting his as the "best performance of the day on the track" after he beat W.T. Coholan of Yale. An intrigued *Washington Post*, the noted newspaper from Taylor's birthplace, claimed in September 1907 in an article simultaneously printed in *The Sun*: "It may be said that there is no athlete more popular with the Celtic Park crowd than Taylor. In fact, it is hard to say whether even Martin Sheridan, well liked though he is, is more highly considered than the Negro lad ... every man of the Irish contingent around the track roots himself hoarse to see Taylor win." The following year, Taylor was picked to travel to London, becoming the first black athlete to win an Olympic gold. Sadly, his stay at Celtic Park was brief, and the reason had nothing to do with racial prejudice. In the late autumn of 1908, he contracted typhoid fever and passed away after two weeks' illness on December 2, 1908, aged just 26.[45]

The needs to compete with the NYAC entailed attracting athletes without Irish ancestry. With New York containing an ever-growing immigrant population and an expanding black community, the GNYIAA/I-AAC had the perfect opportunity to gather plenty of top athletes denied membership elsewhere. But before this happened, Conway needed to create an active organization. He needed a "brand," and the best way to achieve this was to organize athletic meetings that could showcase his new club.

5

"An overwhelming success numerically and financially"
Establishing the GNYIAA Between 1898 and 1904

Whatever they thought of identity, the most imperative thing for Conway and his colleagues was to open an athletic club. The GNYIAA was fortunate it had two previous, albeit unsuccessful, legacies, plus a huge ethnic market to draw on. It had thrown up an athletic stadium in no time and agreed on a club logo to be later known as the "Winged Fist." "The Irish Athletic Club [sic], after due consideration, has decided that the crest of the organization shall be a 'Red Hand' supported on each side by the wings of Mercury," reported the *Irish American Weekly*, "The emblem, while being consistently patriotic, is at the same time emphatically symbolic of strength, fighting powers, speed, athletic agility, and is undoubtedly the ideal adornment that should decorate the breast of an Irish athlete of modern times."[1]

When the day of reckoning came, the club was prepared. Tuesday, May 30, 1898: Memorial Day. Eleven track and field events were featured, attracting an impressive 238 entries and 5,000 patrons, including 3,000 seated in the grandstand. Harvard's Dick Grant was the star, winning the half-mile handicap race. John Flanagan won the 16LB hammer handicap, while the Thomas F. Meaghers beat the Emeralds in hurling, 1–3 to 0–1, and the Kickhams overcame Enterprise, 2–4 to 1–3, in Gaelic football. The Irish-born Long Island City Magistrate Henry Brann made an opening address, and the stadium was decked out with American and Irish flags, while Somerset's Band was hired to play music.[2]

Celtic Park's facilities were immediately recognized by the Metropolitan Association of the AAU. They chose the Queens location for their annual championships, two days before July 9, owing to the management of the original venue, Ambrose Park, failing to maintain the track. The *Sun* noted that the MA's Track and Field Committee "decided to change the location rather than invite a fiasco through incomplete appointments."[3]

This championship was particularly important because the major New York clubs had foregone the Nationals in Chicago due to cost and distance. There was plenty of Irish interest, particularly in NYAC's John Flanagan taking on James S. Mitchell, now wearing the "Brazilian cross of the Pastime AC." Flanagan triumphed in the 16LB Hammer and the 56LB Weight, while his club won every contest except the half-mile. However, the day was a slight disappointment for the GNYIAA: A poor crowd attended, while the heavy morning rain made the track sluggish. Still, the *New York Times* chimed in that Celtic Park "afforded a satisfactory and picturesque arena in which to decide athletic honors," dismissing the slow track on its "newness." Further events were penciled in for 1898 as other clubs used the stadium to host "monster meets." The Pastime, New West Side and Star Athletic Clubs teamed up to hold their own "Triple Meet" two months later—labeled a championship for the smaller clubs—as 2,000 spectators boosted the GNYIAA's coffers.[4]

The following year saw the club organize a number of events: the Memorial Day Games; Fourth of July "Athletic Festival"; Labor Day "Grand Athletic Carnival"; Star and Pastime ACs "Monster Meet" with Xavier AA as the third club; Thanksgiving Day "Carnival of Sports," comprised of rugby, hurling and Gaelic football and which was attended by the visiting IPP leader, John Redmond. To raise funds, Frawley and Prendergast sought another Irish athletic "invasion." They contacted Patrick Davin and Tom Kiely in Ireland and hoped to have a party in New York for the 1899 Labor Day's Games. The tour failed to materialize, and another effort was made in early 1900, which ended with a few individual athletes coming.[5]

However, competitors at their meets were still exclusively non–GNYIAA members, while the club provided no judges. Frawley simultaneously acted as the Knickerbockers' captain and the GNYIAA's Vice-President, while Michael Cregan, listed as the first athlete to wear the club's singlet in competition, didn't join the club from New West Side until 1900.[6]

That year saw the GNYIAA host another Memorial Day "Carnival of Sport," a Fourth of July "Midsummer Carnival," and finally on Labor Day, with "the gold harp of Erin on a green background and the Stars and Stripes waving in the breeze," its "Annual Festival and Games." These would be the mainstay for future years, supplementing events hosted by other clubs, the GAA or Irish organizations. Notable GNYIAA wins included Cregan taking first place in the 100 and 220Yds races in May, while William McCarthy won the 3Mile handicap race in September.[7]

In early June, Celtic Park hosted the 15Mile marathon qualifier for the Paris Olympics. Arthur Newton beat 24 other athletes—none GNYIAA members—in a race shortened because of the belief that two good marathon runs in two months would be impossible. The 69th Regiment used the grounds in April, and St. Francis Xavier College held its annual games there on June 21.[8]

St. George's Athletic Club hosted their meeting at Laurel Hill on July 28, while the New York Lodge No. 1 of the Benevolent and Protective Order of Elks also hired out the grounds the Saturday following Labor Day. Finally, a "dual meeting" between the Star AC and St. Bartholomew's AC in late October saw the Irish visitor Denis Horgan as the star of the event. His American record for the 16LB shot was disqualified when the missile weighed in at 15 pounds and ten ounces.[9]

After being postponed from May 26, the 1901 season opened up with 8,000 patrons attending the Memorial Day Games and the opening of the new clubhouse. June saw an "interstate" Gaelic football match between the Worcester Shamrocks of Massachusetts and the local O'Connells and the St. Bartholomew's AC Annual Games. With almost 500 entries from the Star, Pastime, Union Settlement, Xavier and West Side YMCA clubs, and competitors from as far away as Ithaca and Philadelphia, indicated to the *Sun* "a decided revival of interest in track and field contests." The *New York Tribune* went further, quoting retired athletes remembering the lean years: "Many of the old-time athletes who were present remarked that they had never witnessed such a large number of athletes taking part in one meet in ten years."[10]

Independence Day saw the 69th Regiment Games replace the traditional GNYIAA carnival, and was remembered chiefly for John Flanagan beating Alfred Plaw's brief world record for the 16LB hammer (within a nine-foot circle) by almost four feet. The day was concluded with Gaelic football, a regimental parade and a fireworks display. August saw a cycle "outing" under the control of the Royal Arcanum Wheelmen of Manhattan.[11]

Then came the news of a major coup in strengthening the club's athletic squad. Following the Met Championships on July 27, where he collected firsts in the 16LB hammer, the "Fifty-Six" and the discus, John Flanagan finally decided to jump from the NYAC. A brief notice appeared in the *New York Times* of August 7, declaring, "John Flanagan will compete Saturday under the colors of the Irish-American AC at the carnival of the Olympia AC ... and will endeavor to break the world's record for throwing the 56LB weight." Rumors circulated that Flanagan had been "expelled," but the *Brooklyn Daily Eagle* dismissed the story as "a statement so incorrect that it is amusing," adding that he had even been feted by the NYAC on the night of his resignation. However, a three-month period of being unattached beckoned, with the AAU Registration Committee's chairman, John Steil, stating, "The rule is clear.... Flanagan has been in athletics long enough to know it, and if he competed in the Olympia AC games on Saturday for the Irish-American AC he will suspend himself without any action by the committee."[12]

With Flanagan a member, the Labor Day Games was now the year's highlight. Top local athletes, a selection from Yale, and the recent arrival of Peter O'Connor promised an enticing lineup for fans. The *Tribune* claimed that the event "promises to be unusually attractive," while the *Evening World* suggested that with "the pick of America's athletes, both collegiate and national, as well as World's record holders, the Labor Day sports of the Greater New York Irish Athletic Association ... promises to be as interesting as any held in late years." Watched by 5,000 to 6,000 fans, Flanagan once more broke his record for the 16LB hammer with a throw of 171 feet nine inches, but O'Connor, labeled by the *Brooklyn Daily Eagle* as "the principal attractions [*sic*]" on what was his first public outing in America, injured himself in the long jump and failed to make the final six. The *New York Times* noted that some spectators "could not easily conceal their chagrin." Four days later on September 6, 1901, the same day that President William McKinley was mortally wounded nearby, O'Connor represented the GNYIAA at the Pan-American Games despite his injury. Part of Buffalo's World's Fair Exposition, with his chief rivals, Prinstein and Alvin Kraenzlein, both absent, the Irishman beat the NYAC's Harry P. McDonald in the long jump.[13]

Autumn saw the "Annual Fall Games" and Thanksgiving Day Games wrapping up the year. The first event, scheduled for October 13, invited Arthur Duffey for the 100Yds handicap dash, while the Pastimes entered their "Seneca Indian," "Jerry" Pierce, in the 3Mile handicap. A Gaelic football game between the John Dalys of Brooklyn and New York's Young Irelands, with the winners playing the Rovers of Washington, D.C., in the national final, would conclude the games. Poor weather postponed the event for a week, then Duffey failed to arrive, and O'Connor would soon return to Ireland still recovering from injury. John Flanagan was the only athlete left to shine, breaking James Mitchell's 56LB world record. The second meeting included just a tug-of-war between the Eccentric Firemen's Association and the Brewery Employees Association, who won after the event was switched to the clubhouse cafe due to the cold weather. A hurling game between the T.F. Meaghers and John Dalys saw one spectator, John O'Brien, knocked unconscious with a nose broken "by a blow from one of the sticks in a discussion after the conclusion of the game."[14]

* * *

A similar pattern followed in 1902 with the Memorial Day "Annual Carnival of Sports" marking four years of existence, while the club's Autumn Games on October 19 ended the season. "Hitherto this athletic association has brought out some good athletes, and when it throws open its gates one of the most attractive athletic programs in its history will be carried out," hailed the *New York Tribune*. It added that the Memorial Day games "will be one of the important athletic meetings of the season. The entries ... have already reached an unusually high mark, as many leading clubs have entered their best performers." With the Knickerbockers failing to host a meet, a total of 234 athletes entered, including the visiting English runner, J.C. Purcell, competing in the 1- and 3-mile handicap runs, and listed as a GNYIAA member. Highlights included Martin Sheridan (Pastime AC) breaking his discus world record, while Purcell quit the 3-Mile run after two laps.[15]

The club's July 4 Games were given greater importance when Conway announced that it would include the AAU National All-Around Competitions, with the club's new signings, Flanagan and Prinstein, competing. However, the *New York Times* speculated about the Limerick man's chances against Princeton's John R. De Witt, Richard Sheldon and F.G. Beck in what was the first time Flanagan had faced this trio at once:

> [His] friends claim that he can take matters easy in seven of the events and still win the championship ... [although] Old-time aspirants for the all-around honors are inclined to laugh at the pretensions of Flanagan, for the simple reason that the records show that the event was never won by a specialist. They say that Flanagan will find, after he has gone through several of the events, that he will not be in the best of condition to throw the weights.

The *Brooklyn Daily Eagle* came to a similar conclusion: "It is doubtful if he will be found tceing [sic] the mark. He certainly would stand no show in the runs, and would lose in the jumps. He, of course, depends on the weights, but as he is to compete on the same day against Sheldon and De Witt, in the weights, he would do well to save himself for these opponents."[16]

Prinstein meanwhile faced "an excellent array of talent" including current AAU All-Around champion Adam B. Gunn, Ellery H. Clark, J.E. Peters, and Edward S. Merrill. "Much is anticipated of ... Merrill. He is an all around athlete, and has a fine record both in field and track contests," opined the *New York Tribune*.[17]

Come the day, Clark and Flanagan withdrew their applications for the track events. The Irishman won three out of the four weight-throwing events and took the weight throwing title, while Gunn won the Athletic Championships ahead of Merrill and Prinstein. In a special 3-Mile Race, Jerry Pierce and A.C. Bowen, the University of Pennsylvania 2Mile Intercollegiate champion, fought themselves to a dead heat. The good weather held, but the *Evening World* reported a disappointing attendance:

> Although the day was all that could be asked for, the crowd which attended the games was not by any means as large as was expected. Everything in connection with the meet was to the standard, the best athletes in the country being entered, while the track and field were in perfect shape for the different events.

Meanwhile, the *New York Tribune* disagreed: "The day was perfect for the sport, and every inch of the grandstand and field, where standing room was allowed, was occupied. The enthusiasm manifested throughout the contests spoke well of the interest taken in the games."[18]

Once more, Celtic Park hosted countless sporting festival stages by a diverse number of organizations. Purcell was set to return for the annual field games of the Knights of Columbus on June 21, along with De Witt and Ray Ewry. Frank W. Smith of the Knights claimed that 5,000 tickets were sold, with over 10,000 predicted to attend, though the games were eventually postponed for two weeks by bad weather. The intriguingly named "Chattahoochee Tribe No. 95 of the Improved Order of Red Men" also held their first-ever Athletic Games on August 3. The St. Bartholomew's AC Games on August 23 received 375 entries, mainly due to the Mets being held at Celtic Park the following week, "and the men wished to accustom themselves ... and have a try out before the championships." A month later, September 7 saw the GNYIAA's grounds host the Annual Games of the Grocery Clerks' Union.[19]

Then the Met AA decided to host its Annual Championships at Laurel Hill for the first time since 1898, with the *New York Times* predicting "one of the most keenly contested [championships] ever held in the country." At stake was the $350 Spalding Trophy for the team points champion, which would be retained by the first club to win it three years in succession. "All the clubs have been strengthening their teams, and it is doubtful if there is an athlete in this district who could possibly score a point who has not been enrolled under the colors of some one of the organizations in the association."[20]

While the Pastime AC provided 71 athletes out of the 270-odd entries, the Knickerbocker AC 63 and the NYAC 50, the GNYIAA seemed to have a minimal presence at best, although Victor Dowling was selected as its "Honorary Referee." But the Irish punched well above their weight and showed the first green shoots of what would come. With 13 points, they came in fifth behind winners Knickerbocker AC, NYAC, Pastime and New West Side. Prinstein won the long jump, defeating the incumbent champ W.S. Edwards of the Knicks, while Flanagan came in a disappointing second in the 16LB hammer to De Witt. The *New York Tribune* added, "The games were a success in every way. The weather was perfect, the entry list one of the largest in the association's history, and the attendance large also. The handsome grounds never looked prettier and the track was in fine condition."[21]

All that was left for 1902 was the Labor Day "Carnival" and the Autumn Games a month later. With Dowling as director, Labor Day proved a success, closely equaling the Mets for entries. With "close finishes, holding the spectators' undivided attention to the end, and sending them home well content with their day's outing," the *New York Times* reported the strong "club rivalry, and each had out its full quota of rooters, encouraging their entries to their best efforts in the race for the point prize." The Knicks beat the New West

Side AC for the points trophy, while Albany Medical College alumnus Dr. B.J. Mulligan broke W. Ford's standing broad jump world record by almost three feet. Matters were concluded with the Dalys beating the Garry Owens, 2–4 to 2–0, in hurling.[22]

October 19 saw the season's closing meet, with a special five-mile race, and a soccer match between the Settlement AC and Hollywood Inn AC amongst the events. The *Brooklyn Daily Eagle* reported, "P.J. Conway ... has certainly done a great deal for the cause of pure amateur athletics since he has taken hold of that popular Irish organization. During the present year he has run off at Celtic Park ... no less than four open athletic meetings beside many hurling and foot ball contests." The Canadian Étienne Desmarteau was scheduled to compete against Flanagan, while a hurling championship between the Dalys and Meaghers would conclude the day. It was, however, the match-up between Flanagan and Mitchell that attracted the most attention: "Mitchell's admirers are confident that he will do more than duplicate his feat of the metropolitan championships," noted the *New York Times*. "This talk about Mitchell's prowess does not feaze Flanagan's adherents, who say for him that he was in no condition when Mitchell beat him, but he conditioned himself in the meantime, so that world's records are bound to fly, as they always do when he is in perfect condition."[23]

Four thousand fans watched John Joyce—representing Pastime—win the 5Mile race. However, Mitchell's performance, coming second to Dick Sheridan in the 56LB weight handicap after Flanagan dropped out, was the talk of the meet. The weather, reported the *New York Tribune*, again caused concern. "The black clouds that gathered shortly before the time for the beginning of the games made it look as if they would be marred by rain, but when the hour came to begin the weather was almost perfect." The soccer game was abandoned when the hurling game overran, leaving insufficient light.[24]

There was disappointment with the GNYIAA's performances here, since the club had come in second, with 13 points to the NYAC's 74, at the AAU National Championships. Prinstein's victory in the running broad jump, Flanagan's first in the 16LB hammer, and A.C. Bowen's second in the 5Mile run, after he "plunged forward and snatched the second prize amid the greatest excitement" at the finishing line, was enough to push the Pastimes into third place.[25]

Celtic Park remained open in the winter mostly for Gaelic football and hurling: An Interstate Gaelic Football Championship between the O'Connells and the Worcester Young Irelands on October 12; the Irish Athletes of America Games on October 26 that was interrupted by police (see Chapter 14); the New York Gaelic Football Championship between the O'Connells and Kickhams on November 23; a Thanksgiving Day Games hurling clash between the Dalys and Wolfe Tones; and a hurling game between the Tones and members of the Fifth U.S. Artillery based in Fort Hamilton, Brooklyn.[26]

* * *

Conway and the GNYIAA were keen to capitalize on the growing popularity of athletics. With the brief arrival of James Edward Sullivan, elected the club's Athletic Committee chairman at the November AGM, a winter "Monster Carnival of Sports" at the city's largest indoor venue, Madison Square Garden, that would "long be remembered in the history of American athletic sports," was announced for two days after Christmas Day. The Garden had been the venue for the heady nights of "pedestrianism" in the late 1870s, while in recent years the now virtually defunct Knickerbocker Club had hosted events there. The *New York Tribune* announced that there would be a four-man "intercity team race," with Boston and the University of Pennsylvania entering. Future I-AAC coach Ernie Hjertberg indicated that he would select the New York City team, before the NYAC announced that they would send their own quartet. Arthur Duffey, in his first run since his recent return from Britain, would race Patrick Walsh and Arthur Kent, while an indoor Gaelic football match between the Centrals and Young Irelands would also take place, "and to those who have not seen an Irish football game," commented the *New York Times*, "this event should prove more than interesting."[27]

Prizes were impressive too. The *Evening World* suggested that the "diamond watch fobs offered" were the reason athletes were now "endeavoring to get themselves into the very best of condition" for the event, while the *New York Times* noted that "the preparations being made are as rigorous as would be exacted of professionals," adding that the club planned to "eclipse anything in the nature of awards given during this or any previous year to successful athletes." Over 300 entries were received, suggesting that "[n]early every prominent athlete in the country" was entering, "and close finishes are assured." The *Evening World* declared as the date approached, "What promises the most successful set of athletic games ever held in Madison Square Garden is that to be held by the Greater New York Irish Athletic Association tomorrow night."[28]

They were not disappointed. The *New York Times* described it as "one of the best indoor athletic meetings ever held in this city," having predicted a large attendance: "There has been such a great demand for seats that in order to give an opportunity to those desirous of purchasing the best points of vantage.... Conway has arranged for the sale by auction of the arena boxes and seats in the lower tiers in the Garden." Five thousand came, the largest attendance for athletics since the Lon Myers "Benefit" in 1883, claimed the *New York Tribune*:

5. "An overwhelming success numerically and financially"   59

> The big Garden was almost as noisy a place as it was recently, when the six day bicycle riders held sway. Among the spectators were hundreds of girls and women who cheered when their friends won.... The management was creditable throughout, the large number of contests being run off promptly and without loss of time.

Duffey appeared twice: He was unable to overcome his handicap in the 60Yds and was unplaced, then failed to beat his world's indoor record at the same distance. The NYAC took the 4Mile team relay, while the football match—played for just 20 minutes a half—was called a draw after what the *New York Times* described as "a continuous free-for-all fight going on from one end of the floor space to the other."[29]

This was a huge gamble, and in years to come commentators would reflect on the risk taken. In 1905, the *Evening World* recanted the predictions of failure from many quarters:

> The first carnival of indoor sports given by the Shamrocks at Madison Square Garden ... occasioned not a little sneering in quarters where "the true sporting spirit" is supposed to be a fetich. These scoffers expected to see the new organization go by the board but they recked not of the stuff that was in it. The meeting was a heavy drain on the resources of the association but there were willing pockets and enthusiastic hearts to meet the demand and the scoffers said: "Wait until next year."[30]

The *Gaelic American* also recalled the risks, although like the *World*, it got the date of the first venture wrong, while also suggesting that the Irish were the first athletic club to utilize the Garden:

> The I-AAC hired Madison Square Garden for a set of games in the winter of 1904, crowded the building from cellar to dome and repeated the performance two months later. When they embarked on this latter enterprise all the "wise ones" confidently predicted failure; it was an overwhelming success numerically and financially, and the I-AAC repeated it in February, 1905, and will continue despite opposition to repeat it, as their next event will be held in the Garden on February 2. Previous to 1904 no athletic club dreamed of taking Madison Square Garden for an athletic meet. The financial responsibilities were too great and the building too large to fill, but when the Irish showed them the way and "delivered the goods" it was easy sailing, and now it is the fashion. Imitation, a great writer has said, is the sincerest form of flattery.[31]

The success of the evening was the cue for the GNYIAA to host more indoor events, spurred on by praise from the *New York Tribune*:

> Admirers of track and field athletics are justified in rejoicing at the splendid showing made at ... Madison Square Garden on Saturday night. When the Knickerbocker Athletic Club ceased to exist, the holding of the annual athletic meeting at the ample amphitheater did not appeal to some of the more pretentious clubs in the district. Then the Greater New York Irish Athletic Association announced that it would take the Knickerbocker's place and hold the affair on the abandoned date. The officers of the association can congratulate themselves on the outcome of the undertaking, for

the attendance was larger than at any previous athletic gathering held in the district in the last dozen years. The enthusiasm was well maintained from the firing of the first shot, starting off the sprinters in the fifty-yard dash, until midnight, when the game of Gaelic football was finished."³²

An event was organized for March 14, the Saturday prior to St. Patrick's Day. Conway told the *New York Times*, "Our reasons for giving another meeting are many. The club is anxious to encourage all branches of amateur athletics, and we also appreciate the fact that the public supported us liberally.... I have received many letters from prominent Irish patrons of sport who requested the Irish club to hold another meeting." The *Evening World* uttered enthusiastically, "As the last meet held by the Irish AA was the most successful ever held indoors by an athletic association, they are sure they can make the next more successful."³³

Meeting with the *New York Tribune* in February, Conway was sanguine:

> If you will stop to think of the boom that athletics is enjoying at the present time, and look back to the success that attended our maiden effort at the Garden on December 27, you will agree with me that the next games at the Garden will be the greatest success athletics will ever have had both financially and in an athletic sense.... If there is not a full house at the Garden on March 14 next, then you may say that present signs were all wrong and that I have been greatly mistaken in my calculations.³⁴

Indeed the *Tribune* was equally excited when the games were officially announced:

> Prompted by the enthusiasm displayed both on and after the last set of games ... and encouraged by the wishes of the members ,,, the [GNIAA] proposes to hold another athletic carnival to surpass its former efforts.... Practically everything athletic that could gladden the heart of the athlete and please the sport loving public is on the program.... [Conway and Sullivan] say that this will be the greatest indoor meeting ever held in this country. And the Greater New York Irish Athletic Association deserves all the encouragement that may be given to it. It has to its credit in the last year the holding of more athletic meets than any four clubs combined, while Celtic Park, its country grounds, has been the scene daily of all manner of athletic contests.³⁵

A 2Mile-intercollegiate relay race was planned with teams from Yale, Penn, Cornell, Columbia, Fordham, College of the City of New York, and New York University, a list that left only, according to the *New York Times*, "the entry of the Harvard team [who were still being courted] to make this the most memorable contest ever held indoors." Also a new game called "Pushball" was to be showcased between the Metropolitan and Central Flyers of Yonkers teams, while the Dalys and Tones clubs and the O'Connells and Young Ireland would conclude the night with hurling and Gaelic football respectively. The AAU also decided to throw in its 10Mile Championship, declaring to the press: "In giving this event at its games the [GNYIAA] is actuated by a desire to promote long distance running and to encourage those athletes whose bent lies in that direction to keep up the good work." A dirt track would replace the regular boards, as Conway predicted that the race "will be the greatest event of its kind ever given by the Amateur Athletic Union."[36]

On the night, John J. Joyce—then with the Pastimes—took the 10Mile Championship in a race that had 49 initial runners, while Columbia won the team relay. "Women and young girls were present in abundance," noted the *New York Tribune*, "and the enthusiasm they showed went far to encourage the athletes in their efforts." Indeed, James E. Sullivan, in a rare diversion from all things wonderful being American, recognized that Irish "sports" could be a financially successful athletic attraction, a "Mecca for many non–Irish athletes," and would include them at the Olympic Games a year later, while eventually giving the club the impetus to revive the Tailteann Games.[37]

Now with the 1903 summer season only a couple of months away, Celtic Park's diary was already full. "Nearly all the important athletic fixtures this year will be held at Celtic Park," reported the *New York Times* in January, with the AAU All-Around Championships once more included in the Independence Day Games, and the Met Championships also returning to Laurel Hill. "Aside from this, many other organizations will hold their annual games on the club grounds, among others the games of the Central Labor Union, the County Tipperary Men's Association, the Red Men, the Clare Men's Athletic Association." Others included events of Star AC, Grace AC, St. Bartholomew AC, the Knights of Columbus, the Galway Men's Association and the Journeymen Horseshoers' Union.[38]

The GNYIAA also assembled a lacrosse team, grabbing nine men from the previous season's Orange AC ensemble, while Conway also suggested that the club would enter wrestling competitions. The *Brooklyn Daily Eagle* said, "Earnest in its endeavor to foster every form of amateur athletics the [GNYIAA] has decided to place a lacrosse team in the field.... The [GNYIAA] is a formidable one, as the line up below will show, for nearly all the men are ex college players." However, the *Brooklyn Life* was less complimentary, claiming that the "so-called Irish-American team" comprised "for the most part" graduates from Cornell and elsewhere "with no special affinity to the Emerald Isle."[39]

Their first game, against Columbia at South Field on April 11, resulted in a 4–0 defeat. The *New York Times* reflected "that the players [being] so very good individually served to injure their game as a whole." The GNYIAA had signed too many "star men" who tried to "execute too many individual plays," leaving little teamwork. Things improved: A week later saw a 3-all draw against the College of the City of New York at Celtic Park, before gaining their first victory with a 3–0 win over Crescent AC's second string on May 9 in front of "a large gallery of spectators."[40]

It was also listed for the Memorial Day Games. "This is the first time lacrosse has been played in connection with the athletic games, and it looks as if the innovation would prove interesting to the spectators," noticed the *New York Tribune*. More significant were the prizes on offer: For first place "a handsome gold Roman gypsy ring, with genuine diamond and two sapphires," causing it to be called the "Diamond Meet," while the second- and third-place finishers would receive gold and silver medals respectively. "If nothing else were to attract the entries of the athletes the incentive of the prizes to be given for the Memorial Day meet ... would be sufficient. Famous as the club has always been for the beauty and value of its prizes, it seems to have outdone itself this time." Five thousand people attended, with Joyce beating Xavier's Edward Powell Carr in the 5Mile special race and Prinstein taking the host's only honor in the long jump. Flanagan was, however, "handicapped too heavily to cut any figure" in the weights, leaving the Pastimes and the New West Side clubs to battle for the point trophy. However, while the Tones beat the Meaghers in a hurling match, lacrosse was seemingly absent.[41]

Next up, the Fourth of July Carnival saw the AAU All-Around Championships complement a lacrosse defeat to the Crescent AC: "A large crowd flocked to see the men in their efforts.... Green and American flags were numerous on the grandstand, and the space at the entrance of the park, where the dancing pavilion, picture gallery and merry-go-rounds did a big business," recorded the *Tribune*. Conway had supplied five prizes, as Ellery Clark won the athletics title. In the weights division, Sheridan and Flanagan tied with 112 points each, despite the former breaking the world record for the discus that was later disqualified by the AAU for the lack of an iron circle. Meanwhile the *New York Tribune* laughed that Flanagan, now a cop, "looked as though the position was agreeing with him, for he has grown very fat," hindering his "oldtime form."[42]

In between July 4 and Labor Day, the Met AA held its championships at Laurel Hill on August 22. With an attendance numbering thousands, Celtic Park "never looked more inviting from an athletic standpoint," said the *New York Times*. "The field was absolutely clear of all incumbrances, the track was in rare condition, but a strong wind blew in the faces of the sprinters, which made record times in the runs almost impossible." The NYAC took the Spalding Trophy ahead of the Pastimes, while the GNYIAA came third with 37½ points. Flanagan won both the 16LB hammer and the 56LB weight, while coming second in the discus behind Dick Sheridan. Prinstein won the long jump, Charles Bacon was second in the 880Yds and third in the 440Yds, and Richard Cotter took second in the high jump. In the Junior Championships,

Lawson Robertson took the 100Yds dash title, Bacon the 880Yds, Cotter the high jump, and Joseph T. Mahoney the pole vault.[43]

The Labor Day Tailteann Games revival on September 7, 1903, promised top athletes like the Leahy brothers. Events included javelin, "striking the hurling ball," archery, shooting, 42LB stone throwing, the 56LB weight and the 16LB "sledge," which would be both thrown "with unlimited run and follow" as per "Gaelic rules." Dancing concluded a day where three world records were broken, with one disallowed: Ray Ewry of NYAC in three standing jumps; James Mitchell broke Tom Kiely's 56LB weight (one-handed) Irish style record, while H.L. Hillman failed to improve the 440Yds hurdles mark after knocking down the last hurdle. The Dalys and Buffalo's Emmetts Club contested a sport where "the ball was dribbled by a stick resembling those used in hurling and when off the ground would be hit for distance."[44]

At the AAU Championships at Milwaukee's State Fair Park later that week, the Irish showed that they still had some way to go. While the NYAC took the points title with a score of 50, the GNYIAA, with Flanagan missing, collected just three from Prinstein's second place in the long jump, coming in tied for sixth. The club did better in the Junior Championships the previous day, when they came fourth behind the Milwaukee AC, the University of Chicago and the Central YMC, with firsts in the 220Yds and 880Yds for Robertson and Bacon respectively. Eight days later, Meyer Prinstein took the Canadian Athletic Championships long jump title in Montreal.[45]

The GNYIAA was fast approaching the end of its fifth year in business and was competing at the highest level with just two top athletes. But two wasn't enough, and despite some promising faces coming through the junior ranks, other athletes needed to be convinced that the GNYIAA was for them. Back in the "auld country," the GAA was starting to wash its hands of athletics while simultaneously embroiling itself in a turf war with the more apolitical or pro–British—depending on your own point of view—IAAA. Ireland was no longer a place for top athletes, and the GNYIAA/I-AAC was calling out for them. The club was thus about to change. In a little over a year, it would get rid of its long and somewhat cumbersome name for something snappier; it was also going to acquire some added muscle that would finally make it the best club in America.

6

"A roistering carefree set of hellions"

The Irish Immigrant Athlete and the I-AAC

Arthur Daley, arguably the most colorful American sports journalist of the twentieth century, came up with the name to describe a group of Irish-born weight champions who represented the USA at the early Olympics. As ever, it was not Daley who would be the source of the name, but someone the man with more sporting anecdotes than anyone on the planet had once overheard. It was a waiter taking athletes to Stockholm in 1912, astonished by their capacity to eat and having "grown bowlegged from carrying heaping trays to [their] table," who complained: "They're not men, they're whales."[1]

Indeed the "Irish Whales," as Margaret Mary Hennessey argues, "used their talents to elevate" the Irish in America: "The Irish press heralded their achievements, and Irishmen living in the slums made weekly pilgrimages ... to cheer on their heroic throwers." They came to term the triple X-size, Irish-born cadre of cops who belonged to the I-AAC, as Ian McGowan writes:

> Some of these athletes attained a following that can be likened to modern day professional athletes. They were primarily members of the Irish-American Athletic Club or the New York Athletic Club and most were members of the New York City Police Department. They were known as such because of their athletic prowess, physical size, voracious appetites, and their impact on a generation of sports fans.

James S. Mitchell, for some unknown reason, declined to wear the Winged Fist vest, while Pat Ryan, described as a "whale" by the *New York Times* as early as 1915, was never a cop: "Somehow, Ryan escaped the charm of the police force when he came here," said his *New York Times* 1964 obituary. His only contact with New York's finest, according to Katchen, was the exercising of his generous stature by exhibiting "his capacity for throwing six policemen around." Mitchell, Flanagan and Sheridan did not travel on that boat in 1912.[2]

William Dooley wrote of these men: "America has never had, since or before, hammermen of the extraordinary power and ability of this group." Numbering no more than half a dozen, these were "a roistering carefree set of hellions," according to Daley. Being of a more bulky disposition and hardly reaching the expectations of what top athletes look like today, they participated in sport purely for the fun of it: "And fun they had. They were all weight-throwers and never had to worry about their waistlines or training. They ate enormous quantities of food. Beer never affected them. It was like water."[3]

Dan Ferris, a former I-AAC runner and Sullivan's successor at the AAU, recalled the "whales" never taking training seriously: "The moderns train hard and lift weights to develop their muscles. The whales never trained at all and they never lifted anything heavier than glasses of beer, something they did quite expertly." Bozeman Bulger, of the *Evening World*, once interviewed Flanagan trackside at the 1905 I-AAC Annual Fall Games, and it shines some light onto the athletic workings of these men:

> Do you keep in training for this work [Flanagan] was asked. "Not exactly," replied the big fellow. "I guess we ought to but we don't have time to do all that. Still I keep in practice. Hard training, you know, would change this," and he laughingly touched his stomach. Just then somebody yelled out, "Flanagan [sic] next!" "Wait a minute," he said. "I'll give you an idea of how we throw this weight." The big athletic officer then stepped into a little circle, picked up a still wire attached to a sixteen pound iron ball and began swinging it slowly around his head. The ball rapidly gained momentum and he was soon swinging his massive body around with it. Suddenly his feet left the mound and the iron ball shot into space. It landed 169 feet and 10 inches away, within three or four feet of the world's record. "You were just practicing then were you?" I innocently asked. There was a laugh at my ignorance and [Flanagan] explained that he was in the contest, and that his last throw had won the gold medal. Nobody rooted. In fact nobody said anything until the announcer walked out and told the crowd what happened. To a baseball fan this was amazing. I wanted somebody to yell. They simply commented in an undertone, and the affair passed on to the next number on the program.[4]

* * *

From the mid-'90s to around 1908, a wave of Irish athletes arrived in America. With a de facto athletic civil war between the Irish Amateur Athletic Association and the GAA, coupled with the latter's increasing disregard for athletics, poor opportunities except for the privileged pushed these men across the Atlantic. As the *New York Times* would later write of Ryan in 1916, "[r]eports of wealth and fame to be gained in the States drew Ryan away from his beautiful Irish home." The aid given by the I-AAC was also a significant reason for emigrating. However, this exodus further damaged Irish athletics.

Mark Quinn, biographer and great-grandson of Peter O'Connor, argues: "The extent of sporting talent that Ireland lost due to emigration in the final decades of the nineteenth and early twentieth centuries is inestimable and it could be argued that Irish athletics and field sports in particular never recovered."[5]

The first of these arrivals at the GNYIAA was Flanagan, who signed for the club in the summer of 1901. Arriving in early 1897, born in January 1873—the older brother of Tom, boxer Jack Johnson's manager, and founder of the Canadian-Irish Athletic Club—this native of Kilbreedy, County Limerick, disembarked in New York having already smashed Mitchell's 15LB hammer world record in London at the AAA Championships in April 1896 and the unlimited run and follow hammer title at the English capital's GAA Games a month later.[6]

According to an article on police athletes in the *New York Tribune* in October 1907, Flanagan had "no peer" throwing the hammer: "He has a development which is the envy of a prizefighter or a football player. His build is

Cigarette card featuring John Flanagan. Joining the club from the NYAC in 1901, he was the GNYIAA/I-AAC's first star athlete (Mecca Cigarettes card).

ideal for his favorite sport. His chest, arms and shoulders are nearly twice the size of those of the average man." The *Evening World* said in 1905:

> One man attracted the eye upon entering the inclosure and the whispered tips of several enthusiasts were unnecessary for the visitor to know that he was John Flanigan [sic]. Of gigantic stature and a face almost as mild as a boy's.... Expecting to see a raw-boned athlete trained down to the minute, and cross from overwork, the surprise was great. But for his massive muscular legs and the ponderous shoulders [Flanagan] has the build of a good humored bank president or perhaps an alderman. His arms have lost some of their fatness and his stomach has a curve of easy living and contentment.[7]

There is no specific reason written why Flanagan moved across the Atlantic, but he had a huge impact not only on the I-AAC but on American athletics in general. In a 1924 letter to Flanagan, John Devoy wrote: "It is one of my pleasant memories to stand in Celtic Park watching John's splendid figure whirl the hammer and sent it flying into space.... I always held you as the fresh type of old Gallowglass, winning glory for Ireland ... so long as Ireland produces John Flanagans there is hope for the future."[8]

After he joined the NYAC, his first major event in the country at Bayonne, New Jersey, at the end of May 1897 saw him smash his own record in the 16LB hammer in a seven foot circle, before relieving Mitchell's eight-year hold on the 16LB hammer national title that August. He then won gold in the hammer at the 1900 Olympics, improving on Alfred Plaw's "three-turn" method after seeing him perform it in what he considered a crude manner. Dooley observed, "Flanagan's style was a treat to look upon and many of the aristocrats on Fifth Avenue were in the habit of visiting Travers Island and other New York venues to see John, and John alone, pivoting in the circle."[9]

Another future cop, Martin Sheridan, who according to Alan Katchen "embodied the Irish heritage of talented athletes" stretching back to the birth of the "Tailtin [sic] Games," soon joined Flanagan at Celtic Park. Hailing from Bohola, near Foxford in County Mayo, Sheridan had come to the States in 1901 to join his brother Richard, the 1900 national 16LB hammer champion who had arrived about the same time as Flanagan. Martin was a streetcar driver in his early years, where a 1908 *Evening World* cartoon illustrated him working out by reaching over the front of the vehicle and throwing people out of the way as he trundled through lower Manhattan. He eventually joined the NYPD with what Dooley claims was a 99.1 percent score in his "physical test."[10]

Sheridan would claim that his athletic talents came from his father, who was "the greatest leaper in Ireland," who with just "a twinkle in his eye" once jumped across a valley "leaping from hilltop to hilltop." The 1907 *Tribune* article on NYPD athletes described Sheridan as arguably the World's greatest athlete at that time: "[L]ess than thirty years old, six feet tall and has about 180 pounds of solid bone and muscle. There is not a better proportioned man in the [NYPD]." An article in the *Gaelic American* noted, "There is no secret in Sheridan's success. It is simply a combination of snappy, nervous force, and an intelligent control and disposition of his feet, arms and hands, which is a characteristic of all our famous Irish weight throwers."[11]

Joining his brother at the Pastimes, his first mention in the New York press came in August 1901, when he beat Flanagan in the handicap discus at the Union Settlement AC's Games at Celtic Park. Within a month, New York's newest athletic sensation had smashed this record at the Entre Nous AC Games at Paterson, New Jersey, with a throw of 120:7:75. He broke it again at the Met AA championships the following year when he threw 127:8:75, going on to rewrite the discus record three times in one afternoon at the Pastime's autumn games, with a final distance of 129 feet, three inches, although none were accepted officially.[12]

Sheridan had to wait a further two years before taking the first of four AAU National Discus titles, but he would also be credited with "resuscitating" the All-Around athletic event, winning the national titles in 1905, 1907 and 1909. Frank Zarnowski claims that he was "so dominant ... [James E.] Sullivan had to dredge up straw man entries to maintain the appearance of a competition." Dooley adds that had the decathlon been officially recognized by the IOC back in Sheridan's prime, he probably would have collected three extra golds.[13]

The third famous whale who represented the Irish-Americans was Matt McGrath. Another cop, born in Nenagh in 1876, he arrived in the United States as a 21-year-old greenhorn in 1898, "one of those huge, iron-muscled athletes that have been Ireland's glory." It took him almost a decade to reach the stage where he was described by the *New York Tribune* as the "next greatest hammer thrower in the world after Flanagan," though some considered him superior: "A year ago he was not known in the sporting world. He is a regular Hercules. The muscles on his back, arms and shoulders stand out in big bunches, and his strength is enormous. A thief in his hands would have as much chance as a mouse with a cat. He could tuck a 'drunk' under each arm and walk with them to the police station."[14]

According to Dooley, as "a youth in Tipperary he was known to walk ten miles to see 'the father of modern hammermen,' John Flanagan ... at a Sports meeting, walk home again, and then immediately repair to a field with an old-fashioned hammer, in an attempt to turn with it after the fashion of the Kilbreedy prodigy whom he had that day seen perform for the first time." By 1908 he was breaking records with aplomb and taking his first national hammer championship. A six-footer "of massive proportions," a much bigger man than Flanagan, he grabbed 14 national titles in equal numbers for the

(*Left to right*) Ralph Rose, Pat McDonald, Matt McGrath, John Paul Jones and Abel Kiviat. McDonald and McGrath were two of the Irish-born "Whales," while Rose, from San Francisco, was goaded into not dropping the American flag in London, 1908, by some of these "Whales" (Library of Congress).

hammer and the "Fifty-Six," plus an Olympic gold for the hammer in 1912, and two silvers in 1908 and 1924.[15]

The number four whale was Pat McDonnell. Born in Doonbeg, County Clare, he left Ireland as a 19-year-old in 1899. On arrival, an immigration officer at Ellis Island misunderstood his brogue and put his name down as McDonald. A policeman, McDonald is best remembered, along with the swimmer Norman Ross, for leading the 1920 "Matoika mutiny." This protest was against the awful conditions spent on board the *USS Princess Matoika* en route to the Antwerp Olympics, which almost didn't make it in time for athletes to acclimatize.[16]

The fifth and final I-AAC whale was Pat Ryan, who arrived from Pallasgreen Limerick in 1910. At that year's I-AAC Fall Games, Matt McGrath announced: "Ireland has sent us another great hammerman ... perhaps the greatest of all." Ryan had already won several national Irish championships and had now blossomed, according to Dooley, "into perhaps the greatest natural hammerman that Ireland, or the world, has produced."[17]

The *New York Times* in 1916 would describe Ryan as "colossal in stature, gigantic in strength, yet as fast and light on his feet as a toe dancer.... He has a pugnacious face and is of the fighting type when aroused." Standing a little over six feet, two inches and weighing up to 300 pounds, Ryan was "as touchy" about his weight "as some women are about their years," arguing that he never exceeded 270 lbs. Lawson Robertson countered that he was always 20 pounds over whenever he was weighed. The *Times* reported Ryan saying that in Limerick he paved the way for his attainments of the past few years by developing "as fine a pair of flexible steel legs as ever danced on the 'ould sod.'" This was a man who "can whirl on his toes like a Pavlova" and was "far superior" to any hammer thrower in the World:

> Many thought John Flanagan was the most skillful and scientific hammer thrower that existed, but Ryan upset all these theories when he first exhibited his remarkable accuracy and ability in this country.... He has become master at his chosen sport. He has it down to a science; he studies every throw, every move. Nothing that will improve his form is overlooked.

According to Dooley, Ryan was "one to speedily turn his trainers grey-haired." "What John L. Sullivan was in boxing, Ryan was in athletics, almost to the letter," while he admitted to the *New York Times* that his biggest regret was not having taken up the sweet science.[18]

Additions to the weight men have to include Denis Horgan and Con Walsh. Born in Banteer, County Cork, Horgan was one of Ireland's greatest athletes of his era, securing 13 British AAA shot put titles between 1893 and 1912. In America, he was a "touristic" rather than a permanent resident, first arriving in the summer of 1900 as the shot put world record holder, returning intermittently up to 1908.

In August 1900, the *New York Times* disclosed that the "last foreign mail brought news that Denis Horgan, the Irish shot putter and holder of the world's record ... for the sixteen-pound shot, will leave Ireland for America on the 15th." According to Dooley, Horgan's reason for going to the United States was his defeat to Dickie Sheldon at that year's AAA Championships at Stamford Bridge, where exhaustion and seasickness from traveling overnight from Ireland prevented him from showing his best:

> Feeling he had struck an "off" day, he decided to get to the American Championships by hook or crook, for a second trial of ability with Uncle Sam's representative, and, at the last moment, made a decision which stamped him with the hallmark of greatness. There was no luxury liner for him; no travelling expenses; no guarantees. He had not been to America previously, but, no other means being available, he voyaged into the unknown, working his passage on a cattle-boat to Boston. Disembarking there he travelled through the night on a "sleeper," arriving in New York a few hours before the great meeting on Columbia Manhattan Field. Although his entry had been received he was not expected, he having entered the United States unheralded.

On September 15, 1900, Horgan won his sole American championship, beating W.W. Cox in the 16LB shot.[19]

He joined the I-AAC soon afterwards, and at the dual Star and St.

Bartholomew Athletic Clubs meet at Celtic Park on October 21 he broke C.R. Gray's 1893 American record for the shot put with a throw of 47:4:375 feet. The *Brooklyn Daily Eagle* hailed him "The Invincible Celt" following the Eighth Regiment Company G and Pastime AC Games at the Eighth's Armory, and he remained a GNYIAA member until he returned to Ireland in 1901.[20]

After his two-year suspension for alleged "professionalism" ended on August 1, 1903, hopes were raised that he would return for the AAU Championships in Milwaukee. Instead, he wouldn't arrive until October 1905, signing with the NYAC. He was almost killed in 1907 by an Italian fruit peddler, Clement Lug, who attacked him and his housemate, fracturing Horgan's skull with a sharp-edged weapon. He recovered in time to compete for Britain at the London Olympics, losing to Ralph Rose in the shot put. Another weight man was Con Walsh, the 1908 bronze hammer medalist, representing Canada. Originating from Carriganimmy, County Cork, he moved to New York around the winter of 1906, competing for the I-AAC the following year. He returned in 1909, joining the NYAC.[21]

* * *

If the "whales" defined the I-AAC's Irish weight throwers, track athletes from home also joined the club. Amongst the first was another "tourist," Peter O'Connor, a future double medalist in Athens. Fresh from his world record-breaking long jump at RDS's Ballsbridge grounds in May 1901—which would remain an Irish record for 89 years—the English-born Wicklowman was almost 30 when he arrived aboard the *Lucania* and was feted as a "celebrity" as he walked onto the quay. The *New York Tribune* commented, "This is his first visit to America and, during his stay here, he will represent the [GNYIAA] in all the contests in which he will take part." His first public appearance was at the club's Labor Day Games, before moving on to Buffalo for the Pan-American Exposition Games.[22]

In an article in the *Evening World* titled "Champion Jumper Athletic Wonder," the newspaper waxed lyrical about the huge talent that had arrived:

> Talk about athletes. Here is a new one. He is 6 feet 2 inches in height and when in condition weighs only 140 pounds. He is as fat as a drink of water, as they would say in the Bowery. John Flanagan ... says this lanky athlete could hide behind a billiard cue.... Despite O'Connor's shadowy like build, he is an athlete all over. As one would imagine there isn't a bit of superfluous flesh on his body. He is all bone and muscle and is as quick as a wild-cat in every move.... All in all O'Connor is a good all-round man and would figure close to the top in competition embracing all contests on track and field ... [and] is well educated and speaks intelligently on all subjects.

The reporter and a photographer caught up with O'Connor "training industriously" with Flanagan at Celtic Park. His style was described as "entirely original. He runs cleanly and hits the board at the take off with great accuracy. It is no wonder he has smashed all records for broad jumping held by Kraenzlein and Prinstein." When asked about breaking his own world record, O'Connor was upbeat: "I will make a great attempt to eclipse that record on Labor Day. I intend to get into the best condition for the attempt and feel confident of being successful in smashing it. It will only take me a few days more to get in perfect shape. I rarely spend more than seven or ten days conditioning myself." O'Connor's routine was to wake at seven every morning and run five miles after breakfast, before a "rub down." Then some jumping in the afternoon, and he was in bed by ten. To the question of ever drinking alcohol, he swiftly retorted: "Never in my life. I smoke a pipe a great deal. That's the offense I commit."[23]

Middle-distance running in New York was cornered by two Galway men. The first, and for the Irish-Americans the most prominent, was John J. Joyce from Muycullen, who had come to New York as a 17-year-old after capturing the IAAA mile steeplechase championship title and Irish record in 1899. Competing initially for the Pastimes, he joined the Irish-Americans in early 1904. He never participated in the Olympics but did bag himself a number of Metropolitan and National titles.[24]

The other was John J. Daly, from Dawros near Ballyglunin, whom the *Evening World* described as "a product of that movement in Ireland, which, during the past ten years has brought to life again the old athletic games and sports of the Irish people." Initially a broad jumper, he "soon discovered that he could run and from that time on he bowled over Ireland's best men as fast as they appeared." Daly had competed at the third International Cross-Country championships in 1903 in Scotland, coming in third behind the English duo of Alfred Shrubb and Albert Aldridge, and would be fourth the following year, before beginning a spirited rivalry with Joyce following the 1904 Olympics. He would return to Ireland in 1905 and rejoin the I-AAC in the summer of 1906.[25]

"Tourist" athletes were the only European athletes at St. Louis. The high cost and the then-low reputation of the Games prevented the British from sending over a team, with their only "representatives" being Irish. Along with Daly, John Holloway, from Bansha, Tipperary, who had won his last Irish title in the pole vault in 1898, represented the I-AAC in the All-Around Championship, coming in fourth to another "tourist," Tom Kiely.[26]

Born in Balyneale in August 1869, Kiely was one of the greatest Irish athletes. As Dooley offers, "If he were afforded the opportunity of competing in International All-round trials in the 90's there would appear to be little question regarding his superiority over all and sundry." The *Evening World* welcomed Kiely with a huge complimentary paragraph about his prowess:

> If one may judge by past performances, as horsemen do in picking race winners ... the Irish all-round athlete, stands a good chance of winning the all-round competition of the world at the Olympic games.... In appearance Kiely is the ideal athlete. He is tall and rather slender built much on the same lines as Bob Fitzsimmons, although not so broad across the shoulders as the lanky pugilist.[27]

America first witnessed him perform at the Kickham AC Games at Celtic Park on June 5, 1904, as 4,000 onlookers came "to accord a rousing welcome" to the Tipperaryman. Sadly he was below his best, with the *New York Tribune* suggesting that "after his ocean trip ... he acquitted himself well ... but none of his performances yesterday give any idea of his prowess as an athlete, as he was fully seven pounds below his normal weight."[28]

He spent almost four months with the GNYIAA. On September 28, 1904, at Sulzer's Harlem River Park, three days before he left for Ireland, he received a 14-inch-high "loving cup" from Police Commissioner William McAdoo "on behalf of the many friends he has made during his stay in this country." He told onlookers that he "expects to return," and in 1906 he captured the AAU All-Around Championships in Boston, remaining in America for two months.[29]

There is undoubtedly strong evidence that the I-AAC provided a home away from home for Irish athletes. From big names to minor immigrants who took up track and field, most Irish naturally joined a club that would provide ethnic support and camaraderie in a strange land, aiding the difficult rural to urban transition thousands of miles from their birthplaces. But this was a relatively small flow of migration that had slowed considerably since the 1850s. Irish athletes alone were never going to provide the club with the power to go out and compete against the NYAC, but together with others they were laying the foundations for a club aiming to rule the world. A crucial year, 1904, was arriving.

7

"The banner organization of the United States"
St. Louis and Onwards, 1904–1906

On a sunny June evening in St. Louis, 1904, finally clearing from earlier rain, Pat Conway walked to the President's box of the Louisiana Purchase Expedition's Francis Field athletic arena to collect a special "red silk banner" from Alice Roosevelt, the President's daughter. The portly Irishman must have afforded himself a huge smile as the club members gave three cheers: The emigrant from Limerick had just seen his team of around 21 athletes take the nation's athletic championship, effectively breaking the Mercury Foot's decade-long stranglehold on the AAU Championships, whose next win wouldn't be until 1919.

Earlier in the day, he had witnessed "Big John" Flanagan win the "Fifty-Six" while coming in second behind Martin Sheridan in the 16LB shot. Sheridan had also taken the discus, while John J. Joyce won the 5Mile title. However, non–Irish athletes had also come through: Lawson Robertson won the 100Yds, judged to have beaten San Francisco's Pacific AC's Ole Snedigar and W.D. Eaton despite some vociferous onlookers claiming that Chicago AA's William Hogenson had won. Robertson also came in second in the 200Yds race, as Frank Castleman did something similar in the 120 and 220Yds hurdles events. Prinstein collected his seventh title by winning the broad jump. Charley Bacon (880Yds), Harvey Cohn (1Mile), C.C. Naismith (2Miles), and W.C. Lowe (running high jump) had all come in second, crucially ramping up the points to 61 against the NYAC's 45.

The day's proceedings had almost never occurred. Heavy rain leaving "deep pools of water on the field and tack" reduced the crowd watching the earlier junior events. "Fires were built on the field to dry places … while a brigade of men with sponges and buckets scooped the pools from the track," reported the *New York Tribune*. For Conway, however, everything was clear: Six years on, his dream of creating America's best athletic club was reality. Nobody caught his thoughts that Saturday evening, but it's clear to presume he was over the moon.[1]

The GNYIAA/I-AAC's first AAU Championships were a key point in its history, where they could forget about the Memorial Day Games being the year's highlight. Michael Cregan's AGM report had earlier suggested that the club was moving in the right direction, despite James E. Sullivan leaving to organize the Olympics, with 13 athletes collecting 317 points in 1903: Prinstein (71½), Flanagan (56) and Charley Bacon (40¾) were the top three. On top of that, the club would be boosted by the arrival of Pastimes defectors John J. Joyce and George Bonhag—whose mother was reportedly Irish—while another of the Indians' top men, Martin Sheridan, would also be lured away by Memorial Day.[2]

* * *

The Olympic Games, at the same Missouri venue, were less than three months away, and the challenge for the club was to return and pick up where they had left off. Once more attached to a "World's Fair," the 1904 Olympiad was primarily noted for its few foreign athletes. "Britain's" three competitors—John Daly, Tom Kiely and Jack Holloway—were all born in Ireland, and as the Olympics allowed individual clubs to enter, the first thing the GNYIAA did was to try and grab this trio. "STRONG TEAM OF IRISH ATHLETES FOR WORLD'S FAIR" ran the *Sun's* headline of April 8, quoting Sullivan's prediction that the GNYIAA would bring a party bolstered by visiting Irish athletes, "some of whom have international reputations," including Horgan, O'Connor, Pat and Con Leahy, John Daly and Jack Holloway. By the end of April, Conway suggested that 15 would compete, and a tug-of-war team would also go.[3]

Tom Kiely arrived on June 2, but no club official met him at the White Star's *Teutonic*, nor did any newspaper mention that the GNYIAA had signed him. In St. Louis on July 4, he took the joint Olympic/AAU National Championship All-Around event, beating six other American-based athletes with a total of 6,068 points. Holloway, competing for the GNYIAA, came in fourth with 5,273 points.[4]

In later years, a story appeared claiming that Kiely adamantly rebuffed offers from both the British and the GNYIAA to compete in St. Louis, while Frank Zarnowski asserts that this All-Around event was an American and world title, not an Olympic one. Even though the *New York Times* had reported that Kiely had come for the Olympics, the event was only included in Olympic records in 1954: "[A] half-century after the fact and 3 years after he had died, Tom Kiely, without ever competing at the Olympic Games,

The St. Louis World's Fair "Great Pike." The 1904 Olympics were added on to a "World's Fair," as it was in Paris four years earlier (Library of Congress).

became an 'Olympic' champion." While no other athlete deserved Olympic recognition more, Zarnowski adds that the tale about turning down a trip with the British was just that:

> An important US club, the Irish-American AC, invited the well-known 34 year old Kiely to compete in St. Louis, and several other American clubs also appealed to him to represent them. There is a charming, yet apocryphal, yarn that the British team offered to pay Kiely's fare and expenses.... As the story goes, Tom turned them down flat, and went on his own to represent his native country of Ireland. In fact Ireland was not an independent nation in 1904 and had no Olympic committee. And the British sent no team, not even a single athlete.... Even the Olympic founder,

7. "The banner organization of the United States" 77

Baron de Coubertin failed to attend. Kiely, like others before him, just took himself over to the States and travelled down to St Louis.[5]

It is probable that Kiely would have accepted the GNYIAA's aid, but either his membership was submitted too late or he was compelled to compete unattached. At the "Irish Games"—an inclusion to the Olympics by Sullivan—the Tipp man was the star competitor, winning five firsts in the putting the 42LB stone, the 56LB weight, the 16LB hammer, the 120Yds hurdles, and the running two hops and jump, while coming in second in the long jump to Holloway, all while competing for the GNYIAA.[6]

Officially the GNYIAA won seven medals at St. Louis, four of which were gold. On August 29, John Flanagan came in first in the 16LB hammer, breaking his own Olympic record by nine inches with his first throw. Three days later, on September 1, Prinstein completed the double in the long and triple jumps, while Flanagan, performing under-strength, lost the "Fifty-Six" to Étienne Desmarteau. Sheridan also broke his own world discus mark by almost five feet with a throw of 132:9 feet in a warm-up handicap event. On September 3, he and Ralph Rose fought each other in the discus. With both on equal bests of 128:10:5 feet—an Olympic record—as joint golds were forbidden, a deciding round concluded with Sheridan throwing more than seven feet further than what the Californian could muster. John Daly, listed as competing for Ireland, picked up a silver for the 2,590m steeplechase, being beaten by the American James D. Lightbody, despite having led most of the race. By the time the athletes returned to New York, the season was almost over. Prinstein, Sheridan, Flanagan and Daly competed at the Labor Day "Tailtin games" on September 5, all taking firsts as 4,000 fans welcomed them back.[7]

There were plenty of other distractions for 1904. The club, according to the *Evening World*, would continue playing lacrosse with "the same strong aggregation of players which represented it last spring, with the addition of some former college stars, including Moran, of Cornell, Kegelman of CCNY and O'Rourke of St. Francis Xavier." They also suggested entering a team into the Metropolitan Association's Basketball Championships tournament. The indoor season's highlight was a "monster meet" at Madison Square Garden on the Saturday before St. Patrick's Day, while the summer season started with a tug-of-war between the Eccentric Fireman's Team and the Roanokes of Boston for the championship of America.[8]

The Memorial Day Games, despite the black clouds gathering, didn't deter 5,000 fans from flocking to Celtic Park. The Irish athletes won six of the 13 events: Flanagan, who according to *New York Tribune* "doffed his police uniform," took both the 16LB hammer and "Fifty-Six" events, while coming in second to Sheridan in the discus with a five-foot handicap. Harvey Cohn took first place in the 1½ Mile Run, William Frank won the 3 Mile Run, and Meyer Prinstein won the long jump.[9]

July Fourth's "Monster Carnival," described by the *New York Times* as one of "the most important" of the numerous meets of the day, attracted "all the principal local athletes and a crowd of about 4,000 spectators." The *Evening World* reported that all "the finest quality of Irish brawn and muscle in this country" turned up:

> The perfect weather and the beautiful condition of the track encouraged the spectators with the hope that records might be broken, but the breeze which blew up strong from the south was against the runners at the finish.... The attendance was large, the grandstand being filled when the first event was called. The presence of the fair sex was noticeable, and there were seen rosy-cheeked Irish girls who cheered lustily as their favorites crossed the tape.... The New York police force was well represented at the games. Flanagan, the hammer-thrower, and some half dozen other lusty cops being among the contestants for honors.

However, handicaps hampered the top athletes and hindered the spectacle, with the *New York Tribune* claiming that "the honors went to longmark men of lesser reputation." Although Sheridan won the discus, Flanagan failed to win any of his four events, while Prinstein, starting from scratch in the hop, skip and jump, came in third.[10]

The next major date at Laurel Hill was the Junior Met Championships on August 13. The GNYIAA took five first places, including future senior competitors Cohn (1Mile), William Frank (3Mile), and Claude Allen (pole vault)—beating the New West Side AC, 38 points to 30. The GNYIAA took its first senior title a week later at Travers Island, beating the NYAC with 81 points out of a possible 165. However, there were threats that the points would be "materially altered," not only by complaints about the scoring system but also accusations of professionalism against Sheridan (see Chapter 10). Other winners included Prinstein (100Yds), Robertson (220Yds), Bacon (880Yds), Cohn (1Mile), Allen (pole vault), and Flanagan (56LB weight and 16LB hammer). Afterwards Richard Sheldon was suspended by the NYAC for failing to turn up, which in the opinion of the *New York Tribune* "did much for the Mercury Foot organization's defeat."[11]

One of the most successful events held at Celtic Park that summer by an independent organization was the United Irish-American Societies of New York Games on July 31, which the *Evening World* championed beforehand as "one of the greatest events in the history of Celtic Park, which has during the past few years become the Mecca for athletes and lovers of athletic sports." Six to 7,000 people witnessed Flanagan break his 16LB hammer world record, extending it from 171 feet nine inches to 173 feet. When the new mark was announced, the spectators were briefly silenced:

But when the fact had finally percolated through the minds of the majority a shout went up such as probably used to shake the hippodrome of the Caesars. "Three cheers for ould Ireland," shouted an old man, who seemed to have tripped back over many years to younger days, and the cry passed from tongue to tongue.

Such was the commotion that a bemused crowd overlooking the ground on a nearby hill joined in the celebration. Afterwards "four stalwart young Irishmen lifted [Flanagan's] powerfully muscled form to their shoulders and bore him to his dressing room," amid cheers from the crowd.

> With his fists buried in the hair of two of his bearers to steady himself, Flanagan smiled and nodded his curly mop to the admiring throngs on every side. If he had been running for office he would have received every vote on the grounds. For fear of a slip many would have voted twice and no doubt there would have been such stuffing and repeating as would have made the skies weep.

A lad from Philadelphia's Brown Prep, Mel Sheppard, also took first place in the 1,000Yds run. Flanagan broke his 56Lb weight world record the following month at the Pelham Bay Games, throwing across field rather than down the slope to ensure the record stood, making a mark of 38:7:375 feet. But Sheridan lost to L.D. Klous, a schoolboy from Dwight School with a handicap of at least 15 feet.[12]

The Fall Games on October 30 attracted upwards of 10,000 patrons for a dour day's athletics of four events—one of which was a sack race—with hurling and Gaelic football games concluding. It, however, gave birth to the rivalry between Joyce and Daly, one which the *Gaelic American* later claimed "established [Celtic Park] as the foremost athletic center in Greater New York." With both wearing GNYIAA colors, the pair squared off in the 5Mile run. As the bell rang for the last lap, with both running neck and neck, Joyce, upon passing Daly, the *New York Times* reported, "was interfered with and thrown," leading to him falling over, recovering only to finish second. He had treated the race as a joke by wearing a heavy sweater until the final laps, and according to the *Sun*, when "he saw matters getting serious, he whipped off the garment, [and] buckled into his work," closing the gap at the four mile mark.[13]

Joyce protested that Daly's shoulder barged him, but the *Sun* defended Daly, claiming: "[He] has an awkward method of swinging his arms and might have struck Joyce unintentionally." Betting on the race was large, showing that this scourge had now entered Celtic Park, with potential for disorder. The *Evening World* had little sympathy for Joyce: "'TWAS A LITTLE SLIP THAT DEFEATED JOYCE" ran the headline followed by the claim that he had fallen over a discarded broken hurdle:

> A little slip as the laurel of victory was within his grasp was the undoing of John J. Joyce, the hitherto unbeaten long distance runner.... Never since the days when the

invincible McNamarras, the famous Firbolgs of Irish history, used to jump across a whole county to meet and beat back the raids of the Danes, was there such interest evoked in a Gaelic athletic contest as was shown in this struggle....

The race concluded with a great roar "greater than any that ever echoed from those grounds before ... [Joyce] was lost and he knew it, but was on his feet in a jiffy and amid a dim that could be heard for miles he used his wonderful spurting gift and came in only four seconds behind Daly." Meanwhile the GNYIAA's John McCarthy sniffed, "Joyce kept his sprint up his sleeve too long. He should have 'got on the job' sooner."[14]

The referee ignored Joyce, thus entailing, as the *Evening World* retorted with understatement, "at best ... an unsatisfactory race." Pressure began for a rerun, and Conway immediately "got on the job" to arrange another race. A date was set for November 20 with the *Evening World* anxious to promote "the long-distance running championship of all the World" with maximum hype, promising the winner a "valuable trophy ... a massive loving cup and a testimonial worthy of the prowess of a champion such as will come out of the contest," adding:

> There's to be a foot race on Sunday week worth going further than Celtic Park to see ... to prove whose limbs are the fleeter of the two, and whose heart will outlast a breaking, tiring five-mile grind.... Long distance men have been as scarce as the thoroughbred stake horses of bone and heart, which used to do four mile and repeat races with as much ease as the three-year-olds in these days do their mile. It is because of this that the eyes of athletes throughout the Union and in Ireland and England are on Joyce and Daly.[15]

Coverage continued unabated in the fortnight before what the *Irish World* called this "heart-breaking trial of wind and limb." The *Evening World* continued:

> The caliber of the contestants, their records and the determination of each to win the title and the trophies which go with it insures a slashing race. Not only have Joyce and Daly speed, but they are full to their throathatches with that sand which a man must possess to be a successful runner.... In a quarter of a century, perhaps, two men of such high class as Joyce and Daly in their branch of athletics have not appeared.

Daly, weighing 192 pounds, hefty for today's middle distance runners, was described as "ponderous; and a good judge of sports, not knowing him, would take him for a hammer-thrower or shot-putter, but never a runner.... His muscles are as fine as whalebone and laid on his limbs like elastic bands. He is bony, with the ranginess of an Irish thoroughbred timber-topper." Joyce meanwhile weighed 165 pounds, "molded on altogether different lines than Daly. He is what a horseman would call 'neater,' and as one of his County Galway admirers expresses it, has 'the speed of the divil himself.'" Such were the dizzy levels of hyperbole reached by the newspaper that it even suggested that 30,000 fans would watch.[16]

Celtic Park was packed with around 10,000 people, while the *Evening World* refused to let up:

> Never in the history of athletics was there such an enormous gathering in attendance at a contest ... for the massive silver cup presented by the *Evening World*. There was the wildest sort of enthusiasm displayed by the adherents of both men. The men were so evenly matched that it was difficult to pick a choice, but the betting was slightly in favor of Daly on the strength of his record.

Streetcars couldn't cope with the crowds, leading to scuffles whenever a tram left. Most patrons arriving by ferry from Manhattan preferred to walk.

> Every ferry-boat that landed at the slip after noon poured forth hundreds of men and women who massed up on the sidewalks and waited to go through the ordeal of getting aboard a car. Hundreds of the timid ones faced the long tramp to the park, which is directly across from Calvary Cemetery. At the park itself the unusual throng was too much for the facilities to cope with it, but the good nature of everybody was unbounded, and allowances were made for all shortcomings ... the grandstand was jammed with the sturdy sons and winsome daughters of Ireland, and the grounds outside the track were lined with lovers of pure sport half a dozen deep."[17]

The race proved as close as the other, without any of the controversy. Daly hit the tape first by a yard, his strength and stride being decisive in the final stretch, as the *Evening World* explained:

> The scene that followed was one to be remembered for a lifetime. The two men ran as if linked together as they rounded into the turn for home. The thousands of men roared out their encouragement, and the women waved flags and handkerchiefs and screamed for their favorites. But the men tugged on without appearing to hear a sound. They strained every muscle, tendon and nerve. Their eyes were ablaze, their hands clinched, and their mouths wide open as they gulped in the air that was pumped out again by every stride. And so they entered the stretch. "Joyce has got him" yelled the Irish American contingent as their man tugged for the lead. "The devil he has," responded the Daly men, who were almost as numerous as the Joyce following, and they were right.

Joyce conceded with some excuses: "The track was against me. The time shows that it wasn't a record-breaker, and therefore the track was slow. A slow track was a big advantage to Daly, whose strength is much greater than mine, but he is the most wonderful runner on the face of the earth."[18]

The two men would race each other four days later, with Daly, and "that long, loping stride, peculiar to himself," making it an easy three out of three by taking the Met Senior Cross-Country Championship, beating his nearest rival, Ed Carr, by 22 seconds. Joyce limped off in the first lap after twisting his ankle. By early December, just prior to his return to Ireland, Daly met Carr in a three-mile race at Celtic Park. Here the track was cleared of deep snow wide enough for the pair to run. Daly confided: "Faith, I'll try to add another cup to my dresser, and if I feel as well as I do now I'll be able to put up a good race Sunday. The weather is just the right sort for a good race, and I hope it will keep this way so that all my friends from the 'Ould Dart' can come over to Celtic Park and see how I'll try to win." John McCarthy, who reputedly had translated "The Six Books of the Bretons," was quoted as saying that his research showed "that no man in Ireland in ancient times could beat the records of the Galway 'blazers' today." Meanwhile, Carr was downplaying Daly's hopes of taking the race: "Ay, but there's many a slip 'twixt the cup and the lip." He was right, beating Daly by around five yards.[19]

* * *

The club had ended 1904 with 1,014⅘ points, a figure accumulated under the AAU points system (five points for first place, three for second, and one point for third) by the athletes' positions in all the meetings and championships the GNYIAA had entered. The weight-men were the biggest grabbers, with Flanagan taking 138 points and Sheridan 83. The *Irish World* hailed the advances:

> This Gaelic association is the banner organization of the United States, and never has there been one, since amateur athletics reached their present plane, which has been able to emblazon on its colors in such a short time…. The handful of Irishmen and Irishmen's sons who seven years ago saw the need of such an organization in this city as the [GNYIAA] has become, and who had the initiative to effect it, little dreamed that with the opening of the 1905 such a record as that would be theirs.

The *Evening World* wrote that the club's success was due to "honest endeavor on the part of its athletes and fairness in all sport have been the keynotes of the policy of the [GNYIAA]. No matter what others might do; no matter how unfair others may have been, Pat Conway saw to it … that policy was pursued consistently."[20]

Work commitments, accusations of professionalism, and the long distance to Portland, Oregon, forced the club to forfeit defending its National Championship in 1905. The year started with the third Madison Square Garden indoor games, an event about which the *Evening World*'s headline from January 4, 1905, screamed: "NOTED ATHLETES WILL COMPETE IN CARNIVAL: Famous Champions of Successful Greater New York Irish A A Will Be in Competition at Garden Next Month." "There is not a follower of athletics to-day," the newspaper said, "who will gainsay that in all likelihood this meeting will surpass in interest and importance anything of the kind ever attempted in this country, not excepting the recent carnival at the St. Louis Exposition," adding two days later that the "greatest collection of athletic stars that have ever competed in a single set of games in a single night will line up before the starter's pistol in Madison Square Garden." Hailing the club now "holding twenty-six championships and with seventeen champions in its ranks," and Conway's stewardship, the *World* observed:

> By unceasing effort and with the assistance of the men with whom he has surrounded himself in the administration of the affairs of the association it has been brought through many dark days. It was only a year since that the success so bravely fought for came within the grasp of the association. The winning of that point where the club might say its head was above water was but a milestone in the journey that it has set out upon.[21]

In the meantime, another matter needed to be tidied up. Ever since the first Irish-American Athletic Club was founded, there had been a desire for continuity. While the GNYIAA was seen as part of this, its name wasn't. Now as the club rose to greater levels of success than its predecessors, there came the fear that the name would confuse this heritage. Officers within the club for several months had been calling for a succinct alternative that drew on the history of all three clubs, and at a meeting on January 29 the Greater New York Irish Athletic Association ceased to be, struck down by changing Article I section 1 of the constitution, to be reborn as the Irish-American Athletic Club without any opposition.[22]

Conway told the *Sun*: "Old Name Too Hard on the Wind." Probably unaware of the previous club's name, the newspaper was unimpressed:

> The Greater New York Irish Athletic Association, organized and incorporated in 1897, went out of commission officially yesterday, and from its ashes a new organization styled the Irish American Athletic Association reared its head.... It was said that the old name was trying on the wind, being too long, and that it also jarred on some of the palates of those not accustomed to deep gutturals. Many persons present yesterday could not see much difference between the two and admitted that it was as difficult to get the tongue around the new name as the old one.

Newly printed letterheads had listed the club as the "Irish Athletic Association," suggesting that management felt optimistic about getting the name change. Athletes would also wear a new emblem, with the Gaelic slogan "lair laidir aboo"—in fact, "láimh láidir abú"—which in English, the *Evening World* was informed, means "strong hand forever," a "parody on the ancient war cry of the Clan O'Neill of Ulster 'Lair Dearg Aboo [sic]' or the 'red hand forever.'"[23]

On the night of the carnival, honors were taken by the club with the new name. The Xaviers were second and Pastimes third, suggesting that the NYAC didn't enter, while the Buffalo team had been caught up in a railway derailment at Utica. Still, the *Evening World* called it "the most successful and best conducted indoor meet ever held in this city." Flanagan made a new American record in the 28LB weight, while Joyce won the 10Mile AAU championship—Daly wasn't expected to return to America until April. Future

I-AAC sprinter John B. Taylor ran the final lap for Penn in the 1Mile intercollegiate team relay to loud cheers from spectators. The *New York Tribune* reported: "The boxes were filled with men and women in evening dress, who took a keen interest in all the contests, but especially in the relay race of the schoolboys ... there were a dozen team entered from as many public schools in New York and Brooklyn, all of whom had their admirers in the great audience.[24]

The traditional opening of summer, the Memorial Day Games, attracted over "5,000 admirers of brawn and muscle and athletic effort": "On every hand nature flaunted a Celtic green, and the fine spring air put valor into the heart and ... limbs of the champions of cinder path and field, whose vaunted prowess brought to this park" reported John Pollock of the *Evening World*, "but it was not only a day for the folk of the 'ould sod' and their color bearers." Representatives from Yale, Penn, Columbia, Syracuse, Georgetown and the New York City universities captured four first places in various handicap competitions. The only Irish victories were Joyce beating Frank in the 3Mile race, Robertson's win in the special quarter mile (440Yds), and Flanagan with the 16LB hammer. Still, Conway was upbeat, telling Pollock, "Sure! Galway never beheld a finer day."[25]

The Fourth of July Games saw the NYAC triumph, suggesting that they would take the Mets. The *New York Times* claimed that "the wearers of the "Mercury Foot" emblem [have] been performing brilliantly this season," but with most events handicapped, this was misleading. The Irish could only count on S.C. Northridge winning the 300Yds run, and Bonhag's taking the 5Mile invitation run. Sheridan—under suspicion for "professionalism"—won the AAU All Around title in Boston, breaking Harry Gill's 1900 US record with 6,820½ points.[26]

Other top events at Laurel Hill included the Galway Men's Association Games, where on June 11 Joyce beat the visiting Irish cross-country champ, the "Galway Cyclone," Tom Hynes, in the 4Mile race. While some put the gate as little as 8,000, the *Evening World* claimed that 20,000 "sons and daughters of Erin crowded and jammed Celtic Park ... as its confines never had been taxed before." The race was thrillingly close, despite Hynes having persuaded officials to shorten it due to his insufficient time to acclimatize, with Joyce winning by just 18 inches. The *New York Tribune* noted, "At no stage of the contest was there more than a few feet between the pair." In his column, Robert Edgren asked, "Is this going to be a great year for athletics? ... Just wait until Hynes and Joyce meet again, probably on June 25. By that time the newcomer from Erin will have become more acclimated, and if there are not 30,000 persons present to see the struggle it simply will be because Celtic Park will not hold them."[27]

The rerun at the Mayo Men's Association annual picnic was farcical.

The predicted huge crowd failed to appear—6,000 according to one source—and the abstainers proved correct. Joyce dropped out halfway through, complaining of a "stitch," which the *New York Times* suggested was "an unsatisfactory termination of what gave every promise of being a splendid contest." The *Sun* insinuated that Joyce was faking: "Whether such was really the case no one could tell, but when Joyce pulled up he was running strong and seemingly was not in distress." The Labor Day "Tailtin Games" were even more disappointing: Just 1,000 people attended, disgruntled—despite the presence of American Olympic bantamweight wrestling champion, Isidor "Jack" Niflot—that Flanagan was absent. A heavy downpour left the track in a poor state too.[28]

Following the decision to skip Portland, the Mets took on added significance. By September 9, the stage was set for the clash between the old and new for the supremacy of Gotham's athletics. Both clubs were "marshalling their forces, and the struggle promises to be a keen one. Several minor organizations will send representatives, but stellar honors are certain to go wither to the Mercury Footers of the Irish athletes." The NYAC, which had not "in a decade" been as "strongly represented as at present," were favorites, and "on paper" it looked like they would win "by a narrow margin." Flanagan, however, warmed up by breaking his 56LB weight "without a follow" world record at the Pastime AC summer games in August, with a throw of 31:5 feet, shooting down a remark in the *Evening World* that he "had done nothing throughout the season, with the exception of one good throw."[29]

Sadly, the event would be remembered for protests and counter-protests of professionalism against Castleman, Sheridan and Joyce, as the I-AAC took the Spalding Trophy with 117 points against the 97 of the NYAC. Castleman won the 120Yds high hurdles and Sheridan the discus, while Joyce came in third behind Cohn and James P. Sullivan in the 3Mile run, making it an Irish "one, two, three." Added victories were accrued by Sullivan (1Mile), who became the first American to run the distance in four minutes, 22 seconds, earning him the nickname "4:22 Jim," S.C. Northridge (220Yds), Claude Allen (pole vault), Flanagan (16LB hammer), and Prinstein (long jump). The following week at the Canadian Championships in Montreal, the NYAC beat the Irish by three points, despite Sheridan's increasing his discus record by five feet. Then two weeks later at the NYAC Games, Flanagan came within almost a foot of breaking his 16LB hammer record. The *New York Tribune* noted that numerous times "Flanagan caused the group of officials to hustle out of the way as the weight hurtled through the air and fell where they had been standing."[30]

At the I-AAC's Fall Games, in front of 5,000 patrons, Sheridan further broke his discus world record, raising it to 138:25. The *Gaelic American* hailed the club achievements: "Since the Irish-American, or rather the Greater New

York Irish Athletic Association of former years began making athletic history, the present season has been their best and proudest, and their meeting on the 15th will ring down the curtain till next year on a season's record of unparalleled triumphs." It added that the event would also be free: "Entry Fees are never paid in Ireland, the audience and subscriptions of friends ample to run a meeting," adding that athletes were collegians or low-paid "and the unpopular 50 cents entry fee is exorbitant." Flanagan also won the 16LB hammer and "Fifty-Six," while the visiting English runner, T.W. Morton of the South London Harriers,

Cigarette card featuring James P. Sullivan. "4:22 Jim" became the fastest American-born athlete in the mile in 1905 (Mecca Cigarettes card).

took the special 120Yds handicap. With a points victory of 83 to the New West Side's eight, Bozeman Bulger of the *Evening World* wrote: "What a relief from professional sport! Without a thought of batting averages, bi-weekly pay days or public opinion not less than 200 athletes were heroes at Celtic Park yesterday. There were no wild-eyed, leather lunged fans to make things howl, but records were smashed, great races run and everybody had a royal good time."[31]

* * *

As the New Year approached, the battle to combat charges of professionalism came close to forcing the I-AAC out of mainstream athletics. It would ride a storm over the coming years and continue gaining strength. Athletes were opting for the Winged Fist over the Mercury Foot, and spectators flocked to Celtic Park. Harvey Cohn came in second to the NYAC's W.J. Hail in the National Cross-Country Championships on November 30, but redeemed himself by winning the Met event in late December, through the six-mile "veritable quagmire" of the Mohawk AC's grounds, the I-AAC team taking both races' points titles.[32]

Once again the Irish hired Madison Square Garden for another of what the *Irish American Weekly* argued was, in the face of competition from the NYAC and Columbia University, "the greatest indoor event of the year." With some of the best college runners present, and Flanagan extending his 28LB indoor record, it was Joyce's and Castleman's return from suspension that attracted the biggest cheers, though Joyce's forced rest had left him unfit to defend his 10Mile title. Starting well, he retired after a mile and a half. Castleman came in third to Charles Bacon and Xavier's John J. McLaughlin in the 300Yds, both having ten- and eight-yard handicap advantages on him. Another receiver of a huge ovation was Mel Sheppard, as he ran the last mile of the 4Mile relay "in such magnificent style he was cheered to the echo, and again when the crowd learned he had made the mile in 4:22 4–5, three seconds better than his own [AAU] championship time." Together with Sullivan, Bonhag and Cohn, the relay team broke Cornell's 4Mile world indoor record. The *Evening World* described Sheppard as the second Tom Conneff: "Students of the runners say that in Sheppard the Irish club has got hold of a boy that will excel that wonderful record of that clever little bustler." Sheppard had already smashed Andy Walsh's indoor mile record at the Columbia meet at the same venue, with the *Evening World* noting him as the "schoolboy" running in the colors of the I-AAC: "This lad was pitted against some of the fastest runners that have ever taken part in an AAU event.... When the announcement was made that Sheppard had broken the record a mighty shout went up from the large crowd who had watched the youngster lead his opponents across the line."[33]

The year 1906 also saw the Greeks hosting the "Intercalated Games," celebrating ten years of the Olympics' revival. For the first time ever, only national Olympic committees could enter, but a rivalry was brewing that threatened the calm of American athletics, as the NYAC looked on at the I-AAC's rise, over the past two years, from a bunch of Irish enthusiasts to national champions, in utter horror.

8

"The social element in Clubs is like 'dry rot'"

Snobbery and the American Athletic Club

In 1885, Frederick Janssen, a former hurdler with the Staten Island AC he co-founded in 1877 with six others, was in retirement. He began compiling a record of track and field in the United States through his *History of American Amateur Athletics*. His work spends most of its time on the rules and regulations of America's first athletic body, the NAAAA, British and American records, and sections on various clubs, mainly in the metropolitan areas.[1]

On the final page, however, Janssen attacks what he saw a cancerous growth within athletics: He termed this disease the "social element," arguing that it was corrupting athletics. No longer was the athletic club home to young, competing men. It was a shell-like organization, "athletic only in name," where retired "athletes" congregated to network and decent, but socially inferior men, were excluded by various ruses, like large initial and annual fees and the need to be proposed and seconded by members. "The social element in Clubs is like 'dry rot' and eats into the vitals of Athletic Clubs, and soon causes them to fail in the purpose for which they were organized," concluded Janssen.

To back up his argument, Janssen listed a number of New York clubs—the Harlem, the Scottish-American, the Astoria, the Short Hills, and others—which he claimed were known "by name only, if at all." He claimed that members of these clubs were either too old to compete, were "occasional" athletes, and poor ones at that, or "did not engage in competition at all," pessimistically predicting that athletics faced oblivion:

> It is like an octopus that squeezes the life-blood out of the organization by burdening it with debt. Palatial club-houses are erected at great cost, and money is spent in adorning them that, if used to beautify athletic grounds and improve tracks, would

88

cause a wide-spread interest in athletic sports and further the development of the wind and muscles of American youths. About five years ago athletic sports were at their zenith, since then they have been on the decline. The youths who participate in health-giving competitions, as a rule, cannot afford the expense of membership of the so called Athletic Clubs and they retire in favor of the wealthy young man whose sole claim to athletic distinction is his connection with a 'high-toned' club.[2]

* * *

Regardless of their humble image or Janssen's words of caution, the GNYIAA/IAAC needed to take on rival clubs in the lounges and smoking rooms as much as in the stadium. It's not immediately obvious what were the members' initial intentions with regards to "status," but in future years it likened itself as the "poorman's club" that didn't discriminate, even if it took on some trappings of an elite club. While the Irish had slowly been pushed up society's social ladder by Italians and Jews throughout the '90s, they remained an immigrant group. As the historian of Irish-American emigration, Kerby A. Miller, writes, even those who succeeded were forever tainted by the memories of being poorly treated:

> Even if they aspired to higher status, most Irish males probably worked at least part of their lives in North America as canal, railroad, building-construction, or dock laborers. Those who later rose to more remunerative or respectable employment remembered bitterly that as "Laboring men" they were "thought nothing more than *dogs* ... despised & kicked about" in the supposed land of equality.[3]

As the "athletic phenomenon" spread across the country, most cities with a population over 100,000, according to Richard O. Davies, claimed at least one athletic club that "offered members social exclusivity, along with athletic facilities." The first two I-AACs were largely suspicious of emulating elite clubs, often eschewing joining national bodies, and eventually distancing itself from the AAU through much of the second club's existence. By accommodating soccer, baseball and Gaelic football rather than rowing or yachting, they concentrated on more affordable pursuits when the athletic season was over. But while the number of Irish athletes in New York continued to grow from the "invasions" of 1885 and 1888, Irish-run clubs failed miserably to attract cash to provide facilities comparable with the "elite" clubs.[4]

Meanwhile, in the 19 years between the founding of the first and third I-AAC, the other top clubs fought a "race for status, prestige and the title of the 'leading' athletic club." The Manhattan, Knickerbocker, Berkeley, Crescent and the University ultimately conceded to the New York Athletic Club, primarily because it would be able to run its own affairs successfully and attract some of the city's top sponsors. Others folded, merged or simply became irrelevant.[5]

The NYAC was formed in September 1868 at the Knickerbocker Cottage, a Sixth Avenue tavern, by three Civil War vets: Henry Buermayer, the son of

German immigrants and an outstanding amateur athlete, later known as the "father of American athletics"; John Babcock, a noted rower; and William Buckingham Curtis, the future editor of the sports newspaper, *The Spirit of the Times*, and AAU treasurer. According to the NYAC website, these men were all "accomplished athletes with a singular commitment to the growth and development of amateur sport" in the USA. "Furthermore, they possessed the foresight to realize that the time was right to introduce some organization—and uniformity of measurement—into sporting endeavors across the country, if not around the world."[6]

The *New York Times*, two months after the club's initial meeting, observed that the club was founded "by a number of gentlemen who are fully aware of the benefits to be obtained by healthy and strengthening pastimes.... The New-York Athletic Club intend, next year, to procure grounds of their own, on which a running track and gymnasium will be constructed." To help with funds, the first of its numerous semi-annual games were planned for the opening of the Empire City Skating Rink on November 11, 1868. Along with the New York Caledonian Club, entries were expected from Troy, Paterson and as far away as Toronto and Montreal.[7]

It adopted the "Winged Foot" or the "Mercury Foot" as its emblem, supposedly that of the Greek messenger god Mercury, suggesting great speed: "The color of the foot is red, with the shadings of the toe nails, wing feathers, &c., in white. It is usually worn upon a black shirt or jersey," the *Times* would note a quarter of a century later. It is interesting that the I-AAC was keen to imitate this badge, something that Rebecca Jenkins believed was "intended to contrast with the famous "winged foot"...[but] also indicated the strong nationalist sympathies of its core members." Indeed, it is clear that the badge with an upright clenched fist was perhaps more a mark of defiance than deference, something that now looks dangerously akin—given the "Red Scare" and McCarthyism of later years—to the communist "salute."[8]

From 1877 to 1893, the other senior New York athletic organization was the Manhattan Athletic Club. Known as the "Cherry Diamond" on account of its red logo, it was not until 1879 that the club made its mark with the legendary athlete Lon Myers. Janssen wrote of the MAC:

> The club was very successful in developing athletes and not long after its first days of open competition, was it before many of the fastest men in the country would make their appearance on the different cinder paths in [its] colors.... In the short space of six years it has risen to the position it now holds, that of the leading athletic club of America, while its name and the record of its members are known over the whole world.[9]

While there were other clubs in the city, none could come near this pair in either success or prestige following the AAU's formation in 1888. Other clubs, like the Pastime AC, founded around 1877, produced notable men, but

8. "The social element in Clubs is like 'dry rot'"

the cream of Irish athletes—if invited—had little choice but to join either top club. It wasn't just the facilities that attracted them, but the connections promising good jobs.

Joe Willis and Richard Wettan, in their paper on the social stratification of these clubs between 1865 and 1915, shine plenty of light on the transformation of the humble amateur athletic club into an exclusive establishment with plush, downtown Manhattan premises, and an affluent membership with aspirations to be seen at all the major highbrow non-athletic clubs in the city:

> Prior to 1880 athletic clubs essentially functioned to promote the athletic participation of their members. Shortly thereafter the clubs began to acquire more and more of the characteristics of social clubs. As this trend accelerated clubs became more selective of membership and seemed to develop an insatiable penchant for luxurious clubhouses and other trappings which symbolized wealth and success.

Interestingly, Willis and Wettan fail to mention the GNYIAA/I-AAC, even though in the final decade covered by their research, it was the top athletic club in the city.[10]

* * *

What we gather about the third I-AAC was that it was a "broad church" not just in the social and ethnic status of its athletes, but its members' social composition too. Its directors were primarily the sort of new-money chaps who had worked their way up in the judiciary, politics, construction, grog shops, or like Conway, a successful businessman: People who should've been able walk into any club.

The battle over the purpose of an athletic club somehow mirrored in many ways the battle of the public school system in Britain, where the mission of educating the poor was overtaken by the financial rewards from taking in former pupils'—now in the upper middle class—children. Thus around 1882, the NYAC became more exclusive during the transition from the institution *Outing Magazine* described as "a purely athletic one" where "if a man did not take an active part in physical development, he would have very little use" for it, into a "social club," where the wealthy, retired athletes outstripped active ones.[11] As Willis and Wettan see it:

> The recognition of social position as a requisite to belonging to the elite athletic clubs is evidenced by the membership policies of the leading clubs. The classic description of the purpose of social clubs of the 1890's was also appropriate in characterizing the membership policies of the elite athletic clubs, that is, clubs were formed not primarily to get people in but rather to keep people out.

Concerned active members caused the NYAC to split in 1886, while the Brooklyn AC expelled Austin F. Remsen, a member critical of the encroaching "social element" who sang "objectionable" songs.[12]

Central to keeping out the riff-raff was a hefty "initiation fee" and "yearly charge." Logic deemed that if costs "were kept high enough, undesirables ... men with 'unclubbable' qualities would be discouraged" from joining. An example of the exorbitant costs can be seen from 1893, when both the New York AC and the even snootier University AC—its membership was conditional on possessing a degree and "[a]lthough not an official policy, the specific college or university was undoubtedly important to the club's membership committee."—charged a $100 initiation fee and a further $50 annually for membership. In today's money, that counts as in excess of $2,500 and $1,300, respectively. The Manhattan AC—reputed to be even more selective than the NYAC according to Steven A. Riess—then reformed as the Knickerbocker AC, with a $50 initiation fee and $40 yearly charge.[13]

Of course, this only went so far. There were plenty of "unclubbable" men in New York City—Irish pugs-turned-politicians John "Old Smoke" Morrissey and "Boss" Richard Croker, "Big" Timothy "Dry Dollar" Sullivan, or the gambler Jere Dunn, a known multiple killer who had his membership in the Freemasons in 1887 blocked, when the thought of having a man with the blood of at least three men on his hands was all too much for the funny-handshake brigade—who were able to cough up any initiation fees from loose change lying around after a night of gambling. Therefore, sitting members needed also to block applications, as Riess illustrates: "Membership criterion was strict and candidates could be blackballed for no reason.... Acceptance into such a restricted club proved certification of a candidate's high social standing."[14]

Willis and Wettan point to the NYAC's 1886 "Constitution, By-laws, Rules and Alphabetical Lists of Members" as a clue to how the club kept out undesirables. Prospective members were required to submit a "written application, dated, stating full name, residence, and place of business of the candidate, signed by the members proposing and seconding him, with such references and remarks as they may have to make." Thus this information would allow "the membership committee to accurately place an applicant in the social hierarchy and determine if he met club standards."[15]

The NYAC's discrimination and snobbery were highlighted by the *New York Tribune* in 1902, indicating further layers of exclusivity within its membership, where an inner club of 190 resided:

> At a stated period each year there are gatherings at the handsome clubhouse of the New York Athletic Club to which are admitted only members of the club who belong to a tribe generally classified as "Indians." Some call them "good fellows" and others say just "boys" but they themselves prefer to be called "Indians" for that is their real title. They are a wheel within a larger wheel—which is the club. The official title of the organization is the Huckleberry Indians and the tribe was formed on December 7 1899. Since then, the tribe has secured Huckleberry Island, in the

Sound, about a mile away from the regular country home of the club, at Travers Island.... The Huckleberry Indians are becoming bald and gray, many of them, but they spurn the idea that a single one of them will ever grow old.[16]

Earlier the same year, the *New York Times* disclosed the long waiting list for athletic membership, particularly the Union, Knickerbocker, and University clubs. "The Union may extend its limit number when it gets into its new house. This will not be before January." But like first class travel, these obstacles inevitably created a false air of snobbish security, shattered when members of the loud and crude lower orders somehow managed to get themselves in to the high-priced seats. Any loosening of unofficial entrance criteria would generate uproar amongst those who were led to believe that membership entailed not having to rub shoulders with the uncouth.[17]

The same newspaper highlighted in a report on the "rift within its lute" and "serious dissension in its ranks" at the Manhattan AC in 1891. As the MAC opened its doors, accepting "almost everybody who offered himself," and increasing its membership to three thousand "names," a few undesirables gained admittance, including a janitor "of a big down-town office building." The unnamed source of the interview with the *Times* lamented loudly:

> They did not knowingly pass undesirable men, but they did not exercise enough caution in the matter, and in the fifty to one hundred and fifty men they elected at every meeting there are many of unclubbable qualities and no social position.... I have no aspersions to cast on men who work for their living with their hands, but they are not exactly desirable members for a club which wants to establish itself on the plane of social clubdom. Besides the unclubbable men we have a lot of boys who scarcely know how to behave properly in a club. This is the inevitable result of letting down the bars too far in a club boom and the better class of members are suffering from it. The unclubbables find nothing to grumble at in their new environments. We do.[18]

The late '80s and early '90s were known, as Riess calls them, as the "glory years of the athletic clubs," where "membership ... became an important link in a web of associations that constituted an exclusive community." But like the distant iceberg facing the Titanic, disaster was inevitably coming, and nothing was done to change course. Clubs spent lavishly on luxurious property, with the NYAC splashing out $150,000 on its Manhattan home. Meanwhile the MAC had overstretched itself by obtaining Berrien's Island as a country retreat and yacht basin in 1890, but by July 1893, laden with debts, the club went bust, and its assets sold for $456,000.[19]

Such snobbery obviously disappeared if it threatened to get in the way of a good deal. When the Democratic Club bought the NYAC's home on 55th Street and Sixth Avenue for $190,000, the deal was brokered between Croker and the NYAC president, James Whitely, by James H. Haslin, who was a member of both organizations and was the Chairman of the Committee on Admissions at the NYAC.[20]

When it came to Irish members, the waters were certainly muddy. McGowan writes:

> When the Irish immigrants who formed [the I-AAC] arrived in the United States, Irish immigrants were still largely distained in amateur athletic circles. Amateur athletics in New York were dominated by the almost entirely Protestant New York Athletic Club, the oldest private athletic club in the United States, which was founded in 1868.

Kevin McCarthy opines that exclusion existed because the "difficulties for the Irish in gaining acceptance among the elite of such as the [NYAC] led the immigrants to effectively set up their own club." However, Irish athletes like Tom Conneff, Mike C. Murphy, Mike O'Donovan, James Mitchell, John Flanagan, Thomas E. Burke, and John Francis Cregan all became successful members of these establishments.[21]

As competition against other clubs opened up, working-class, but high-performing athletes of "good standing" were admitted. As Davies notes:

> As the New York clubs engaged rival clubs in athletic competitions, the more aggressive clubs began to admit members whose social standing and income level were suspect but whose athletic talents were exceptional. Others found it expedient simply to pay outstanding performers to represent them in competitions, or to grant them free memberships. These efforts meant that young men of working-class status were often representing exclusive social clubs in their track and field competitions.

Indeed, as McGowan concludes, the notion of athletics being a "rich man's leisure activity, largely influenced by the Victorian and Edwardian perceptions of athleticism," would ultimately be redefined by "a successful athletic club that was dominated by working class athletes."[22]

James Sarsfield Mitchell, the original Irish Whale, who arrived with the Gaelic Invasion, was to remain with the NYAC for almost all his American career, eschewing any temptation to move to Celtic Park. At the MAC, the club enticed Tom Conneff in early 1888, helping the Cherry Diamonds take their first national championships in September 1889. Prior to joining the GNYIAA in 1901, John Flanagan won four championships for the NYAC, while P.J. Walsh and Matt McGrath also wore the "Mercury Foot." The only athlete to have let "the side down" was William J.M. Barry. Remaining in the United States following the Irish tour in 1885, the 16LB hammer world record holder competed for the NYAC until expelled over an unpaid bar bill.[23]

At its third club meeting on April 24, 1898, the GNYIAA discussed the matter of attracting athletic talent and expensive membership. One suggestion proposed, according to the *Brooklyn Daily Eagle*, was an "unlimited athletic membership" where "every facility will be afforded to athletes who will represent the organization in public competitions":

> In the past years a series item in the majority of athletic clubs has been the annual dues. In all cases it has proved almost too much for the limited exchequer of the youngster, consequently, they have stayed away from athletics. But a real remedy will be offered in the instance of the Irish Athletic Club. Athletes can become members for the nominal sum of $1 per year. The dues of regular members will be $5 per annum, with the initiation fee waived for the first 500. After that an initiation fee of $5 will be charged, but the dues will remain the same.²⁴

Over a decade later in 1910, the I-AAC would continue keeping fees low, announcing that "in an effort to increase its membership," its initiation fee after May 1 would be $10, "with the dues $12 for the rest of the year, proportionate to the date of admission," and including free entrance to Celtic Park. By 1912, the club still charged members $10 yearly membership, compared with the NYAC's doubling of fees in 1907 to a $200 "admission fee" and $60 annual dues.²⁵

The club had the sympathetic ear of Curtis, who claimed "the pernicious registration rule of the AAU," which previously kept out professionals, was now deterring young men, "not too liberally endowed with worldly goods," from athletics. They were now either taking up other sports or confining themselves to competing at unaffiliated picnics. James E. Sullivan pointed his finger at the clubs themselves: "They are afraid of losing money, and to these clubs, and not to the AAU, is due, in a measure, the deplorable condition of athletics."²⁶

* * *

In September 1902, the Knickerbocker Athletic Club folded. It "had taken over affairs of the MAC" and its Red Diamond logo in the mid-'90s, the New Jersey's Athletic Club's former grounds at Bergen Point, and an opulent Manhattan clubhouse gifted to them by Henry Genslinger in 1896. Its years of existence were "fraught with many surprises and sensations," according to the *New York Times*, despite a membership of up to 2,000 "in its palmy days."²⁷

When the principal backer of the club's Manhattan home, J. Herbert Ballantine, the man with the finances behind the lessees of the building, the Piqua Association, found himself in financial trouble, the premises was handed over to public usage. Only the library and smoking room on the second floor would be left for members' temporary use before the building was eventually sold for $550,000 the following March. An announcement in the *New York Times* claimed: "[A]s an organization, in the real sense of the word, [the KAC] ceases, and will in reality become a popular public athletic organization." A meeting of prominent members was called eight hours after the deeds had been filed on September 17, with club president Gilson S. Whitson saying "he thought the club would surely be reorganized, and that it would then look for a home."[28]

It never did, and in time the need to fill the role of rival to the NYAC and revitalize the city's athletics was taken up by the Irish-American Athletic Club. By 1908 the *Irish American Weekly* had observed: "The opposition the IAAC has offered to the New York AC on the athletic field has aroused the tremendous interest manifested in athletic sports in the metropolis today." Undoubtedly the clubs were as different as chalk and cheese, but if imitation is the greatest form of flattery, the Irish would do this mostly on the track and field, with the newspaper adding three years later:

> When the NYAC was in the height of its glory, sweeping in all the records (and incidentally all the athletes) of the country, its membership was crowded with the wealthy and prominent citizens of this town and neighborhood. It was enabled to build a splendid clubhouse in town and purchase and equip a lovely summer place near Glen Island, with club house, track and water. The New York Athletic Club is still a great club, but it has had to lower its colors to the Irish-American on many a well-fought field.[29]

Soon accusations arose of unsporting and underhand practices by both clubs, creating an uneasy rivalry. A *Gaelic American* article in September 1906, hardly an unbiased source, claimed that Conway had telegrammed Cohalan from the Canadian championships with the message: "Glorious victory under the enemy's flag. We pay back insult given our people four years ago." The newspaper added:

> This telegram refers to the fact that in St Louis and at Travers Island the [NYAC] designated the [I-AAC] as "a bunch of harps" and a "crowd of Micks," and when President Conway demanded an apology it was not forthcoming. He then told the New York Club that the "harps" and "Micks" would beat them on every field where the two clubs met, and he has "made good."

Now the tables were turned: "Their clubrooms are overcrowded with the trophies of their victories, and they have demonstrated if, indeed demonstration was necessary, that as athletes the Irish race have [*sic*] never been surpassed."[30]

The incident, providing it occurred, was never publicly reported, but the 1905 Met Championships duly exposed the friction between the clubs. The *Brooklyn Daily Eagle* reported about the "bitter rivalry," and both clubs "were so anxious to win that they took advantage of every opportunity, and protested some of the leading stars on the least technicality." The Irish claimed that the Mercury Foot athletes had failed to sign their registration forms individually, before Matt Halpin accused Sheridan of competing for cash at Boston the previous July.[31]

8. "The social element in Clubs is like 'dry rot'" 97

Inevitably, the I-AAC would see the whole affair as an exercise in putting them in their place. Conway hit back, offering his belief that a conspiracy by the AAU and the NYAC was being hatched.

> We can outpoint the NYAC at any time, in any set of games, and Mr. Sullivan knows it; so we don't care much about what he does, but we want him to do something. Last Thursday night, at a meeting of the Registration committee held at the New York Athletic Club club-house, I protested practically the whole New York Athletic Club team entered to compete in last Saturday's games. The committee decided the case without leaving their seats and the team competed. But they have been fooling along with the cases of our men for three months and more, and they will have to get busy or they will hear something drop.[32]

The following January, the *Gaelic American* tore into the NYAC with a not-so-subtle swipe at what it called the "nothing doing" accusations against I-AAC runners Dan Frank and John Joyce, and the 1906 I-AAC Winter "Carnival" at Madison Square Garden, while also displaying a bout of inverted snobbery about its rise in American athletics:

> The "stall fed" representatives of millionaire athletic organizations reap easy glory and the self-satisfied autocrat [Sullivan] indulges in Utopian dreams of an Anglo-Irish-Australian-American Athletic Alliance, of which, incidentally he shall be the dictator. *Moryah!* Well, so it is, and as long as it does not hurt, "don't you care," the [I-AAC] will hold an athletic carnival ... which will be but a repetition of their former successes and will show to the public that the organization of Celts which had grit enough to fight its way to the top of the ladder from a shoestring, is not going to be kept down by a cabal of nincompoops who were never known to throw the hammer beyond the distance of their own shadows, which is very much the largest part of them mentally and physically.[33]

As the AAU began to look into accusations of professionalism—the NYAC also had athletes investigated—the 1907 Metropolitan Association of the AAU Junior Championships, perhaps not exactly the top event of the year, was still a place where both clubs could do battle. Altogether there were 50 protests, mostly against college men masquerading as bona fine members. John L. Eisele, a graduate of Princeton now with the NYAC, was one whose status was approved, but others from both clubs were subsequently barred, with Sullivan threatening to shut down the event if the abuse continued. John B. Taylor was prevented from entering the Met Championships through an unsatisfactory residential status, while Harry Porter, a Cornell graduate, applying through both the NYAC and the Irish-Americans lists, was not allowed to compete.[34]

The Irish narrowly and controversially lost the AAU Junior Nationals in Pittsburgh in 1912 by one point, almost causing "a riot by their kick over a decision in the javelin throw." During the last event, sitting in second place, the I-AAC's Thomas Lund's javelin string became unfastened, and a protest was launched. Sullivan ignored Lund's pleas to retake his throw. The *New York Times* commented sarcastically that if both clubs "scrap over points at home as they did in this city this afternoon ... it is no wonder that athletic events are so successful."[35]

Reprisals were taken through boycotts. When the NYAC sent just three athletes to the 1906 Labor Day Games, Robertson hit back, claiming it was the work of Halpin and Charles H. Sherrill, and banned his athletes from attending further Mercury Foot events:

> [The I-AAC] will not enter a single athlete in any set of games given under the auspices of the [NYAC]. It is unfortunate that men like Sherill and Halpin, who pretend to be such good sports, cannot take a beating without showing such bitterness of feeling. They have started this trouble, and it is up to them to take the responsibility of their action.[36]

In September 1908, the NYAC refused to send a cadre to Celtic Park, so once more, the *New York Tribune* noted, "Not more than half a dozen Irish-American athletes competed" at the NYAC's Fall Games. "It was said that the lack of Irish entries was the result of the failure of the [NYAC] to send its athletes to compete in the Irish-American Club's games on Labor Day." Flanagan did attend, coming close to breaking the 16LB hammer world record. Only one I-AAC athlete competed at the NYAC's Games in September 1910 after the hosts refused the entry of the I-AAC's R.J. Egan, a NYAC member only weeks previously, claiming he had been "stolen." Amateur principles were thrown out the window as the *New York Tribune* reported, "Those who had any knowledge of the situation were emphatic yesterday in their statement that the New York

Matt Halpin, pictured in 1908, the scourge of the I-AAC, was seen as running a campaign of harassment against the club on behalf of the NYAC (Library of Congress).

Athletic Club was acting wholly within its rights." Sometimes there was a certain amount of oversensitivity by the Irish: When John Joyce and Thomas Hynes were accused of professionalism in 1905, part of the evidence was provided by an Irish-born priest, hardly a bluenose NYAC agent.[37]

This rivalry began threatening American success at the Olympics. When Halpin was named manager for U.S. team in London, there was an uproar from the Irish. As one anonymous athlete's letter to the *Sun* during the 1908 Olympics complained:

> [T]he Western fellows appear to be more imbued with the real American spirit than the fellows from the East. They are out for the Stars and Stripes and their club or college is only a secondary consideration. Among the New York AC and the Irish AAC there is a bitter rivalry, the latter, except John Flanagan, being out for the Irish club only.[38]

The 1904 National Championships win was no fluke, and with the I-AAC taking championships with aplomb after 1906, the NYAC saw the I-AAC as its worst nightmare. It wasn't clear what was more alarming: The fact the Irish were winning so much, or that they had done so with a bunch of largely working-class children of immigrants. Prejudice or not, they suspected that the I-AAC were breaking the rules. And things began to unravel almost 5,000 miles away from New York.

9

"The first, if not the foremost, athletic club in the world"
The I-AAC Between 1906 and 1908

Athens, early May 1906: The first-ever American Olympic team, competing under one management and flag, had gathered to celebrate their Intercalated Olympic Games "victory" with a hotel meal. A successful two weeks for the Americans—11 gold medals, six silvers, six bronzes—had been accompanied by a managerial shambles. By the American coach, Matt Halpin's, own admission, "Maintaining discipline among the athletes ... was quite a task."[1]

Halpin was detested by athletes, and not all American. Peter O'Connor accused him of falsifying Prinstein's first jump, thus depriving him of a second gold, while James B. Connolly, the first American gold medal Olympian, described Halpin having "never done anything which might indicate he could half fill the job" as a U.S. coach, labeling him an "incompetent trainer, a man of impossible manners and child in travel." Graeme Kent would later write that the "prissy" Halpin had to endure "many outspoken" I-AAC athletes in his "unsuccessful attempts to curtail their lavish lifestyles and his complaints against the loose way they conducted their sporting activities."[2]

It wasn't just I-AAC athletes. At the Hotel De Napoli, in Naples, Robert Leavitt, the 110m hurdles gold medalist, got so tanked he "smashed furniture, insulted women, and otherwise conducted himself along the lines of a rowdy, or according to his own ideas of a gentleman." Halpin paid the damage out of AOC funds and prevented Leavitt from being arrested, while his fellow Bostonian, William Eaton, attempted to hold Halpin up for money, which he refused to grant. He had previously caught the pair late at night, smoking and drinking heavily, on the ship, where the threat of being sent home failed because the other athletes wouldn't back him.

Still, Halpin thought it was time to put these things behind them. What better way to conclude matters than with a congratulatory telegram from President Roosevelt? Halpin gave W.A. Schick the paper to read out before he passed it to a nearby athlete, who then sent it down the table to be never seen again. Halpin would later tell the *New York Times*, "The cablegram did not pass more than two members of the Irish-American Athletic Club, when it disappeared and has not since been seen, although I have repeatedly demanded it from the athlete in whose hands it was last seen."[3]

* * *

While these Games' results are no longer recognized by the IOC, they played a critical role in keeping the Olympics alive. They were the first competed solely with national teams, and the I-AAC was keen to contribute, Conway telling members at the presentation of the Annual Report: "I have such a spirit of forgiveness in my heart that I move the appropriation by this club of $250 to be applied to the expenses of the American athletic contingent going to Olympus ... toward defraying the expenses of the American team to Athens." The donation was described as "a liberal one, very liberal indeed, and adds materially to the amount of money now in the possession of the committee."[4]

It was money well spent: The I-AAC had five of their eight athletes take a total of ten different metal medals, amounting to what the *Gaelic American* claimed was the largest score of any club, and almost half the Americans' tally. Before departure, the *Irish American Weekly* jested that "as far as Irish affiliation is concerned you can rarely go by any safe rule of nomenclature in this very mixed community, but it would certainly seem to be desired that we should have as our champions at Athens something with a little more of Celtic flavor about it." Only Charley Bacon, Harvey Cohn (one caught tonsillitis and the other a ruptured left ear drum on the journey over), and Jimmy Sullivan failed to win a gong.[5]

Martin Sheridan collected an astonishing five: a gold in the shot put and the discus free style, which resulted in a new world record of 41:46m, and three other silvers in the standing high jump, standing long jump and the "Fifty-Six," although he had to retire from his favorite event, the All-Around (Pentathlon). Of the others, Lawson Robertson won a joint silver with Sheridan and Leon Dupont in the standing high jump, and a bronze in the standing long jump, while William Frank came in third in the marathon.[6]

However, it was Bonhag's and Prinstein's golds that caused the most controversy. Bonhag took gold in the 1500m walk despite never having competed in the event previously, and repeatedly broke into a jog. The *New York Tribune* dismissed O'Connor's objections to Prinstein as sour grapes, adding that he was a political agitator for his role in a "flag controversy":

P O'Connor of the British team has lodged a formal protest against Myer Prinstein ... on the grounds, first that though Myer Prinstein's number was 40, he jumped third in order to take advantage of the smooth track before it was cut up; second, that Halpin, in the absence of the official measurer, assumed the duties of judge and measurer; and third, that while thus acting Halpin declared two of O'Connor's jumps foul, the claim being that one of these jumps exceeded Prinstein's. The protest was not allowed but the matter has excited warm feeling. O'Connor had previously caused excitement by claiming to represent Ireland as a distinct nation, and when he won in one event he produced Irish flags, asking to have them waved instead of the British flag. This request was not granted.[7]

The I-AAC would have collected more medals if Mel Sheppard—accused, then cleared of professionalism—had been allowed to travel. As late as March, there was fleeting optimism that he would be cleared in time, as an angered *Evening World* pondered the case:

No charges have been made against the youngster—no protest has been filed. There is no tangible kick on any side against his standing in amateur circles. All that has been recorded is an anonymous and incoherent remark by somebody not concerned in athletics to the effect that sometime in the dim past Sheppard ran in a set of games run by the Caledonian Club at Maspeth, LI, and that in these games some of the events were contested by professionals. There is no allegation that Sheppard then or at any other time competed for a reward or with opponents who were professionals.[8]

At the meeting where the donation to the AOC was announced, "the member for Mayo" had shouted in reply: "I move in addition that when the check is forwarded, the secretary be instructed to ask Mr. Sullivan why Sheppard, who wears our colors, is not going to have the jaunt to Greece ... to have a crack at that mile." Sullivan had, however, given the subject short shrift, according to the *Evening World*:

Sheppard's name is under a cloud, he says they say. They don't want to send any cloudy proposition over there, he says they say. A man has written a letter to him saying that he ran in a race with Sheppard where money was paid, he says the man says. But no charges have been lodged and no protest made against Sheppard, everybody says. And that's why Sheppard will not see the Maids of Athens this year.[9]

On April 1, Sheppard was finally denied clearance. Confusion reigned when the Met AA Registration Committee refused to either confirm or clear him, declaring instead, the "evidence produced on both sides ... is not deemed satisfactory to the committee for the purpose of dismissing or sustaining the charges." The *New York Tribune* assumed Sheppard had been "exonerated" and "returned to full amateur standing," while the *Sun* was unsure. Meanwhile the *New York Times* claimed it was the "Scotch verdict of 'Not Proven,'" with the right "to reopen the case at any time should further evidence be forthcoming." The boat to Greece was departing the following day.[10]

9. "The first, if not the foremost, athletic club in the world"   103

Conway broke the bad news after making an exhausting number of offers and pleas in vain to the committee. The *Sun* recorded, "The Irish AAC backed up Sheppard aggressively ... [and was] willing to pay Sheppard's expenses to Athens, but whether this plan will meet with the approval of the Olympic team management could not be learned." It wasn't; Curtis chillingly replied to the suggestion, "I would prefer for America not to be represented at Athens rather than have any man go whose record is questioned." Conway backed down, bitterly admitting that "it was decided by the committee of selection that this would be an impossibility."[11]

Mel Sheppard (date unknown) missed out on a trip to Athens in 1906 following unproven charges of professionalism (Library of Congress).

An anonymous sports writer in the *Evening World* sarcastically reported:

> Thanks to the dilly-dallying of the Registration Committee of the AAU, Melvin E Sheppard, the fastest miler in America, or perhaps in all the world, will not represent this country in the Olympic contests in Greece.... And so the flying wonder, a sure point-getter for the team, is left at home, despite the fact that the professional runner who made the charge against him ... admitted at the final hearing yesterday that he had testified to a deliberate lie.

The only good news was that Robertson would be added to the party waving goodbye from the *Barbarossa* to 2,000 cheerers on April 3, as the I-AAC and the 13th Regiment chartered a tugboat, *Robert Palmer*, to follow the liner "down the Narrows, and there waited until the big liner disappeared in the haze."[12]

Their return a month later was greeted equally enthusiastically. Conway was key to organizing a suitable reception when at a directors' meeting, it was decided to invite all the clubs in the vicinity "in giving a great welcome home to the American team of athletes, who distinguished themselves at Athens." He co-opted 50 members to help. "Honors are to be showered thick and fast on Martin Sheridan ... and his comrades of the Irish-American Athletic Club when they arrive home," said the *New York Tribune*. "Steamers will greet them down the bay and banquets will be given in their honor." An I-AAC delegation met the White Star Line's *The Republic* on May 25 and took the athletes back on the Iron Steamboat *Cepheus* as Albert Spalding, Frawley, NYAC president Bartow Weeks and Curtis watched on from another tug.[13]

The following night, 400 people attended a banquet at the Hotel Astor. The *New York Tribune* witnessed "justices of the Supreme Court, city officials, bankers and lawyers and merchants and writers" who, prior to the meal, mingled with the eight I-AAC athletes. Conway acted as toastmaster, while the Wexford-born New York judge, John W. Goff, saluted "Ireland's Influence on Athletics." It was an occasion, according to the *New York Times*, to pay a "patriotic and enthusiastic tribute to the skill and strength of the Irish-American athletes who aided the American Olympian team ... win its wonderful triumph.... They gave homage again to the men of the Gaelic race who made records when Greece was barbarian. They crowned once more the athletes of the club, who sat in the place of honor as the heroes of Marathon."[14]

* * *

Having the Olympics so early in the year meant that the summer season would be unimpeded by any exodus. Celtic Park opened with Gaelic football between Tipperary and Kilkenny on April 1, with the *Gaelic American* reporting that the early opening was due to "the unusual number of meetings arranged for this year," while the Annual Report, published in May, revealed "that the club is growing like Jack-in-the Beanstalk's tree," with the venue booked throughout the summer "by athletic clubs from all over Greater New York." The *Gaelic American* noted that both financially and sportingly, 1905 was the club's greatest season so far: "Celtic Park this year promises prosperity, and ... Conway, in view of Martin Sheridan's success at Athens, says the Gaels can be transplanted and to their world in any clime." The directors told members, "We feel we have passed the experimental stage, and the permanency of our association is assured." The club certainly wasn't impoverished. Assets of over $33,473.02 were now held, while plans for a Western tour with meets against the top clubs from Detroit, Chicago and Kansas City were also suggested.[15]

By the I-AAC's Spring Meet, Celtic Park had already hosted the ICAU annual field day, the Queens Borough High School Athletic Association, the Meath Men's Association, the Forty-First and Forty-Second Districts' Public Schools, and the Men of Galway. Tom Kiely had returned on May 26 with the intention of competing at the All-Around Championships in Boston on June 23. Billeted in Flushing, he had promised not to compete before Beantown, but appeared at the Men of Galway Games the day after his arrival. Five thousand fans were hoping to see him, but unfortunately he had been told by the organizers in the morning that the event was cancelled due to heavy rain. However, when a huge crowd braved the downpour, the day went ahead without Kiely, amidst a disgruntled crowd.[16]

The Memorial Day Games saw "sensational records and exciting finishes" according to the *New York Times*, although all the I-AAC Olympians—except Sheridan—were handicapped and beaten. Still, the crowd was not disappointed when Yale's prodigious future inventor, Alfred Carlton Gilbert, broke Norman Dole's world record for the pole vault. During the summer, Celtic Park hosted various diverse organizations, with some significant athletic performances. At the city's Clan na Gael annual picnic and games on July 1, 10,000 spectators saw Flanagan's new world record in the "Fifty-Six" disallowed as an "exhibition." Sheridan also spoiled a chance of a new discus world record, with a throw of 140 feet, by stepping outside the circle. In a heady seven days, records were broken in three events. On August 19, the Athletic Games of the First Regiment of Irish Volunteers, one of the biggest crowds yet at Celtic Park with 15,000 spectators, saw Sheridan improve the discus world record "in a seven foot circle" with a throw of almost 138 feet, but the mark wouldn't be accepted. The following Saturday, at the first day of the Ancient Order of Hibernians "Athletic Carnival and Midsummer Festival," fans witnessed Denis Horgan, now with the NYAC, beat Sheridan and Flanagan in the 28LB stone event, breaking William Read's 18-year-old record event. A day later, in front of the 7,000 rain-soaked onlookers at the AOH Games, Sheridan broke his discus record with a throw of 134:4 feet, while Flanagan rewrote the 56LB weight record with a lob of 43:5 feet.[17]

Come September, the Irish athletes were ready for the highlights of the domestic calendar on the month's first two weekends. Leading up, there was disappointment for the Irish in the Met Junior Championships, with the NYAC winning by 63 points to 58, a crucial moment being the fall of Ralph Young at the fourth hurdle of the 220Yds hurdles final. However, with the NYAC going into the Met Seniors with some absentees, the Irish were favorites by providing the majority of the 127 entrees. The I-AAC beat the NYAC by 120 points to 97 in front of just 2,000 souls at Travers Island, with St. Barts and Xavier sharing third place with just four points each. Mel Sheppard ran his first 880Yds, and as the *New York Times* noted, "He spread eagled his field and won as he pleased." However, as in the previous year, there were protests by the NYAC, claiming that the I-AAC's Cornelius Van Duyn, a school physical instructor, was a "pro."[18]

While the AAU National Championships at Travers Island received entries from California, Canada, Greece, Australia and Ireland, it ended in a tussle between the two major New York clubs. At Celtic Park between both championships, Flanagan had broken his record for the "Fifty-Six" with unlimited run and follow at the Eccentric Firemen Games. A previous throw at the Pastime AC Games was disqualified when the weight was found to be several ounces too light. Meanwhile, the Labor Day Games proved a "family affair" with only two NYAC athletes attending. The *Gaelic American* observed that patrons "as usual, [were] mainly Irish and Irish-American, but there were many men of other races," as a thousand Greeks came to watch discus Olympic silver medalist, Nikolaos Georgantas.[19]

On the day before the Senior Championships at Travers Island, the I-AAC took the National junior title by a close margin of 48 points to NYAC's 45. The senior title was less tight with a result of 63 points over the Mercury Footers' 38. Flanagan was the only man to win two events: the hammer and the 56LB weight. Sheppard took the 880Yds with little trouble, Ralph Young the 220Yds, Sheridan the discus, and Prinstein the long jump. The *Gaelic American* reported that the team and supporters afterwards sang a disparaging song called "The Irish Won't Let Them," where they said "the winged foot as a club/Are good 'nough socially in the Hub/But as athletes in New York they should skidoo/For a lemon they will get/And a soft one you can bet/And as 'has beens' after this it's up to you."[20]

One last chance for the NYAC to take a major championship floundered at the Canadian Championships on September 22, where New York sent 31 representatives to Montreal, of whom 19 were from the I-AAC. Sheridan bettered his discus world record with a throw of 134:4 on his first attempt. The *Evening World* rightly predicted that New York would dominate the games: "The championships should prove little more than a dual meet between the two New York organizations. Of late years the Canadians have made a miserable showing when pitted against the cream of our metropolitan athletes."[21]

The *Gaelic American* meanwhile focused on other matters, particularly the incongruous behavior of the local crowd:

> The Irish Athletic Club men never got a bit of applause for their work. When the final score was announced and it was seen that the I-AAC had won out, the only applause given came from about twenty-five young men who occupied seats in the far end of the grand stand and who seemed to be the only persons present who were pleased at their victory ... dead silence greeted the appearance and performances of such men as Sheridan and Flanagan. This was in strong contrast with the reception given to foreign athletes when they appear at Celtic Park.... One cannot help thinking that in this respect, as in many others, they bear a striking resemblance to their English brothers. At least they seem to be as "hard losers."

The following day, the I-AAC athletes were seen off by a huge crowd of Irishmen who "jammed the great depot to suffocation, held up the train until they showed by their enthusiastic cheers." Only Conway's intervention finally got the train to depart 30 minutes late.[22]

The season ended at Celtic Park with the I-AAC's Fall Games. Denis Lanigan, the Irish triple-jump champion, was the main guest amongst the

400 entries received; a special 600Yds race was added so that Mel Sheppard could attempt to break Thomas Burke's ten-year-old record. Between 10,000 and 20,000 people turned up to see Sheppard, aided by his pacemakers, M. Katzenstein and Harry L. Hillman, come within three-fifths of a second of breaking Burke's record. There were other diversions as the *New York Times* remarked: "The crowd cared less for record breaking ... than for the more picturesque features. Two spectacular events were on the program, the two-mile steeplechase and the obstacle race." A successful day prompted the *Gaelic American* to claim, "The fame of the club has travelled far, owing to its long series of victories, culminating in the great triumph at the Olympic Games at Athens last May, and every true lover of athletics now makes a pilgrimage to Celtic Park when he gets the opportunity."[23]

Winter saw a number of indoor events complemented by the Met AA and National AAU Cross-Country Championships. The *New York Tribune* commented, "on paper the Irish-American Athletic Club team looks almost invincible, with Bonhag, Daly, Frank, Goodsell, Lilley and Cohn ... while Daly, if at his best, will probably be a strong favorite for individual honors." They didn't disappoint: At the Mets on December 8, they won "a close struggle" in freezing conditions, with 37 points against the Mercury Footers 45 (as noted the team with the lowest points won these events: See "Notes on times, distances, abbreviations and scoring"). Fifteen hundred spectators watched the start and finish at Celtic Park, as George Bonhag beat Xavier's Ed Carr by 14 seconds. Covering the six-mile event in a time of 30 minutes and 52 seconds and the *New York Tribune* reported him arriving at Celtic Park, leading "by some fifty yards, and [having] no difficulty in holding this advantage" to the finish line:

> The start closely resembled a football scrimmage, as the runners had to break through the crowd, which fairly filled the road.... Then followed a long wait for those at the finish, until a cry went up that the field was in sight. The crowd formed a narrow lane, through which the runners finished, and interfered with some who were running strong.

The *New York Times* meanwhile reported "dissatisfaction" about the lack of flags marking the "poorly laid out" course: "[M]any of the competitors were unable to find the proper turnings, and several times went out off their course." Once more Halpin complained, claiming that at least three NYAC members "had taken wrong turns, and thereby lost the team championship if not individual honors." Bonhag disclosed that he too had taken a wrong turning at the rail tracks, "and by the time he had returned to the proper course he had been passed by seven contestants."[24]

A week later at Travers Island, the setting would be a more amiable one than the environs of Laurel Hill: "The difficulties experienced in going over the course will be removed at Travers Island, which is one of the best arranged cross-country courses in America," said the *New York Times*. The I-AAC took the team title with 29 points to the NYAC's 34, Bonhag couldn't repeat his form, coming third to Frank "The Buffalo Wonder" Nebrich and John J. Daly. Billy Frank came in fifth, while Joyce, Sheppard and Odell were all in the top 11.[25]

Before these two races, on November 9 and 10, the AAU also staged its first Indoor Championships "in many years" at Madison Square Gardens. Indeed, there was no reporting of any AAU Indoor Championships in the New York press since the only previous Met AA Indoor Championships, in January 1892. These games resulted in a heavy financial loss to the association and a demand of $15 from each club—big or small, rich or poor—to make up some of the shortfall, which many initially refused to pay. Therefore the decision to host the championships was partly due to the success the I-AAC had with their own indoor meetings. Where athletics—the indoor variety at least—had been written off by the *Evening World* in 1892, which noted they were "not near so popular as they should be," thanks to Conway and James E. Sullivan, crowds were now packing the Garden.[26]

The press hailed the strong I-AAC team being sent, with the *Times* declaring, "The 'Winged Fist' athletes, having carried off the honors in all the big outdoor meets during the past season, are being carefully prepared for the indoor events.... In the distance events the Irish should score heavily." Again the I-AAC took the points trophy by 87 to the NYAC's 72, with the *Gaelic American* proclaiming that it "has demonstrated in a most decisive manner its right to be known as the premier athletic organization in this country." On Friday, records were broken by Eller in the 220Yds high hurdles—recently returned after injuring himself in a crash with the police patrol car he was driving—and Sheppard in the 1000Yds, while Sheridan made the first-ever record for the 8LB shot put, while winning the pole vault for distance and the 56LB weight. Robertson won the 300Yds run. The following night, Sheridan claimed the 24LB shot and the three standing jumps, while coming second to Alfred Gilbert in the pole vault. Bonhag won the 5Mile race and Robertson collected the 150Yds. Curiously a week after, one of the strangest world records was broken by Robertson and his NYAC rival Harry L. Hillman at Brooklyn's 13th Regiment Armory, marking a time of 12 and three-fifths seconds in the 110Yds "three-legged race." Bonhag also lowered his indoor record for the 3Mile run at the 23rd Regiment Games on November 24.[27]

* * *

Nineteen hundred six was another momentous year for the club, and the Irish community thanked the club with a special reception by the United

Irish-American Societies on December 27 at the Grand Central Palace. Originally intended as a reception solely for Sheridan and Flanagan, the Mayoman thanked the organizers for the proposed honor, but requested at a club meeting—to huge applause—that all athletes be honored. Both Irishmen were presented with bronze statuettes of themselves by Cohalan, who then gave "a glowing tribute to the abilities and sterling character of the men." Alongside I-AAC officials were numerous Tammany stalwarts such as "Big" Tim Sullivan, "Silent Charlie" Murphy, and Senator Patrick H. McCarren. The *New York Times* commented, "The achievements of Sheridan and Flanagan are too familiar to need recapitulation. Both have repeatedly broken world's standards in the various events in which they contest ... [Sheridan's] achievements at Athens alone stamped him as the foremost athlete in the world today."[28]

Early in 1907, the I-AAC AGM's financial report showed a net profit for the year of $3,100. Projects proposed included upgrading the grandstand, a new pavilion, new quarters for the athletes, and "a general overhauling of the grounds and track" which was predicted to cost $20,000. The club's Athletic Committee chairman, Michael Sullivan, declared at the end of the presentation:

> In its achievements for the last year the Irish-American Athletic Club has established the right to the title of the foremost athletic club in the world. A designation bestowed on it by James E. Sullivan, the best authority on amateur sporting matters now living. Our club now holds forty-eight championships and six of our members hold twenty-one of these. This is a record unparalleled in the annals of sport.[29]

The first date organized by the I-AAC for the year was its Indoor Games at Madison Square Garden on February 3, with sixteen events planned. Twelve months earlier the *Gaelic American* had roared its approval at the event's growth over three years: "This great athletic organization was the first to arrange for an indoor athletic meet in Madison Square Garden ... and was a huge success. Since then this great athletic reunion has become a permanent factor in the indoor season of American athletics."[30]

The ten-mile run was being halved from previous years, according to the *New York Times*, "with the expectation of attracting a stronger and better balanced field." However, the dark rumors of the "stock watch" returned when the *Times* added that "in order to bring out a big field, five prizes are offered for the event." In the end, there were 765 entries, with 94 for the 100Yds, while the 1½ Mile had 86, leading the *New York Times* to comment: "In point of numbers and quality the list is one of the largest that has ever been received for an athletic meet in this country."[31]

Five thousand fans attended what culminated in a "Riot At Irish Games," according to the *New York Tribune*, while the *Sun* described it being "topped off with a free for all fight." The *New York Times* said, "Row breaks up Garden Game: The Irish-American Athletic Club gave an athletic carnival in Madison

Square Garden last night, and before it was over a row broke out which ended in a free-for-all fight." Trouble occurred not with the athletics but with the Tipperary versus Kilkenny exhibition indoor Gaelic football match that closed the meet. Because it was inside, both teams agreed that if the ball crossed the back line, a point would be awarded. However, one of the Tipperary subs was unaware of this and greeted one award by jumping onto the pitch and protesting, before punching a rival in the face. The *New York Times* noted that spectators clambering over seats and railings to join the "general fist fight," before inevitably referring to Ireland's infamous festival of violence by claiming: "The floor of the Garden was converted into a Donnybrook fair." In his wisdom, NYPD Inspector Hussey brought four plainclothes detectives with him to quell the disturbance, only to find themselves getting punched as much as the next man, and "lost in the melee." One of his charges managed to get nine policemen from outside and to call for reinforcements, who managed to quell things and turn everyone out onto the street. Before the excitement, the Quakers' quartet, including John B. Taylor, won the intercollegiate 2Mile relay. In the final athletic run of the night, George Bonhag beat his old indoor record for the 5Mile with a time of 25:52:2. Although Nelson had "jumped away in the lead at the crack of the pistol," maintaining the lead for two laps, he ran out of steam. Bonhag lapped him at three miles and again half a mile from the finish, finally beating him by two and a half laps. Bonhag broke his own 3Mile indoor record a week later at the 74th Regiment Games in Buffalo with a new time of 14:43:6.[32]

Celtic Park opened for business on April 7, while the Memorial Day Games were hailed by the *New York Tribune* as "filled with high class athletes." The club had already lost Ernie Hjertberg, who had defected to the NYAC in mid–February, and after "scouring the country" the I-AAC announced that they had secured Williams College's Bernie Wefers. The *New York Times*, reporting on the late May meet, declared, "The appearance of the cracks, the prospect of records being smashed, and the propitious weather made an irresistible combination that attracted fully 10,000 persons to the grounds." The NYAC beat the I-AAC, 30–27, but once more the controversy of handicapping raised its head. The *Times* reporter pointed out that it prevented the real winners from taking top spots, rather than leveling the playing field: "Although Flanagan and Sheridan gave their stout arms an extra twist and hurled the iron at a great distance, they were nevertheless beaten."[33]

Still, I-AAC athletes continued to break records during the summer. Martin Sheridan broke the discus world record at the Mayo Men's Games with a distance of 136:10 feet on June 23, while at the AAU All-Around Championship on July 4—switched to Laurel Hill from Jamestown—he broke the record with 7,130½ points in a two-man contest with fellow I-AAC athlete Richard Cotter after John J. Dalton failed to turn up and the Irish athlete

Dennis Murray declined an invitation. Speaking to the *New York World*, Sheridan complained, "There was nobody to push me to make me do my best. No man can do his best unless he feels he is against somebody and has fear in him that he has to go his limit to beat the other fellow." The previous Sunday, Con Walsh broke his own 56LB for height world record with a throw of 15:2:5 feet at the Cork Men's Association Games. Mel Sheppard broke Howard Valentine's two-year-old world record for 900Yds at the AOH Midsummer Games, in a special race with pacemakers. After his defeat at the Waterbury AOH Games the previous day in the half mile, experts predicted his participation was "hazardous": "[B]ut Sheppard did not show any effects from that race when he appeared on the track yesterday," said the *New York Times*. "In fact, those who have seen him in all his greatest effort, contend that he never showed better running qualities." At the Labor Day Games on September 2, Taylor, running in the Winged Fist vest, won the 500Yds handicap, as the I-AAC took the point trophy.[34]

The first major opportunity to skip handicaps was the Mets at Travers Island in late August. Played out in front of a poor turnout of 1,000—half of them arriving an hour late due to train delays and the lack of transport from Pelham Manor Station—Hjertberg conceded to the *New York Tribune*: "On form the IAAC should beat my team." The *Sun* agreed: "For the last few years the Irish have succeeded in carrying off the palm of this meet and they repeated the trick again yesterday.... It was simply a dual meet, for no other club made a point." The *New York Times* was unforgiving in its report, claiming that the Irish had "spreadeagled" the NYAC, as Keating (100Yds, 220Yds), Sheppard (880Yds), Sheridan (16LB shot—beating Denis Horgan—and discus), Sullivan (1Mile), Edward Cook (long jump and high jump), Flanagan (56LB weight), Bonhag (3Mile run), Allen (pole vault) took firsts as they won the Spalding Trophy with 87 points to the NYAC's 48: "When in the first three events, upsets put the winged-foot favorites out of it, there was nothing more to the meet as far as the team competition went. It was a question merely of only how large a score the Irish club would win by, and it nearly doubled New York's score." William Joseph Keating, "the boy sprinter," son of Irish immigrants born in the coal mining belt of Pennsylvania, received special praise from the *Evening World*:

> Keating has been the special pride of [Wefers] ... for weeks. Wefers taught the sprinter the flying start which enabled [him] to clip seconds off the sprint records of his day and which are still standing.... "He's the champion sprinter of the world right now" enthusiastically exclaimed Wefers, as he led Keating to the dressing room, "He will lower the 100-yard before the season is over."[35]

However, the *New York Tribune* was unimpressed with Matt McGrath, following his victory over Flanagan in the 16LB hammer, being hailed as another "champion of the world":

It was an unsatisfactory transfer of the title, as the athletic field was soggy and soft and the giants slipped and slid as they swung the heavy cannon ball over their heads. McGrath was the steadiest of the contestants on his feet, and after three trials he made his distance. Flanagan was lighter, and the best he could do was thirty feet behind the world's record made by himself and which many had expected to see him beat.... The heavy track and field favored the Irish-American team in that they are all big men, heavier than the [NYAC] contestants, and therefore better able to stand on their feet and make headway in the mud. But though it favored the heavyweights, it necessarily spoiled any attempt at new records.

However, the *New York Times* condemned the "farcical" team competition: "It showed merely that in the unseemly scramble for college material, the Irish-Americans had corralled the more ringers. Athletic officials admitted that the rules were being evaded and ineligible men competing.... Every one realized that laxity of rule had gone so far as to be an absurdity." O.F. Langan, Banderman, A. Zink and Fred Bellars all ran "subject to protest."[36]

William Joseph Keating, "the boy sprinter," son of Irish immigrants from Pennsylvania's coal mining region, was one of many NYPD cops in the I-AAC (Mecca Cigarettes card).

Two weeks later, the Irish party traveled on the steamship *Monroe* to the AAU National Championships at the Jamestown Exposition Grounds, Norfolk, Virginia, along with other top brass of the Met AA. In the Junior Championships on Friday, Pat McDonald took the 56LB weight title, while Cook came within four inches of the pole vault world record, giving the I-AAC the points title.[37]

The Irish then completed the double the following day by defeating the NYAC, 62 to 21, in the seniors, which the *Gaelic American* ballyhooed as "really the world's championships." Taking eight firsts, Sheppard and Daly bettered their half mile and five miles records respectively, while Eller equaled Harry Hillman's record in the 220Yds hurdles. Flanagan, according to the *New York Tribune*, threw the 56-pound weight "further than it had ever gone before" at a distance of 38:3 feet, although the record wasn't recognized. He also took the 16LB hammer title but not before breaking the leg of a judge, John J. Walsh. There were further wins for James P. Sullivan (1Mile), Sheridan (discus), and Cook (pole vault). Meanwhile, Taylor was not allowed to compete for the Irish and instead wore Quakers' colors in his 440Yds victory.[38]

As the *New York Tribune* remarked, the East had "the cream" of the America's athletes: "The Irish-American Athletic Club outclassed its rivals and won the meet with plenty to spare.... When three men from the same club finish one, two, three, in the five mile race, as did the Irish-Americans, it is a pretty sure sign that that club is about the best there is in the country." The *Irish World* concluded that the Irish were here to stay: "It take [sic] a number of years brilliant work to beat the Irish team, and until Flanagan, Sheridan, Sheppard, Daly, Bonhag, Cook and Allen retire from the game the Celtic Park club will have a team of stars which can gather in enough first places to insure victory at any set of games." After returning by the *Jefferson*, the Irish club "received a rousing reception." The *New York Times* observed, "The National Athletic Club band had been secured for the occasion and the victorious athletes were met by a large delegation of club members.... Two sightseeing automobiles conveyed the athletes and the members of the Reception Committee from the dock to the clubhouse ... where an informal reception was held."[39]

I-AAC athletes also began attending meetings as far away as Kansas City, Missouri, and interest in athletics led the AAU to revive old competitions. On October 12, John J. Daly "scored a hollow victory" in the 10Mile AAU Championship run at the Polo Grounds, where he beat Thomas Collins by a quarter of a mile and a minute and a half at the finish. Eighteen athletes competed—Billy Frank was the only absentee of note—in the first such championship in 12 years. The following day, the Galwayman ran at the I-AAC Annual Fall Games. With a strong wind battering the grounds, breaking records proved impossible. McGrath beat Flanagan with a three-foot handicap in the hammer, while Sheridan not only won the discus but beat Claude Allen in the pole vault through his handicap. But it was the steeplechase race that "held the principal interest," according to the *New York Times*: "The Liverpool had a fascination that was compelling, though every time a runner landed in the icy waters cold, sympathetic chills ran down every spectator's back. Daly ran from scratch, and wore down his field in the first mile, having no difficulty in finishing a winner."[40]

The Irish-American athletes ended 1907 having scored a total of 1,696 points, "the greatest number of points ever scored by an athletic club and stamps the winged fist stars as real world beaters," according to the *Evening World*. The NYAC's athletic total of 1,395 points with 68 athletes was overtaken; Sheridan topped the squad with 194 points while Sheppard was second with 158, and 14 records were broken by the club.[41]

* * *

The winter events produced mixed results. The Irish retained the AAU Cross-Country Championships with a tally of 25 to 42, despite NYAC's teenage sensation Fred Bellars taking first place. The placing of Daly, Collins, Crowley, Bonhag, Joyce between third and seventh securing enough low points. The indoor season opened with the AAU Championships at the Garden on October 25 and 26, with the Irish keen to make a clean sweep of the major titles as they had the previous year. On the first night, Sheridan broke the world mark for the pole vault for distance, while Porter (high jump), Sheppard (1,000Yds), and Bonhag (2Mile) took firsts, helping the Irish lead the Mercury Footers, 40–36. On the second evening, Bonhag won the 5 Mile and Claude Allen took first place in the pole vault, but disappointingly Sheridan—who was said to be entered in nine events—came in second in the 24LB shot put and third in the three standing broad jumps. Keating and Bonhag both missed out on first in the 150Yds run and 3Mile walk, while Sheppard's loss to E.B. Parsons in the 600Yds caused the most surprise. The final score was 76 to 70 in favor of the NYAC.[42]

However, Mel Sheppard's form, and more critically, his behavior, would take a turn for the worse. At the Company I, First Regiment, Pennsylvania National Guards track meet in Philadelphia, competing in a two-night series representing New York City on January 24, 1908, trouble started on the first night in the 1,000Yds event. His chief rival was Penn's Guy Haskins, who had previously beaten Sheppard in Philadelphia without incident. Sheppard led the student from the second lap but was beginning to tire, and as Haskins tried to pass him on the sixth lap, the men began jostling. When Haskins started to break away, Sheppard "swung round and, seizing Haskins around the neck, deliberately threw him to the floor." Suddenly, according to the *New*

York Tribune, there was a "mini riot" in the City of "Not So Brotherly" Love. Haskins' supporters, seated near the track and close to the finish line, furiously ran out to confront Sheppard, who, suddenly thinking discretion the better part of valor, responded by trying to take flight: "Some one hit him fairly on the chin, and in a moment he was jostled and being punched and kicked. Friends of Sheppard ran in, and for a moment there was danger of a serious free fight. A dozen policemen forced their way into the crowd on the floor and rescued Sheppard, whom they escorted to one of the company rooms in the armory." George Orton, the race referee, disqualified Sheppard, who excused his behavior to the *New York Tribune* on being "tired and irritated and did not know what he was doing."[43]

There was suddenly "great interest" in the second night's event. But eventually the Quaker coach, Mike Murphy, stated that he wouldn't let Haskins run against Sheppard on the Philadelphia team which eventually won. The Penn student was later due to run against Sheppard at the Pastime AC Indoor Games in New York, but there were rumors that Sheppard would be suspended, and sure enough the Middle Atlantic AA of the AAU barred him until March 1. While he apologized to Haskins and "confessed his guilt" to the Mid Atlantic AA, the AAU Registration Committee refused to rescind the suspension when asked.[44]

The Irish-American's own "Monster Indoor Carnival," set for February 8, was now significantly devalued, with the *Evening World* predicting that Sheppard's suspension would "put a crimp in any aspiration the Irish-Americans might have had." The *New York Times* claimed that the suspension "has created an unfavorable feeling in New York," due to tickets being sold not only for the Irish club's event, but also the Pastime AC's at the same venue, on Sheppard running, while noting that the Philadelphians made their profit by suspending "Peerless" Mel after their events: "Several thousands of dollars had been taken in for the advance sale, the purchasers expecting to see Sheppard run. The Philadelphians protected their own meet, but totally disregarded the Pastime games." Optimism briefly returned with the arrival of Swedish Olympic pole vault silver medalist Bruno Söderström, who embarked in New York in early February. Listed as King Gustav V's "representative" and "accredited ambassador ... to investigate and report on amateur athletics as they are conducted here, particularly indoors," Sheridan was immediately dispatched to the Met AA's offices to convince Sullivan to allow the Swede to compete at the Garden. The *New York Times* recorded that Söderström was to "add an international flavor to the carnival," while the Unicorns of the Boston Athletic Association were in town to run a Match Relay race. On a night where up to 10,000 attended and 600 athletes entered, Forrest Smithson, "the famous Western sprinter and hurdler" now with the 22nd Regiment AA, equaled S.C. Northridge 60Yds hurdles record.[45]

Conway was "satisfied" with how the evening progressed, the *Evening World* reporting that

> while there were no records broken, nor anything approaching sensational competition ... the games proved that athletics is far from being dead. Properly promoted and conducted as were these games, athletics might be made as popular as of old.... [Spectators] saw a great set of games, in which the cream of the athletic world competed and it showed the enthusiasm that can be aroused by good healthful and fair sport with its roof-rousing cheers at the slightest provocation.

Taylor took a tight two-man race from Bacon—Hillman dropped out through injury—in the 660Yds run, and Pat McDonald won the 56LB weight handicap with Flanagan, despite the best throw, coming in third. Boston beat the Irish in the match race, while the I-AAC in turn outran the NYAC in the 2Mile relay race. Cornell beat the University of Pennsylvania's quartet that included Taylor in the 1Mile intercollegiate relay.[46]

There were some innovative acts, including what the *Evening World* described as "the cruelest happening of all the night." Here Patrolman Hickey was disqualified from the Half-Mile walk for policemen in uniform:

> What of it if he did skip and run a wee bit every once in a while? He was determined to get home in front to the tune of "H-A-RR-I-G-A-N," and he did. When he was told he was disqualified for running he seemed the most dejected man in the Garden. "Don't I get nothin'?" he asked. George Bonhag didn't have the heart to tell him no, but Hickey felt he wouldn't. "Where's Martin Sheridan?" he demanded as he broke through the crowd to get some satisfaction from the all-round champion.

The *World* concluded, "The Irish-American athletes, through, perhaps, a sense of decency, didn't win the majority of events, as they usually do in similar meets.... In explanation Martin Sheridan, the busiest official on the floor, instead of a competiter [sic], for a change, said: 'We do as well at our own games. We want to give the other boys a chance.'"[47]

The event was attended by possibly the largest attendance for an indoor event at the Garden: "All told the games proved more successful than the club itself had hoped, and adds another story in the building up of American athletics through the efforts of the Irish-American AC, which, starting insignificantly some years back is now of the first, if not the foremost, athletic club in the world." A week later at the Columbia Track AA games, Harry Porter, a new recruit from Cornell, broke the indoor record for the high jump at the same venue, beating Michael Sweeney's record with a jump of 6:03:5 feet.[48]

Good news arrived that Hjertberg's sabbatical at the Mercury Foot was ending and "The Wizard" would be returning to Celtic Park on March 1, collecting $500 over his NYAC salary. "It was an open secret that Hjertberg would not be with the New York AC aggregation next year, but the announcement that he will again take charge of the Celtic Park crowd will come as a surprise," said the *Washington Times*, as Wefers looked like going the other way. Meanwhile the I-AAC's Forrest Smithson broke the world indoor record for the 70Yds hurdles at the NYAC Indoor Games at the Garden.[49]

The year 1908 would be an Olympic year in which the I-AAC hoped to see many of its members representing Uncle Sam. But there would be problems before the big event. On March 4, at the Met AA versus Mid Atlantic AA "Inter-City" meeting at the First Regiment Armory in Philadelphia, Sheppard "marred" the meeting through his actions in the 660Yds race. The *Evening World* reported, "The ill feeling that has existed between Melville Sheppard ... and Guy Haskins spoiled what otherwise might have been a grand race last night at the First Regiment Armory." Haskins firstly had a false start, which led to a three-yard penalty, before Sheppard joined him "ostensibly to show that he wanted to be on fair terms with [Haskins]." Sheppard jostled and crowded the Quaker for most of the race, until the final lap when Haskins finally broke free, which led to Sheppard suddenly walking off. Bacon won the race with fellow I-AAC member Bromilow coming second. Sullivan, as referee, called it a "no race," ordered a re-run and disqualified Sheppard, leading the other New Yorkers to refuse to participate.[50]

Sheppard would seriously test the patience of the AAU with his feud with Haskins, his temper nearly ruling him out of another trip across the Atlantic. He should have been a shoe-in for Athens two years earlier, before disaster struck, being accused of the most heinous crime an amateur athlete could commit in 1906, something akin to how we view doping today: Professionalism.

10

"If you see an Irish head, hit it"
The I-AAC and Accusations of Professionalism

Irish Bostonian Arthur Duffey was one of the finest American sprinters at the turn of the century. Despite missing out on a medal at the Paris Olympics, he would add the 75Yds in 1903 and 50Yds in 1904 to the 100Yds world record he broke in June 1902 with a time of 9:6 seconds. The 100Yds time wouldn't be beaten until May 1930. However, Eddie Tolan knocked a tenth of a second, not off Duffey's time, but that of future I-AAC long jumper Dan Kelly, who in June 1906 had merely equaled the Beaneater's best. By then Duffey was an athletic "non-person," his records wiped away from history.[1]

The reason for this was that in October 1905, two months after he retired, Duffey did something shocking. He confessed to Bernard McFadden of the magazine *Physical Culture* that he had been accepting money for running since 1898, igniting arguably the most high-profile "sporting" scandal of the twentieth century before drugs: Arthur Duffey was to shamateurism what Ben Johnson was to doping.

This interview confirmed many suspicions about false "expenses." Duffey argued that three factors made the "evil" possible: The popularity of athletics; the event managers; and the athlete who succumbs, where "he can easily afford to compete for [expenses] alone, irrespective of the intrinsic value of the trophy," allowing him "to travel all over the world in order to take part in contests and return to the land of his birth with a bank account of a very comfortable nature indeed."[2]

Many were furious. The *New York Times* angrily called this an "exposé of the pseudo-amateur and the methods whereby he is able without means to live and travel in comfort, if not luxury, and have a sufficient supply of pocket money," without jeopardizing his status as an amateur:

10. "If you see an Irish head, hit it"

The subterfuges and evasions, which all have known were practiced, are to be laid bare without mincing words. While the information may enlighten some who still hold to the belief that the majority of the "stars" that tour the world are bona fide "simon-pures," most of these who have been in close touch with track sports know the methods quite as well as the champion and understand their limitations in attempting to prove the charges against any particular man. None knew the facts better than the Amateur Athletic Union officials, and the impossibility of securing evidence.... While most of those in the know have believed this for some time, it has never been possible to establish it, so it must be assumed that Duffey has himself at last torn the veil from his false pretense.... The existent conditions described do not call so much for rule changes as for a greater prevalence of common honesty, and the creation of a sentiment among athletes that shall mark the man who accepts bribes to pose falsely as unclean for until the men themselves root out the evil, it will always continue to exist. The only rule change needed is to give the authorities governing athletics the right to disqualify on suspicious circumstances as subversive to the entire fabric of true sport.[3]

James E. Sullivan decided to "ascertain whether or not [Duffey] ... could be prosecuted legally for his action." As editor of Spalding's athletic almanac, he also removed Duffey's records and name from the "winners" list, replacing it with those whom "he wrongly deprived of the honors"; "No punishment that can be meted out is too severe for Duffey. His name has been fraudulently placed upon our records and he has been given events that he himself admits

James E. Sullivan, in the center, with athletes en route to Stockholm, 1912. A one-time I-AAC official, the "czar" of American athletics and alleged cousin of Matt Halpin became a figure hated by the club (Library of Congress).

he was not entitled to." He described Duffey's disclosure as "the most startling ever made in athletics," claiming that widespread money-taking was a lie: "There may be isolated cases of crookedness, but any wholesale practice would certainly come to our knowledge."[4]

Duffey replied by threatening to reveal names: "If they thought my story would end with a rehearsal of my own doings they've shot wide of the mark.... I know the men who have yielded to the temptation and thus violated both the spirit and the letter of all amateur rules." He then backtracked, distancing himself from McFadden. If he was looking for mercy, he could forget it. At the 1905 AAU's AGM, Joseph B. MacCabe declared, "The man who deliberately accepts excessive expense money is a professional of the worst type, and the seal of amateur condemnation should be placed upon him forever." In February 1906, his varsity records were deleted; "No such stigma should be allowed to cloud the fair name of the American college athlete." Duffey would move into sports journalism, working for the *Boston Post*.[5]

* * *

Amateurism in athletics was a touchy subject. Following the "pedestrianism craze," the world of athletics had been taken over by amateur clubs, meaning that this was the last sport that remained—theoretically at least—untainted by the passing of lucre. In practice, amateurism served more as a tool to discriminate against undesirables from the lower classes. And like so many discriminatory and snobbish practices, it arrived less from the British aristocracy, than through their sycophantic middle-class admirers, who defined an "amateur" narrowly to those who had never done paid manual labor, as "college" men often found it hard to compete with those who had.

In May 1905, the *Evening World*'s John Pollock wrote about the disparity between the privileged varsity athletes, who relied on generous "handicaps" to win races against the earthy New Yorkers of the I-AAC:

> There were athletes from all the greater universities ... and trained though they were for the honor of their colleges, not one but had to "extend" himself to hold his own with the lads from the shops and mills and markets of New York City, who chiefly made up the membership of the Irish-American Club. The college men learned that not only is it in the university gym and on university campus and training grounds that men are best fitted to win laurels of athletic fields.[6]

Initially, the NYAC had been at the forefront of imposing the "British" concept of amateur, someone "who has never competed ... for public or admission money, or with professionals for a prize ... nor has at any period in his life taught or assisted in the pursuit of athletic exercises as a means of livelihood." In 1894, the NYAC questioned whether so-called "Class B" bicycle riders should represent the club. John C. Gulick, the club's Bicycle Committee Secretary, told the *New York Times*: "[T]o my mind Class B riders are semi-professionals, and sooner or later they will be full-fledged professionals. This is an amateur club, and the feeling among the members is against that class." However, American athletics' first national body, the National Association of Amateur Athletics of America, paid the price for adopting this rule. In 1888, many clubs walked out to set up the rival Amateur Athletic Union.[7]

Richard O. Davies argues that Americans could never commit to such narrow definitions:

> Too many members were hard-driving businessmen who lacked the detached perspective and social self-assuredness of the hereditary British elite. Few had inherited their wealth; rather, most had obtained it in the aggressive business world. They tended to apply the same competitive attitude toward sports as they did to their economic environment. Nonetheless they invoked the amateur concept when it suited their needs.

Rules were loosened to allow both laborers and "expenses" to "out-of-town" athletes.[8]

As this "poor-man's club," the I-AAC eschewed elitism for good reasons, because as Katchen argues, they couldn't survive otherwise. Top "unclubbable" athletes—Irish or not—were welcomed by a club that Kent celebrates, not without some justification, as a "cornucopia of extroverted star athletes and relaxed atmosphere towards its members accruing 'expenses.'" This open-door policy would create resentment, as the club was not averse to sharp practices. At the opening of the Pelham Bay athletic ground in September 1904, the GNYIAA won the 1Mile relay handicap after changing the original lineup at the last minute. By including Lawson Robertson, they altered their own handicap, having, according to the *Sun*, "executed a clever trick." When the NYAC discovered "the sharp act," they immediately protested to the referee, James E. Sullivan, who had no choice but to disqualify the Irish.[9]

John Flanagan and Matt McGrath moved over from the NYAC and brought questions about what incentives they were given. Soon accusations of professionalism surfaced. But during this period of athletic "McCarthyism," other factors should be considered: Athletes found amateurism hard work when the financial rewards of other major sports were enticing, and as most I-AAC athletes—especially those born in Ireland—had never attended any "college," this luxury was something not easily affordable.[10]

Despite what Sullivan said, by mid–July 1905 the AAU was suspicious of certain aspects of athletics. The *Washington Times* claimed that "the public has been bamboozled long enough" by the press and clubs advertising top athletes' attendance, only for them not to come, or worse, participate at a different event elsewhere on the same day. The Met AA were clamping down on what the *New York Times* claimed were "the flagrantly loose methods which have recently prevailed" around its catchment area, where clubs listed contestants with no intention of competing and "patrons of the sport have been misled." Sullivan added that he thought the "offenders were so artful in evading detection ... that it had been an impossibility to mete out to them the prescribed penalties." Everyone, it seems, knew the rules were "being flagrantly violated." The *Times* continued, "There is to be something in the nature of a thorough housecleaning" within the AAU. "Drastic measures" were to be taken "against offending amateur athletes." Several leading athletes from a number of clubs, including James P. Sullivan, were suspended after changing their club affiliation at a Decoration Day event in Albany.[11]

Already under suspicion was Martin Sheridan. After capturing nine of the GNYIAA's 81 points at the 1904 Mets, he was immediately protested and accused of professionalism by the NYAC, temporarily halting the Irish's first-ever Spalding Trophy win. The charge against Sheridan—who had once been suspended for failing to pay an entrance fee to the GNYIAA in 1901 while with the Pastimes—was that as the manager of "the new public athletic field in Pelham Bay Park," he had at hand the facilities to train whenever he wanted. He was reinstated in July 1905, in time for that year's All-Around Championships, but then the I-AAC lost more men.[12]

First their new recruit from Colgate, Frank Castleman, noted by the *Sun* as "one of the most versatile athletes of the time[, a] fine hurdler and sprinter ... a crack baseball player and brilliant halfback, and no means an inferior basketball player," was suspended, accused of playing summer baseball for money. Then, following their absence from the Fourth of July Games, Thomas Hynes, the visiting Irish runner, and John Joyce were both banned, the official announcement reading: "Suspicious circumstances ... are sufficient to make [their] amateur status ... a matter of reasonable doubt." One charge centered on "a so-called manager" of one or both men demanding money from organizers. Another was that both had agreed to appear at Celtic Park yet ended up in Boston instead, allegedly receiving $100 each. "Other suspicious circumstances will be investigated in connection with recent races ... including betting," reported the *Evening World* ominously, as Robert Edgren also stuck in his two cents: "What excuse is there for going all the way to Boston to compete in a match race there when just as good a match was arranged to be decided here in our own Celtic Park? Maybe Hynes, having heard a lot about the Back Bay district, wanted to see it."[13]

The AAU's Torquemada in investigating professionalism was Matt Halpin. Not only was he a long-time Mercury Foot member and administrator, he was also Sullivan's cousin, a prime example of the "keep-it-in-the-family," pseudo-incestuous structure of sport's hierarchy at the time. Indeed, while the accusations against Joyce and Hynes were brought by the I-AAC, the club was disgusted by Halpin's protest against Sheridan. At the 3Mile race during the Pastime AC Games, the NYAC spoiled another fine day by claiming that Charles Daming was a professional, which led to officials withholding the points trophy won by the Irish.[14]

So when, at a meeting of the Met Championship Committee on September 7, 1905, three athletes were refused entry, the club hit back with all it could muster, leading to a courtroom encounter. The evening was taken up with both major clubs protesting against each other: The NYAC continued complaining about Sheridan's job at Pelham Bay and Van Duyn being a physical fitness instructor. Then Conway "sent a bomb flying into the meeting," according to *The Sun*, demanding that Edgren, Hillman, and Mitchell should all be declared professionals because they were sporting journalists. With Halpin in the chair, both Castleman and Joyce were barred from the Mets, while on the following night, the eve of the event, the Registration Committee suddenly found George Bonhag guilty of competing "under an assumed number" since February and banned him for a year.[15]

Such endless kvetching infuriated the I-AAC, who considered themselves being unfairly targeted in this "war" on professionalism; their men, "more sinned against than sinning," were suspended without sufficient evidence. They accused the AAU of "favoritism in the administration of rulings in regard to offending athletes, and so many more things that it would take a book, and a fat volume at that, to deal with the various phases of their complaint." Behind this campaign against the club was Sullivan, who had "had it in" for the Irish ever since they refused to send him as their delegate to the MA's annual convention prior to the 1904 Olympics.[16]

The *New York Times* reported that the I-AAC was "preparing for a bitter fight" in courts: "[T]hey are firm in the belief that Joyce and Castleman will prove themselves to be amateurs in the truest sense of the word. But should they get the 'word of the deal,' as they put it, they will at once take steps to further the organization of an amateur athletic body that will threaten the supremacy of the [AAU] and its forces."[17]

Seeking the advice of lawyers, they obtained from the New York Supreme Court "a mandatory injunction ordering the officials to allow [the athletes] to compete" at the Mets. The *New York Tribune* reported:

> As a final expedient the [I-AAC] on Friday made application for a writ of mandamus to compel the registration committee to reinstate the men. Justice [Leonard A.] Giegerich proposed, as a compromise measure, that they be allowed to compete, under protest, holding that the case was wholly outside the jurisdiction of the court, as the [AAU] is a "voluntary unincorporated body" and there is no implication of a duty imposed by statute.

Giegerich granted the I-AAC one week to find a "precedent on which a definite ruling may be based."[18]

The event descended into what the *New York Times* lamented as "a battle of protests, with the majestic dignity of the Supreme Court looming threateningly in the background." Meanwhile the *Tribune* couldn't hide its sarcasm: "The picturesque country home of the New York Athletic Club, at Traver's [sic] Island, Pelham Manor, never looked more attractive than it did yesterday.... Brightly as the sun shone, however, there were lowering clouds upon the athletic horizon. In place of the usual good fellowship, court orders and bitter feelings were rampant." The Irish-American officials spent most of the day objecting every Mercury Foot entry, while Joyce and Castleman rubbed the court judgment in the NYAC's faces, by being "potent factors in the victory of the Celtic organization over the New York Athletic Club." Adding "to the unpleasantness," Halpin again loudly accused Sheridan of receiving payments in Boston, naming dates, places and amounts charged. The Mayoman eventually "only took the field under protest." Then the I-AAC's J.E. Gerrity was prohibited from participating as "he had not obtained a written release" from the Pastime AC. The *Tribune* sighed in conclusion:

> All in all, it was a fine mix-up, and the whole affair reeked decidedly of unsportsmanlike tactics from start to finish. What the outcome will be is problematical, but it is likely that the [AAU] will allow the courts to decide the Joyce-Castleman case, now that it has gone to that stage. It is to be hoped that once the present difficulties are straightened out the squabbles of those who pose as amateur athletes will not be aired so publicly.

It added grudgingly that when "the numerous protests are decided, these figures are likely to be materially changed," the removal of the trio's points would still mean that "the [NYAC] team will hardly win."[19]

The *New York Tribune* didn't conceal its disgust over the whole "sordid and repugnant" affair: "Accusation and recrimination are publicly flung back and forth, charges are followed by counter-charges; and instead of an honest rivalry we have a free display of jealousy and unfair competition—anything but the spirit of true sport." It conceded that it was impossible to ascertain if there was any truth in the charges, but continued, "the mere fact that the charges were made—and publicly made—is in itself almost as disgraceful as proved guilt of them would be."[20]

The I-AAC was keen to see the three athletes cleared before heading off to the Canadian Championships, with Conway briefing the *Evening World* that he had a majority of New York's clubs behind him:

> We shall insist that something be done tonight. The cases ... have been hanging fire for mero [sic] than three months. I charge that they have been held up in order to benefit the New York Athletic Club by order of [Sullivan].... Either the three men under consideration are amateurs or they are professionals. We purpose to find out.... We are no quitters. We don't hold back and send a team to compete only when we think we have a clinch. I received a letter to-day from J.C. Russell, manager of the Central YMCA baseball team, in which he suggests that the Irish AAC call a meeting of all the clubs in the metropolitan district to enter a protest against the

unfair methods of the powers that be in the AAU. Scores of amateur athletes of high standing and many writers have commended our course in going into the courts.... We did not want to drag this matter into the courts, but after three months of shilly-shallying it was the only course open to us.

Nine days after the Mets, at the New York Supreme Court, with Daniel Cohalan representing the Irish, Justice Charles H. Truax, a NYAC member, declared, like Dowling before him, that he was disqualified from taking the case.[21]

The Irish-American press was naturally angry. In an article called "'Knocking' Irish Athletes," the *Gaelic American* declared:

"You can't keep down the Irish," that seems to apply particularly to the [I-AAC] nowadays. It requires only a semblance of fight to put the Irish on their mettle anyway; it is characteristic of the fighting race, hence when that autocratic and truly august body, the Registration Committee of the Metropolitan Association of the American Amateur Athletic Union, by "Divine Right" saw fit to put Johnny Joyce and Frank Riley Castleman out on the specious plea of professionalism or some other, the I-AAC started in to "build up their fences," and began over again to win new laurels for the "Winged Hand."..[The case] still lays dormant for the simple reason that the committee of the AAA [sic] having the matter in charge seem to be afraid to face the music.[22]

However, by involving the lawyers, the I-AAC was playing for high stakes: The AAU, like any sporting body, detested outside legal interference in its business. One writer for the *Boston Evening Telegraph* predicted that the Irish might need to leave the Metropolitan Association, as resorting to the courts was "in violation of the rules of the [AAU]." Sure enough, as Giegerich's judgment moved closer, an MA meeting declared that it would grant "ten days of grace" before serving a notice that the I-AAC either cease "the injunction proceedings" or face suspension for "insubordination."[23]

Cohalan left the meeting furious, telling the *New York Tribune*: "The notice served on me ... is one of the most remarkable papers I have ever seen. While the decision of Justice Giegerich is pending we are commanded to withdraw the proceeding under threat of charges of insubordination. I believe that to be contempt of court, and we will take action accordingly." The threats he added were a ruse to interfere with the I-AAC indoor games at Madison Square Garden on February 3. Meanwhile Sullivan made a pithy statement to the press: "Let them go to court. I have built up my reputation during twenty-five years of honest effort, and I need not go to these men for a bill of character. I am not worrying, and they can take us to court for contempt. They must obey the rules."[24]

The threat was greeted in the *Gaelic American* by a caustic article titled: "THE REIGN OF SULLIVAN: Trying to Hold His Own at the Expense of the Irish-American Athletic Club":

Mr. James E. Sullivan, the self constituted autocrat of the athletic world, is quoted in an evening paper of Friday last [January 11] as follows: "Let them go to court.... Let them get out of the AAU if they don't like it. Why don't they abide by the constitution? We are not incorporated, and they must obey our laws or suffer in consequence. What's that? Have I any animus? Certainly not. The secret of this trouble is that the men at the head of the Irish Club are ignorant and do not know anything about American athletics." "But is it not true that they have many champion athletes?" asked the reporters. "Who are they?" demanded Mr. Sullivan. "Well, there is Martin Sheridan." "He is under protest," snapped Mr. Sullivan. "The Irish Club declares that was another injustice inspired by animus." "How about John Flanagan?" "He is an ex-champion." "You can say for me that I am not worrying," concluded Mr. Sullivan. "Let them take us to court for contempt. As a matter of fact they do not want a decision. Why? Well, they must obey the rules."

The columnist "Killarney" continued to list the club's success since 1898, especially bringing indoor athletics back to Madison Square Garden, while attacking both Sullivan's ability to run American athletics as well as his apparent disdain for his own ethnicity:

Certainly not! Mr. Sullivan or his press agent—we believe they are identical—who built up his reputation said it was so and there you are. But will this architect of reputations tell us of one athletic club in which he continued for any lengthy period as a member or officer and he has consistently held office that has been successful. He cannot claim to have made the Pastimes what they are, and who has heard of the Catholic Club, Jersey City, in athletics in the past ten years. Where! Oh where! Are the New Jersey AC, the Knickerbockers and the once famous Manhattan AC? These are a fair share of failures for even an autocrat in twenty-five years. "Let them get out of the AAU," he says. Certainly! That is what Mr. Sullivan most desires; he knows he is in for a fight but can he afford to engage in one? We think not, the weapons he is using at present would win no fight for him or anyone else. "Let them live up to the constitution." Certainly, the I-AAC should live up to the constitution, and we should like to know why it is if they have violated it, that august body (the AAU) have not brought them to trail and given a decision on their case. There is we believe, a rule in the constitution of the AAU which makes it obligatory on all affiliated clubs to run at least one set of open games each year. Why is that rule not lived up to? How many clubs in the Metropolitan District (affiliated) are there which have never been known to run a set of games, and are there not some clubs erroneously posing as athletic, which have no competing athletes in their membership, but whose delegates have both voice and vote in the councils of the AAU? Mr. Sullivan says: "The secret of the trouble is that the men at the head of the Irish Club (the I-AAC) are ignorant and do not know anything about American athletics.".. Imitation, a great writer has said, is the sincerest form of flattery. If the I-AAC are ignorant of American athletics, why are they imitated? Ignorance and success do not belong in the same category. Success the Irish AC certainly has had, it is glutted with it from a social, financial, and last, but not least, from an athletic viewpoint. Then, Mr. Autocrat, where does the ignorance come in? Ignorance of the Irish! And this from a man named Sullivan, the recreant son of an honored Kerry clan! If the forbears of this know-it-all could only come back to mother earth again for a short time it is but fair to them to say that they would treat him to the familiar spanking, and in addition, a good ducking in the limpid waters of Lough Lein.[25]

Back in court, it looked like Giegerich was procrastinating. In a busy courtroom on January 13, 1906, the I-AAC was left disappointed as he failed to deliver. Four days later, he shocked everyone by taking their side, accusing the MA of ignoring the AAU's own bylaws, "which provide that, within ten days after the evidence has been closed where charges have been made, the committee shall file its report with the secretary of the union, which ... shall be submitted to the board of governors at its next meeting. In case no decision has been reached by the board within ninety days after the charge was first filed the person accused shall be deemed to have been acquitted and the charges dismissed as though final action had been taken to that effect by the vote of the board of governors." He concluded that 90 days had passed.[26]

The *Evening World* ran the headline: COURTS DECISION BLOW TO AMATEUR ATHLETIC UNION: "Irish A A Wins Out in Fight for Athletes Castleman and Joyce." Afterwards Conway told the newspaper:

> This decision means that Joyce and Castleman can enter any games. It also means that the powers of the Registration Committee of the AAU are not unlimited and, that athletes who are treated unjustly can get redress in the courts. The Registration Committee has ruled supreme for a long time. We are the first who have ever brought them to time.

Conway vented his spleen: "The purpose of that letter was very clear. Sullivan and his registration committee have been throwing obstacles in our way for a long time, and they were evidently determined to spoil our midwinter games." The Registration Committee had retracted "its arbitrary stand," demanding that the I-AAC withdraw its injunction, but sent a second letter to Conway demanding that the club comply by February 6, after the Madison Square Garden event. The *Evening World* concluded that the AAU "fought the injunction on the ground that [they were] not incorporated and the Irish club had to obey the bylaws which gave the committee undisputed power," only for Giegerich to overrule, adding sarcastically: "It is believed that Mr. Sullivan will contest the matter further for the purpose of maintaining his undisputed rule."[27]

Despite Giegerich's decision, it was also expedient that the I-AAC should refrain from further court action. On February 1, it jointly agreed to a trio of arbitrators—Gustavus T. Kirby of the Intercollegiate Association of Amateur Athletes, the NYAC's hardly impartial Patrick J. Walsh, representing the Met AA, and Dr. Luther Halsey Gulick, the Public School Athletic League secretary—to deal with the case. Joyce and Castleman were cleared to compete "under protest" just in time for the I-AAC's indoor games two nights later. The *New York Tribune* greeted the news with the headline: "SETTLED

OUT OF COURT: Warring Athletic Factions Agree to Arbitrate Differences," claiming that the Met AA and the I-AAC had "buried the hatchet and settled the differences."[28]

Cohalan met Weeks to iron out a settlement. At a hearing on March 15, the case against Joyce and Castleman was heard. The *New York Tribune* summarized that while the case against Joyce was "not particularly strong," Castleman's amateur status looked in peril. His responses to Weeks' questions "astonished the few who were allowed at the hearing," admitting to being "a special student" at Colgate, where he hadn't actually enrolled. He also participated in "unsanctioned" games at Elmira, New York, and Pittsburgh in 1904, and conceded that while captain of the Colgate track team, he had never read the rules covering intercollegiate athletics or the AAU. He also played baseball with a Yale man debarred for being a professional, and against a team from Malone, in upstate New York, who were allegedly taking pay.[29]

When the verdict was returned in May 1906, there was relief at the I-AAC. The three-man committee ordered the reinstatement of the pair, despite Castleman being found guilty of playing for a hotel baseball team for money and "articles of jewelry not suitably inscribed and not authorized by the registration committee and ... [competing] in games where more than three prizes were given in one event." The MA's report found that "an opportunity for serious misunderstanding among competitors and a misleading of the public has resulted from the unauthorized entering of athletes in games in which they have no intention of competing," and recommended that the AAU consider "legislative enactments" to ensure that only the competing athlete signed their entry blanks.[30]

Yet while this case was being settled, another witch-hunt began, this time preventing Mel Sheppard from travelling to Athens for the Intercalated Olympics. The charge, unsubstantiated, was that Sheppard had run as a 16-year-old schoolboy at the Caledonians Games event at Maspeth, Long Island, where there were also some professional contests. Sheppard was not "exonerated" until a meeting at the Wyandot Club on May 18, where the AAU's Registration Committee finally decided that the accusation was groundless.[31]

Two years later, the question of acceptable "expenses" became entwined with what James B. Connolly would later call the "stock" watch, called because the day after an event, the watch would be returned to a jeweler's "stock" in exchange for cash, asserting that the AAU "knew both [these prizes'] origin and destination." The I-AAC had a reputation of attracting top athletes with good prizes: "[They] are considered the handsomest ever offered," said the *Irish American Weekly* of the upcoming Memorial Day event in 1903, consisting of "a solid gold Roman gypsy ring set with a genuine diamond and two sapphires for winners." The 1909 Indoor Carnival was widely hailed for the prizes' value: "With the announcement in bold letters across the top that the prizes are the costliest ever presented at an amateur set of games," reported the *New York Tribune*. While the AAU limited prize values to $35, by reason of "a special dispensation" the 4Mile run's first prize "will be a diamond ring valued at $100," with a gold stopwatch for second place. The *Gaelic American* had highlighted the club's generosity as early as 1906, insisting that the I-AAC didn't shirk on gongs: "The Irish-American Club has never yet been accused of presenting inferior prizes, and any athlete who has ever been lucky to secure one of their prizes was always eager to compete for another."[32]

Who needs to turn professional with awards like that? "Expensive travelling bags, toilet seats, marble clocks, barometers," wrote the *Gaelic American*, "pianos, bicycles, jewelry, music boxes ... are more acceptable to the athletes than a collection of worthless medals ... he can never regard in the same light as a war veteran does his treasures." Inevitably, complaints were made about the stinginess or deceit of organizers, and remembering we're still talking about amateurs, a number of athletes—among them Matt McGrath, Mel Sheppard and Hannes Kolehmainen—brought a case against the Tipperary Men's Association and its organizer, former I-AAC distance runner Bill Powers, following their Celtic Park meet on September 29, 1912. According to the *New York Times*, all athletes "agreed they were poor indeed." However, at the meeting to discuss the charges, what the *New York Times* would later call "one of most sensational [cases] in the history of AAU trials," the Registration Committee's chairman, Jacob Stumpf, asked the rather awkward question whether Kolehmainen had done any paid work since arriving in the States. The Finn, through an interpreter, retorted that that was none of Stumpf's business, and he was there to answer solely questions about prizes. Meanwhile, McGrath remarked that "he was so accustomed to getting cheap prizes that he didn't care what they were like, and as a matter of fact he only received two or three good prizes during the progress of a year's competition." Powers was later kicked out of athletics for "misrepresentation," the *Times* chuckling that those missing prizes were later brought to the AAU, where "through the trial there was hardly a wink of sleep in the old Astor House" as it resounded to the ringing of the clocks' alarms.[33]

The "handicap" system was also open to abuse. In November 1905, at a meeting at St. Bartholomew AC's rooms, local athletes claimed that favoritism in handicaps was rife, while the *New York Times* condemned the practice following the 1906 Eccentric Firemen's Games at Celtic Park: "The unaccountable tendency to award big handicaps in the games spoiled the chance of making good contests in all the track events." Two years later, the *Evening World* perfectly summed up the potential for corruption by describing a downtown meeting between Conway and Flanagan:

"What's the matter John?" asked Conway. "Arrah, man, look at that biteen of a ring on my finger. That's what I got for smashing the record with the 28-pound. It's a funny thing, but it's true, that whenever I break a record I never cop the first prize. The handicap is too much. That's why the other fellow, with a throw of 31 feet 8 inches, gets the split season gold watch, while I, with 34 feet 4 1–2 inches, fall in for this gold band, and I never wore jewelry in my life, at that, but I need a good watch in my business."[34]

* * *

The Olympics were now less than two years away, and the British athletic authorities demanded action. At a dinner in his honor in early 1907, a seemingly irritated Sullivan offered a dire warning about the failure to combat professionalism, promising that if any man's amateur status was rejected, he would withdraw America from the Games. The *New York Tribune* claimed this was the result of a recent cablegram that stated that the standing of Olympic entrants was the responsibility of the national associations, adding tongue-in-cheek:

> There is nothing in this, perhaps, to arouse any antagonistic feeling beyond the implied suggestion that some of the American competitors might not be strictly amateurs.... The English Olympic committee need not worry about the standing of our athletes. If they are vouched for by James E. Sullivan, Casper Whitney and the balance of the American committee they will be amateurs in good standing. The water may appear to be slightly ruffled for the present, but it is only temporary.

Two months later, the AAU, headed by Sullivan, announced an amendment to its Rule 6, hoping it would tighten up controls over dubious expenses. Athletes and organizers would now send in separate, signed, itemized expense statements to the AAU's Registration Committee, with those failing being suspended.[35]

In the period leading up to the 1908 Olympics, questions were asked about the I-AAC latest acquisition, the Cornell student high jumper, Harry Porter, one of the club's earliest college steals from the NYAC's traditional hunting ground. The *New York Times* revealed a letter from a prominent New Jersey "divine" in September 1907, who was "aroused by the recent exposure of proselyting [sic] methods in athletic clubs," namely poaching. An "investigation" into Porter had "laid bare only what has been recognized by thoughtful observers" for years: "The evils of professionalism, so called, are not merely about taking the money, it is the spirit which the contending for money produces the taking advantage of every subterfuge of ever dveice [sic], honest or dishonest, in order to win."[36]

There was no hard evidence that Porter had been given an inducement to join the I-AAC, so these allegations were conjecture at best, libel at worst. The *New York Times* suggested that the colleges were working to eliminate the aggressive snatching of their athletes by the New York clubs, although nobody pointed out that students were supposedly at the university to study. While the I-AAC had clearly increased signing students, the question was why the concern when the NYAC had been doing likewise for years. In fact, the NYAC could equally bend the rules: A *Jersey Journal* report in 1897 let slip that when Flanagan arrived in America, he was sought by a number of clubs. But as good jobs were scarce, "the [NYAC] made him the best offer," which included securing him a good post and waiving his membership fee.[37]

Post-London, the I-AAC lost two stars to money. Marathon winner Johnny Hayes sought to cash in on professional races, while cyclist George Cameron also turned pro. On December 29, 1908, the New York sporting columns reported another scandal involving shamateurism. "There was a shake-up, in fact an earthquake in amateur athletic circles last night," reported the *New York Tribune*, "when announcement was made of the suspension of six prominent athletes, five of whom took part in the recent Olympic Games…." Four—Sheppard, Bacon, Porter and Bonhag—were I-AAC athletes. All except Bonhag, said the *New York Times*, had been accused of failing "to file an itemized account of their expenses to games out of town."[38]

The latest incident had followed the 74th Regiment Games in Buffalo on December 12. An insight into what athletes were able to claim is highlighted in Sheppard's own list of "expenses" which came to $33.50. Of these, the train fares were $18.50; sleeping compartment $5.00, meals and hotels $10. Furthermore, his prizes were worth $35 for coming in second in two events. Then there is the letter by Porter claiming he couldn't provide an "itemized" bill at present, before adding with no little arrogance:

> I spent something in excess of the amount charged, as I took advantage to have a good little visit at their expense, which I consider perfectly legitimate. You don't imagine for an instant that a busy man like me is going to leave his business and go off so far to an athletic meet without being perfectly compensated in the amount of recreation and sport afforded.

Meanwhile, Bonhag was accused of demanding a second-place prize worth $50, $15 above the maximum first-place limit. The *New York Times* could only surmise, "Besides the implied charge of excess expenditures … many of the prominent amateur athletes have been demanding what is called appearance money—that is, a certain amount of money in excess of legitimate expenses for competing in big events."[39]

The Met's Registration Committee chairman, Herman Obertubessing, had suspected this for some time, stating that Major Charles J. Wolf of the Army had furnished a statement showing that Porter, Sheppard and Bonhag had been paid far more than "ordinary expenses." He added that he had received information from "reliable sources" that coaches had been demanding money for their teams to appear at meets. "This will not be tolerated….

A warning has been sent to all amateur athletes that they must not allow themselves to be parties to such deals under the penalty of suspension on professional grounds."[40]

Sheppard and Porter, who were travelling to Pittsburgh with Sheridan and Cloughen, were immediately suspended. But both insisted in competing, claiming they hadn't been informed, and it took the stern intervention of the event referee, William L. Jones, to insist they sit things out, although Sheppard was finally allowed to run a 220Yds dash against time. Once more the I-AAC was apoplectic: John J. Dolan told the *New York Times* that he didn't understand the charges and refused to comment further, adding bellicosely: "If the members of this club are not fairly dealt with ... the club will see that they are, no matter to what extreme it is forced." Once more the accusations were proved false or trumped up. Sheridan represented the athletes at a Registration Committee meeting where accusations that the trio, and NYAC's Fred Bellars, had been overpaid in Buffalo were rebuffed, although Bonhag was given a warning for cheekily asking for a special prize.[41]

Yet accusations continued. The *Chicago Record Herald* claimed that another "reliable source," Dr. George K Herman, President of the Central AA, began an investigation in 1909, which, "if proved, will result in a wholesale declaration of professionalism." Along with Matt McGrath (still with the NYAC), Sheridan was accused of taking $500, in addition to expenses, out of the $7,000 gate at Chicago's Gaelic Park, while Dan Ahearne, Flanagan, the NYAC's Con Walsh, and two unnamed New York long distance men were offered to the Illinois GAA for the sum of $950. Sullivan scratched his head in disbelief: "Such accusations are astounding, and I don't believe a word of them." He told the *New York Times* that Martin Sheridan, whom "he has known him for many years ... was not the type of a man to receive or demand pay for his services at athletic meets." Like so many others, this accusation was quietly dismissed.[42]

Then Sheppard was suspended for the umpteenth time, this occasion by the Military Athletic League following an indoor meeting in Philadelphia on December 11, 1909, when a Captain Joseph Klapp Nichols accused him of "unfair dealing ... unbecoming language ... demanding excessive expense money ... refusing to deal directly with the management of the games," and along with William J. Hayes, refusing to compete. The I-AAC made a request to run Sheppard "under protest" at its 1910 indoor games, and the suspension was removed on February 2, but then immediately renewed by the MAL, which seemed keen "to make a determined stand" and kick Sheppard, a national guardsman, out of amateur athletics to fight off any I-AAC threats of court action.[43]

Conway demanded that Sheppard's suspension be lifted until he was "tried" and looked to get an injunction to compete at Madison Square Garden.

Meanwhile, the *New York Times* had scant sympathy for the runner, claiming: "It has now become known that Sheppard has only himself to blame for being charged with making an exorbitant demand for expenses for competing." Sheppard was eventually allowed to run by agreement of all parties to "avoid a controversy and possible legal enlargements."[44]

On the evening of February 19, 1910, the night after Sheppard competed in the Spanish War Veterans' Games "under protest," where he was greeted with huge applause, his "public" "court martial"—only counsel, friends and reporters were admitted—was held at the 71st Regiment Armory. Sheppard was charged with "taking exorbitant expenses ... and using language unbecoming a militiaman." Supported by his own personal counsel, John D. Connolly, Terrence Farley and John Cloughen, with Conway observing, Farley opened by claiming that the MAL "was an illegal body" that used its armories to host events and receive money "to which it was not entitled." He also questioned the MAL's right to try the case, as the incidents occurred in Philadelphia, leading the court chairman, Colonel William L. Garcia, to overrule Farley. The rest of the hearing was largely argument and counter-argument, with Captain M.J. Pickering claiming that Sheppard had called the Philadelphians "mutts," although Sheppard did admit wanting ten dollars more than the $20 offered as expenses. An adjournment was declared as the *New York Tribune* observed that "Sheppard ... did not seem at all perturbed as to the probable outcome."[45]

Three weeks later, Sheppard was found guilty of two of the nine charges and suspended for 60 days, backdated to January 28: Using "profane language to a number of the officials" and of "not having told of his expenses to Philadelphia at the first hearing." Sheppard had testified that despite being kept in his running suit from ten o'clock until 11:45, he didn't use "violent or abusive language ... and talked in a gentlemanly manner," merely urging officials to run the race. Two Philadelphia friends, Thomas O'Donnell and James Hepburn, testified that they were with Sheppard most of the evening and "that his manner was not excited, nor did he, so far as they knew, use any violent language to the officials." As for excessive expenses, he never asked for more than the $30 offered nor received any prize, even returning the check "when he found that he did not need to spend all of the money which had been allowed him." The *New York Times* described the "trial" as "one of the most colossal bits of poor judgment which have marked the athletic firmament" recently: "Guilty though he may have been of using language which he should not have spoken ... there was no doubt that the Olympic champion received treatment in Philadelphia which would have made any athlete of any spirit resent." Additionally, the accusation that Sheppard had caused "a small sized riot on the floor of the armory" was actually due to a drunken soldier. Concluding, the *Times* went as far as questioning the integrity of the tribunal's chairman, claiming that Luscomb's objections were continually sustained, while Farley's were all overruled. Amongst all this, Harvey Cohn threw in the amateur towel and took up a post at a prep school in Brooklyn.[46]

More cases came as Robert Cloughen was rapped over the knuckles for competing in Canada without a permit. Even boxing didn't escape: Two amateur pugs, including the I-AAC's heavyweight, John J. Garretson, "disqualified themselves from further amateur competition" after boxing at a professional exhibition. Finally in November 1911, a court martial "dishonorably discharged" Sheppard from the 22nd Regiment for "neglect of duty" by refusing to drill with his company, having been presented before "the delinquent court" the previous winter "for non-payment of fines and inattention to duty." His superior officer, Captain Porter, confirmed the discharge: "Yes it's a fact.... He was given every opportunity to do the fair thing, but for reasons best known to himself, failed to avail himself of the chance to clear himself with his commanding officers.... I am very sorry that he took such a means of breaking his connection with the National Guard of this State."[47]

The following January, he was barred by the MAL from running at any armory in the state, rendering him ineligible to compete for the I-AAC at any indoor meet. The ban was lifted for 1912/1913 indoor season, but attempts at rejoining the army, through the 14th Regiment, were stalled; he was told he would have to wait five years, and also ordered to return any prizes won while representing his regiment.[48]

In the meantime, yet another bout of suspensions of I-AAC athletes was handed out. The *Sun* of November 15, 1912, described the club as "up in arms over the recent actions of the registration committee" in sanctioning three athletes; Tom Collins and J.J. McNamara were suspended for competing in the unsanctioned Mayo Men's Games at Celtic Park, and H.C. Feber was disciplined for "disrespectful language" to the officials at the St. Agnes Games. The I-AAC was once more unprepared to take things lying down and was ready to turn to its learned friends:

> Officers of the Irish club stated yesterday that there was petty jealousy behind the action of the committee, which had been induced to take these steps in the interest of a rival organization. They threaten to take the cases of Collins and McNamara to court and to ask for an injunction to restrain the registration committee from refusing the entries of these men.

Lawson Robertson reportedly popped in to see the chairman of the AAU Championship committee, asking him for the form for the upcoming Senior Cross-Country Championships, and immediately tore it into shreds, telling him they wouldn't compete in the Senior Cross-Country. He told the *Sun*: "It would be useless to have the team compete when four of the best men were under suspension or ineligible and he had no hesitation in ascribing the suspensions to malice." Both Cross-Country races were eventually entered with I-AAC teams, Robertson sheepishly returning for a replacement form. But once more the I-AAC was livid, with the *Sun* noting, "In fact the Irish take the position that the policy of the registration committee appears to be 'If you see an Irish head, hit it.'"[49]

* * *

On the same day this was happening, the I-AAC was admitted into the Amateur Hockey League, replacing the NYAC. But even within this sport, there was no hiding place from accusations of professionalism. In January 1917, a meeting of the AHL at St. Nicholas Rink declared four Irish players— Patsy Sequin, Aleck Wellington, Dick Whitten and Tom Bawlf—professionals: "If the charges of professionalism and ineligibility were sustained," the *New York Tribune* reported, "the loss would be irreparable to the local team." Accusations were made by the Hockey Club of New York that the four had played professionally in Pittsburgh the previous year. Bawlf and Wellington maintained that it was a misunderstanding. Sequin, who was employed at the St. Nicholas rink as a "skate sharpener," couldn't be classed as a professional as the concession was leased, while Whitten was still ineligible due to the three-month residency rule.[50]

The Irish and Crescent AC were tied for first place when the AHL refused to reinstate Wellington, so the I-AAC "protested practically all the other clubs in the league," in particular indicting four Crescent players. These included the Canadian future NHL star Tommy McCarthy, who was accused of overcharging on a trip up to New Haven and Boston years earlier, when playing with the I-AAC. The Crescents manager, George Hallock, then refused to let his team go onto the ice against the Irish on February 13, in a game the *New York Times* predicted "had every promise of being just about the most nerve-tingling clash of the year." In front of a large crowd, Patsy Sequin scored the first goal, and officials gave the game to the Irish, 1–0.[51]

At the Crescent AC three days later, a secret AHL committee meeting dismissed the I-AAC's accusations. The *New York Times* had already suggested "ROW MAY MEAN END OF HOCKEY LEAGUE" and the game in New York: "Diplomatic hockey relations have been severed between the Crescent Athletic Club and the [I-AAC]," said the *Brooklyn Daily Eagle*, while the "New Mooners" were also boycotting the St. Nicholas Rink due to its Irish connections. Rumors surfaced that the New York Hockey AC, the HCofNY and the Crescents would either ask the Irish to leave or form another organization without them. "One thing is certain, the other three active clubs and the [NYAC], a non-active organization, are tired and sick of the action of the [I-AAC] players and league representatives both on and off the ice."[52]

The problems were more than charges of professionalism. On February

12, one I-AAC player apparently punched an AHL governing committee member in the locker room after a game, while another insulted two members of the executive committee where "his flow of Billingsgate" was only halted by teammates. By now a "prominent member of the Amateur Hockey League" told the *Eagle*:

> We always had trouble with the [I-AAC]. We have nothing against the club. Unfortunately, it has let its hockey department drift into hands that have caused us unending trouble. Under the name of the Wanderers, many of the same crowd caused trouble. Finally the Wanderers retired from the league. Then the [I-AAC] appeared. It caused trouble from the start.

The official also accused the I-AAC of "playing rough house hockey," concluding, "Either the Irish club has to get out of the league, or other clubs will leave the league alone to the Irish organization."[53]

The row subsided into what the *New York Times* scoffed was a "love feast." The AHL committee absolved all players, while adding that the I-AAC "was justified in protesting all the players in question from the information it had." The Irish "waived its right to claim a victory," and the rematch ended with the Crescents triumphing, 5–1.[54]

Perhaps there was some evidence that I-AAC athletes were coming close to contradicting the Corinthian athletic spirit. But this was not just about accepting payments, but increasingly wrongly filled-in forms and competing at meetings that either had professionals entered or were run by unattached bodies. It was even, it seems, about a spot of swearing when well-wrapped-up officials left athletes standing in the cold. It was also checking if your opponents, who were constantly putting in complaints, were doing the same. It is ironic that at one of the last major athletic meets hosted by the I-AAC, they themselves, along with the AAU, were subject to an injunction when they were ordered to admit a Bronx Church House athlete, recently labeled a pro, to its 1917 Winter Games.[55]

Before that, the Irish-American athletes were to enter that bastion of honest "sport" for probably the first time ever, where it would be given a lesson, never to forget, on the meaning of "fair play." A few, especially those born in Ireland, were already aware of where the NYAC got its ethos of snobbery and suspicion of the lower orders from. For the others, the 1908 Olympics would prove an eye-opener.

11

"You carry the Stars and Stripes proudly!"
The I-AAC Athletes at the 1908 Olympics

On Friday July 24, 1908, in a crammed West London stadium, spectators waited expectantly for the arrival of a bunch of athletes running the 26 miles from Windsor Castle. The first to run, or rather stagger, in was wearing a handkerchief hat of a working-class Englishman on the beach and looked like a drunk falling out of a pub. Yards from the line, to gasps from onlookers, this 22-year-old Italian shop assistant began to collapse before their eyes. His life appeared to be extinguished, like Pheidippides two and a half millennia earlier, when after running a similar distance to report the defeat of the Persians at Marathon, cried, "Joy to you, we've won," before dropping dead.

The words "He's dying" reverberated around White City. Suddenly in stepped two men, one wearing a boater hat while simultaneously struggling to keep hold of a loudhailer, the other a portly Irishman in tweeds and cap. But these men weren't there to administer first aid; instead, both men gently aided Dorando Pietri over those final yards, where a third man beckoned him and cheered as if his own life, not Pietri's, depended on the Italian crossing the finishing line. Spectators, officials and even the Bobbies erupt in cheers as he won the marathon.

The two men who helped Pietri cross the line were Jack Andrew, the supposedly impartial race referee, and Michael Bulger, its chief medic, who forgot his Hippocratic oath to treat Pietri. Indeed, the high-jumper Ray Ewry would later dryly observe, "I believe if ... it was a runner from the United Kingdom who was in second place, they would have been willing to hit Dorando over the head rather than have him cross the line."[1]

Running behind Pietri was Johnny Hayes, a five-foot, three-inch, 22-

year-old New Yorker, whose father Michael was from Nenagh, Tipperary. He had taken up the sport as a starry-eyed ten-year-old after watching James B. Connolly make his way through New York wrapped in an Irish flag, following his triumphant return from Greece in 1896. Running for St. Bartholomew's, Hayes came in third in the 1904 Junior Cross-Country Championship. At Yonkers in November 1907, he won his first marathon, grinning at the end of the race, "Never underestimate the luck of the Irish." In London he needed no help, let alone luck, to cross the finish line.[2]

* * *

In the I-AAC's brief history, the London Olympics were arguably its finest hour. In the words of Kevin McCarthy, this was the "high point for Olympian promotion of Irish identity" within the U.S.: "It gave a simultaneous and huge boost to Irish pride, to American acceptance of the Irish as 'Americans' and, indeed, to the Irish embracing of their American identity." It also gave the club huge exposure not only across the United States, but the world. The experience would produce an enduring legacy. Twenty-four individual track and field events were contested by members: They won nine of America's 14 individual golds, while Sheppard and John B. Taylor were members of the triumphant medley relay squad.[3]

However, competing in London almost never occurred. In early December 1907, it was announced that Matt Halpin would continue as American team manager, confirming to some the inordinate NYAC influence within American athletics. Inevitably matters would explode, and smelling blood, the I-AAC, through its secretary Charles E. Kenny, dredged up Athens to object to his appointment. Conway even threatened to ban his athletes from travelling. When cornered for a response by the press, he replied curtly, "No one objects more strenuously to Halpin than I do. The way he treated the American team at Athens was, to say the least, very unsatisfactory.... It was not only members of the [I-AAC] that complained. Even members of the club to which he belonged came to me and told how badly they had been treated." Conway contested that the athletes' fury was kept under wraps until they were back home, but were furious that they couldn't complain about Halpin at the Astor reception. "I will certainly protest against Halpin managing the next team. As president of this club, I say that no Irish-American athlete will be managed by him. Any athlete who represents this club, whether he be rich or poor, white or black, must be treated fairly while I'm at its head. I would resign before sanctioning the appointment of Halpin."[4]

Strong words indeed and likely to put the I-AAC on a collision course with the AAU, AOC and James E. Sullivan. A day later, Sullivan, while not being drawn into lengthy debate, quickly dismissed any suggestion that Conway was going to dictate matters: "The American team, with Mr. Halpin as manager and adviser, went to Athens last year, and ... carried off first honors by a wide margin ... the successful manner in which Mr. Halpin conducted the team was recognized by every member, and his selection for the position again was unanimous." Ominously, he added that any athlete who objected to his appointment might "have the pleasure of staying at home," claiming they didn't know for sure yet if they would be picked. Others came to Halpin's aid; William Curtis, one of the Executive Committee who selected him, declared, "[I]n Athens last year, Mr. Halpin proved to be worthy in every respect." When asked by the *New York Times* about an I-AAC boycott, he snapped, "Well, they can stay at home," telling the *New York Tribune*, "I know nothing and care less." A colleague, who refused to be named, angrily responded, "[S]o Halpin is not popular with the athletes. Well if the real truth were known why he is not popular it certainly would reflect anything but credit on our representatives of track and field." Edward Bushnell, an athlete in Paris in 1900, suggested, with a heavy dose of snobbery, in the Washington, D.C., *Evening Star*, that some athletes, what the newspaper later slammed as "a bevy of overfed champions," had nothing to complain about on their free trip to Europe: "The task of taking a bunch of high-strung athletes to Athens was a most arduous one.... Some of these men apparently forget that they were extremely fortunate to have been taken with the 1906 team. But for ... [being] chosen without any trials and to the exclusion of all college men, many of them would never had made this trip."[5]

Conway refused to buckle: "I do not think that it is a good plan to send an unpopular man with the team that is to represent our country in the next Olympiad. A number of the boys have told me that they will under no circumstances become members of the team if Halpin is to be in charge again." Opposition came not only from Celtic Park. William Eaton told the *Washington Times*, "Most of the more than thirty men who crossed to Greece with Manager Halpin, soon discovered he was not in the least acquainted with the duties of his position. He played favorites, and the few in his favor received the best treatment."[6]

Lawson Robertson was quoted in the *Los Angeles Herald* saying that there was never a day when Halpin was not quarrelling with some athlete. Sheridan also threw in his two cents: "I certainly am dissatisfied with Halpin's appointment. Personally I think highly of Halpin, but as a manager of a team of championship caliber I say most emphatically that I believe him incompetent. Under his charge I shall certainly refuse to compete in the next games if I make the team."[7]

By the end of December 1907, the I-AAC voted to put forward an official protest to the AOC against Halpin, based on what Kenny described as an "almost unanimous" report by club athletes:

> The record made at the games by the [I-AAC] members ... which won the honors for the United States on that occasion, are matters of universal knowledge and gloriously treasured by our organization. The charges of uncivil and sometimes boorish treatment which some of these young men received from Halpin have been fully proved to the satisfaction of this organization.... It is the opinion of the [I-AAC] that, as it proposes to send to London next year another great point winning body of athletes, several of whom earned honors at Athens, a protest in their behalf should have some weight. The conclusion is impressed upon the club that Halpin is not a fit person to represent the United States abroad on such an important mission either by temperament, education or personality. In making this protest we desire to be distinctly understood as having no candidate to offer for the place.[8]

The *New York Tribune* suggested that the AOC had been wrong-footed for not taking Conway seriously, adding that the protest "will have to be acted on," although it doubted it would. The AOC and the AAU wanted things to calm down, hoping any dissent would blow over as London moved closer. Halpin, in contrast, was furious; no persuading was going to make him bite his tongue. He told the *New York Times* that complaints were the "outcome of spite work" by the I-AAC because he protested Sheridan. Like the recent Mount Vesuvius, whose eruption had moved the games to London, Halpin was in full flow:

> In all likelihood the many rabid statements made concerning my treatment of certain men on that trip emanated from the [I-AAC] which has not had a kindly feeling for me since I was a factor in the protesting of [Sheridan].... I am free to confess that I think that the bitterness then engendered has never died out.... [W]hen this matter is thrashed out before the Olympic Committee that not alone will I be able to make good for my seeming harsh treatment of these certain men, but will also be prepared to prove many things to their detriment.

Charles H. Sherrill, a former athlete and future ambassador and IOC member, argued that any lack of criticism would suggest that Halpin had let the athletes do exactly what they wanted. Weeks, another AOC member, added:

> There is only one way to deal with the Halpin matter, and that is for the men who are dissatisfied to lodge charges, so that we may investigate them.... I can hardly believe that the description of Halpin in the Irish-American protest can be an accurate one. The best team manager in the world would, of course, find some trouble in taking.... Halpin may have found it necessary to use plain words at times, but a manager is not necessarily boorish or uncivil because he enforces discipline.[9]

Halpin distanced himself from the chaotic travel arrangements to Athens, claiming they were made before his appointment. He added that athletes shared the "quarters in the Zappion" offered by the Greek Crown Prince, which even satisfied the British Oxbridge men, and was ashamed that some athletes had even complained. He accused eight principal detractors, of whom only one—Martin Sheridan—was an I-AAC man, while three—Ray C. Ewry, Harry L. Hillman and H.V. Valentine were NYAC members. The others included "those cultured gentlemen from Boston," Leavitt and Eaton, D.A. Sullivan and his brother, "Montana Jack," and Robert Edgren, the *Evening World*'s sports editor, whom the paranoid Halpin accused of being a puppet: "Can it be possible that some one in authority over him, or the Irish-American Athletic Club, is using pressure to make him write and publish what he knows to be untrue?"[10]

As for the I-AAC, Halpin was indignant:

> Realizing that I have been placed in a false position by my recent determination not to publicly defend myself against the venomous attacks and libelous criticisms of members of the Irish-American Athletic Club and others.... I have reconsidered to the end of the subjoined statement, in which I attempt to cover every point on which I have been assailed.... The motive for the bitter and venomous attacks that are now appearing in the newspapers throughout the country is understood by every member in the [MA AAU] to be the continuance of the bitter quarrel for athletic supremacy in the Metropolitan Association between the [NYAC] and the [I-AAC], and made more bitter by my protesting of Martin J. Sheridan.... Furthermore my activity in quest of evidence which will undoubtedly result in the cleaning up of the semi-professional element in the Metropolitan Association is not relished by the Irish American Athletic Club.

He'd continue to rid the sport's "questionable amateurs," regardless of what the AOC would decide: "[B]efore the American team left New York the antagonism of the Irish American Athletic Club members reached such a state that Martin J. Sheridan was requested not to permit any of the members to use physical violence on me during the trip to Athens and return." Halpin concluded by exposing his prejudices, hinting that he would never have had this trouble had he not been handed a team packed with plebs: "It is a significant fact that my management of the American team has not been criticized by the college element that took part at Athens.[11]

Many who read Halpin's comments were aghast, but there was also sympathy, even from Edgren. The *New York Times* said, before releasing Halpin's statement:

> There is general regret felt in athletic ranks that this affair should have assumed proportions because either side of it could have been stopped on its course by a little judicial consideration. Had the Irish-American Athletic Club adopted some other method of manifesting its disapproval of the selection of Halpin by the American Committee, or had the latter body read the signs of times rightly and appointed a manager who would have proved less objectionable ... no such prominence would have been given to this teapot tempest.

It signed off by lamenting: "The controversy savors more of a schoolboy quarrel, than between men of intelligence and wide experience.[12]

Halpin was left alone until early March, when he was pushed upstairs to "manager," while coaching was handed to Mike Murphy. The AOC had finally lost faith in him: E.R. Bushnell of the *Detroit Free Press* dryly noted that Murphy's appointment made a "ten-strike," silencing criticism of Halpin, by relegating him to "business management." The *Evening World* described it as hitting "three birds with one stone," satisfying the I-AAC, adding a top coach to the party, and putting Halpin "in a position remote from the team, where he can do no harm." Conway was sought for a reaction and used the occasion to put one final boot in: "The action of the executive committee last night in selecting Mike Murphy ... was the very best thing that could have happened ... Halpin? Oh, yes. Halpin will go along as manager, and say, this is tough weather, isn't it, for a fellow with the gout?"[13]

Choosing the athletes finally began through "trials," and on current form the I-AAC was optimistic. Celtic Park hosted the last of the major winter championships, with the MA Senior Cross-Country title going to the Mohawk AC, as no Irish-American entered. The annual Memorial Day "monster festival," held by the Firemen's Memorial Fund, was predicted by the *New York Times* to be the "greatest set of amateur contests" in New York since the visit by the London AC in 1895, as numerous Olympic prospects promised to attend. Instead it was postponed due to poor weather.[14]

At Philadelphia's Franklin Field, the I-AAC athletes shone at the Eastern Olympic "try-outs." Martin Sheridan improved his free style discus world record, before losing it to the NYAC's Arthur Dearborn's throw of 139:11 feet. He made up for this loss by beating the Greek style record with a throw of 115:4 feet, while Sheppard won the 800m, Robertson took the 100m dash, Taylor the 400m, Bacon the 400m hurdles, Porter the high jump, and new recruit Lee Talbott the hammer. A week later, the initial 75 men were chosen, and as the *New York Times* pointed out, "Ireland's former sons form no inconsequential part of the list," while the *New York Tribune* added, "America's greatest athletes seem to be of Irish descent, and a glance at the names of the members will prove this. Here are a few of them: Flanagan, Sheridan, McGrath, O'Connell, Morrissey and Hayes. And nearly all of these will be point winners." In the *Irish-American Advocate*, Martin Sheridan argued with hyperbole for the team's strong "Irish" composition: "Indeed if one were to go right through the team the difficulty would be to pick out those who haven't at least some strain of Irish blood in them." Perhaps not that difficult, but they were certainly the largest ethnic group. In contrast, the *Evening World* saw the selection through purely American patriotism, suggesting that it was perhaps "the greatest athletic team that ever competed under the colors of any country."[15]

Nineteen I-AAC athletes were initially picked: Further names would be added, as Sheridan and Robertson tried to get "several deserving athletes"

11. "You carry the Stars and Stripes proudly!" 143

like Harvey Cohn—who eventually did travel—and Claude Allen added. But money was short and some—like Bill Horr, who broke Dearborn's discus record at Torrington, Connecticut—had to pay their own way. Then NYPD Commissioner Bingham announced that he wouldn't let any policeman go, but the I-AAC dismissed this, claiming that Mayor George B. McClellan would straighten out Bingham after returning from Grover Cleveland's funeral. A rumor that Sheridan preferred to get married than compete for Uncle Sam also proved false.[16]

Flanagan didn't participate in any trials, but he was clearly on form. At Torrington he took Matt McGrath's world record for the 16LB hammer with a throw of 175:0:75 feet, having just missed out the week before at Travers Island by stepping outside the circle. Edgren was impressed: "Flanagan has come back into splendid athletic condition, and will undoubtedly make a new record this year, unless McGrath beats him to it." The party finally set sail on the American Line's *Philadelphia* on June 27. Sheridan was nowhere to be seen until he "was observed pushing his way through the crowd on the dock, and as he boarded the ship a great cheer arose." A week and a day later, the party arrived at Southampton: What could possibly go wrong?[17]

* * *

The answer to that: Plenty. While the I-AAC grabbed the majority of the athletic honors, the Games soured sporting relations between America and Britain. The non-dipping of the Stars and Stripes on the first day, a perceived deliberate insult to the British monarch, accusations of biased officials and cheating athletes, and the help Pietri received, led to James E. Sullivan being branded locally a pantomime villain, while feted a hero back home. Myths were made, Arthur Daley's invention in the *New York Times* of July 6, 1952, the most infamous, claimed that Sheridan demanded of Ralph Rose that "this flag dips to no earthly King," even though as McGowan contends, there was "no evidence that Sheridan ever uttered the infamous words."[18]

In his 1908 Olympics history, John Bryant pictures Sheridan relaxing over a pint with Ralph Rose—a man who wasn't, despite Bryant's claims, either Irish-American or an I-AAC member—the night before the opening ceremony. Discussions swung to leading the American team, with the consensus being that Rose, the biggest and strongest, should carry the flag. Sheridan explained to Rose the etiquette an American should use when passing the British Royal family: "Don't think you have to bow and scrape to that bunch.... You carry the Stars and Stripes proudly."[19]

Graeme Kent describes the decision, "arrived at over a few jars in some ill-lit bar," more succinctly: "[T]he truculent Sheridan ... had threatened to put Rose in hospital if he even considered acknowledging the presence of the

British monarch." Rose acquiesced; while other nations politely dipped their flags in respect as advised, Rose passed the royal box stiff-armed.[20]

The stage was set for Rose's lack of action being rehashed into one of the biggest American Olympic legends by the following fortnight's events. Daley later wrote, adding a disclaimer that the story was "only a legend but," that the plan was devised in some dingy London tavern, involving solely ethnic Irish athletes: "None of their ancestors came from Lower Slobodia. They were much too close to the Ould Sod." Now you didn't have to be Irish in 1908 America to suffer from Anglophobia. As Kevin McCarthy writes, whether deliberate or not, that Sheridan was part of it, or that snooty Americans saw Rose's actions as bad manners, didn't matter: "What was central was that it typified both the tensions in Anglo-American relations of 1908 and the degree to which Irish anti-monarchical sentiments were indistinguishable from popular American ones at this time." Certainly, Sheridan wouldn't have allowed Rose to show the same disrespect had the Olympics been held in Rome, and probably suggested that Rose didn't grovel to the British. Quoted later in the *Irish World*, Sheridan was unrepentant: "Ah! When I saw the Stars and Stripes go marching by without going down, my heart took a great leap for joy."[21]

Daley, though, had other angles to write about: perfidious Albion and rebellious Ireland. Tempers were stirred by the Irish athletes competing for Britain, rather than "for Ireland as the embittered Celts desired. The rebellious Gaels flatly refused. Score victories for 'perfidious Albion?' Are you daft, man? They'd win 'em for Ireland or not at all. It was not at all. They sat it out." However, the Irish didn't sit out the Games, competing for either Britain—as Martin Sheridan would later, bitterly complain—or other countries:

> The night before the Olympics opened, the legendary Irish-American whales were relaxing over a spot of ale in a near-by English pub. The grievances of their ancestors mounted with every passing hour and their brooding grew more intense. "Tis a disgrace, it is," said Pat McDonald in his soft County Clare brogue, "to think that our glorious American flag will be dipped tomorrow to the crowned head of a kingdom." "And him an English King, too," said Flanagan. "George Washington, the Lord have mercy on his soul, freed America from the yoke of a British King," said Sheridan. "Ireland must also be free some day," said Gillis, which showed how their minds were working. "We can't permit our flag to dip," said McGrath, pounding the table with brawny fist until the pewter mugs danced. "Ralph me lad," said McDonald, drawing himself up to his full 300 pounds and 6-foot-5. He transfixed huge Ralph Rose with baleful glare.... "'Tis thinkin' I've been. The American flag bows to no man, King or peasant. Should you be dippin' it to the King I'll break you in half with me own two hands."[22]

Daley, however, wasn't finished embellishing. Sixteen years later, he reiterated his schmaltz when Janice Lee Romary, flag carrier in Mexico City, kept it upright and "faithfully observed a practice that began at London" in 1908:

> The backbone of the United States team that year was supplied by the brawny weight-men from the Irish-American Athletic Club of New York, all with deep roots in the Ould Sod. They took a rim stand and issued explicit orders to the flag-bearer: "Ye won't bow the American flag to a British King," bellowed Martin Sheridan, the discus champion. "It didn't bow then and has not bowed since."[23]

The story served to embody everything America believed positive of itself. As Bryant concludes, "The chances are this quote was embellished, rehashed, and grew with the years, that it was tidied up and used as propaganda. As a piece of propaganda, the story and the Martin Sheridan remark were too good not to be true, and these days the legend has evolved into truth." In fact the 77th Congress took note, passing Federal Law 829 in 1942, which demanded the flag "should not be dipped to any person or thing."[24]

In London, the incident attracted little attention amongst a British press corps more concerned about the weather; Rose had simply forgotten. While Kent describes "horrified gasps from those spectators who had noticed the slight, followed by delighted raucous laughter from those Americans in the crowd who were aware of the missing Stars and Stripes in the stadium and guessed that this was payback time," Captain Charles Dieges, who was present, told the *New York Tribune* that Ralph Rose was unaware what to do "and had no intention of committing the childish breach of etiquette into which the incident has been turned in some quarters."[25]

Insults are, however, pointless unless the intended know about it, and the Royals weren't paying attention. And so the press were informed instead. Initially East Coast dailies, with the exception of the *Evening World*, the most Anglophobic newspaper outside the Irish-American publications, were uninterested. Sheridan had been providing—hopefully unpaid—eyewitness accounts through the *Associated Press*, yet he made no mention of it in his *Evening World* report of July 15, concentrating on the mundane journey over. Rose, Flanagan and McGrath had "caused a panic in the pantry at the first meal," as McGrath tucked into "five plates of soup, four orders of fish, three broiled chickens, two steaks, six English plover, seven cups of custard, three pieces of apple pie, four cups of coffee and two pounds of cheese…. His record for eating still stands." Meanwhile Dan Kelly was a victim of a "funny joke" when Tom Moffitt told him he was wanted on the phone. Kelly went outside and asked a steward where the call was to be taken, to which he was curtly told, "A shark by the ship had it in his mouth." None of this was intended to get readers to throw their tea into Boston Harbor.[26]

Instead Edgren took the lead, describing King Edward sitting in his royal box "fat, happy and smiling," surrounded by "a hundred thousand loyal

English subjects ... calmly waiting for the great parade of athletes of all nations" to march by:

> Then came a section of the column that marched along with a loose swinging step, light and airy, like the step of a khaki-clad rough riders dancing up San Juan Hill. The Americans! No hide-bound training military here. Everything free and easy and debonair. At the head of the American column tramps a Goliath of a man.... It is Ralph Rose, bearing the American flag. King Edward smiles more and more. It's a long time since an English king has had the pleasure of seeing an American flag trailing before him. He smiles a little more, and then some, and then—Ralph Rose stalks, his nose in air, six feet five inches from the ground. The American flag never bobs or wavers, but flutters overhead. The Americans pass with singing step. On the great Stadium a sudden horrified silence falls. "My word!" exclaim a hundred thousand Englishmen. And again, "My Word!"[27]

Amos Alonzo Stagg, the famous college football coach, writing in the *Chicago Tribune*, was unimpressed. "There is one incident of the Games which has received little comment in this country but which may explain in part the markedly noticeable unpopularity of the Yankees ... aside from the fact that they were winning a majority of the events." Bryant added that Sheridan was quoted in the *Chicago Record-Herald*, admitting that Rose had failed to dip the flag without giving any reason. As for the Irish-American press, they were emphatic. The *Irish World* published a cartoon across its front page of Rose holding the flag upright, accompanied by possibly George Washington doing likewise, with the caption "Inspired by the Spirit of '76."[28]

* * *

On July 14, the "first real business day," began, and I-AAC athletes were immediately in the thick of things. Flanagan not only broke his Olympic hammer record with a distance of 170:4:5 feet, he'd finally "overcome his hoodoo" of constantly being beaten by McGrath. "From the first time he met Matt McGrath in the seven-foot circle, John has shown a degree of nervousness that spoiled his best throws," said the *Evening World*. "McGrath defeated him consistently until at last every one thought the big NYAC athletes had John's number. But John has made good in the world's greatest competition." McGrath led going into the final throw, when it appeared his leg gave way as he threw. It was enough for Flanagan, a man the *Sun* described as "bordering on the Osler climacteric and almost qualified for a dash of chloroform," to grab a third gold hammer medal, causing "thirty minutes of flag waving, singing and cheering." Then Sheppard won the 1500m with time of 4:03:4 and what the *Sun* called an "exercise of the most magnificent generalship." Sheppard was fourth entering the final lap, and with 60 yards to go, Harold Wilson looked certain for gold. But he had sprinted too early, and Sheppard beat him by just under a yard in a time that equaled the Olympic record despite a strong headwind. The following day, Bonhag and Cohn received silver as part of the 3Mile Team Race. Then on Thursday July 16, Sheridan won the discus free style gold with a distance of 40.89 meters, while Horr took bronze behind Merrit Griffin.[29]

Midweek attendance had been disappointing, but a better crowd was drawn for Saturday, July 18, "similar to that," the *New York Times* noted, "which attends football matches on half holidays." Sheridan hoped to grab his second gold, this time in the Greek style discus, but as Edgren later wrote, there were doubts the Mayoman still had it in him:

> In the American tryouts and in the few contests he entered before the team sailed Martin didn't shine. Many people thought that the great champion had at last come to the end of his winning streak and that new and perhaps better champions would take his place among the record breakers. Sheridan is a light man among the weight throwers. It seemed likely that heavier men like Horr and Dearborn would best him when they had mastered the knack of throwing the saucer shaped missile. But just before the team sailed Martin with his quiet smile whispered to me: "I can let out a few links yet, Bob. They'll have to go some to beat me in the big test. Horr is likely to beat anybody, but I feel sure I can beat the rest."

By the end of the competition, Sheridan had broken all previous records with a distance of 37.99 meters, while Horr came in second. Writing for the *Evening World*, he commented with notable modesty, "I surprised myself at the result."[30]

The second week started with Sheridan continuing his medal quest. On Monday July 20, he took bronze in the standing long jump behind Ray Ewry and the Greek Konstantinos Tsiklitiras, making him, according to Robert Edgren, "the most reliable point winner in the world." The following day saw a golden double for the I-AAC: Mel Sheppard won the 800m, beating Emilio Lunghi with a world record of 1:52:8 in a race that, the *Sun* said, was "what every one agreed was the finest performance the stadium has ever seen or is likely to see." The *New York Times* added, "He proved himself entirely too fast for Just, the English champion, who was absolutely done up by the tremendous pace." The two British runners, Theodore Just and Ian Fairbairn-Crawford, thought they could set a pace that would wear out Sheppard, but the early running seemed to be what he wanted, and Fairbairn-Crawford didn't even finish. "The American let Fairbairn-Crawford set the speed as high as he liked and kept right at the Englishman's heels. Just followed close at hand, but the plan miscarried for the latter, who expected to come up in the stretch and pass Sheppard, had no reserve speed left and was not only beaten by the American, but also by Lunghi." Harry F. Porter captured the high jump, smashing Irving Knot Baxter's Olympic record with a jump of 1:90 meters. After confirming that he was the winner, he went after the world record with the bar set at 6:5:75 feet, an eighth of an inch higher than Mike Sweeney's thirteen-year-old record, "but it was just a shade too much for him." "'Ten more points for Uncle Sam.' That was the slogan of the American athletes as they left the field after the conclusion of the Olympic Games this afternoon," reported the *Evening World*. "And the ten points were gained by members of the Irish-American Athletic Club of New York." Wednesday witnessed more medals for I-AAC athletes. Dan Kelly nipped Canada's Calvin Bricker by a centimeter to take silver behind Frank Irons in the long jump, but the performance of the day came in the 400m hurdles final, where Bacon broke the world record with a time of 55 seconds, beating Harry Hillman.[31]

* * *

However, things had been running far from smoothly for the Americans. Apart from the flag incident, the tug-of-war team, containing three I-AAC members—Flanagan, Horr, and Talbott—was controversially beaten in the quarter-finals by the Liverpool Police squad wearing "heavy boots with strong built heels," in contrast to the Americans' "light athletic heels." Edgren screamed, "'British fair play' is becoming a joke the world over." Daniel Cohalan also chided, "Spiked shoes were not allowed in France, in Greece or at the Olympic Games in St. Louis, but the English officials have made up their minds to win fairly or by some other method, for which they are notorious."[32]

Lord Desborough, the Games' president, explained that the Liverpool Police wore "their usual boots," to which John Devoy replied caustically in his *Gaelic American*: "[He] might just as well have said, 'Why, my dear sir, these are exactly the same boots that Lancashire men kick their wives with,' for all its relevancy to the charge of unfairness." Meanwhile, Sheridan diverted his attention briefly from haranguing the British, to snipe at Halpin: "This should

Cigarette card image of Emilio Lunghi. Born on the eve of St. Patrick's Day, 1887, he joined the club in 1909, breaking Lon Myers' 27-year-old record at the club's Tailteann Games that year (Mecca Cigarettes card).

have been done for by the American Commissioner [Sullivan] who was on the ground two weeks before the games were started, or by the alleged manager [Halpin] of our team. The disagreeable tilts that arose might have been avoided had this precaution been taken."[33]

There was also Sullivan's obsession with the "Championship Trophy," an unofficial title granted to the winners with the most points. He was upset that the American system—five for first, three for second and one for third—was ditched for the British system of just one point for the winner, while also wanting the other categories—rugby, soccer, field hockey—that the Americans weren't going to win, "events of minor importance which would give the British and [sic] overwhelming victory," said the *New York Times*, excluded. In the end, the mysterious "trophy" was withdrawn as there was no consensus to its format.[34]

Anglo-American relations got decidedly even hotter with two late events: the 400m final on Thursday, July 23, and the marathon the following day. The 400m semi-finals had included seven American athletes, including John Baxter Taylor, out of the 15 runners: Three—John Carpenter, William Robbins and the I-AAC's John B. Taylor—joined Britain's Wyndham Halswelle in the final, by which time the I-AAC contingent had already bagged another silver with Cloughen second in the 200m. As the four runners set off, Robbins and Carpenter immediately led, but into the final stretch, a trackside judge, Roscoe Badger, claimed that the pair had obstructed Halswelle's efforts to pass. Taylor, running last, found himself "roughly" dragged off the track by excited officials shouting "No race." In the *Evening World*, Taylor spoke of the injustice of the decision: "Being behind, I could see everything.... If either I or Halswelle had had it in us we would have passed inside, as there was lots of room.... If there had been any fouling I certainly would have seen it, being in the rear." As for his man-handling, Taylor was equally scathing. "This shows what a state of mind he was in, when he could not restrain himself from laying hands upon poor me who was a long way behind." After 30 minutes of arguing, Carpenter was disqualified and the race was declared void and rescheduled, with the Americans apoplectic, immediately refusing to participate further. When the marathon began, the Games were so badly poisoned by bitterness that few believed anything could top what Edgren called "the crowning outrage ... the crooked work pulled off by the English officials."[35]

In the aftermath of the marathon, Hayes was rightly awarded the race. Even the British press could no longer deny that there was foul play. The *Daily News* said that the help given Pietri was "a gross infringement of the rules and a scandalous interference" with the race:

> That the victory should have gone to the American is the very best thing that could have happened.... It is sad for the sportsman who made such gallant effort; but it is even sadder for the reputation of the official body of the Stadium—which has hith-

erto confined itself to more or less innocent forms of mismanagement—that the necessity of disqualifying Pietri should have arisen at all.[36]

Porter bitterly reflected on the battles Americans had throughout the games, not only against other competitors, but also "prejudiced" officials:

> The judges may not have been intentionally unfair, but they could not control their feelings, which were antagonistic to the Americans. This was especially true in the field events, where the boys came in closer contact with the judges. The Americans were continually nagged and made uncomfortable. The officials were discourteous to our men, and further, by their encouragement of the other men, tried to beat us.[37]

As for Hayes, he was an instant hero. Back at his workplace, Samuel Bloomingdale immediately ordered the building decorated in his honor and held a reception for him on his return. There were two last events for I-AAC members to grab more medals. Arthur Shaw took bronze in the 110m hurdles, while Sheppard and Taylor won golds in the medley relay. Taylor's medal was a milestone in itself: The first black athlete to win gold at the Olympics.[38]

* * *

In the Games' aftermath, the I-AAC athletes were penciled in for a European tour that would include a dual-meet in Ireland on August 1, before travelling on to Sweden. Arriving at Dublin's crowded Amiens Street Station on July 30, the *Evening World* described how "thousands lined the streets, fairly blocking them, along the route to their hotel. The demonstration displayed recalled the triumphal entry into the city of Parnell when he was at the height of his popularity." The *New York Times* added that it was "all the more remarkable because it was entirely spontaneous, the mere announcement of the hour of their arrival bringing many thousands of persons to the station to meet the athletes. The streets along the route to their hotel were completely blocked by the Dublinites." The *Evening World* concluded, "The city is wildly enthusiastic over the appearance of the Irish-American Athletic Club's team of victorious athletes fresh from their laurels in London. Sheridan, Flanagan, Robertson, Cloughan [sic], Kelly and the rest are being lionized on every side and the boys are simply overwhelmed with the warmth of their greeting." At their hotel, Joseph Devlin, Member of Parliament for Belfast West, greeted the party, saying "that wherever they went in Ireland a similar welcome awaited them." Robertson admitted that while he expected "an Irish welcome," what he'd witnessed took his breath away: "The Americans could not have done without the Irish lads in the games at Shepherd's Bush, and now the Irish capital had given them their first taste of a welcome home." Crowds did not disperse until around midnight.[39]

Johnny Hayes traveled onto Nenagh, where he met his grandfather and was "seized by his admirers ... carried, shoulder high, to his carriage to an accompaniment of cheers and the discharge of innumerable fireworks." The

Chicago Tribune reported, "When the train drew in, the athlete was greeted by the town officials. Horses were removed from the carriage which was pulled triumphantly by the crowd through the streets." Hayes didn't compete at any meetings but did give exhibitions.[40]

However, even here athletes were once again bogged down by pettiness. Upon finding that some meetings were under the IAAA's control, Conway, with his GAA connections in the United States, urgently cabled Robertson not to attend their meets. Robertson was having none of it, feeling "honor bound to compete, as ... agreed" at Ballsbridge on August 1. Immediately the GAA declared the meeting "illegal," but the *Evening World* concluded that "opinion is general that the dispute should not be allowed to mar the harmony of a national welcome to the Irish-American champions." The following day in New York, the *Sun* ran with the headline: "IRISH ATHLETES REBEL: Bound in Honor to Compete at Dublin Despite Club's Instructions."

Johnny Hayes, probably photographed on board the ship traveling to London, 1908. Eventually he was given first place in the marathon at the 1908 Olympics following the unlawful interference in the race by British officials (Library of Congress).

As a compromise, Robertson proposed that the team compete as individual athletes, adding that when arrangements were made, he "knew nothing of any dispute." Still, the *New York Tribune* predicted some sanctions, "The Gaelic Athletic Association threatened to disqualify all American athletes who took part in the games, and may do so, but this will probably worry no one concerned."[41]

Ten thousand spectators, including former Tammany "Boss" Richard Croker, gave the visitors a rapturous welcome. Winners included Sheppard (half mile) Porter (high jump), Cloughen (100Yds), Talbott (hammer), Taylor (440Yds), Bacon (120Yds high hurdles), and Bonhag (4Miles). Two days later at the Dublin Metropolitan Police Games at the same venue, Flanagan broke Matt McGrath's world record for the 16LB hammer from a nine foot circle with a throw of 173:11 feet.[42]

Sheridan had refused to participate. He was honored two weeks later with a 2,000-strong "torchlight procession" by the GAA to his hotel, headed by Dublin's mayor: "The demonstration was intended as an expression of gratitude to Sheridan for his support of the Gaelic Athletic Association in its recent dispute with the Amateur Athletic Association," declared both the *Evening World* and the *New York Times*. On August 16 he competed at a GAA meeting at Dungarvan, County Waterford, against Tom Kiely, a contest that ended in a draw. He also traveled to Dundalk on August 23, where he broke the world record in the discus (free style) with a throw of 142:5 feet that subsequently wasn't recognized. Perhaps the only time that the I-AAC athletes didn't cause controversy was when several offered an impromptu performance on Queenstown's promenade for well-wishers before leaving for home.⁴³

Meanwhile, Conway was busy organizing a reception for the returning athletes, what the *Irish American Weekly* believed would "make up for the scant courtesy they received at the hands of the Britishers on whom they visited so many ignominious defeats." Pay-Jay called for an "official welcome" in what would be perhaps the biggest civic reception for sportsmen ever in New York: A huge parade where, according to the *New York Times*, businesses "will be decorated with flags and bunting, and citizens will be requested to hand out emblems and flags bearing welcome legends, especially on the line of march," with flags from "almost every seat of learning of prominence in the United States." The procession would end with a reception at City Hall with "as remarkable a tribute and testimonial to the trained athletes as ever recorded." Every member of the New York County judiciary would be present. His major headache was that many athletes were still in Europe. On July 26, he cabled Robertson to cut short his tour, but Robertson refused—or possibly was unable—to comply. The eventual date came almost a month after the Games finished.⁴⁴

Most athletic clubs, the YMCA, and the PSAL were keen to participate, and a meeting was arranged at the I-AAC clubhouse on Friday, July 31, to select "working committees." The *New York Times* reported that the date would be determined "when positive information reaches this side as to the sailing of the athletes now in Europe." Plans were for the parade to form at Madison Square before marching south to City Hall. To pay for the day and present the athletes with "suitable testimonials," subscriptions were solicited. Conway also sought to include Roosevelt and Governor Charles E. Hughes along with upcoming Presidential and Vice-presidential nominees. New York military regiments, "boy athletes from the public playgrounds," and others would add to the pageant's list. In addition, the I-AAC would have its own banquet for their athletes.⁴⁵

Conway soon became overwhelmed. He issued orders for a special club meeting for Monday, August 17, where uniforms for members attending the march of "White Duck, Green facings and white duck cap" with the club emblem across the breast, were proposed. Meanwhile, the lack of finances and contributions meant money was fast running out. William D. McLaughlin announced through the *New York Times* that only $8,460 had been collected, adding, "unless the contributions improve materially next week, it will be necessary to eliminate several features." In fact, only $4,000 of the $12,000 needed had been collected, with the organizing committee claiming the response "has not been received in the broad, patriotic spirit it is worthy of." The Irish-Glaswegian tea magnate, Thomas J. Lipton, chipped in with $500, declaring, "Better sportsmen never crossed the ocean."[46]

Getting the athletes together forced Conway to change dates twice, finally settling on Saturday, August 29, when he predicted "all the athletes who represented this country will have returned and all will be included in the celebration." But some athletes would still arrive as late as the day before the parade. William L. Jones and Halpin were appointed to sort things out following a disturbing message Jones received from Dolan that the I-AAC party wouldn't be back until August 31. Jones cabled Robertson, demanding, "Cancel all arrangements. Be here at any cost. If transportation secured, transfer can be changed for other steamer. Serious disappointment to general public if team not here."[47]

Hayes arrived aboard the White Star Line's *Oceanic* on August 19 and was greeted by 2,000 cheering worshippers at the dock and Bloomingdale's 50-piece band, while a steamer, *Massasoit*, had been chartered by the I-AAC officials and Hayes' friends to greet him. As he walked down the gangway, he was overwhelmed by the public and, the *Evening World* reported, "propelled by a dozen pairs of stout arms belonging to members of the Irish-American Athletic Club," as Conway cried, "And now give him an Irish tiger and a cheer for his dad":

> There is just nothing to it. From the moment the hat of little Hayes appeared just above the rail of the towering steamer ... there were cheers from steamer and dock. Then fluttered a handkerchief on which were the figures "26" ... and an Irish harp in green, which enthusiastic admirers aboard stretched across the breast of the midget athlete, who had been lifted upon the rail. Cheers were redoubled then and the little fellow wiped away the moisture which had gathered in his eyes at the joyous greeting.

Hayes, overcome with emotion, announced, "I am glad to get back to my own country, and it is the proudest moment of my life to be able to bring back with me the much prized Marathon trophy."[48]

To reporters he regaled his trip to Nenagh, "where they were just as happy over my Marathon victory as here," although he was more guarded about British tactics:

> We've cleaned them out, and therefore should be generous. I have no kick coming. The press was manifestly unfair, but I do not think the English press truly repre-

sented the English people. The papers conceded us no chance whatever in carrying off the Marathon prize, and when we did win, the pill was consequently all the harder to swallow.

Hayes returned as the smiling little kid he was when he left: "The feeling I experienced when I entered the Stadium, with 100,000 persons looking at me, is difficult to describe. Every fiber of my body tingled. And I never expect to experience a similar feeling."[49]

Along with other I-AAC Olympians, Hayes attended the Eccentric Firemen's Games at Celtic Park four days later, where he was given a rousing reception by 25,000 fans, one of its biggest crowds there ever. Mobbed leaving the dressing room by "a wildly enthusiastic crowd," it was only through the efforts of the Firemen's band, who placed him on their shoulders, that he managed to force his way through.[50]

On the morning before the parade, the final batch of 14 athletes arrived. Everything was now set for what *New York Times* predicted would be "a national celebration." That evening, George M. Cohan invited the athletes to his Knickerbocker Theatre to watch *The Yankee Prince*, and offered extra drama for the audience. Midway through the second act, Gilbert Gregory, playing Uncle Sam, appeared on stage with "flags formed by cutting off a section of Old Glory and adding a harp of Ireland ... neatly printed on silk," as a tribute to the Irish-Americans. Feeling insulted, an audience member, Marion Alexander, loudly protested and demanded Gregory's arrest, before being shouted down by a soldier, who insisted, "That flag doesn't mean anything but a compliment to the boys." With the audience taking the soldier's side, Alexander left in disgust.[51]

Up to a quarter of a million people lined New York's streets on the day of the parade. Catholic athletic clubs, GAA teams, and Irish regiments "acted as a guard of honor to the American athletes, who rode in automobiles," escorted by 15,000 troops and civic workers for five miles from 46th Street and Broadway, passing "banked behind lines of blue-coated policemen ... [and] thousands of enthusiastic spectators." The *Sun*, in what appears a spoof titled "Mrs. Casey's Observations," a "fruit and candy stand" seller who had spread a green flag across her stall, gave her opinions on the march: "'Twas a gr'reat day for Ireland. And there was a lesson for one and in that same p'rade. 'Tis bether for to be bor'rn Irish than lucky. Those that ar're bor'rn both ar're Irish-American." At City Hall, Board of Aldermen president, Patrick F. McGowan, addressed the athletes, offering congratulations from the city and the nation, before concluding, "But you won. You Won! All the people of the United States are proud of you, and this great demonstration in your honor is the best evidence of the gratitude of the American people." The *Sun* reminded readers that only a few months ago, Hayes was a $20-a-week store clerk: "He was Irish, therefore good humored, quick witted and game as a fox terrier ... but the idea of little

11. "You carry the Stars and Stripes proudly!" 155

Olympic athletes arrive at City Hall to celebrate their successes at the 1908 Olympics in London, where the I-AAC won most athletic medals (Library of Congress).

Johnny Hayes, Kid Hayes, Johnny Half Portion Hayes, winning the Marathon made them laugh up in Harlem." When grabbed by some aldermen, "squirming in painful embarrassment," Hayes muttered a few inaudible words that were "understood to mean that he was very much obliged and very happy and all that, and wouldn't they please put him down so he could get under the table."[52]

At Celtic Park the following day, 15,000 spectators welcomed a number of the Olympians at the AOH Annual Games, where Flanagan broke Matt McGrath's 16LB hammer (nine-foot ring) world record by almost 15 feet. On Monday, August 31, Theodore Roosevelt, who declined an invitation to City Hall, invited the Olympians, along with Sullivan, Halpin, Conway and Murphy to his home at Sagamore Hill, on Long Island. There Conway offered the President honorary membership of the I-AAC. He gladly accepted. Sheppard and Flanagan each gave Roosevelt one of their medals, which the President was only convinced of accepting when the pair explained that they had others. Afterwards the party moved on to Donnelly's Grove, College Point, where "Big Tim" Sullivan hosted a picnic.[53]

The following weekend, up to 20,000 patrons watched the I-AAC Labor Day Games and AAU All-Around Championships. Some spectators climbed onto the grandstand's roof for a better view, causing events to be halted as officials, fearing it would collapse, called the police in. Princeton's John Bredemus took the All-Around title with 5809 points, well below Sheridan's 7,120½ from the previous year, while Rose broke the 16LB shot put world record.[54]

Olympic athletes are greeted by President Theodore Roosevelt (center top row, in white shirt) at his Long Island home in 1908. Pat Conway (left of Roosevelt) granted the president honorary membership of the I-AAC, while Sheppard and Flanagan gave the president one of their medals.

The I-AAC honored its own members on September 21 with a banquet at the Waldorf Hotel. James E. Sullivan declared in front of 500 guests, "I would like to pay a tribute to the most remarkable athletic team that was ever brought together. Too much credit cannot be given to the Irish-American Athletic Club ... [it] could have won the world's championship without the assistance of any other organization." The club later gave 21 athletes life membership.[55]

Some people were less than pleased with the make-up of the American medalists, as correspondence to the *New York Times* showed. A letter on July 31 from an "E Pluribus Unum" in Easton claimed that while he was "naturally proud of the achievements of the 'American' athletes" in London, he had to point out:

> But it not be well for us to temper our celebration of their victories by consideration ... that most of the victories won by our team in the track events were won for us by foreign-born athletes, or by men whose immediate ancestry is foreign; and that one club, the Irish-American of New York, composed for the most part of foreign-born athletes was the greatest point getter on our side.... I submit that this

fact should weigh far more than the conventional and purely adventitious fact that our flag was hoisted so many times, when we come to consider how many foreigners are included in the "American" wins in the Olympic games of 1908.

In reply, S.L. Harbinson of New York argued: "There were twenty-seven events decided in the Stadium, of which we won fifteen.... Only three of these were won for us by men of foreign birth.... It is an extraordinary perversion to call an American of foreign descent or even of 'immediate foreign descent' a foreigner. All of us except the Indians are of foreign descent."[56]

John Schaeffer would later describe how the 1908 Olympics aided the rise of Irish acceptability in the States:

> By competing under the American flag, Irish Americans were able to demonstrate their loyalty.... Turning middle class Americans against the English naturally increased the visibility and respectability of the Irish on the United States Olympic team. The victories of Irish Americans at the Games gave the Irish ethnicity an enhanced value in America. By claiming the victories of the Irish Americans as their own, those previously considered "native" Americans were implicitly inviting the Irish to join their ranks—at least in the sporting world. This process occurred not by instilling any change in the Irish Americans, but by embracing the very qualities that had previously been despised in Irish Americans. The pride America took in its Irish American Olympians' physical vigor and competitive spirit transformed them into a valued part of American society.[57]

While the I-AAC had supplied the backbone of the American team at the Olympics and dispatched their brand around the world, the feeling continued that the club had discarded much of its own Irishness behind. What the I-AAC stood for with regards for Irish identity after ten years, and what had it achieved in that time in promoting Irish sport, was a question worth answering.

12

"Blood stirred by its games and sports"
The I-AAC and Promoting Irish Sport and Identity in America

March 27, 1903: the New Star Theater, Lexington Avenue and 107th Street. A performance of an Irish melodrama, *McFadden's Row of Flats*, was just beginning, when one member of the theatre's orchestra blew a whistle. Suddenly, around 200 men and women of the 2,500 present opened fired with a deluge of rotten eggs, fruit and vegetables upon the cast. Describing the protesters as AOH and CnG members, the *Evening World* claimed that the actors were caught by surprise: "They were aware that the celebration of Easter was apt to begin a little early on the east side and sometimes to last over night, but they hardly looked for it to start two weeks ahead of time."

The theatre was thrown into chaos. When the pelting began, everyone stood to see who was causing the disturbance, making it impossible to spot the perpetrators. One policeman had to stamp out a burning rag in one of the aisles as the protesters attempted to burn down the place. The *New York Tribune* reported the following day:

> At least two hundred eggs went across the auditorium landing on all parts of the stage. They struck everywhere. Not a person on stage escaped being hit by at least two or three, and some of them got more. The donkey was a ludicrous sight. The scenery was ruined by the numerous eggs which missed the players and smashed against the make believe windows, doors and walls of the saloon. After the egg shower the throwers drew out apples and threw them at the players who lingered on the state. Then they threw vegetables of various kinds, the goods landing with a peculiar sound against the stage and scenery and falling down and rolling this way and that. It seemed as if the two hundred persons who were throwing had thrown each five times, making a thousand eggs and other articles flung at the players…. It was the wildest uproar imaginable, and a fire panic could hardly have been more uproarious.

The *Evening World* noted that the "green-whiskered" policeman's line, "Chure, this is a free country, but kape off the grass," started the mayhem:

> Almost before the shrill notes of the alarming whistle had died away he was a walking omelet [sic]. He carried a full line of eggs in all styles and of all ages.... The donkey at first appeared to take a more cheerful—even a hopeful—view of the proceedings. Hope died, however with his first sniff of an egg which had struck his flank, caromed to his left ear, and dropped at his feet. He gave expression to his feelings in prolonged and weird braying, then broke for the alley.

Four "ringleaders" were arrested before the play finally restarted, with time for one last act from the audience. An Irish electrician, Michael J. O'Brien, stood up and screamed, "I denounce this play as a shame and a disgrace, and its ridiculing the Irish race," before hurling one final egg.[1]

* * *

The cause of the demonstration was, according to the *Evening World*, an outrage over the growth of the "coarse caricatures of the Irish." This demonstration "intent upon avenging what [the demonstrators] considered an insult to their race," was led by an amalgamation of New York's Irish bodies. The *Irish American* had already called for action, albeit without violence: "A boycott on all such theatres and players as offend in this manner will have a healthy and quick effect in putting a stop to the evil."[2]

However, the disturbance also showed how much the GNYIAA/I-AAC embroiled itself in other matters. This was, after all, "more than a club" in the political manner that Barcelona FC would claim decades later, fighting for more than athletic honors. They were also defending the honor of Irishness on a number of fronts, not only from stereotypical depictions, but also from Anglophile incursions into America. The *Irish American* said that *McFadden's Row of Flats* "received the attention from an organized effort carefully planned by members of the [CnG] and the [AOH], reinforced by members of the Greater New York Irish Athletic Association." Indeed, among those who arrived at Harlem Police Station to arrange bail and act as advocates were Conway and Cohalan.[3]

This was not the last time assaults on Irish identity were countered by I-AAC membership, protesting against other plays like *The Irish Servant Girls* in 1907, a "brutal and disreputable 'sketch' ... [a] gross, vile, indecent and an outrage on the Irish people." In 1909, the United Irish-American Societies met at the clubhouse to campaign against an article in *McClure's Magazine* by George Kibbe Turner on Tammany's alleged control of New York's Italian and Jewish criminal gangs. Even the proposal to name the new bridge over Blackwell's Island the Queensboro Bridge attracted anger from the I-AAC, with Conway telling the *Evening World* that the I-AAC was a "heavy taxpayer" in Queens, which qualified it as an objector. "Besides," he sniffed, "Queensboro cannot hold. 'Boro' is not properly spelled."[4]

Daniel Cohalan was perhaps the most tenacious club member with regards to Irish identity. Born in Middletown, New York, in 1867, the eldest of five sons of County Cork immigrants, Cohalan studied law at Manhattan College, playing for the college baseball nine before being admitted to the New York bar in 1888. He was one of Tammany boss Charles F. Murphy's chief advisors until as late as 1906, the Grand Sachem of the Tammany Society from 1908 to 1911, and a major face within Clan na Gael, co-owning *The Gaelic American*—the Anglophobic organ which advertised for subscribers' gatherers by offering a rifle "delivered, express paid, to any address," in return for 50 names—organizing much of the Easter Rising's funding and being one of John Devoy's closest friend.[5]

Both Irish speaker and regular visitor to Ireland, Cohalan's antipathy to Britain fueled a staunch American isolationism that never subsided throughout World War I. He also deftly combined the Old-World politics with the new, a sort of dual patriot who "walked a tightrope between respectable and revolutionary politics." Writing about race relations in America in the first

Daniel Cohalan (*second from left*) alongside (*left to right*) Judge John W. Goff, Eamon De Valera and his close friend John Devoy. An I-AAC director, judge, and reputed planner and financier of the Easter Rising in Ireland, Cohalan would fall out with both Woodrow Wilson and De Valera (Library of Congress).

four decades of the twentieth century, Matthew Pratt Guterl wrote of "the quintessential Tammany Hall man" and "ruthless politician" Cohalan: "He was also a devout Irish nationalist—one of the faithful whose quixotic belief in an independent Ireland seemed, for a time, to be the grandest delusion of all."[6]

Cohalan was a friend of Tom Clarke, the leader of the 1916 Easter Uprising, who was also a member of the I-AAC when he lived in New York. Cohalan sent Roger Casement, who was in the States when war broke out, over to Berlin to procure arms, leading the British to accuse him in 1921 of conspiring with the Germans even after the United States had entered the war. He was the principal organizer of the Irish Race Convention and had been chief witness before the Senate Foreign Relations Committee arguing the Irish case with regards to the League of Nations. He would clash with both Woodrow Wilson, over his antipathy to Irish independence, and Eamon De Valera; the issue of how the $5 million raised on De Valera's U.S. tour should be utilized sparked a soured relationship that declined further as Ireland fell into a Civil War.[7]

Cohalan's ability to pull off a high-profile protest against British interests was shown in November 1905, when along with Dowling and the American senator Charles A. Towne, he appeared on the cover of the *Gaelic American*, denouncing the upcoming visit of the British Fleet and Prince Louis of Battenberg—whose son, Louis Mountbatten, would be killed in Ireland by the IRA in 1979. Dowling presided over a huge meeting at the Cooper Institute where Cohalan concluded with "a spirited 'Irish speech,'" both speakers juxtaposing their dual identities, the old of Ireland and the new of America, without any apparent contradiction. Dowling declared that this was not a personal snub of Battenberg, but of Britain: "With the personality, charming as it may be, of the gentleman who visits our shores, we have no quarrel.... But we have a serious protest to enter against those who would make what seems to be merely a social visit an omen of danger to the peace of the world and omen of insecurity to the future of our country."[8]

In contrast, Cohalan spent most of his speech railing against Perfidious Albion:

> We have had one persistent and consistent enemy from the time when the liberty of this country was wrung from an English king and an English government, and England has been our enemy either openly or secretly ever since, openly when she dare do, secretly when she did not dare, or when she thought her interests would be advanced more by being apparently an open friend of ours ... knowing those things it is not necessary to speak as Irishmen, but as Americans solely. Knowing the part of our people have played in upbuilding the institutions of America and in bringing the American republic into existence and the part our race is playing now in this same country ... we will say, as our fathers said before us, we want no alliance with any nation.[9]

Cohalan often used the success of the I-AAC, of which he had been a member since at least 1902, to further his anti–British sentiments. He embroiled himself in the 1908 Olympics controversy, exploding in more than one newspaper about the English notion of "fair play" and the underhanded tricks he knew the British would pull. In the *Evening World*, he "spoke his mind" following the controversial tug-of-war event: "Our athletes expected just the sort of conditions with which they are meeting. The English have scheduled events in which we have no entries and for which there have been no preparations by the American team. Thus far the English have fallen down lamentably as sportsmen." He added in a rival paper: "Oh, no one ... will be surprised at this little matter of favoritism.... It's quite typical of the English, who are always talking about fair play, that they don't know the meaning of the word, and would go far out of the way to keep from learning it."[10]

Sheridan, in his *Evening World* Olympics column, slammed the Irish-born athletes—Leahy, Horgan, Walsh and Roche—who had represented Britain. Their actions had caused "the only bitterness displayed by the boys" because they had let their "scores" go to "John Bull." Sheridan's ridiculous argument was that the U.S. was somehow more representative of Ireland, and that if these athletes weren't lucky enough to compete for the U.S., they should've boycotted the games altogether:

> All four of these men claim that they were scoring points for Ireland, but this contention while patriotic is not practical because the very object they seek is defeated by themselves. The Irishmen want to beat England, and the only way they could do that would be to stay at home. The eight and one third points scored by those men were taken from the American team and recorded for England. No amount of patriotic argument can change that fact.

Later, Dowling told guests at an I-AAC banquet for the athletes at the Waldorf Astoria:

> That English King who, when he heard of the victorious charge of the Irish Brigade at Fontenoy, cried, "Cursed be the laws which deprive me of such subjects," might have a prototype today in some sprig of English royalty who, seeing the victories won for the United States by Irish-Americans, might well exclaim against the tyranny which drove those men or their ancestors from Ireland to seek asylum in this country. Some of these men of Irish blood who won points against the British must have taken a malicious pleasure in seeing ... the United States flag raised over the red flag of England.[11]

Indeed, the Irish-American press, normally quite reticent on non–GAA matters, was quick to praise the role of the I-AAC in London. Following the Olympiad, the *Irish World* displayed a woodcut of Flanagan, Sheridan and McGrath, wearing tops with a large shamrock in the middle, as they stood with their hands on each other's shoulders. A five-verse poem was dedicated to the trio, with the final verse declaring: "Brave 'Kelly and Burke and Shea'/ Flanagan, Sheridan, McGrath/True Anglo-Saxons are we/Ha, ha, ha, ha, HA, HA!" At the *Gaelic American*, E.P. McKenna penned a poem titled "How the Yankees Beat the World," which praised the club's athletes' Irish-American identity while simultaneously attacking the British:

> But they never met on turf or track such men of brawn and bone/So Flanagan and Sheppard, McGrath and Sheridan/Showed them all the kind of stuff's in a good Cork Yankee man.... A blinding whirl, a might swing, and like a falling star/The hammer fell a good spear length beyond the farthest bar/Then Flanagan shook hands in glee, and dusting off his clothes/ "I learnt that trick, me boys," sez [sic] he "where the blue bright Shannon flows"/A man of god-like beauty then stepped out before the throng/So lithe, so trim and handsome, so sinewy and strong/He held the discus in his hand and hit the sod and swat/Then did a speedy stunt or two and let it go at that/The dukes and earls, who looked like girls, screwed their monocles tight/And said, "Ba Jove, th' bloomin' thing has gone up out o' sight"/Marty gazed upon the crowd who gave him cheer on cheer/"No man can hate that throw," sez [sic] he, "since me father isn't here...."/At jumping too, and running they showed the English tricks/Although they knew John Bull could sprint since back in '76/They chewed them up, and spat them out, and trounced them good and sound/That's how the Yankee beat the world in good old London town/So let the Eagle scream, me boys, from 'Frisco to New York/From Dublin town to Galway Bay, from Derry down to Cork/Hang out the starry banner and never take a dare/For they still raise brawny Yankees in Donegal and Clare.[12]

* * *

Cohalan demonstrated that the politics of the I-AAC was very close to that of the Ancient Order of Hibernians and Clan na Gael. Indeed this trio— and the GAA—were "so closely interconnected it was hard to see where one began and the other ended." Understandably, as New York's biggest Irish-owned center for outdoor events, political organizations utilized the grounds for their own picnics and rallies, and top athletes also competed and broke records at them.[13]

Both political groups had a large cross-membership separated by only minor differences. The largest was the AOH. Founded in New York in May 1836, it "developed in the nineteenth century as a provident association devoted to the advancement of the interests and welfare of Irish immigrants." Despite its current reputation as a conservative body, it spread initially as a strongly radical, working class, ethnic movement that fed on "the economic and social grievances of canal and railroad laborers, and the nationalist sentiments of [Irish] workers everywhere." It embroiled itself in Irish labor struggles such as the "Molly Maguires" in Pennsylvania, through to the "Orange" riots of July 1870 and 1871 that cost a total of 70 lives. Its first recorded sporting event in New York City was hosted by the Brooklyn AOH in 1855.[14]

Founded by Jerome Collins in 1867, Clan na Gael, unlike the AOH, was less exclusively Roman Catholic, with Dr. William Carroll, a Donegal-born Presbyterian, its main figure alongside Devoy. It was America's principal "physical force" organization until Noraid emerged in the 1970s, with one source claiming that $100,000 was handed over to the IRB between 1913 and 1916. More prone to splits, it was divided by the 1890s between its egotistical leader, John Devoy, in New York, and William Sullivan in Chicago. What had "struck fear—and terror—in the heart of the world's most formidable empire" was now, as Devoy's biographer, Terry Golway, claims, "little more than two rival factions led by men with revolvers in their pockets."[15]

Sport was a means to both improving youth fitness and patriotism, as Paul Darby discerns: "Of all the nationalist groups that were associated with the GAA in the late nineteenth century, Clan na Gael had perhaps the clearest vision about how best to harness the mobilizing power of Gaelic sport to generate support for their militant agenda." But they also saw picnics as a great way of building their names and creating camaraderie within the Irish community. Hosting its first-ever "Annual Games" in New York on August 17, 1870, under the auspices of the Fenian Brotherhood of the District of Manhattan, 5,000 people traveled to Jones' Wood near the East River.[16]

By the time they moved their events into Celtic Park, both organizations' meetings achieved as high a standard as any held under AAU rules. In July 1906, the *New York Tribune* reported of the CnG Annual Picnic: "Many prominent local athletes took part in the contests, and the events were of the kind that kept the crowd yelling like mad from the time they began until the final one was decided." Two years later, the AOH Annual Games saw Flanagan break the 16LB hammer world record, while 20,000 attended the Brooklyn and Long Island Clan Games in July 1913.[17]

Other times, Celtic Park became the venue to raise money for Irish causes by separate organizations headed by club members. An athletic tournament in aid of a Christian Brothers seminary in Clontarf was arranged by the UIAS on July 31, 1904, with the organizing committee including Frawley. Kiely, Flanagan, Alexander Grant of the NYAC, and Arthur Duffey were scheduled to compete. The attendance consisted mostly, according to the *Evening World*, of "Irishmen or the American-born sons and daughters of Irishmen ... [who] had their blood stirred by its games and sports," adding that there was more than mere enthusiasm in this crowd: "It was patriotism, love of country and pride of race that shone in their faces and rang in their voices at the sight of the strong-limbed men and lads who ran and hurled shots and hammers and did the broad jump as only the Irish know how." Meyer Prinstein would have won the broad jump but for the "liberality" of D. Frank's (NWSAC) 26-inch handicap, which caused "much comment," according to the *New York Times*:

12. "Blood stirred by its games and sports"

It was a day for Irish people. When there were no contests of brawn to keep the eyes of the spectators engaged, their ears were filled with music strains of Erin—such music as makes the heels and toes keep time, no matter how hard one tries to keep still. The New York Catholic Protectory Band was on the green and the tunes and bars it struck went home.[18]

The following year, 15,000 people helped the I-AAC's Fourth of July Summer Games profits go to the completion of the Daniel O'Connell Memorial Church at Cahersiveen, County Kerry, birthplace of "The Liberator." The *New York Times* commented:

Perhaps it was that feature of the affair that gave an aspect of a fair day on the Emerald Isle to the gathering. It was an enthusiastic crowd, and next to applauding the athletes it cheered the flag, the one of the Stars and Stripes and that of the Green and the Golden Harp, while the fine band of St. John's Orphan Asylum played the stirring melodies of "Killarney," "Wearing of the Green," "The Harp that Once Thro' Tara's Hall," and all the others that cause the pulses of Irishmen the world over to beat a little faster.[19]

* * *

One of the key reasons for a senior Irish athletic club in New York was the desire to promote Irish identity through Irish sports. In 1902, Conway was reported in the *Irish American Weekly* as proposing a "National Association for the advancement of Gaelic sports" to bring the country's GAA clubs closely together. But there was some confusion about what exactly were these sports. Hurling and throwing certain weights—the "fifty-six" is the only Olympic event performed in ancient Ireland, rather than Greece—were clearly Irish in origin, but what about the hop, skip and jump?[20]

Only one event, a sporting festival that hadn't been hosted for over 800 years, could bring any legitimacy. The Tailteann Games hold a special and mystical place in Irish sporting history; beginning around 1900 BC until the Norman invasion, they predated both the Celtic invasion and, by 1,200 years, the Greek Olympics. Named in honor of Tailté, the Iberian-born wife of the King of the Firbolgs, Eochaidh Mac Erc, the annual event gathered athletes from all over Ireland to the now anglicized Telltown, Meath. A festival of culture and intelligence as much as one of muscle, sports consisted of hurling, football, throwing various weighted objects, dancing, wrestling, and horse and chariot racing.[21]

Naturally the resurrection of the Games was seen as a crucial aim for sporting Irish nationalists and was the reason for the GAA's 1888 "Invasion." Michael Davitt, the Irish Land League founder, outlined his intentions in a letter to William Prendergast, reprinted in the *Boston Globe*:

The contemplated invasion is but a means to an end, the end being a projected international Gaelic festal here in Ireland in 1889. It has been promised that an effort on a national scale be made next year to reestablish the old Taltean [sic] games, or something approaching the festival which under this name was a national institution in ancient Ireland centuries anterior to the fame Olympic tournaments of Greece.[22]

Briefly organized in Ireland in 1924 as a short-lived affair, Boston's Irish Athletic Club had previously attempted reviving them, the first "official" "Tailtean [sic] Games" being held on July 25, 1889, at Oak Island. But the Tailteann games in the United States were to be a temporary arrangement, less a Hibernian rival to the Olympic Games and more an Irish-American answer to the Caledonian Games, until Celtic Park would provide it its very own Panithinaiko Stadium.[23]

In July 1903, the Greater New York Irish AC announced that after nearly 800 years—ignoring Boston—the "Tailtin [sic] games" would return. "Celtic Park will be the Mecca to which all true loyal sons of Ireland and their children will turn on Labor Day," said the *Irish American Weekly*. "In resurrecting the games, the organization has in view the perpetuation of this ancient athletic festival of Ireland." Conway would spare "no effort" in making the games a success. The *Brooklyn Daily Eagle* noted that he "has mapped out a very elaborate athletic carnival":

> It will be a revival of the celebrated Tailton [sic] games of Ireland. This will be the 2,950th celebration of Ireland's ancient athletic festival.... President Conway and his committee have gone through the annals of Irish sport and have duplicated as near as possible the original program. America's most foremost Irish citizens have decided to become patrons of this event, and President Conway has been promised the prizes for all the events. This will insure the winners of prizes that will be well worth winning.

The *New York Tribune* argued that this would be an ideal occasion to showcase Irish sport. "There has been much skepticism among the Irish-Americans concerning the prowess of their fathers in athletics, and this is a great chance for the fathers to 'make good,'" while the *New York Times* suggested optimistically that "henceforth, every year will witness a set of these games until they become an annual institution."[24]

Despite the rival Caledonian Games nearby at Maspeth, the event was a resounding success. A then-record crowd of 8,000 turned up, and the club decided to make it an annual Labor Day event. At the following year's Games, according to the *New York Times*, 3,000 to 4,000—the *Gaelic American* put the attendance figure at 10,000—sporting aficionados "filled every available seat and all the desirable standing room" to watch "the modern revival of Ireland's famous athletic contests, as the Olympic games are the revival of the ancient Greek sports." Clog dancing and Gaelic football were included in the program.[25]

The Labor Day Games reverted back to a standard athletic meet, containing little Irish sport, in the eyes of the American press until 1909. Only the Irish-American newspapers continued to call the event the Tailtin [*sic*] Games: Although the *New York Tribune* referenced the 1907 games as "the revival of the ancient Tailtin [*sic*] games," others made no mention of any connection.[26]

Following the athletic fever generated by the 1908 Olympics, Emilio Lunghi was the star attraction for 1909. The *New York Times* promised the event would "surpass any of its Tailtin [*sic*] games made famous by the Irish race." The 1910 games were the most successful since 1903, with 10,000 spectators watching three world records broken, two being recognized.[27]

This was the last time that the I-AAC would call their Labor Day event the Tailteann Games. Despite attempts at imitating de Coubertin's Olympics, this I-AAC rebranding was essentially a parochial affair. It didn't bring together all of America's ethnic Irish athletes, let alone match the Olympics for internationalism. Few athletes competed who were not from the Metropolitan area, with the Clan na Gael political splits having as much influence on this as the distances from Chicago or San Francisco. It was left to the Chicago Irish-American AC to continue hosting the Tailteann Games with an ultimate failed revival; the final Games in 1915 were won by the city's Danish-American AC. Even this most Irish of sporting festivals couldn't remain a purely Hibernian event without the aid of other ethnicities.

13

"Condemned for wholesale proselyting"
The I-AAC Growth Between 1908 and 1912

Home from London, the I-AAC Olympians in September faced the two top domestic championships within a week of each other at Travers Island. At the Mets, for the second year Taylor's residency qualification was questioned. He refused to attend a Registration Committee meeting, but the Winged Fist retook the team award for the fifth year running, with 89 points to the NYAC's 43. Flanagan broke his own record in the "Fifty-Six" with a throw of just over 39 feet, while falling just short of exceeding his 16LB hammer record. Keating (100Yds and 220Yds), Eller (120Yds hurdles and 220Yds hurdles), Sheppard (half mile), Allen (pole vault), Porter (high jump), Horr (16LB shot and discus) were the other first places.[1]

A week later, and a day after they had beaten the Mercury Foot, 35–31, in the Juniors in front of just 500 spectators—Bobbie Cloughen (100Yds) and Dan Ahearne (broad jump) were their only firsts—the Irish won their fourth National title, defeating the NYAC, 55–29. The day was remembered by the *New York Times* for the "mismanagement of the most flagrant description" after officials, neglecting to find out the number of laps to a mile—four or five—wrongly rang the bell on the final circuit of the 1Mile race. It was rerun later in the week. No records were broken, but the I-AAC captured six championships: Sheppard (five miles), Keating (220Yds), Eller (220Yds hurdles), Porter (high jump), Horr (discus), and Flanagan (56LB weight).[2]

Sheridan failed to appear at either event, but the following month he broke Dearborn's discus world record from a two and a half-meter circle at the Pastime AC's grounds, with a throw of 140:5:5 feet. Meanwhile at the Alesian AA Games at Elizabeth, Flanagan once again failed to officially break the 16LB hammer record. Here a chord was used instead of an iron hoop,

13. "Condemned for wholesale proselyting" 169

and the throw was slightly downhill. In between these two meetings, the I-AAC's Fall Games wrapped up a memorable season. Ten thousand people witnessed two records being officially broken—Bacon's 440Yds high hurdles and Eller's 220Yds high hurdles. Matt McGrath's hammer record was disallowed because the wire handles "stretched an inch between the start and finish of the event."[3]

As winter commenced, the Irish steamroller rolled on. While Bellars took first place at the AAU Senior Cross-Country Championships, the team trophy went to the Irish, a "foregone conclusion" before "the pistol was fired" according to the *New York Tribune*, as the club took six places with Joyce second. The Thanksgiving Day Yonkers Marathon, "probably the most spectacular event of its kind ever held in America," was also won by James F. Crowley, cementing his reputation as a the "King of the Marathoners" in the era of the "marathon craze" by beating the favorite, Sam Mellor of the local Mercury AC, by over six minutes. Afterwards he declared to onlookers, "Boys, I did my best. I started out to win, and—well, you see I've done it. I did it for the Irish-Americans," while a big onlooker shouted that he was a "worthy successor" to last year's winner, Hayes.[4]

* * *

The indoor season also saw the Irish continue their dominance, taking the AAU Nationals at Madison Square Garden. While the *Evening World* wrongly suggested that the two New York giants would find things difficult,

James Crowley following his Yonkers Marathon victory in 1908 (Library of Congress).

"owing to the caliber of entries made by the other great organizations of the country," the Irish triumphed 84–36, over the NYAC. Tom Collins broke Edward Colston Carter's 21-year-old American indoor record in the 5Mile run. The *Evening World* reported enthusiastically, "You can't keep the Irish down when it comes to making records.... Once more a son of the Emerald Isle has been crowned champion of America, and this time it is for both indoor and outdoor honors.... During several stages of the journey he would sprint to the front and then come back, letting some one else take the lead." Collins made light of the win: "Sure, a month ago I won the girl of me choice, and the lightness of the heart has added wings to the feet." As 1908 closed, Robertson told the *New York Tribune* that his athletes had won 46 track and field championships and scored 2,261 points. Sheridan led with 181 points, while Sheppard was second with 148.⁵

Once again the club's own indoor meet, on February 6, was deemed the foremost gig of the winter season. The *Evening World* cooed, "Only the classy athletes will compete at the games ... it is likely that indoor records will fall before the mighty strides of the winner," while the *New York Times* echoed, "Seldom has ever an athletic meet brought together such classy athletes as those who will compete tonight at the carnival of sport of the [I-AAC] at Madison Square Garden." Sheppard was one athlete cited as having his sights set on Charles H. Kilpatrick's half mile record, while the club limited handicaps to reduce the meeting's length.⁶

Just two new records were made: Collins broke Bonhag's 4Mile mark with a time of 19:53:2, while Pat McDonald exceeded Flanagan's 1904 record in the "Fifty-Six" by three and a half inches. Other indoor records broken during the winter included Cloughen lowering Wendell Baker's 1886 record for the 130Yds dash at the 47th Regiment Games in February. Robertson surpassed L.B. Dorland's 300Yds indoor record by nine-tenths of a second with a time 0:32:6, while Bonhag broke the 5-, 3-, and Collins' 4Mile records at various events. Then at the 22nd Regiment Armory, during the Fordham University Games' "special seven mile event," against Jimmy Lee over the first four miles and Bellars for the following three, he broke times for the 5½, 6, 6½ and 7 miles, beating Carter's "outdoors" 7 mile record with a time of 35:50:6. He now held all indoor records between two and seven miles.⁷

The Decoration Day Games attracted 5,000 fans, with the I-AAC five-man relay team beating the NYAC, setting a new American record of 3:17:5 through the "splendid running" of new signing William Robbins, while Cloughen, Northridge, Sheppard and Rosenberger made up the rest of the quintet. The Clare Men's Association took the July 4 slot at Celtic Park.⁸

Records started falling as early as May 2. At the Pastime's grounds, Sheridan broke Horr's discus record with a throw that the *Evening Star* of Washington described as "nothing short of phenomenal. Six times he toed the mark and six times he sent the weight hurling through the air to record distances." A member of the crowd had shouted out before one throw, "Now for a new record, Martin." The big Mayoman replied with a smile, "Now, don't kid me like that. I never felt better but remember this is my first time out. I'll make a good throw all right, but that's all I hope for." The newspaper's reporter described what happened next:

> An instant later the discus was hurling through the air. It seemed even to the initiated that it would never land and all hands grabbed for the tape. It was a regulation steel measurer. As it was unwound Martin followed it down the field. He said nothing, but watched every inch as it measured the ground. When Horr's mark was passed and 135 feet 5 inches were recorded he blurted out: "I'll bet I can't do it again."[9]

Sadly, the record was not recognized owing to "technicalities." At the San Salvador Council of Knights of Columbus Games at the same venue three weeks later, he recorded a throw of 138:11:75 in a strong headwind: A proper steel tape was also provided. His throw, at the New York Post Office Clerks' Association, of 144 feet was rejected, while a similar record in early September at "the big Hibernian [AOH] athletic meet" near Waterbury, Connecticut, was rebuffed as it had been made on inclined ground, aided by a strong wind, and without a steel ring. Two days later at the Orange Playground Festival, Sheridan broke the discus record with a mark of 141 feet, 1 inch. This time AAU officials accurately measured the throw, but again the throw was rejected. Sheridan finally made a new mark at the Canadian Championships a week later, throwing the discus 139:10:5.[10]

However, the discus wasn't Sheridan's only preoccupation. As All-Around champion, he also broke the world record for points at the United Scottish Clans Annual Games at Celtic Park, exceeding his own record by 154½ points, with a score of 7,285. The *Tribune* commented, "The big fellow was in excellent form, and won nine of the ten events." Opposition consisted solely of the West Side YMCA's Theodore L. Matsukes. E.L. Farrell of South Boston and E. Payne of the Mohegan AC didn't compete, while the Irish-Americans' William McLead was denied entry after turning up late.[11]

Flanagan also spent the season breaking records with aplomb. In front of 4,000 spectators at Celtic Park on June 6, during the Bricklayers Union No. 27 Games, he "defeated his protégé and bitter rival," Matt McGrath, in the 16LB hammer, breaking McGrath's 1907 world record with a distance of 174:3:375, the *New York Times* sniffing that it was the first time a steel tape was seen at Laurel Hill since Decoration Day. But the record was gone in less than a week. Ten thousand fans filled Travers Island to see Flanagan add six inches with a new distance of 174:10:175, the *New York Times* declaring:

> Never was the big weight thrower in better form.... There was probably not any more interesting or picturesque event on the varied program of the meet than the hammer throw, and as the spectators saw Flanagan come up for his turn those in the stand directly opposite instinctively forced themselves further back in their seats, for it looked as if the weight, with its lashing handle, would land directly among them. There was always a feeling of relief as the iron ball buried itself out of sight close to the edge of the track.[12]

Later in the month it was gone again, with an uphill throw of 180 feet at the New York Press Club AA Games at the American League baseball park: Matt McGrath only managed 164 feet. Flanagan wasn't finished: For the fourth time, in "magnificent form," giving a taster in practice with a throw of 182 feet, Flanagan made a new world mark with a throw of 184:4:0 at the New Haven CnG Games at Savin Rock. "It was expected that [his previous] throw would stand for some time," the *New York Times* said, "but to-day's record shows that the giant New York policeman has not yet reached his limit." To top things off, he broke his "Fifty-Six" world record at the Rhode Island Clan Games, but once more the lack of rudimentary accessories—this time a ring— meant that the record wouldn't stand.[13]

The third I-AAC athlete to re-write the records was national junior champion Dan Ahearne (or Ahearn). Born in Athea, County Limerick, and the younger brother of 1908 Olympic hop, step and jump gold medalist Tim Ahearne, who had competed for Britain in London, the pair had traveled to America in 1909. While Tim was enticed over to the NYAC—he did later join the I-AAC in 1913—Dan joined the Irish-Americans and spent the summer of 1909 trying to break the 21-year-old hop, step and jump world record held by fellow Irishman Dan Shanahan. At the same Post Office Clerks Games where Sheridan's record was disallowed, Ahearne broke the event's American record with a distance of 49:8:0, but "as the takeoff was not accurate and the addition of a strong breeze aiding the jumper," it went unrecognized. A week later at the Kerry Men's Association Game, he made a longer jump of 51:04:75, which was also refused as a linen tape was used.[14]

It was only a matter of time: At the Clare Men's Games, his leap of 50:01:375 stood a chance of recognition. "If the record cannot be accepted by the [AAU] the club is likely to get into trouble," cautioned the *New York Tribune*. It was recognized, but controversy returned in August. A day after his record at the Knights of Columbus Boston picnic, Ahearne was once more "robbed" at Celtic Park, as the *New York Times* put it, by the absence of a steel tape at the Clan na Gael picnic to measure his 50:06:5 jump.[15] This failure to supply correct measuring equipment was mostly due to negligence rather than malice, a product of a sport run for amateurs by amateurs. As we see here, even Celtic Park's officials often failed to provide the necessary items to properly validate their athletes' claims to breaking records.

The year 1909 once more saw Celtic Park practically booked out, with festivals such as the American AC's "International Athletic Carnival" on July 11 being "one of the most important of the year." The I-AAC's foreign signings, Wilson and Lunghi, ran in Irish society picnics, while other athletes were competing out of town. Three world records were broken at the "Tailtin Games" on Labor Day, with Lunghi beating Shep in the 700Yds special run and breaking Lon Myers' 1882 record with a time of 1:31:00. Eller broke Al Copeland's 1888 120Yds low hurdles record with a time of 0:14:6, while the NYAC's Platt Adams bettered the standing hop, skip and jump mark.[16]

However, one disappointment was the club's absence from the national championships. In an attempt to spread the athletic gospel further and tag it to a World's Fair, the games were attached to the Alaska-Yukon-Pacific Exposition. Boosterism was optimistic that the Irish would attend: "The struggle for first honors will probably lie between the [NYAC] and the [I-AAC] of New York.... Each is sending an array of stars such as never before visited the coast," wrote one local hack in the *Evening Statesman* of Walla Walla, some 260 miles from the Emerald City. While the NYAC sent a squad, the difficulty in getting cops released at the height of summer ensured that the Irish-Americans stayed away. The *New York Times* concluded that their absence "will be severely felt," but that hosting the games in Seattle "will do more for the cause of athletics in that section of the country than anything else."[17]

So the Mets was their only major title to fight over. Despite the NYAC not having captured the Spalding Trophy since 1903, the *New York Times* was beefing their chances: "The Irish American Athletic Club will have a hard fight for the trophy this year.... The Winged First [*sic*] captured the championship last year and wants to annex it again, but their road is not likely to be

Cigarette card featuring Dan Ahearne. The summer of 1909 was taken up by the County Limerickman's attempts at breaking the world record for the hop, step and jump (triple jump) (Mecca Cigarettes card).

as smooth ... many good men have sprung up in the smaller clubs, and the fight promises to be interesting." Immediately both Wilson and the NYAC's Con Walsh were denied entrance due to being resident in the city less than six months, but the Irish still initially entered 91 men to the NYAC's 85, shortened to 50 and 40 on the day.[18]

With 13 first places, the *New York Tribune* reported, "Once more the Irish-American Athletic Club showed its superiority ... by sweeping everything before it." The *New York Times* called it "an almost unprecedented string of victories" as the Irish hammered the NYAC, 96–45, with "the phenomenal schoolboy" Abel Kiviat taking the mile. In the final lap, with the NYAC's R.M. Davis leading the pack and Kiviat at the rear, the Staten Islander broke through to win with ten yards to spare. The club's other firsts were Rosenberger (100Yds, 220Yds), Eller (120Yds high hurdles, 220Yds low hurdles), Robbins (440Yds), Daly (5Mile), Flanagan (16LB hammer, 56LB weight), Sheridan (discus), and Dan Ahearne (broad jump; HSJ). The *Times* added days later: "The [NYAC] is feeling somewhat sore over the result ... and the athletes are all training hard for the indoor championships ... when they expect to turn the tables on the Winged Fist contingent, as conditions will be different."[19]

As the indoor season beckoned, the I-AAC record-breaking continued. Lunghi marked a world's best at the Canadians, reducing Charles Fitzpatrick's 14-year half mile time to 1:52:8, helping the club with the point trophy by an incredible 167 points to the NYAC's 12. Ten days later, Sheppard, Charles Cassasa, Rosenberger, and Robbins established a new world record for the 1Mile relay at the NYAC Fall Games with a time of 3:20:6. Sheppard had previously written to Sullivan about breaking records in the 1000Yds, asking for timers at the 500-, 600- and 700-yard marks. The *New York Tribune* opined, "'This shows conclusively that Sheppard, who is a good judge of pace and a judge of his own ability, knows perfectly well that the ... records are all within his grasp." Sullivan acquiesced and requested that the Mercury Foot Captain, Jeremiah T. Mahoney, "as a special favor to Sheppard and also in the interest of American athletics," arrange nine timers. In the end, for some unknown reason, Sheppard opted not to run.[20]

The I-AAC Fall Games on Sunday, October 10, were also expected to provide a great day's entertainment to close the summer, with 14 events scheduled. The *New York Times* noted, "Never has any athletic meet held in recent years had such a varied program as here assembled." The 10,000 people who attended were far from disappointed with six records—five world—broken that afternoon. Lunghi smashed W.G. George's 1882 record in the ⅔ Mile in 2:45:6, while Sheridan again extended his discus record to 142:10:5, before grabbing one of James Mitchell's American records, in the 42LB stone, with a throw of 27 feet, 9 inches. The I-AAC quartet of Collins, Riley, Bromilow

13. "Condemned for wholesale proselyting"

and Kiviat reduced the University of Michigan's 4Mile relay record to 18:04:8; Flanagan extended his 16LB hammer with unlimited run and follow with a throw of 188:08:0 feet; and finally, Northridge and Cassasa clipped six seconds off the 26-year-old 220Yds three-legged run. At the Monument Club Games two weeks later, the "fever for establishing new world's records continued unabated" as Flanagan switched from the "sixteen" to the 12LB hammer, breaking Talbott's record by "a trifle more than seventeen feet," with a new distance of 207:07:75, throwing into the wind, "so that there could not be any question of the throw being favored."[21]

The indoor season had already started. The AAU held its annual national championships early at Madison Square Garden on October 4–5. Although Wilson and Lunghi disappointed, the Irish took a close championship, 69–62, over the NYAC. Keating (75Yds), Porter (high jump), and Dan Ahearne (hop, step and jump), triumphed on the first night. Sheppard made a new time for the 600Yds of 1:11:6, Eller shaved a fifth of a second off his 150Yds record, and Collins (5Mile) and McDonald (24LB shot) clinched matters on the second night.[22]

Over a three-weekend spate, the outside winter distance championships were also dominated by the Irish. On November 6, Bonhag won the 10Mile AAU Championship, beating Jim Crowley second place and breaking Willie Day's 1889 American record with a time of 52:34:8. A week later, the I-AAC beat Mohawk AC, 39 to 40, to take the National Junior Cross-Country Championship, despite Acorn AA's Billy Kramer coming in first. Finally, on November 20, the Irish edged Mohawk by one point (27 to 28) to take the AAU Senior Cross-Country Championship, thanks to Crowley coming in second to Kramer, Daly third, and three top ten placements close behind. In amongst these events, Crowley broke his own records from ten to 16 miles in a special 20Mile race under "lantern light" at Celtic Park. However, Xavier's James Clark broke the I-AAC man's record for the total distance, after Crowley "stopped almost to a walk" before finishing fifth. As the new year approached, Everett C. Brown, Sullivan's replacement as AAU president, told the *New York Times*, enthusiastically, "with such splendid teams as those represented by the Irish-American Athletic Club and the New York Athletic Club, new records are promised, and there is no reason why the year 1910 should not show the climax in athletics never before reached in this country."[23]

Three new marks were made at the Irish Indoor Games on February 5. Bonhag shaved three and three-fifths seconds off the 4Mile with a time of 19:39:8. Eller set a time of 0:08:4 for the 70Yds hurdles, while Bromilow, Schaff, Robbins and Kiviat set a new world's best for the 2,400Yds relay with a time of 5:06:2. "The Garden has not held such a gathering to see an athletic event in many a day ... it being estimated that there were 6,000 persons in the big amphitheater," reported the *New York Times*. The *Tribune* recorded, "As soon as the doors were opened the 'gallery gods' swarmed up the stairs to their accustomed roosts beneath." At the games of the Dominican Lyceum in early May, E.A. Frey set a time in the 90Yds of 0:09:4, while Keating and William Slade ran the 90Yds three-legged race with a time of 0:10:2, in what was the first race ever at that distance indoors.[24]

* * *

Celtic Park reopened on April 3, and the star of 1910 was Mel Sheppard, who seemingly broke records almost every weekend at Laurel Hill. However, once again the I-AAC refused to compete in the Met AA Cross-Country Championships. The Memorial Day Games suggested to the *New York Times* "a general expectation" that "old records in several events" would be broken. Two world records indeed were, while another was equaled as "Peerless Mel" lowered the time for both Lon Myers' 1880 660Yds and Emilio Lunghi's 700Yds, running the extra 40 yards to make the mark. The *New York Times* scoffed that as Myers had broken the record in a longer ½ Mile race, with a time of 1:11:0 for 600 yards, he wouldn't have taken another ten seconds to cover the extra 60 yards: "'Shep' cannot lay claim to the fact that he is a better athlete."[25]

On June 26, at the Clan na Gael's Games, Sheppard broke Harry Hillman's 550Yds world record. Three weeks later, at another Clan event, he broke Lon Myers' 1881 1,000Yds global best with a time of 2:12:4. He took Lunghi's ⅔ Mile record with a time of 2:45:4 at the Eccentric and Standard Engineers' Association Games on July 31, then, in a special 900Yds race at the Cavan Mens' Games a week later, with Kiviat as pacemaker, he broke the seventh record of his career, slashing three seconds off Andrew Glarner's record with a time of 1:57:2. One wonderful afternoon unfolded on August 14, during the Irish Volunteers Games, as Dan Ahearne finally broke Shanahan's hop, step and jump world record with a distance of 51:02:875, and Sheppard lowered Tommy Burke's world record times at 500, 550 and 600 yards during one single race. He broke his 2/3Mile record again at the Games of the Knights of Columbus, near Newark, on August 20 with a time of 2:44:4. Finally in this astonishing run, at the St. Mary's AC Games in Poughkeepsie, he took Myers' record for the 800Yds, with a time of 1:43:4, failing however to beat Lunghi's ½-Mile mark.[26]

At the same meeting, Flanagan beat Étienne Desmarteau's world record in the "Fifty-Six" with a throw of 39:08:25. But while crowds flocked to see Sheppard, the weight categories were suffering. The *New York Times* observed drily, "The advocates of the abolishment of the hammer throw ... added another point to their contention yesterday at Celtic Park." Problems occurred when spectators encroached onto the field as Flanagan was about to throw:

Flanagan, whirling around, sent the sixteen-pound weight flying through the air. It flew directly at the crowd of people standing on the track and struck a young fellow a glancing blow on the left hip. Fortunately, he spied the missile in the course of its flight, and jumped just in the nick of time. He was removed to St John's Hospital, not very seriously injured but badly scared.[27]

There was also a growing consensus that some records were bogus: "The epidemic of world's records had its continuance yesterday afternoon," commented the *New York Times*, as an unknown, Julian J. Elliot, set the first-ever world record in the 5LB shot, throwing the oversized bullet over 76 feet at the Pastime AC Spring Games. "Never before has such an event been held in the world, and, therefore, the best throw made yesterday was all that was necessary to establish a record." One observer joked, "Perhaps the next time they want a world's record for a set of games they will have a four-and-a-half-pound shot or perhaps a sixteen-and-three-quarter-pound hammer."[28]

The Labor Day "Tailtin Games" also saw two world records broken, with Cloughen lowering Wendell Baker's and Luther Cary's joint 110Yds mark in 10.8 seconds, while Riley, Bromilow, Sheppard and Kiviat set the 2Mile relay record. Disappointingly, Eller's new record in the 250Yds low hurdles went unrecognized as only two timers were present.[29]

* * *

As the major championships approached, the Irish were confident that they'd secure their seventh Met title in a row and retake the Nationals. However, the Irish were stunned on September 10, as the NYAC snatched the Spalding Trophy, 76 to 69. "The enthusiasts of both clubs were on hand to cheer their favorites to victory," observed the *New York Times*. "The Irish-American delegation came up to [Travers] island in two sightseeing automobiles and the lower stand was filled with the 'wearers of the green.' The winged-foot rooters turned out as they never have done before, and the red and white of the Mercury Foot Club was in evidence everywhere. The meet resembled a regular college gathering." Sheppard failed to partake in the 440Yds, leaving Richard Edwards unopposed. Bonhag broke Carter's 5 Mile American record as well as the outdoor marks for 4, and 4½ Miles, while Cloughen (100Yds, 220Yds), McDonald (16LB shot, 56LB weight), Flanagan (16LB hammer), Sheridan (discus), and Brood (javelin) finished first.[30]

Other events would now seriously test the I-AAC's ability to reign in New Orleans. The following day, Flanagan broke the world record for the "Fifty-Six" at the Pastime AC Games, which wasn't recognized, while Bob Eller's 90Yds mark was also dismissed. Within a month, the Limerick athlete "threw a broadside into the ranks of the [I-AAC]" by announcing his decision to return to Ireland following the death of a relative. "'Genial John' says that a relative died recently, leaving considerable property, and that he has the commission to manage the estate," reported the *New York Times*, predicting that this would probably lose the I-AAC ten points at the Nationals.[31]

That was the second bombshell. The first came on September 21 when the *New York Times* reported that Sheppard was quitting the I-AAC. "Amateur athletic circles were somewhat disturbed last night over a rumor ... [Sheppard] would withdraw from membership of the [I-AAC]. Those who are close to the Olympic champion stated last evening that he ... would compete unattached." Reasons given were numerous. The Irish apparently blamed Sheppard for losing the Mets, after arriving late for one event and quitting in another because "the opposing runners beat the gun at the start." Sheppard had countered that the accusations were "unfair: "It was stated that he asked for a vindication or explanation from the Irish-American Club officials, and because it was not forthcoming, he has threatened to withdraw from the club." The newspaper concluded, conveniently, "None of those concerned in the controversy could be found to discuss the rumor last night." Sheppard ran his next meet at Dexter Park, Brooklyn—in which another Sheridan discus record was turned down due to a slope—"unattached," confirming the rumors.[32]

Two days later, Sheppard failed to appear at the I-AAC meeting to discuss the team for New Orleans. Though entered in all his "favorite events," the fallout from the Mets put his competing in doubt:

> It had been anticipated that a rather warm session would be the outcome of the meeting, contingent upon the insistence by Sheppard that some apology be made to him by the club for the supposed slanders which, he said, had been uttered against him. In view of Mr. Sheppard's non-appearance the committee could take no action in the matter, as nothing of an official nature had come to the attention of the club.

Luckily, a lack of quorum prevented the Directors' meeting, and thus the proverbial pouring of more petrol on the fire. A week before the championships, Sheppard declared that he would skip the trip to the Crescent City. The *Times* reported, "He declines to state just what his reasons are, but rumor says he finds a slower application to business more to his liking than hiking around the country winning what to him must now be empty honors." With the absence of Flanagan, Sheppard's withdrawal, the *New York Times* concluded, "more than ruins any chances" of the Irish winning the points trophy. Then came the news that the Commissioner, William Baker, wanted the police athletes to stay (see Chapter 14). It looked like the Irish were sending a skeleton team to the Big Easy.[33]

Suddenly, Sheppard decided to board the steamer *Creole* to New Orleans, with his wife, daughter, and 15 clubmates, with the "apparent ill feeling" between him and the I-AAC forgotten. Conway, other club officials, Sheridan—who had a date at the I-AAC Members Fall Games, where he would once more break the discus world record, at 142:02:0 feet—and the remaining athletes would travel on an "athletes special" train the following Tuesday.[34]

Against the odds, the Irish left New Orleans taking both the junior and senior titles. The former saw the Winged Fist beat Chicago AA, 51–17. The Senior title, in contrast, was by just one point over the NYAC. "By the light of the moon tall Dan Ahern [sic] this evening won the hop, step and jump, and with it the national track and field meet of the [AAU] for his team," reported the *Evening Star*, the battle going down to the wire after Sheridan, Sheppard and McDonald failed to deliver in their events. "In a week which just bristled with exciting periods, the result of which from a team standpoint was in abeyance until the concluding event," said the *New York Times*:

> Never before in the history of National athletics have there be so many upsets, supposed "sure things" going down like ten pins before a sure "strike" man. The Irish and New York AC contingents were kept on the tiptoe of expectancy throughout, and the hop, step and jump, with Dan Ahearn [sic] the winner, and Platt Adams second settled all existing claims in favor of the Irish.

Rosenberger (100Yds) Brodd (javelin), Jack Monument (1Mile), and Eller (220Yds low hurdles) were the other victors. The party returned home over a week later and were met by a large crowd at the landing pier.[35]

The AAU Indoor Championships on November 1 attracted athletes from Canada and across the country. But unlike at New Orleans, the NYAC took the title, beating the Irish, 77–67. "When the battle for team supremacy ... ended last night in the Madison Square Garden," said the *New York Times*, "it was found that the Winged Foot ... had reached the top-most ring of the point ladder just ahead of their Winged Fist rivals." Cloughen (60Yds, 75Yds), Monument (2Mile), Robbins (440Yds hurdles), Dan Ahearne (hop, step and jump), McDonald (24LB shot), and Collins (5Mile) all took top spots.[36]

Surprisingly, given their recent successes, the I-AAC failed to enter the 10Mile AAU Championships at Celtic Park, won by NYAC's "Win" Bailey. Then they performed badly at the National Cross-Country Championships, the NYAC triumphing, 37–51, as Bellars took first place. Yet despite these final disappointments, the Irish completed a fruitful season, their athletes collecting a total of 2,096½ points. Mel Sheppard gathered the most (122), followed by Sheridan with 120, then Ahearne (116) and Flanagan (111). Meanwhile, the *New York Times* claimed a smaller figure of 2,001 points, but added that the I-AAC "had put to its credit a score said to be greater than that of any similar aggregation of athletes during any single year."[37]

The New Year saw Robertson replace Hjertberg—appointed by the Swedish to prepare their athletes for the Stockholm Olympics—while Frank Riley was elected captain, at the club's "annual dinner" at Mouquin's. This was hotly disputed by members who were either not present or couldn't afford to go; Riley was re-elected at a later special meeting.[38]

The club's stars had also grown in 1910. Egon Erickson jumped from Mott Haven in July, giving the club a top high jumper. This was what the *New York Times* reported as "the first of a number of important accessions which the Irish-American AC has in view.... Several pole vaulters of prominence were said to be on the point of signing, and if the club gets the men in view it will have a particularly well balanced team." The national 220Yds champion, Texan Gwynn Henry, joined later, while the "corralling" of the former Mercury Foot middle-distance runner, Harry Gissing, raised eyebrows. Gissing had left the NYAC to compete in England, but then returned to America when things soured, joining the Irish and a threat to bump either Shep, Rosenberger, Pepis or Schaaf from the club's quartet at the Labor Day Games. The *New York Times* commented mischievously, "Several of the clubs hereabout have been dickering for the middle-distance indoor title holder, and it was thought that he would go back to the Winged Foot organization. The wires became crossed, however, and he will from now on be found in the camp of the champion athletic club."[39]

Robertson spelt out his vision for 1911 in an *Evening World* article titled "CHAMPIONS UNDER COVER FOR COMING ATHLETIC SEASON: Irish-American Trainer Says He Will Spring a Few Surprises This Year." "A Couple of new champions will be added to our long list of record-breakers before the coming outdoor season is concluded," Robertson predicted, as he "closed a big book that contained the names of the new athletes and locked it up in the safe." He reflected that while the NYAC had beaten the club in the "Mets," the Irish would return to show "'em a trick or two.... We will have a few new men who are the class—not college athletes, but just a few new and experienced men." The *Evening World* opined that the "Mets" loss came as a "great surprise to followers" of athletics: "The winged-foot organization's unexpected strength sort of upset some of their old rival's best men, and there's a chance that the Irish-Americans didn't train very hard for the games, for they, too, were a greatly strengthened team." Hadn't the club developed Bruno Brodd, Jack Monument and Bob Eller—brother of Jack—into champions virtually overnight? So there was optimism for the new season: "All of the club's old champions say that they are anxious to see the Irish-American AC come back and retake the championship of the district, and most of them will work harder than ever before to get into the best of shape." Shephard was equally sanguine; "I suppose I'll be defeated by most of the boys in the first few races I run," he told the *Evening World*, "but I'll take things easy, the way I did last year—take 'em easy until I get back into shape, and then watch out!"[40]

Six thousand people turned up at the Garden in early February to witness "the pick of the athletic talent of the East, [with] a plentiful sprinkling of college men being seen in the score of events." A month later at the Seventh Regiment Armory, George Bonhag broke John Svanberg's world indoor record for the 3,000m during the Dominican Lyceum Sports, with a time of 8:52:4. On the same night, at the Twenty-Second Regiment Armory, Bob Eller beat the previous record in 65Yds with a time of eight seconds. On the international front, the club's Canadian long-distance runner, Mike Ryan, left for England to compete in the Polytechnic Harriers Marathon Sporting Life Cup on May 27, run from Windsor Castle to Stamford Bridge stadium to find "practically the world's amateur champion." Ryan came second to Surrey AC's Harry Green.[41]

* * *

With Celtic Park open for Gaelic football from April 2, the Decoration Day Games saw the club "endeavoring to corral the leading sprinters of the land for the 125-yard scratch race," with the still unattached Gwynn Henry breaking Sherrill's record over the distance. Two other records were broken: Jack Eller broke George Schwegler's 250Yds hurdles record in 0:29:2, while Dan Ahearne beat his own hop, skip and jump world record with a jump of 50 feet 11 inches. Two weeks previously at the Pastime AC Spring Games, Sheridan had emerged from his short-lived retirement and "showed that his arm had not lost its cunning in respect to discus throwing." At the New York Post Office Clerks' Association Games, at Celtic Park the Sunday prior to Memorial Day, he "demonstrated his competitive worth by snatching victory out of defeat in his last trial by scaling the Grecian missile the hitherto unprecedented distance" of 141:4:375, a new world record. At Willard Park, Paterson, the following month, Sheridan broke the record again with 141:8:5 feet: "There were no crowds near enough to harass the mighty Sheridan, and yesterday's work is said to be but the forerunner of a series of increasing of marks, which will ultimately be put at 150 feet, according to the record holder."[42]

The same month at the NYAC Spring Games, Bonhag lowered Willie Day's 3Mile American time with a record of 14:32. More records went at Celtic Park: On June 1, the Bricklayers and Masons' Union Games hosted Dan Ahearne's new hop, step and jump world best of 51:4:5, while Eller "smashed" the 75Yds low hurdles with a time of 0:09:2. The following month at the Guttenberg Games, he broke the 250Yds hurdles record in a two-man race against J. Malcolmson of the Seattle AC. Jim Rosenberger also overcame Lawson Robertson's mark for the 220Yds by a fifth of a second with a time of 0:22:6. Finally at the Labor Day Games, packed with 10,000 visitors, three world records were broken. In what the *New York Times* described as "probably the greatest mile relay race ever run," the I-AAC quartet of Schaff, Sheppard, Rosenberger, and Gissing—making his debut in the Winged Fist vest, but listed as unattached—broke the club's own world record with a time of 3:20:6. Recent signing Matt McGrath, also officially unaffiliated, broke Flanagan's "Fifty-Six" record with a throw of 38:08:0 feet, while South Paterson's Louis Scott smashed the 5,000m world mark.[43]

The Junior Met title was taken by the Mercury Foot, but the Irish beat the NYAC to take the National Juniors the following week at Forbes Field, Pittsburgh, 37–27. The following day, July 1, Irish athletes broke two records and secured the Seniors for the sixth time in eight seasons, 58–28, over the NYAC. In front of 25,000 onlookers, including the Tyrone-born Pennsylvania Governor, former baseball player and National League President, John K. Tener, Sheppard knocked a second off the 880Yds championship record with a time of 1:54:2, while Abel Kiviat broke the American record for the mile in 4:19:6. Arthur Shaw (120Yds hurdles), McDonald (16LB shot and 56LB weight), Sheridan (discus), Dan Ahearne (hop, step and jump), Bonhag (5Mile), and John Eller (220Yds hurdle) also won their events.[44]

The Met Seniors in September also promised an exciting finale to the season. Although Ahearne and Eller (sprained ankles) and Shaw (as a physician, he was unable to attend) were absent, the Irish took the title with ease, 93–52, against the Mercury Footers. "The meet was made notable by the presence of a number of title holders of bygone days, most of who marveled at the keenness of the competition and the fine work of the contestants," noted the *New York Times*. Meanwhile, the *Sun* criticized the lack of a contest: "The keen fight for the point championship of a year ago was sadly missing." Meyer (100Yds, 220Yds), Sheppard (880Yds), Eller (120Yds hurdles) Kiviat (1Mile), McDonald (16LB shot, 56LB weight), Gissing (440Yds), Ryan (16LB hammer), Brodd (javelin), and Sheridan (discus), came in first in their events.[45]

* * *

The dominance of the two monoliths was attracting increasing scrutiny over their recruitment activities. New York's smaller clubs had lost key members to them and were now using their collective power to change transfer rules. In February, James E. Sullivan gave notice that he wanted to do away with these "practices of a proselytizing type which meet with general condemnation in many circles." Or stir "up a hornet's nest," as Robert Edgren called it.[46]

Conway was cautious, quick to blame any previous unsporting approaches to keeping up with the NYAC: "I am thoroughly in favor of Mr. Sullivan's ideas in relation to the abolishment of the release rule," he told the *New York Times*. "Our organization is ready at once to discontinue reaching out for men who are, or have been aligned with other clubs.... But we have simply been following the lead of a club which is our strongest opponent." He was confident that the I-AAC would develop its own athletes and knew that the chief target of the change—college athletes—was an area, due its proletarian and ethnic roots, that the club rarely capitalized on:

> We are ready and willing to show that we can develop men, and hope the proposition will go through just as suggested. While we have had college men on our roles there has never been a time when we could not do without them. I venture to assert that as many men have been developed under our colors as we have ever obtained through reaching out and picking them up.

Conway claimed that he wanted to see more spreading of points in championships, arguing that if "the little fellows could be assured of having a look-in at the championships," attendances would grow through more cranks from other clubs:

> [T]here is always sure to be a certain amount of jealousy where a man is brought in from some other organization, particularly if he is a good man competitively. On the other hand, where the boys of a club have followed the progress of a lad whose track and field existence has been passed with them there will be found that good fellowship which is so often found wanting when men are gathered from other clubs. I'm for the new rules.

Understandably, the NYAC's Paul Pilgrim argued against any change: "I ... think it would be a bad thing to bring about. Even if we did not want to take up some boy who showed promise, but was aligned with some other school, college or club, I have found times out of number fellows who wanted to become members of the New York AC."[47]

In June, Sullivan spelt out the detail, but even for Conway, it made uncomfortable reading. Rule changes regarding transfers between clubs would force athletes to run unattached for two years. "Both the New York AC and the Irish-American AC are to be condemned for wholesale proselyting," Sullivan told the *New York Times*, "and one is as deep in the mire as the other." Referring to the 1911 Met Junior Championships, where both clubs grabbed 120 of the 162 points available, he spoke of "the futility of the smaller clubs ever getting a look-in." "A fine showing, considering the class arrayed against them" was how the athletics czar described the third-place Mohawks, who bagged just 18 points, adding snidely: "The important feature ... is that the men who scored them were all developed by the Bronx club."[48]

One case—the Swedish runner Alexis Ahlgren, from a small club in the Catholic Athletic League, Ozanam AC—showed the I-AAC's ruthless, and somewhat embarrassing, recruitment practices. Ahlgren was compelled to write an open letter to Conway claiming that on February 9, the Met AA Registration Committee, "against my wishes, transferred me from the Ozanam Association to the [I-AAC].... As you know, I never joined your club, nor represented it, and while I have the greatest respect for it and its members, I will not represent it." The Swede demanded his release so that he could continue representing Ozanam. At an appeal, there emerged no evidence that Ahlgren had ever joined the I-AAC. In fact, Terence Farley, now the Met's Registration Committee chairman, had somehow conned Ahlgren, because he had no knowledge what he was signing. "There was no meeting of the minds, and hence no binding contract."[49]

It took a while, but in September, the 75-club Catholic Athletic League hit back as Farley came up for re-election. "ATHLETIC SKIRMISH ON—Terence Farley Becomes a Bone of contention," was how the *New York Tribune* greeted the campaign. The *New York Times* added that Farley "is bitterly opposed ... by many who feel that they have fared badly at the hands of the committee," while the *Sun* put things more forthrightly: "The Catholic Athletic League ... is out to down Terry Farley, the chairman, on the ground that he is only in the position to further the interests of the Irish-American AC." While the CAL led the field, other smaller clubs, leagues, and the *New York Times* were pushing for Patrick J. Walsh to take Farley's place, claiming he was better suited to "protecting the interests of the smaller clubs from the recruiting agents of the larger clubs."[50]

At a CAL meeting at St. Ann's Hall, Manhattan, on September 8, led by its president, Father Francis Sullivan, the CAL passed a resolution that stated:

> [I]t views with deep concern the possibility of another term of the present committee's chairman, who in our judgement has forfeited all right to the support of those engaged in placing amateur sport upon a higher plane in this district. His decision in the Ahlgren case stamps him as one more anxious to promote his club's athletic supremacy—even if it necessary to pilfer athletes from the smaller clubs—than to further the upbuilding of amateur sport under his jurisdiction....

Although Ahlgren was a member of a non–Met AA-affiliated club, the CAL believed he shouldn't have been transferred without its permission. Conway responded angrily to the accusation: "We are one of the largest athletic clubs in the country and have spent a great deal of time and money in promoting the cause of amateur athletics. We think that our position in the amateur athletic world entitles us to have a representative on the registration committee, and we ask your co-operation in electing him." Conway even accused Father Sullivan of trying to take control of the MA:

> [T]he president of the Catholic Athletic League, in addition to running the [CAL] to suit himself, desires to obtain control of the registration committee, so that his representative can carry out his aims and purposes in the Metropolitan Association. The result will be that instead of the [CAL] being an associate member of the Metropolitan Association, it will control it, and the clubs of the Metropolitan Association will be simply associate members of the Catholic Athletic League.[51]

One hundred reps of the 160 Met AA clubs were expected at the I-AAC Clubhouse, as the *New York Times* observed that "electioneering of the most partisan like nature is being indulged in" by delegates of the "athletic governors who are supposed to guard the interests" of athletes. Conway pleaded for Farley's re-election in a letter: "He has filled that position, we believe with credit and distinction," reiterating that the club's standing in the "amateur athletic world entitles us" to representation. After a "hard fight," Farley was re-elected with 58 votes, along with Walsh and Jacob Stumpf. "Peace and apparent harmony prevailed," the *Sun* noted sarcastically.[52]

While the I-AAC had gotten its way regarding Farley, the AAU abolished athletes switching clubs on a whim at the Hotel Waldorf-Astoria on November 20. The *New York Times* had previously revealed that the new amendment being tabled by the AAU's Legislation Committee would demand that no member "be allowed to compete as a representative of such club in case he has within two years competed as a member of any other club then in this union, unless such other club shall have disbanded or practically ceased to exist, or unless he had taken a bona fide residence in another district of this union."[53]

This was not a rule that affected undergraduates, but struck at the I-AAC's policy of picking up talent from smaller clubs. In his sporting column in the *New York Tribune*, "Herbert" claimed that the rule changes were "a way of correcting an evil which is slowly, but none the less surely, undermining the sport" in America:

> A number of athletes have expressed themselves loudly against these reforms, and some clubs, too, are not in sympathy. I am told that the delegates from the [NYAC] will stand out against the amendments, but this is hard to believe, inasmuch as their adoption would be so plainly a forward step. It has been said that the rules would stand in the way of advancement for athletes and that they would rob a man of his right to join any club he wished. This, however is a fallacy.

As he rightly explained, athletes could still enjoy the benefits of club membership; they just couldn't compete for it, adding that there was "no place" in the sport for athletes who didn't pay for membership: "Seeds of professionalism are sown broadcast by the system of athletic members, which means no dues. If a club cannot get along without buying its athletes it is time for that club to disband."[54]

The two most contentious of the ten proposed changes were the two-year unaffiliated rule and the prevention of school or college students from running with athletic clubs. The first was eventually carried with just a one-year penalty, as the *New York Tribune* acknowledged that the evening proved a disappointment for "those who have worked hard ... to do away with proselyting [sic] and the attending evils" as "out of town" delegates voted down the other motion.[55]

Celtic Park concluded 1911 on October 21 with a four-club meet and a

Gaelic football game between Kerry and Cork. Pat McDonald set a new record, breaking Ralph Rose's 24LB shot with a throw of 38:10:875 feet. The Finn Frans Johansson, "a rangy Swede," won the AAU Junior Cross-Country title for the Irish, while in the Seniors, despite Kramer, now with the Long Island AC, taking first place, the I-AAC won the team prize over the NYAC, 34 to 36. Sheppard missed the race after being operated on for a growth on his neck that interfered with his speech, but news came that Dick Edwards, "one of the best quarter milers in this section of the country" and the 1910 NYAC points winner, was deserting to the I-AAC.[56]

By the time Sullivan picked his All-American Athletic Team, which included Eller (220Yds), Sheppard (880Yds), Bonhag (5Mile), Dan Ahearne (hop, step and jump), McDonald (56LB weight), and Sheridan (discus), a new year and another overseas jaunt to Europe beckoned. However, times were changing. A clampdown on alcohol was growing, championed by those who had successfully shut down New York City on the Lord's Day of rest for decades.[57]

14

"Such shameful spectacles would never be permitted in pious New York"
The I-AAC: Policemen, Politicians and Sabbatarians

One day around the turn of the century, Matt McGrath, wandering north of New York City, thought he had left the dank, grime-ridden, bustling streets for the countryside. Finding a lake and going for a swim, he recalled having himself "a wonderful time jumping and throwing boulders" around the place, feeling he had found the Tipperary he'd left behind.

Sadly, this nirvana was Manhattan's Central Park. He was not in a timeless rural wilderness, but one large, man-landscaped patch of unbuilt New York, which had been opened less than 50 years previously. Things suddenly looked like taking a turn for the worse, because McGrath was spotted swimming by an unimpressed mounted Irish cop. After calling him out, readying himself to arrest the burly athlete for violating city ordinances, he changed his mind upon finding that McGrath was from the auld country, chuckling as he listened to the tale of McGrath's mistake and letting him go with a stern but not too serious warning.[1]

McGrath pledged then that he would become a cop. He joined the NYPD in 1902, rising to the rank of inspector and heading Manhattan's traffic control. He saved at least three people from drowning while off-duty—including a jumper in the freezing East River—captured a murderer by attacking his barge "with a deadly rain" of bricks until he gave up, and almost got fired when during "some personal dispute," as the *New York Times* described it, he failed "to count ten before pulling the trigger of his revolver."[2]

* * *

Matt McGrath pictured here in police uniform sometime between 1915 and 1920. McGrath was one of a multitude of I-AAC athletes who were also policemen (Library of Congress).

Amongst the I-AAC's athletes were a large number of policemen; and amongst the "whales," only Pat Ryan was an exception, working instead as a foreman of a gang of Italian laborers. Martin Sheridan became a cop in 1906 and fast-tracked as bodyguard to the Governor whenever he visited the city. Pat McDonald joined in 1905, working as a traffic cop out of Times Square, where his "figure and County Clare brogue became as familiar as the Knickerbocker Hotel, Shanley's, the Victoria Theatre and Dowling's," while Flanagan had signed up two years earlier, the *New York Tribune* commenting at the 1903 AAU All-Around Championship Weight Throwing Championship, "Flanagan has become a policeman since his last exhibition at the park and yesterday he looked as though the position was agreeing with him, for he has grown very fat."[3]

This was hardly surprising. As Hasia R. Diner writes, a cop "may have been the most visible job associated with Irish men" in a city where as early as 1855, 27 percent of its cops were born in Ireland. This perception was to continue for the next 100 years, according to Andrew T. Darien: "The public face of the NYPD in the first half of the twentieth century was a large, burly, tough, blue-collar, Irish man. Some Italian, Jewish Polish, Greek, and other Eastern and Southern European men secured police jobs, but their whiteness afforded them a relatively quiet assimilation and did little to change the public's generally positive view of its officers."[4]

So dominant was this "Irish ideology" within the NYPD that according to Darien, ethnic fraternity groups—the Jewish Shomrin Society in 1924 and the Italian Columbia Association in 1932—never threatened it until the Black Guardians, founded in 1943, led to the formation of the Emerald Society ten years later:

> Previously, Irish identity had been normalized in the NYPD; so many police officers were Irish that it made little sense for them to form a fraternal organization. Irish officers had little difficulty getting white officers of German, Jewish or Italian backgrounds to join the "Irish parade." But the Guardians presented a new threat to whiteness in general and Irish identity in particular.[5]

However, this stereotype of the "Irish cop" was also taken "from the mythlike characters of the Irish Whales," according to Margaret Hennessey. With the *New York Times* claiming in 1916 that out of the 11,000 city cops, 4,000 were athletes and "fully 1,000 could win high athletic honors if they entered the best amateur or professional ranks," a myth grew that all the I-AAC's top athletes were indeed police. In an article from October 1907, titled "POLICE ATHLETES; Many Members of New York Force World Champions," the *New York Tribune* said:

> A large proportion of New York's guardians of the law are of Irish nationality, and the "wearers of the green" generally make fine athletes, especially if they have a strain of American blood. The Irish seem to show most prominently in the weights, long distance running and jumping. Three of General Bingham's men hold world's championships in the weights. Every one of them is a giant.[6]

The NYPD has a long history of Irish athletes. The wrestler Bill Muldoon found the post of cop ideal for a working class athlete retaining his amateur status. He helped organize the Police Athletic Club, which stumbled along for two decades. In 1903, the *Sun* argued that a reorganized PAC could become a potent force: "There are not many Flanagans on the force, but there are perhaps two score men who could be a credit to any athletic club." The new Police Athletic Association often held its annual events at Celtic Park. The *Gaelic American* wrote of the 1906 NYPD games at the American League ballpark, that 95 percent of the competing athletes were "Celts": "[I]f some one said that it was an athletic event held under the auspices of the [I-AAC] he would not be far wrong."[7]

Subsequently Flanagan and Sheridan became the public faces of the force. At the 1906 I-AAC Winter Carnival, a NYPD deputy commissioner reportedly turned to Victor Dowling as Flanagan threw his weight, asking, "Is that lump of lead 56 pounds weight?" When told yes, he continued:

> Then I see a way to save the city money. The Police Department now pays $5 apiece for axes, $2 for jimmies and $3 for picks for use in raiding pool-rooms and gambling joints. I'll recommend that John Flanagan and Martin Sheridan ... should be detailed as a battering ram squad. I'd like to see the door that would stand a wallop of that 56-pound thrown by either of these men. It wouldn't cost the city a cent and would keep both men in training.[8]

In 1904, the *New York Tribune* ran an article titled "Athletic 'Cops'" which covered the New York cops' sporting skills: "[There is no] winner more popular with the crows than the man who 'hammers the pavement' most of the day, and keeps his muscles in shape with dumbbells, Indian clubs or weight machines in a corner of the station house dormitory." NYPD commissioner William McAdoo claimed that a policeman could never have too much athletic training: "The men of the force who do and dare in the many ways in the line of duty know that their efforts will be recognized at Headquarters."[9]

By 1907, one Pennsylvania newspaper claimed that New York was now credited with having "more athletes on her police force" than any other city on earth:

> It seems now that the typical fat, sluggish policeman is bound to go. In his place will come the quick, agile, officer trained to decide and act promptly when called upon.... It is generally admitted that the trained athlete is quicker witted and better adapted to cope with emergencies than the man whose only training has been obtained from books, or the man who has nothing except brute strength. The trained athlete has more control over his temper and his muscles.[10]

The disproportionate number of members included the "Lightning" or "Athletic" Cop, Mike Cregan, John Joyce, William Keating, Jack Eller, George Bonhag, Emil Muller, Billy Frank and John W. Kelly. When Kelly, a traffic cop around Broadway and 46th Street, won the Met AA All-Around Middleweight Championships at the Order of Scottish Clans Games in 1913, the *New York Times* reported:

Kelly showed his athletic prowess ... at Celtic Park a week or so ago, and in the doing helped to add to the fame of those sons of the Ould Sod who have made their presence felt in American athletics. Several years ago he was "a broth of a bye," and, like most of his husky track and field contemporaries on the "forse," he learned at that time the inklings of athletics.

When Joyce was appointed a patrolmen, his precinct commander, Captain Shevlin, proudly told the *New York Tribune*, "I guess I've got one man now who can catch any thief he runs after."[11]

It wasn't just athletes that the I-AAC had as police members. William Prendergast was a cop for 11 years until his sudden resignation in July 1907, when the *Sun* ran the headline: "Rich Policeman Resigns." Prendergast had speculated on Long Island property, especially a large tract of marsh land outside of Flushing that he picked cheaply with a partner, while also possessing property in Sunnyside now wanted by the Pennsylvania Railroad: "On the question of wealth he was dumb yesterday, devoting all his attention to the motormen and passengers on the trolley of Loop 7 at the New York end of the bridge. 'Sure I have nothing to say about it. That's me words; can't tell you nothing about it,' he said to questioners." The sentiment of his colleagues was: "Did you ever see an Irishman before who wouldn't talk about himself in a thing like that," and that his wealth was around $100,000, "a regular fox when it comes to spotting out thirty acres of land or so that look like pretty dingy pickings at the time but bring in a profit around the $100,000 mark five years later."[12]

Inevitably questions were asked about "easy jobs." News broke in July 1910 that Sheridan, Flanagan and McGrath, previously patrolmen, who had been moved to the mayor's marshal's office, suddenly found themselves back pounding the streets. "When the transfers were announced at Headquarters the only reason given was 'for the good of the service.'" Indeed, the light duties afforded to famous athletes led to suggestions of shamateurism, akin to what was later witnessed in Eastern Bloc countries. The NYPD was sensitive to accusations of "phony" posts, and within weeks, the *New York Tribune* ran the headline: "FLANAGAN LEAVES FORCE: Transfer to Patrol Duty Did Not Suit Hammer Thrower." It continued, "For a long time Flanagan was assigned to special duty at the City Hall, and when he was transferred to patrol duty last month he found it was impossible for him to continue his athletic training: He said last night that he planned to go to Toronto, Canada, and go into business with his brother." Sheridan declared that he too was handing in his badge, having allegedly "had a very good business offer from a Western concern," according to the *New York Times*, and was considering taking it up."[13]

While the pair were in the autumns of their careers, this news came as a setback to the I-AAC. Perhaps strings were pulled, but Flanagan and Sheridan were soon promoted back to less arduous positions. The other athletes weren't as fortunate: In mid-season, John Eller found himself being dragged by a runaway grey horse on 125th Street that left his uniform "torn to ribbons." At his station he "convinced the lieutenant in charge that he had better go home." Cut and bruised, he suffered no serious injuries and "declined the ministrations of a police surgeon."[14]

There were other dubious practices, hardly surprising in a force so dominated by the Irish that a shared ethnicity trumped everything as much as blood trumped water, as clean cops never exposed dirty colleagues. Stories surfaced of I-AAC athletes getting favorable treatment if arrested. Katchen wrote about the time Pat Ryan got into a spot of bother "letting off steam," when Robertson and some Tammany politicians persuaded a magistrate to let him off with a reprimand. Unfortunately, still half-cut, Ryan didn't take kindly to the admonishment. When asked if he had anything to say, he replied, "You can go plumb to hell. This case is all fixed." The magistrate shook his head and sent Ryan to another night in the slammer.[15]

An *Evening World* article of 1906, titled "ATHLETIC 'PULL' BEATS A JUDGE'S," seemed to confirm this uncomfortable relationship. It began: "A Supreme Court Justice is a big man in this town, so is the head of a city department, but when it comes to having influence with a policeman greater than either or both of these is the President of the Irish-American Athletic Club." Conway was out in a "big red touring car" with Edward S. Murphy, the city's Superintendent of Buildings, George Cahill, and "a dignified Justice of the Supreme Court," possibly Dowling, when a "vigilant policeman held up the party." Murphy tried to placate the cop by apologizing for speeding and showing his "ornate badge" identifying himself as "a city official and ___." "Aw-w-w," growled the cop, "so you've got one of them tins, too, eh? Where they come from is more than I know." "That's right, officer, do your duty," interrupted the Justice, feeling uneasy, "You are sworn to uphold the laws and should be protected in so doing, but really this is embarrassing because I happen to be a Judge of the Supreme Court and ___." "Now, here," replied the cop, "quit yer kiddin'. Youse can't kid me. I've had many's the drink in your saloon." Falling about laughing, Cahill offered him his card, saying "I'll think you'll find ___" which was met by an increasingly irate: "I'll take nothing," Conway tentatively tried his luck: "See here, Bill," said Conway, "I guess you're all right at that. I'm the president of the Irish American Athletic Club, and I ___." "How are you?" shouted the cop, sticking out his hand. "I see by the papers that Flanagan and Sheridan and the other thirteen cops in your club is doin' fine in the games. If I can get off I'll be over to the park next Sunday. Run along now, and don't let that oil wagon run away with you."[16]

Not everyone in the Police Department was happy with this coziness. Indeed the force's hierarchy was averse to losing cops to athletics, and in 1908 its chief, Theodore A. Bingham, refused permission for Eller, Sheridan and Flanagan to go to the Canadian Championships at Montreal. William F. Baker, commissioner from 1909 to 1910 and future owner of the Philadelphia Phillies, was keen to emphasize that the NYPD was created to fight crime, not house athletes, denying permission to any officer to attend the 1910 National Championships, telling the *New York Times*:

> Under no conditions will I grant any New York policeman a leave of absence for such a purpose. I might consider an absence from duty of twelve hours, but for one which would require the time for a trip to New Orleans, a stopover and return, that's out of the question. No, the men cannot go, even if it was during their vacation time, for police regulations read that a man leaving New York must get permission from headquarters, and I have received no such request. When a man gets permission to leave New York the fact is posted in every station house so that 8,500 men can read, and each wants to know why special favors are granted certain men who are athletically inclined.[17]

The I-AAC would have five athletes missing, including Flanagan, who had gone to Ireland following the death of a relative. Although they lost Matt McGrath, the NYAC had a strong chance to win its first title since 1903. Suspicions were raised that they had somehow gotten Baker, a man accused of interfering in the investigation of gambling in the city, to cripple the Irish-Americans. The city's mayor, William J. Gaynor, told the *New York Times* that he wouldn't intervene, despite receiving a request from James E. Sullivan, stating: "[T]hese are the type of policemen that I know you want to encourage. If all our policemen were athletes the force would be of a high standard." Baker was perhaps asserting his authority, and a more credible counter-argument was that the I-AAC got their contacts at Tammany Hall to order him to retract his edict.[18]

* * *

While the I-AAC's main aim was amateur athletics, its ownership of Celtic Park, and the heavy reliance on the fees from Irish county associations and "Old-World" political organizations, made it impossible to distance itself from Irish politics. Athletic meetings with political connections stretched back to the first club. In 1880, the *New York Herald* organized an event in aid of the "Irish Relief Fund" for the 1879 famine at Madison Square Garden, deemed sufficiently apolitical to entice the Knickerbocker AC, the Union Boat Club and the Scottish-American AC to compete with the I-AAC. Later, when Irish politics moved from the "constitutional" IPP to "physical force," the I-AAC was on hand to help raise dollars, its clubhouse hosting the first Sinn Féin meeting in the city, presided over by none other than Daniel Cohalan himself in August 1907. The proceeds from the "Field Day" commemorating 900 years since the Battle of Clontarf in April 1914, where Padraig

Pearse was due to "deliver an address," were handed over to the future GPO martyr's St. Enda's College. The club had also raised $4,000 for Douglas Hyde's Irish Language Fund eight years earlier.[19]

Celtic Park became home to more events mixing sport and politics than would be comfortable today. At the 1902 Thanksgiving Games, the guest of honor was a Texan Colonel, John Blake, who had led the heavily Irish "Foreign Legion" in the Boer War against the British, while an IRB Veterans Association Games at the 69th Regiment Armory was organized "under the auspices" of the I-AAC. In the summer of 1914, the I-AAC offered Celtic Park for a huge picnic on August 9, and proposals were made to hand over Celtic Park on Labor Day to the Irish National Volunteers Fund Committee. There was nothing hidden about the destination of funds raised. The committee's treasurer, Dennis A. Spelissy, read a cablegram from Ireland at a meeting stating, "arms and ammunition was the help they wanted from their friends in America." The *Gaelic American* claimed that these events were "for the purpose of augmenting the fund which is being raised in New York to arm the men of Ireland.... Those present at the meeting were extremely grateful to the Irish-American Athletic Club for its generosity in placing Celtic Park at the disposal of the committee, free of charge." Indeed, McGowan opines that "it does appear that much of the money that the Clan-na-Gael raised to finance the Easter Rising, came from the admission charged at the gate of Celtic Park."[20]

Two years later in July 1916, the entire net proceeds from the Galway Men's Association Games was sent to Ireland "for the relief of the war sufferers" following the Easter Rising. The I-AAC Independence Day Games attracted 6,000 spectators; Evelyn Plunkett, the sister of one of the executed, Joseph Plunkett, attended. Proceeds were turned over to the Irish Relief Fund. "A flag of the Irish Republic which was carried in the recent Irish rebellion in Dublin attracted much attention at the park," observed the *New York Times*, while the *Sun* said:

> The spirit of revolt that caused the recent Irish rebellion flared up again in New York yesterday.... [As Plunkett] pulled the rope that sent the white, green and gold piece of bullet torn cloth to the top of the flag pole, the band struck into "Ireland a Nation Once Again." Simultaneously 6,000 loyal sons of Erin tore down the fences in front of the grandstand in their eagerness to get nearer to the emblem.[21]

Less controversial political events were hosted. In 1906, William Randolph Hearst was given a "riproarious" reception by 15,000 spectators at a game between Cork and Tipperary, while campaigning to become Governor of New York. Patrons rushed onto the field before a ten-foot fence in front of the grandstand was knocked down, as "jerseyed football players dropped the game and made a rush for him." The *Sun* wrote:

> The whole crowd lost interest ... and surged around him, sweeping the police off their feet and dragging the candidate from grand stand to field and back again.... Hundreds of husky Irishmen, yelling at the top of their voices, broke through the thin police hedge around Hearst, knocked the cops to one side and amused themselves by slapping the candidate on the back, good hard slaps, that made Mr. Hearst wince a bit.

The *New York Times* reported that several people were injured, including women. "That his clothes were not torn off by the good-natured crowd, he had to thank Capt. Hayes and his policemen. He could not take off his hat, but he was not so hampered that he could not smile right and left."[22]

* * *

Connections with the Irish-dominated Tammany Hall "machine" extended far deeper than beat cops. Clearly the Irish-American Athletic Club needed to have some political friends, especially where any sporting enterprise's functionality relied on local government goodwill. But in this case, political friends were more than expedient, illustrated when "Big Tim" Sullivan and Conway got together to organize trains to Philadelphia for the Jack Johnson-O'Brien fight in 1909.[23]

As a lower-middle or working class immigrant club, most members were not wealthy, and athletes needed "jobs" that could accommodate training. Sometimes they involved little actual work, such as the post Conway secured for Johnny Hayes at Bloomingdale's. When he announced that he was going to London, his employer "granted him leave of absence with full pay." Joseph Reilly, following his victory at the 1908 Olympics, claimed that Hayes was "one of the most capable and energetic workers" there, adding that as work "kept him indoors all day, he had been compelled to do all his training at night." But there was another story: Following his Yonkers Marathon victory in November 1907, Hayes left the St. Bartholomew AC for the Irish-Americans, not only for their better facilities, but also their better political connections. He needed time to train and an income to supplement it. Conway dismissed any thought of Hayes continuing his work in the sewers, where being knee-deep in water would hamper his chances in London. Instead, he secured him a "dry job" at the department store as a messenger or a shipping clerk, being photographed training on the store's roof. In reality, he just collected his wages. As John Bryant wrote, "[F]rom the moment Johnny stopped being a sandhog, he became a full-time athlete." Upon winning gold, the Bloomingdale Brothers promoted Hayes to the manager of the sporting goods department. He didn't need it; soon afterwards he turned professional.[24]

The club's directors also suggested close links with local government and judiciary. The *Evening World*, in early 1908, claimed that Conway spent too much time with the city's leaders to be considered an "ordinary Joe" anymore. A bout of gout he was suffering was blamed on a bad combination of two contrasting indulgences: Corned beef and cabbage, washed down with champagne. Speaking to a reporter over a glass of Lithia water, Conway sighed, "In the days of my youth, when I was a care free gossoon skipping lightly over the turf on the estate at my ancestors in Ireland little did I think I'd ever have the gout." This was a nutritious dish, Conway explained, that "makes a man supple and vigorous," and added that some of the I-AAC's top athletes "train" on it: "I have eaten enough of it in my time to fill an ocean liner and it never did a bit of harm to me until I began to take champagne on the side." Conway argued that the French wine had no place alongside this Irish dish, regretting now ever being introduced to the drink, which replaced the beer he previously drank: "The politicians downtown are opening wine all the time and they got me into the habit.... As soon as I get well again I'm going to cut out champagne The simple life for P.J. Conway ... with corned beef and cabbage taken in moderation six or eight times a week."[25]

Conway tried hard to get into the Tammany inner coterie, but without much success. In 1909, Charles F. Murphy was urged to back "Pay-Jay" to replace Thomas F. Foley as New York County Sheriff. Years later in 1914, when Conway was proposed as a U.S. Marshal, the *New York Times* claimed that he broke with Murphy for turning him down: "Conway has a strong following among the Irish societies, but there is no particular political influence behind him." In the same year, he became the head of the Democratic Athletic League, an organization that was pushing the re-election of Governor Martin H. Glynn, and furthering the political career of NYAC president, and Tammany member, Bartow S. Weeks.[26]

Other senior members of the club were more successful. The club's attorney, Victor James Dowling, was described by the *Brooklyn Daily Eagle* as someone who "in his youthful days, [was] quite an athlete himself ... it is but natural that he would take a special interest in athletic doings now." Born in New York City in 1866, he became a successful lawyer and Democrat ward leader and was tipped as a possible mayor and even a candidate for Governor, suggested as an alternative to John Alden Dix in 1912. State Assemblyman for the New York County's Sixteenth District in 1894 until ousted by the Republican Charles Steinberg, he was re-elected to Albany as Senator for the 18th District in 1900 and served four terms between 1901 and 1904. Fellow Senator and Assemblyman George Washington Plunkitt wrote of him: "He knows the Latin grammar backward. What's strange, he's a sensible young fellow, too. About once in a century we come across a fellow like that in Tammany politics."[27]

Shortly after leaving the Senate in 1905, Dowling was promoted to the New York City Supreme Court. The *Evening World*, writing of his initial day, gushed about "the tributes of innumerable political religious and social organizations," foremost being the Irish organizations and athletic clubs in New York: "The Greater New York Irish Athletic Association's floral offering took the form of a horseshoe taller than Justice Dowling himself. It bore the initials 'GNYIAA,' and occupied a conspicuous place among the van load of fragrant flowers."[28]

Another "Tammany sachem and loyalist" who served as a director and the "power" on the club's Finance Committee was Daniel Cohalan. Like Dowling, he rose to Supreme Court Justice in June 1911, named by Dix to fill James O'Gorman's departure to the U.S. Senate. On his first day he was presented with a gravel with the I-AAC emblem and its motto, "Strong Hand Forever," by club secretary John J. Manning, who declared, "In presenting the gravel, Your Honor, we are proud of your Irish lineage, prouder still of your American spirit, but proudest of all of that fearlessness and unswerving adherence to your convictions of right, for which we know you so well, and which more than all else maketh a just Judge." Cohalan replied with a short speech: "I thank you, gentlemen of the Irish-American Athletic Club for the honor you have done me and wish that the club may go on growing in strength and reputation."[29]

Victor J. Dowling was another high-ranking politician on the I-AAC's Board of Directors. He was a judge, State Assemblyman and State Senator (Library of Congress).

John Cloughen, the father of Robert Cloughen, was New York City's Commissioner of Public Works and was elected for just three days in 1909 by the Board of Alderman as Manhattan Borough President, to oversee the removal of John F. Ahearn for corruption. At the I-AAC, Cloughen was the Chairman of the Athletic Committee, and the *Evening World* remarked on his death in 1911, "he helped that organization to hold its place as leader in the athletic field." Reportedly born in County Monaghan in 1849, Cloughen emigrated in 1851 and after a basic education became an apprentice plumber and ran a contracting firm, before moving into politics. At the I-AAC,

Cloughen also stood out from most of his peers—if not from the athletes—by being an Irish-born Protestant in an executive heavily comprised of Catholics. His funeral was held at a Lutheran Church and he was buried in Brooklyn's predominantly Protestant Green-Wood Cemetery.[30]

Other minor local political figures included Justice John R. Davies, a former noted athlete and Alderman nominated to the city's Supreme Court in 1914; John C. Fleming, a Killarney-born building contractor who occupied adjoining pews at Manhattan's St. Ignatius Loyola RC Church to Mayor Hugh J. Grant, and described as one of Tammany Hall's "old guard" when he died in 1910; George Murray Hulbert, Congressman for New York's 21st District; Thomas J. Dunn, one-time New York County Sheriff; the magistrate Henry A. Brann; and Lieutenant P.J. McGuire. Then there were two lawyers, Anthony J. Barrett and Terence Farley. Chief of the Transfer Tax Bureau of the Surrogates Court in New York County before being the Law Assistant to the city's courts, Barrett was also Chairman of the I-AAC's Athletic Committee, elected national President of the Irish Federation of the United States in 1916, and wrote under the nom de plume of "Walter Fortescue." Farley was possibly the brother of New York County Sheriff Thomas "Big Tom" Farley, who would become embroiled in the Seabury Investigations of 1930–1931 into New York's police and judicial corruption, and was also later claimed to be connected to the club in a 1932 lawsuit.[31]

James J. Frawley, the nephew of the former Tax Commissioner Edward Sheehy, was probably the best-known I-AAC politician, giving his name to the 1911 "Frawley Act" that semi-legalized boxing in the state. A former plasterer and then building contractor, he was one of the first men elected to the GNYIAA Executive Committee in 1898. He became Tammany Hall's youngest district leader, heading the 32nd Assembly District four years later, while also acting as an AAU boxing referee. After he was briefly accused of "bribery and aiding and abetting false registration and illegal voting" and threatened with arrest along with a John J. Dietz and another man known as "Schemer" Ryan, charges were dropped, and he was elected to the State Senate in 1903, replacing Thomas F. Donelly of the 20th District. Frawley married twice: He obtained a divorce from his first wife, Miriam Morris, in 1905 and married Lillian Gannon a year later, a public disclosure that caused Frawley to get "much excited," according to his *New York Times* obituary.[32]

In 1907, Frawley first proposed allowing legal amateur sparring. Contests, he suggested, should be under the jurisdiction of the Metropolitan AA—he had been on the Board since 1900—and in April 1911, he succeeded in getting a State Athletic Committee to supervise boxing by licensing clubs, forcing participants to obtain a physician's certificate, and banning alcohol sales at events. The "Frawley Act" came under pressure from the start by reformers, following a riot at Madison Square Garden in August 1911. Sup-

14. "Such shameful spectacles"

Club director James J. Frawley (*second from right*), most famous for putting his name to the law that legalized boxing in New York in 1911 (Library of Congress).

porters for its abolition included fellow Democrat, Governor Dix, who the *New York Times* reported saying that Frawley had agreed that the law "had not come up to his expectations." Frawley, however, hit back: "It is true that I told him that if it was shown to me that the new law would not eventually accomplish what it was intended to do I would not oppose legislation for its repeal. I have not yet been convinced that it will not elevate the sport."[33]

Conway agreed and wrote to the State Senate about his concerns over re-banning boxing, "pleading that a law which encouraged the manly art of self-defense should be kept on the statute books of the State."[34] Frawley left the Senate in 1915, succeeded by Irving J. Joseph, and his act was finally repealed in February 1917. Ostensibly this followed the death of the fighter Young McDonald, but the Republicans had for three years stated their intention to eliminate the NYSAC, claiming it was merely a cover for Tammany aficionados. Governor Charles S. Whitman finally declared to the *New York Times*, "In the interest of public morals, I deem it my duty … to ask for the repeal of this statute."[35]

* * *

"Moralists" had thwarted boxing in New York for the best part of the previous century, but that wasn't their only concern. They were a potent force that the I-AAC, no matter how many cops or friends in the Senate they had, couldn't control. The club found themselves embroiled in one of the major social polemics—alongside prohibition and gambling—of the day, with Celtic Park as a major battleground: Whether the Lord's Day of Rest should be allowed to be desecrated by the sounds of people cheering on sportsmen and actors.

The campaign to keep Sunday free from such idolatry—known as "Sabbatarianism"—affected every kind of working class sporting and theatrical entertainment, and was detested by New York's mostly non-WASP population. As early as the 1880s, when the future New York mayor, Seth Low, then Brooklyn's leading politician, learned that immigrant communities wanted "taprooms" open on Sunday afternoons—their only day of leisure—he was prepared to allow taverns to operate as long as they appeared closed.[36]

A report from the *Evening World* in 1907 noted that a quarter of a million German-Americans and labor unionists were mobilizing to demand the repeal of "Blue Laws" and the enactment of one "in keeping with the spirit of the times" that no longer deprived "men of the enjoyment of liberty." Katchen writes that the Irish and Jews, despite rivalry and mutual suspicion, both shared "an aversion ... to WASP urban reformers' campaigning against Sunday sin." For the Irish, Sabbatarianism was "a war against a poor man's recreation, including outings at Celtic Park," while Jews, having Saturday as their Sabbath, saw it as "an attack against their meager livelihoods."[37]

Late-nineteenth century America was riddled by interference in Sunday sport, stretching from baseball to Gaelic football. Indeed, Sabbatarianism had prevented Meyer Prinstein from adding to his Olympic medal haul. Representing Syracuse University at the 1900 Olympics in Paris, he was the favorite for gold in both the long and triple jumps. His dream was scuppered by SU's decision, as an affiliate of American Methodist universities, to prevent athletes competing on the Sabbath. It didn't matter that Prinstein was Jewish; he couldn't compete on the final day of the long jump. Meanwhile, his chief rival, University of Pennsylvania's Alvin Kraenzlein—a Christian—overtook Prinstein, reneging on a reported deal to abstain. Reports came back that Prinstein was so infuriated by the double-cross that he either punched, or was restrained from punching Kraenzlein, when he refused to compete in a "jump-off" the following day.[38]

As for the I-AAC, Sunday was not only the one day it could count on for drawing huge crowds to Celtic Park, but the day most of their athletes could get off work to compete. An example of this was the club's failure to gather enough men for a team at the Met Cross-Country Championship in February 1909, due to the race being held on a Saturday. But while Tammany-appointed judges, many Irish-American, were either apathetic or openly hostile to moralists, this counted for little. While the warriors of Sabbatarianism never wrecked Celtic Park like they did the ICAU's Yonkers project, they tried their best. An October 1902 day of athletics and Gaelic games, hosted by the "Irish Athletes of America," was suddenly threatened by the arrival of 14 of New York's finest. A complaint had been received from a small organization called "The Law and Order Society," and as the *Sun* reported, Captain Anthony Woods and Detective J.J. Rooney "marched" into Celtic Park with their "force of bluecoats" half an hour before the games began, depositing themselves near the finish line of the 100Yds race.

> The attitude of the men in uniform attracted the attention of the spectators, who anticipating the raid, began to have fun with the policemen. A crowd of 2,000 persons surrounded the inclosure and very soon five athletes toed the mark for the 100-yard race, confined to members. With the crack of the pistol sending the runners on their way, Capt. Woods, followed by his men, broke through the gateway to the field inside, and when George B. Goerwitz dashed across the line a winner he was placed under arrest.

Goerwitz, Celtic Park's manager Joseph T. McKane, and games organizer Andrew J. Dargan were taken to Long Island City in a tramcar, where they were arraigned and charged with violating sections 264 and 267 of the Penal Code, before being bailed out for $500 apiece, courtesy of Dennis Gilroy. At Celtic Park, the *New York Times* noted, "the unpleasant incident was soon forgotten in the excitement attending several close finishes in the track events," as the rest of the day continued. The *Sun* added, "No sooner had the guardians of the law turned their backs on Celtic Park than the regular program of ten open events was reeled off."[39]

Of course the next stop was a visit in front of a magistrate, where things got more interesting. The presiding judge was none other than Luke J. Connorton, a second-generation Irishman who detested Sabbatarianism, while defending the arrested was Dowling. Connorton seemed keen to conclude matters quickly. Neither asking for any proof or speaking to the defendants, he dismissed every charge, agreeing with Dowling's opinion that "athletic games on Sunday, when participated in by members of an organization such as amateurs of the Athletic Union, would cause no breach of public peace, and as there was no disturbance in the neighborhood the games were entirely within the law."[40]

Opponents thought such a test case would see off the Sabbatarians, with Conway celebrating the decision at the AAU offices, believing police harassment would cease. The *New York Tribune* hailed it as "a decision that may materially affect" sport clubs in the state that hosted Sunday sport. "It is possible now that this decision will prohibit further interference with cross-country runs, golf matches, bicycle races and other events that are usually scheduled on Sunday for those that are unable to take part in such club pastimes during the week," was how *Sporting Life* thought things would pan out. While hurling returned to Celtic Park the following Sunday with an "unusually fast and dexterous" and, more crucially, uninterrupted game between the Meaghers and Dalys, this was to prove presumptuous and optimistic.[41]

A year later, police were back marching into Celtic Park during the Annual Field Day of The Irish Volunteers. In front of 2,000 spectators, two cops from the same 75th precinct that had turned up the previous year, arrested the referee of a Gaelic football match that was a preliminary to the 1904 Olympics. "The moment Charles O'Connor, as umpire, put the ball in play, Police Officers Kennedy and Donnelly ... placed the umpire under arrest for violating the Sabbath Law," reported the *New York Times*. The GNYIAA argued that as no one was charged, no law was broken; but by coincidence, Connorton was at the game and immediately set up an "impromptu session" that bailed out O'Connor until the following Thursday, when the case would be heard in Long Island City. Unlike the previous incursion, the participants abandoned the game, moving onto what the *New York Times* called an "indignation meeting" where patrons denounced Commissioner Francis V. Greene for the arrests.[42]

In 1905, the Manhattan-based Sabbath Observance Society forced the NYPD back to Celtic Park, arresting Robertson, Hjertberg and a ticket seller. The trio were charged with "alleged violation of the Sunday Laws." Connorton once again handled the case, and once more he dismissed it, scathingly asking the rhetorical question of where exactly the SOS was located: "Let them stay over there and attend to their own business," he suggested angrily, before criticizing the local police, demanding that they should "attend to any violators of the law ... without assistance from societies in Manhattan." They soon forgot his advice. On July 10, police arrested the organizers of the Claremen's Patriotic Benevolent and Social Association Games.[43]

A year later in April 1906, the arrival of two detectives to stop a Gaelic football match organized for the victims of the San Francisco earthquake, between Queens County and Kildare, almost caused a riot when they arrested the referee and the two team captains. Infuriated, spectators "made a rush for the cops with the tender morals," and only through the intervention of "some men of prominence who advised letting the law ... take its course" were they saved from harm. The *Evening World* said sarcastically, "'What?' said these conservators of the city's morals, 'a football game on Sunday? And for charity? Fie, fie!'" The pair had even descended on Celtic Park after "passing in the great and viriuous haste several saloons that were open in violation of the excise law." At Long Island City Police Station, according to the *Evening World*, an exacerbated Connorton "gave vent to a few remarks" about "the overwhelming intelligence" of the police. Back at Celtic Park, the game continued.[44]

Newspapers occasionally ran a disclosure that the authorities were finally getting tough: "Entertainment, as it has come to be understood in this city, will be limited next Sunday. Besides attending church adn [sic] Sabbath school, New Yorkers may ride on the rapid transit lines or stay at home," declared the *New York Times* in December 1907. Some form of clarity was given by Justice James O'Gorman's decision in the New York City Supreme Court concerning a suit called the "Hammerstein Case." "The law is plain, and there can be no excuse for laxity in its observance and enforcement," he announced, adding, "all performances in theatres or other places of public amusement and entertainment on Sunday are prohibited." He concluded:

> The law is well established in the State of New York that the Christian Sabbath is one of the civil institutions of the state, and that for the purpose of protecting the moral and physical wellbeing of the people and preserving the peace, quiet and good order of society the Legislature has authority to regulate its observance and prevent its desecration by appropriate legislation.

The man charged with enforcing the law, Theodore Bingham, was ready to do its bidding: "Under Justice O'Gorman's decision I have no alternative except to continue to enforce the Sunday law ... and we will go right on with the same strict rule every Sunday until the present law is repealed or amended." He even singled out the I-AAC: "The Sunday athletic exercises at Celtic Park make a fine, clean show. But the decision cuts it out."[45]

O'Gorman's decree was largely ignored by everyone except perhaps baseball. For the I-AAC, it took another eight years before the cops returned. This time a schoolboy athlete from Holy Cross Lyceum, Jeremiah Gorman, one of 150 competitors running in a "novice road race," had his collar felt by Sergeant John Casey and was handed a summons, as a number of Irish-American politicians, including Congressman Peter J. Dooling, State Senator Thomas McManus and State Assemblyman Charles D. Donohue, looked on. Seemingly the school had heard that the police were coming, and Gorman volunteered to be arrested. At West Side Magistrate Court, the judge, Paul Krotel, dismissed the charges, concluding "that the individual athlete could not be held responsible if there was a violation of the Sabbath law, and that if an arrest was deemed necessary the officials of the race should have been apprehended." The organizers—the I-AAC—found Krotel's words open to interpretation, and the *New York Times* agreed that there was as much "doubt as ever regarding their right to promote road races in the city streets on the Sabbath."[46]

Sabbatarianism was also linked to public decency. A year after the O'Gorman's decree, I-AAC athletes were arrested not only for running on the Sabbath, but for running around showing off their bare legs. The *Evening World* ran the caustic headline "OH, HORRORS! MEN RAN IN BROOKLYN WITH BARE LEGS: Women So Shocked by Cross Country Runners That They Complained to Police." Fourteen runners managed to get away, due to a shortage of fit cops, but commenting on the six—Harvey Cohn and five members of Trinity AC—presented in front of Magistrate Alfred E. Steers in Flatbush the following day, the newspaper laughed, "You can't run around Brooklyn without your legs wrapped up even if you are an Olympic victor. It's a crime. Brooklyn ladies don't like it." Lieutenant Richard Duffy had been awakened from a nap by a total of five, as the *New York Times* called them, "women of exaggerated sensibilities," bursting into his office screaming "Officer, there are a lot of young men running round here with nothing on but their underclothes. Their—their—that is, their limbs are entirely bare. It is very indecent and it is your duty to arrest them." The *Brooklyn Daily Eagle* claimed he was awakened instead by a phone call: "Say captain, six men shockingly naked, just ran past my house and it is disgraceful to see. Please arrest them." "Duffy summoned his men and declared: 'There a lot of young fellows running round the park naked. Go out and get them.'" The *Times* smirked:

> Not knowing that they had been assigned to overtake Harvey Cohn, the policemen started blithely enough, big ones and little ones, thin ones and fat ones. The latter dropped out before the chase had proceeded half a mile. Far ahead of them sped the runners, and it seemed hopeless to catch them. Some of the policemen stuck to it, however.[47]

Back at the station, Cohn argued that athletes had been training in such garments for decades. Duffy countered, "Custom or not. It's agin' section 265 of the Penal Code and the park rules. Moreover you're shockin' the women. There's been five in here rowin' about it." Cohn retorted, "But I wore this costume at Shepherds Bush before 100,000 people." As his siesta had been cancelled, Duffy was in no mood to listen: "I don't care if you wore them in Canarsie before a million. It's agin' the law and I hold you in two hundred dollars bail each." Mrs. Woods, the nearby Boulevard Hotel proprietor's wife, bailed out the athletes. In court the following day, Steers pontificated with a heap of sarcasm:

> It's pretty tough on you young men, but this is Brooklyn you know. Now if you will only put overalls on or rubber boots the ladies won't object. The women are coming to the front for their rights and you know what would happen if twenty women went round in running togs anywhere off the stage ... the good people of Brooklyn believe in observing Sunday in full length pants. However you are discharged.[48]

The battle for the right to practice sport would continue until July 1917. Inspector John J. Collins, who covered Celtic Park on his beat, intended once more to make a test case of the Blue Laws, using the Knights of Columbus Annual Games. Although attending, mysteriously he declined to intervene. It was now too late. Within a month, Blue Laws were given a damaging blow when one of Irish-America's most famous (or infamous) sportsmen helped consign it to history. The New York Giants manager, John McGraw, came up in front of another notoriously anti–Blue Laws magistrate, Francis X. McQuade, for playing Sunday baseball. McQuade dismissed the charges, adding, "It is my opinion that there was no infraction of any statute. Playing ball on the first day of the week, when not amounting to any serious interruption of the repose and religious liberty of the community, is not a violation.... There is not a scintilla of evidence of any one ... being disturbed." McQuade would later become a major Giants shareholder and treasurer, part of a trio, along with McGraw and Charles A. Stoneham, who bought the franchise from the estate of John T. Brush.[49]

Belated attempts to pursue prosecutions did continue. A couple of weeks later, Collins managed to bring three members of Local Union No. 20 Independent United Order of Operating and Stationary Engineers before the bench, after charging admission at Celtic Park. Irvin S. Cobb sarcastically countered in the *New York Times*, from the World Series in Chicago, played on Sunday, October 7: "It would have broken the heart of a strict Sabbatarian to behold so many people having such a good time on the Christians' days of rest. Such shameful spectacles would never be permitted in pious New York. We are too godly for such things east of Alleghenies."[50]

By the fall of 1917, there were more pressing concerns for the I-AAC than Sabbatarianism, with the U.S. six months into World War I. Of course, nobody saw any of this in 1912 as the club prepared for another Olympics, but it would be the last Games the I-AAC would send athletes to.

15

"In spite of depressing conditions"
The Beginning of the End of the I-AAC (1912–1916)

In 1908, Stockholm was awarded the fifth Olympiad, beating Berlin for the honor. None of the shenanigans that marred the London games would reoccur, but the I-AAC, especially their weight men, would play their part for Uncle Sam, while Lawson Robertson was handed the job of assisting Mike Murphy. In the previous four years, the I-AAC had loosened its tight grip on American athletics only once (the 1910 Mets). Things continued to look good.[1]

In the lead-up, the indoor season had seen more records tumble. At the I-AAC's Winter Games on January 25, Pat McDonald "wiped out" Ralph Rose's 18LB shot world record with a throw of 43:09:0 feet. Bonhag took the 5000m world record with a time of 15:05:8, to add to the 3000m mark of 8:35:0 set at the Seventh Regiment Armory on December 16, while Eller bettered his own world record in the 75Yds hurdles with a new time of 0:09:2 seconds. Bonhag would knock three seconds off the 3Mile record at the Boston Mechanics' Building the following month, too.[2]

However, three days later, Alvah Meyer's 100m run of 0:10:6 at the Loughlin Lyceum Games was "ridiculed" by "experts," and according to the *New York Times*, "is generally viewed as a joke by close followers of the sport who witnessed the games. These athletic sharps are a unit on the proposition that something was wrong." One unnamed "former champion record holder," possibly Harvey Cohn, who was a timer at the event, declared, "If Meyer is handicapped from now on the assumption that he ran 100 meters in 10 3–5 seconds, I'll wager that he will never win another handicap race as long as he lives." Frederick W. Rubien would later declare the record null and void, citing the track as almost—a barely noticeable—five inches short.[3]

As the summer outdoor season started, the AAU announced that Celtic

15. *"In spite of depressing conditions"* 207

Park would host the Pentathlon and Decathlon Olympic qualifiers in May, while the I-AAC's Decoration Day Games would double as the Met's Olympic "try-outs" for many events. Meanwhile, Michael Ryan took the season's first outdoor world record in the Boston Marathon with a time of 2:21:18:2. The *New York Times* reported that the I-AAC was ready for a demanding few months: "Lawson Robertson ... is now on the ground, and has almost completed arrangements for the strenuous campaign which will be necessary to fit the members of the Winged Fist for the tryouts for the Olympic Games ... at the Harvard Stadium June 1." One hack reported back from a training session, where Sheppard and Harry Gissing in particular battled out a competitive 600Yds encounter:

> With the wind blowing half a gale over Celtic Park yesterday afternoon, the members of the [I-AAC], under the guidance of Lawson Robertson ... put in a strenuous session in their preparation for the Olympic try-outs. Seventeen athletes turned out and the practice took on the nature of competitions between runners who have achieved world-wide fame.[4]

The Pentathlon "try-out" on May 18 showcased for the first time the talents of James Thorpe, the doomed part-Irish and Native American athlete who "proved to be in a class by himself." The Decathlon tryouts two days later were postponed as there were just two entries, while the Olympics'

Jim Thorpe chases Thomas McLaughlin of Loughlin Lyceum AC, possibly in the 1500m at the 1912 Pentathlon Olympic Trials, May 18, 1912, which Celtic Park hosted. Gold medalist in this event in Stockholm, Thorpe was banished from athletics for taking money to play baseball. Martin Sheridan's national record, which Thorpe broke, would be reinstated (Library of Congress).

importance had kyboshed an I-AAC plan to send a team to the Eaton AA Games in Toronto, with the club preferring that the athletes compete at a fundraising meet on June 2 instead.[5]

One of the now traditional early-year meetings of Celtic Park, the New York Post Office Clerks' Games, on May 26, saw Kiviat beat Harold Wilson's 1908 1500m world record in 3:59:2, breaking it again the following Sunday with time of 3:56:8 at the Olympic fundraising meet. Martin Sheridan's days of discus dominance were numbered, as the unattached James Duncan came up with a throw of 156:01:0 to take the world record. At the Memorial Day Games/New York Olympic Trials, Meyer (100m), Eller (110m hurdles), Rosenberger (400m), Sheppard (1500m), McDonald (shot put), Brodd (javelin), Kiviat (2Mile) and John J. Reynolds (marathon) were the I-AAC runners who won their events.[6]

All was set for the Eastern tryouts at Harvard's Cambridge Stadium. Twenty thousand spectators saw Kiviat knock a second off his 1500m record with a time of 3:55:8, but there was little Irish success elsewhere. "On all sides after the games the principal topic among the New Yorkers present was the reason for the downfall of the Irish-American AC stars," reflected the *Times*. "Before the sports, the wearers of the Winged Fist were counting on winning, or at least making such a showing that would force recognition by the Selection Committee." While Meyer, Rosenberger, and Eller would all eventually make it to Sweden, "none of these men caught the judge's eye for a place in any of the events in which they started," while Gissing, Ike Lovell, Drew Valentine, J.J. Archer, Cloughen and Walter Conway would, for one reason or another, miss the boat.[7]

The omissions caused consternation in certain quarters. W.P. McLoughlin's "Wurra, Wurra!" column in the *Evening World* had a fictional conversation between Sheridan and Conway, complete with stock "to be sure, to be sure" Irish brogues:

> "What d'ye think o' that Olympic Selection Committee at all, at all?" wailed Martin Sheridan to-day. "Here they go an' leave behind a rigimint ov' sure point winners an' they sind only fourteen min from the Irish-American Athletic Club, altho' we have a couple o' hundred wall-toppers left, an' ___." "What talk have ye?" interposed President Pat Conway. "We've done dam fine. We have more than twice the number o' min from any other club, and every one of our la-ads will be heard from. An' you must know this is not a battle of the Irish-American Athletic Club. It is the United States against all the countries of the world." Martin was flabbergasted. He thought hard for a few moments. "Well," said he, with a gleam in his eye. "Isn't the Irish-American Athletic Club able to lick the whole world?" Conway wouldn't contradict him. So Martin believes it.

Lovell's exclusion was especially galling when he broke the 70Yds hurdles world record at the Pastime Games a couple of weeks later, while Sheridan was left to make a "comeback" of sorts at Celtic Park, in the "handicap" discus event of the International Union of Engineers Games.[8]

Twelve members of the club eventually traveled to Stockholm: Bonhag, Eller, Kiviat, McDonald, McGrath, Meyer, Muller, Edwin Pritchard, Reynolds, Rosenberger, Sheppard and Ryan, who injured his ankle on the ship over. In comparison to London, Stockholm was a disappointment with just two golds captured in individual events, both by "Whales." The first medal went to Alvah Meyer on July 7 when he came in second to Ralph Craig in the 100m final, while Sheppard took another silver the following day in the 800m, losing out to Ted Meredith, despite also beating the previous world's best. On July 10, Abel Kiviat picked up a silver in the 1500m behind Britain's Arnold Jackson, while Pat McDonald beat his fellow Americans, Ralph Rose and Lawrence Whitney, in the shot put. The cop also grabbed a silver a day later in the "Two-handed Shot Put" behind Rose, a heads-up competition where distances with throws from both hands were counted. July 13 saw Bonhag and Kiviat win golds as part of the American team that won the 3000m team medal: Bonhag came fifth while Kiviat didn't finish, exhausted by being the team's pacemaker. The final two days of the Games saw Matt McGrath beat Canada's Duncan Gillis and American Clarence Childs to win the hammer competition, while in the marathon on the same day, neither Reynolds nor Ryan completed the course. A day later, July 15, Mel Sheppard won the last of his four Olympic Golds with the American 4x400m team that established a new world record of 3:16:6.[9]

* * *

Back in the States at the Eccentric Firemen Games, the Irish athletes carried on attempting to break records and preparing for the Met and national championships. Matt McGrath, finally permitted to compete for the Irish, broke John Flanagan's record for the 16LB "hammer unlimited run and follow" that counted for nothing, as once again a steel tape was not on hand. Pat McDonald's record for the 12LB shot was also disqualified. One record that did go was Sheridan's All-Around points record: "When Martin made this total in 1909," the *Evening World* conceded, "it was freely predicted that it would probably be a decade, if ever, before this record was broken." Now at Celtic Park, Jim Thorpe smashed it with a mark of 7,476 points at the All-Around Championships. Sheridan was in a philosophical mood: "I thought I was good in 1909 when I made the record for the all-arounds, but you make me look like a never waser." Sheridan's record's place as a "never waser" would last almost nine months until Thorpe was suddenly kicked out of amateur athletics for playing baseball for cash.[10]

Chaos ensued on September 7, the day of the Met Seniors, when the I-AAC announced that it was following the NYAC, suspending 32 club members "for infractions of the club rules and non-payment" of club dues, and signing entry slips for the Labor Day Games despite competing at other meets. "The names of those who were dropped were not made public," reported the *New York Tribune*, "as the club officials declared it was a personal matter with the members, but it was said that some of the deposed runners had been consistent point winners for the club." The *New York Times* labeled the athletes "delinquents," whose names "could not be learned," but included "several who were eligible to tally points" in the Met Seniors championships. If these athletes were prevented from competing at Travers Island, they had no bearing on the result, with the Irish triumphing, 75–54, over the NYAC, with Meyer (100Yds), Eller (120Yds hurdles, 220Yds hurdles), Kiviat (1Mile), Abe Pepis (440Yds), Walter Conway (220Yds), Muller (discus), McDonald (50LB weight, 16LB shot), and Ryan (16LB hammer) all winners.[11]

Two weeks later, Pittsburgh hosted the AAU National Championships, with the Irish narrowly and controversially losing the Junior title, 31–30, to the NYAC (see Chapter 8). Next day, as the *New York Tribune* reported, "the limber-legged athletes of the [I-AAC], swept all before them," with 67 points, as the Mercury Foot "was far in the ruck" with 34, their rivalry, according to the *New York Times*, making this "the greatest athletic meet ever held in this city." Sheppard, whose recent departure to Canada had fueled speculation that he was one of the suspended, returned to take the 880Yds title. Meyer (220Yds), McDonald (16LB shot), Kiviat (1Mile), McGrath (16LB hammer), Ryan (56LB weight), Eller (220Yds hurdles), and Muller (discus) also took firsts, with Kiviat coming close to taking John Paul Jones' world record. "Kiviat started out at a killing clip," reported the *Times*, and opened up a gap of 150 yards over Boston's J.A. Power by the back stretch: "Some of the [I-AAC] weight men saw the big lead he had and shouted for him to take his time. He slowed down into almost a jog, but when he reached the starting point he was told he could establish a world's record if he tried. He set sail for that honor, and went past two men and almost lapped Power and Noble."[12]

The Celtic Park season wrapped up with Kolehmainen running a "fast five miles" American record at the Galway AC Sports on September 22, with a time of 25:09:4. At the Tipperary Men's Association Annual Games a week later, Matt McGrath threw the 16LB hammer a distance of 191:05:0, beating Flanagan's 1909 mark, and being measured by Stumpf, there was "no question about the allowance of the new mark." Finally, some "sterling performances" were put in at the I-AAC Fall Games, with Pat McDonald overtaking Rose's 21LB shot best with a distance of 42:4:5 feet.[13]

However, that evening, Celtic Park was struck by burglars who took $3,140 in cash—including $1,000 belonging to Celtic Park's manager, Tom Lynch, and $1,300 in receipts from the day—a gold watch, chain and diamond pin from the safe in the club storeroom, before the "expert cracksmen" helped themselves to drinks at the bar. Lynch, who was sleeping on the premises with his watchmen, Joe Solisky and Michael Kenny, had guard dogs, but Solisky found them all poisoned by contaminated meat around 7:30 in the morning after investigating why they hadn't come to him in a normal manner. It was clear, to the *Evening World* at least, that the robbery was "carefully and skillfully" organized: "It was known to them that within the past few months the custom of carrying the money taken in at the park on Sundays to a safe place in Manhattan had been discontinued." Previously Conway would take the cash, escorted by a "bodyguard of husky athletes." That night he received a call that his house was on fire. Instead of leaving, he rang home to his surprised family. But the penny hadn't dropped, and a busy Conway still declined to take the money into town. Sheppard's medals, due to be returned to the Military Athletic League, were rumored to be amongst those stolen. Miraculously, they weren't, with "Peerless" Mel claiming "he was at a loss to know how" anyone could think he'd leave his property at Celtic Park. No one seems ever to have been arrested, let alone jailed, for the heist.[14]

The winter season's first championship was the Met AAU Cross-Country, won by Billy Kramer. The Irish still took the points trophy by 42–64, but there were complaints that second-place Frans Johansson, a recently arrived Finnish Olympian, shouldn't have run for the I-AAC as he was not an American resident. At a later meeting of the Met's Registration Committee, he was declared "a bona fide member" of the I-AAC. When the National Cross-Country Championships were hosted at Van Cortlandt Park on November 30, Kramer again took first place, but while fourth-place Kiviat was the first of the Irish-Americans over the line, the Winged Fist took the team title, 21–58, against the NYAC.[15]

Indoors, the I-AAC also made a mark. At the 13th Regiment Coast Artillery Armory in November, Abel Kiviat beat Kramer and broke the U.S. Indoor record for the 1½ Mile with a time of 6:48:2. January saw the Irish win the National Indoor Juniors at the 22nd Regiment Armory, beating the NYAC by just two points (22–20). Two months later at Madison Square Garden, they took the National Seniors, once more bettering their cross-city rivals by five points (30–25). "Records fell while excitement ran high," said the *New York Tribune*, as over 6,000 spectators "spared not their throats in shouting and cheering." Additionally, "father time was put into confusion" as Kiviat broke the world indoor record for the 1,000Yds with at time of 2:15:8, while Pat McDonald broke the 24LB shot world mark with a put of 39:3:75 feet. Both men captured "double honors," also taking first in the 600Yds and the "Fifty-Six," being the only Irish winners on the night. In between these two events, the I-AAC Indoor Games at Madison Square Garden saw Kolehmainen break a series of distance marks, most notably Bonhag's 1909 5Mile title. Pat Ryan also beat William Real's record of over 20 years in the

56LB weight putting. Then Kiviat lowered Oscar F. Hedlund's three-day-old world indoor record for the mile at the Indoor Relay Carnival of Columbia University on February 15. And before the indoor season was out, Pat Ryan abolished Con Walsh's 35LB weight world indoor mark at the Battery D Games with a throw of 20:09 feet.[16]

* * *

Celtic Park's 1913 outdoor season began on March 28 with a doubleheader Gaelic football/hurling event. The Memorial Day Games saw Ted Meredith beat Kiviat in a special ¾Mile Race by two feet in what the *New York Times* described as "one of the fastest outdoor contests seen at the distance since the days of [Tom] Conneff." In June, the I-AAC team lost the 4Mile relay world record to the BAA, and at Far Hills, New Jersey, the Irish also lost the Met Juniors to the NYAC, 56–35. With the Nationals at Chicago's Grant Park only weeks away, the Irish prepared to send 25 athletes to the Windy City. "The point score promises to be extremely keen, with the Irish-American team having their work cut out for them to lead the Western contingent."[17]

Home-town advantage proved crucial in the Juniors on July 4, with the Irish coming in third to both the Chicago Athletic Association and second-place Mercury Foot. But the Irish kept their hands on their Senior title a day later: "Out of the dust and smoke of battle raised by the Chicago Athletic Association ... rose like a phoenix the rushing forms of the Irish-American Athletic Club's athletes." Scoring 44 points to the Cherry C's 27, with the NYAC a dismal fourth (18), this was, according to the *New York Tribune*, "one of the most bitterly contested meetings ever held in the history of sport." The weight categories proved crucial. "The brawny sons of Erin including Bruno Brodd, a Swede, were in a class by themselves when it came to urging the iron ball out over the green." The *Sun* took a different view, claiming, "Favorites were bowled over with great regularity.... The Irish American AC saved enough from the wreck of what were considered sure winners to carry off the point honors." The only weight event not won by the club was the shot put; Pat Ryan broke the championship record for the hammer, while Brodd (javelin), Kolehmainen (5Mile), Muller (discus), and McGrath (56LB weight) won their events, and Tim Ahearne came in second to his brother, the former I-AAC jumper Dan, in the hop, step, and jump.[18]

In mid–August, Conway returned from Ireland. There he had met with John Flanagan, who told Conway he would be back in 1914 to compete at the Greater New York Fair and Exposition at Yonkers. Greeted by up to 500 club members, including Sheridan and McDonald, as he disembarked the *Celtic*, he was escorted to a reception at the Manhattan, where "in his best voice," he said he had been "sorry to leave the 'Ould Sod'" but was "gratified" to be home. Conway's return preceded the visit of a German Athletic Commission delegation later in the month, which included Carl Diem, the 1916 Olympics chief organizer, who would become infamous as the man in charge when Berlin finally got the Games 20 years later. Rather prophetically, Diem's colleague, Lieutenant Walter von Reichman, compared the Laurel Hill stadium's location with that of the proposed site for the 1916 Games: "Celtic Park [is] very similar to the grounds used by the Berliner Sports Club, which however, will have to be given up within a year or so because of the encroachment of the city."[19]

On the field, Pat Ryan broke the world record for the 16LB hammer at the Eccentric Firemen's Games at Celtic Park with a distance of 189:06:5, beating Matt McGrath's mark of October 1911, while Kolehmainen took Alfred Shrubb's American 3Mile record with a time of 14:32, five seconds off the world best. At the Labor Day Games, the world's "weight-throwing records received a wonderful turnover ... when between them Pat Ryan and Pat McDonald, the two giant weight tossers of the Winged Fist organization, annexed four of the best marks ever accomplished." The 16LB hammer (nine-foot circle), the 42LB stone with follow, 35LB weight for distance, and the 14LB shot records were all gone. "Never before has there been such a wholesale demolition of weight-throwing records," commented the *New York Times*. "The men have been preparing for their onslaught against the marks in the keeping of Father time for several months and their recent showing in the several events has served well for just such doings as were seen yesterday."[20]

Come the Mets on September 20 at Travis Island, watched over by the Germans, who, as the *New York Times* put it, "marveled at ... the good natured rivalry between the two big clubs," the Irish were relying heavily on their weight men. Pat Ryan broke Pat McDonald's record in the "Fifty-Six" with a throw of 42:02:0 feet, as the Irish triumphed, 74–68, over the NYAC, with firsts by Meyer (100Yds, 220Yds), Sheppard (880Yds), Kiviat (1Mile), Kolehmainen (5Mile), McDonald (16LB shot, 56LB weight), Ryan (16LB hammer) and Muller (discus). A month later, Ryan broke the 12LB hammer world record with a throw of 213:9:125 at the I-AAC Fall Games.[21]

However, problems were once more arising over membership and eligibility, while the club's ability to retain athletes was weakening. Dan Ahearne had left the Irish for Chicago in early 1913, joining the Illinois Athletic Club in the Windy City. Although the I-AAC went some way by replacing him with his brother Tim, who was the NYAC's top points scorer as recently as 1911, the older of the brother's form seemed to waning, illustrated by his coming second to Dan at the 1913 AAU Championships in Chicago. At the end of September, Emil Muller suddenly resigned from the Irish, announcing that after a year unattached he'd compete for his home-town club, the Paterson (NJ) YMCA: "The reason announced for his decision to retire from the

Winged Fist organization," claimed the *New York Times*, "is that the club failed to enter him in the [NYAC] games." The following year, the club was embarrassed further when a row broke out about who should pay the entrance fees to the NYAC Fall Games. The *Sun* labeled 23 I-AAC athletes, including McGrath, McDonald, Meyer, Kiviat, Ryan, Tim Ahearne, and Bob Eller, "delinquents." McGrath "hustled to the AAU headquarter" under protest, "blaming the Irish Americans for not having attended to it," while Alvah Meyer declared "unofficially that he would not run again for an organization that did not take care of his entrance money," and would instead run unattached.[22]

Both Muller and Meyer would relent, but soon Kolehmainen was in trouble, questioned in the fall of 1913 about his "source of his income," and the prizes—estimated at $1,000—he had won since arrival. The MA Registration Committee held a secret session at the St. Bartholomew AC to discuss the Finn's amateur standing and declared afterwards "that it had reserved its decision," though it suggested that Kolehmainen had sold his trophies for cash. William L. Jones, in the absence of Terrence Farley, represented Kolehmainen, who with little command of English declared that he wasn't "alarmed." Once more the I-AAC was "indignant" at what they viewed as unnecessary harassment. They were then hit by "a solar plexus blow" by the *Evening World* headline: "Irish-American AC's Two Big Weightmen, [Pat] Ryan and [John] Cahill, Desert Organization." The pair told the paper "that the winged-fisties don't know how to properly treat their athletes and consequently they are seeking pastures new. It is said that they are going to Chicago and will join som [sic] organization there."[23]

As the year wound down, the Irish re-took the Met Cross-Country title at Van Cortlandt Park, Yonkers, 19–45, over the NYAC, with Kolehmainen taking first, as fans crowded the final yards, almost causing a riot: "So eager were the enthusiasts to see Kolehmainen finish that they drove him out of the course." I-AAC officials had received threats to the Finn, and Robertson had brought in 30 members "stretched along the three mile course to catch any evildoers." In the national event at the same venue on December 7, Kohelmainen's absence after pulling up in a Thanksgiving Eve race explained how the club could only draw with the NYAC, 32 points each, despite Abel Kiviat coming in first. 1913 saw the Jewish runner gain the most club points with 165, beating the "indoor bicycle king," Eddie Goodwin, who had 118 points. Sheppard came in second amongst the athletes (107), followed by Meyer (101), McDonald (96), and Kolehmainen (75).[24]

* * *

The year 1914 promised much of the same, with only a few minor issues regarding restless athletes to sort out, but by the year's end, desertions hit the club. Also, despite wanting to step down and allow Harry Bannon to take his place, Conway was persuaded to stay on, re-elected president for the 18th time. Old issues started reappearing, as Kiviat and Kolehmainen were accused of running a "fake race." At the 13th Regiment Armory, they tied for first at the 2Mile Race at the Games of the 4th Company, 13th Regiment, with the *New York Tribune* suggesting, "Had it borne a few more of the outward signs of actual competition the crowd might have gone on its way rejoicing." Instead they were livid, shouting "fake" and "put up job" as hisses accompanied the pair's departure from the track. This was the second time since 1912 that they had finished together, and Sullivan demanded answers, furiously telling the *Sun*: "I have read the report ... and from the clear account of what happened am convinced the race was a fake." Both men were suspended, with John T. Dooling, a specialist sports lawyer, taking the athletes' case to the City Supreme Court, arguing for "an injunction restraining the [AAU] from keeping the two athletes out of competition."[25]

Robertson's success was also causing him to become noticed. The University of Pennsylvania, reeling from Mike C. Murphy's death, wanted the Scot to coach their football team. Team captain Albert Journeay declared, "Everyone knows how badly the football team needed a trainer last year, and we shall be equally bad off next year unless a competent man is secured. Robertson is my choice first, last, and all the time." Robertson hardly hid his enthusiasm: "I will say this, however, that my contract with the Irish-American Club ... would not prevent me from accepting an offer, and that I would like to become connected with the University of Pennsylvania's athletic teams."[26]

Instead his reputation reached further afield. Budapest had been awarded the 1920 Olympics, and the Hungarian Olympic Committee was after a top name. They settled on Robertson, giving him a six-year contract taking him into the Games. "Herbert" of the *Tribune* opined, "Lawson Robertson is not far behind the late Mike Murphy as a trainer, in my opinion, and this country's loss is Hungary's gain." Robertson would earn "a salary which is said to be the largest ever paid to any American to coach a foreign team," rumored at $5,000 per annum, for someone they claimed "undoubtedly has brought out more champions in his short career than any other trainer of the present day." Former Cornell coach William "Sparrow" Robertson, who had previously "prepared the Winged Fist athletes for two months, and turned out a successful squad," was slated to replace the Scotsman. The start of World War I jettisoned Robertson's plans just as he was scheduled to sail for a Europe whose lights had already gone out, costing the jobs of other American trainers like Al Copeland in Austria and former I-AAC official Jim McLoughlin in Denmark: "This will give the Irish-American Club an opportunity to retain his services for an indefinite period," smiled the *New York Tribune*, as Conway affirmed that Robertson's contract would continue. There was delight amongst athletes. Abel Kiviat wrote an excited column in the *Tribune* where he confessed that the club had their "wish" granted by the war: "Robertson cannot very well afford to take a chance with his wife and five-year-old daughter in attempting to get to Austria-Hungary. He has tried all the transatlantic lines and they have refused him transportation."[27]

Yet the biggest bombshell of the year was Mel Sheppard's departure after almost eight years at the club. On March 25, the New York press announced that he would "quit" the I-AAC and run unattached for a year before competing with the Millrose AA, the works athletic team of Wanamaker's New York Department Store, where Sheppard moonlighted as an "investigator." "Members of the Irish-American AC stopped worrying about the disturbance in the old country yesterday to confront a similar situation in their own organization here," commented the *Sun*. "The desertion of British army officers paled into insignificance before the information that was bandied about town that ... [Sheppard] had forsworn allegiance to the Winged Fist and was prepared to enlist under the Millrose AA banner." The first sign of trouble came when Sheppard entered "unattached" at the Second Naval Battalion Games on March 28, but he had previously been connected with the store when at their indoor games, and he had competed in a relay race between its New York and Philadelphia branches. With the Big Apple team due to run in Millrose vests, the AAU stepped in and demanded that Sheppard compete in his I-AAC attire. Pointedly, the *Sun* had suggested that the club had lost its ability to look after its top athletes. "Further it was stated that some of the rank and file of the Irish club would follow in the footsteps of the noted middle distance runner." Future 3000m steeplechase silver medalist in Antwerp, Pat Flynn, was "flirting" with Millrose, as was Ryan, who had only recently rejoined the club. "The loss of these men will mean a serious drawback to the Irish American AC, in point scoring, and the club members are incensed at the desertion of Sheppard after he had been elected captain of the club."[28]

More was to come: the *New York Tribune* opined that the I-AAC wasn't bothered about losing Sheppard, who was probably past his best, but were concerned about him becoming a coach, where "he will use his influence to get other members to join Millrose AA." Conway and Robertson were furious. Accusations started to fly, which some thought were rich considering the previous concerns about the I-AAC's "proselyting." Millrose was accused of "poaching" athletes in Ireland, snatching three jumpers, Michael Hanlon and the Leahy brothers, Pat and Con. The *Evening World* noted, "Hanlon arrived in this country ... a week before Election Day. He intended to join the [I-AAC], but the Millrose AA was first in the field." As for Con Leahy, the newspaper claimed he "has sported the colors of the [I-AAC] for many years, and is now competing unattached."[29]

Kolehmainen then got a spot of homesickness and wanted to return to Finland: "[T]here is a slight possibility of his return to this country, in which event he will represent the [I-AAC] in the National Amateur Athletic Union championships," the *New York Times* claimed optimistically, pointing out that Kolehmainen was not taking his prizes. Sadly, the war forced Kolehmainen to return "unexpectedly" to New York in mid–September. Being eligible for the Russian Army probably swung things, and unsurprisingly, he found it difficult getting out of Finland, arriving back without any luggage and little money. He met his brother "William" in Scotland, who supplied him with funds. "He was obliged to go through a number of daring escapades with a friend who accompanied him as rubber and assistant trainer," the *New York Times* reported. "Though overweight, the little Finn declares he can get ready to run in two weeks, and perhaps may represent the Irish-American AC in the senior Championships a week from Saturday." Arriving about the same time was countryman Ville Kyronen, who was rumored to be joining the Irish.[30]

Sheppard ran unattached throughout the rest of the year, but I-AAC athletes continued to break records and, more importantly, retain the major championships, without him. First up was the AAU National Indoor Championships, where the Irish beat the NYAC, 48–33. Two new world indoor records were made by Alvah Meyer in the 300Yds and Kiviat in the 1,000Yds. Meyer also won the 75Yds with McDonald (24LB shot, 56LB weight for height), Richard Reiner (2Mile walk), Eller (70Yds hurdles) also coming in first. Kolehmainen then established new indoor American record in the 1500m at the Spring Games of the 13th Regiment with a time of 14:57:8.[31]

* * *

The outdoor season began at Laurel Hill with a benefit for Padraig Pearse's St. Enda's School on April 19, while the tenor John McCormack was rumored to be attending the Monument Day Games. But firstly the I-AAC had to settle dues with the Met AA for members' registrations, which threatened to halt the event, while it also had to present trophies it owed from as far back as 1912. It had ten days to pay a bill "which is said to amount to a considerable sum," according to the *New York Times*, "and has been due since September of last year." The Games went ahead, and McDonald broke Rose's 1911 18LB shot world record with a distance of 46:02:75. "The accomplishment of the task came as a great surprise to the followers of McDonald for during the last month he has done little in the way of preparation," said the *New York Times*. Ryan broke the world record for the "Fifty-Six" at the Chicago Irish-American AC Games, beating McGrath's 1911 distance by over two feet, with a throw of 42:10:5.[32]

With no Labor Day event recorded, the national championships at Baltimore's Homewood Field on September 11–12 was the next major fixture for the I-AAC. Once again the Irish triumphed, after losing to the NYAC, 55–24, in the Juniors the previous day. Rain and "the heavy atmosphere militated against record breaking in the sprints, but three championship records were made in the field events" as the I-AAC scored 61 points, 30 more than the NYAC. Firsts went to Kiviat (1Mile), Muller (discus), McDonald (16LB shot, 56LB weight) and Ryan (16LB hammer). In the Mets, due to be held at Celtic Park the following Saturday, but suspended following James E. Sullivan's death until October 3, the result was far closer with a 79–70 victory for the Irish, reversing the 83–23 defeat in the Juniors back in June. Irish winners were Meyer (100Yds, 220Yds), Kiviat (Mile), McDonald (16LB shot, 56LB weight), Ryan (16LB hammer), K. Caldwell (pole vault), and Brodd (javelin). Intriguingly, at Washington Park the following Saturday, the Long Island AC hosted what was possibly the first-ever MA AAU "Small Clubs" championship. It was won by the Pastimes; both the Irish and the NYAC were specifically told not to come.[33]

The winter season began with Kolehmainen taking the AAU Ten Mile Championship at South Field, Columbia University, but he still failed to beat Alfred Shrubb's mark. "Kolehmainen ... did not have a desire to set any new records, despite opinions to the contrary expressed by his coach and others who were supposed to know," the *New York Tribune* concluded. In the Met Junior Cross-Country Championships, the major surprise was the inability of the NYAC to field a team, entering five individuals instead. In contrast, the Irish entered ten, including the future Olympic marathon runner, Frank Zuna, taking the championship, 40–42, against a very strong Bronx Church House combination, although the winner, I-AAC's Arthur Fogel, ran outside the team as an independent. At Prospect Park, Brooklyn, on November 21, Kolehmainen took the Senior Met Cross-Country title, while the Irish won the points trophy by 18–62 over the NYAC. Tom Barden was second, Fogel third and Pat Flynn fourth. Three weeks later at Van Cortlandt Park, the National Cross-Country Championships contained only three teams, Philadelphia's Mercury AC joining the two New York clubs. Once more, as the *New York Times* trumpeted, the "Irish-Americans Score Easy Victory," taking the trophy with 16 points to the NYAC's 49. Kolehmainen took first, while Fogel and Barden came in second, battling it out with Yonkers YMCA's Holden.[34]

The club's Annual Indoor Games, hailed by the *Evening World* as having the "BEST TALENT IN WORLD FOR IRISH-A.A.C. GAMES," was held on November 28. The *Gaelic American* described the upcoming carnival in typical hyperbolic tones:

> If Cuchulain [sic], Oscar, Finn McCool, Goll McMorna and some of the other heroes and champions of ancient Ireland could get leave of absence from Tir na Og, long

enough on the evening of Saturday, November 28, to attend the indoor games of the [I-AAC], how their hearts would rejoice at the prowess that yet brings the sons of the old sod into the front rank in every hosting of champions.

Six thousand spectators saw two non-Irish heroes, Kiviat and Kolehmainen—"the fleet Finn, who doesn't belong to the Finns of Ballyfinn" as the *Gaelic American* described him—as the night's main stars, with Kiviat coming within a fifth of a second of equaling Tom Halpin's world record for 1,000Yds. But more problems were mounting for the Irish.[35]

Emil Muller once again announced his departure—this time for Los Angeles to manage a garage, joining the Los Angeles AC—while Kyronen couldn't be registered in time for the AAU 10Mile Championship, running instead "unattached." Then came the news that Pat Ryan was returning to Ireland for "an indefinite" period. "Ryan has not been well for some weeks," reported the *New York Times*, "and he believes he has been overworked, being forced on numerous days to remain at his position for eighteen and twenty hours at a stretch without relief," believing a return home will "put him in shape again." With it hardly the best of times to travel to Europe, there was optimism that he'd reconsider.[36]

There were further disputes about registration fees. Recently the NYAC had become aggressive about demanding outstanding payments, which didn't go down too well with the Irish, who were continually being knocked for fees themselves: "Much indignation was expressed yesterday by members of the Irish-American AC over the method of procedure followed by the New York AC to collect its debts," said the *New York Times*, "and arrangements were made to immediately wipe out their account with their rival club. According to Lawson Robertson, the Irish club has outstanding accounts for entrance fees amounting to about $3,000. The club has been unable to collect a dollar of this money for some months. It was only recently, Robertson said, that the Irish club received a bill from another club for $7 entrance money, yet this organization was in debt to the Winged Fistites for more than $100."[37]

There were positives as the New Year arrived: Six national championships were captured in 1914, while Meyer, Kiviat, Kolehmainen, Muller, McDonald, McGrath, and Ryan were picked for the All-American athletic team. Conway was again re-elected on February 8, as once more other directors refused to place another man "at the helm of their organization." Thomas J. Cummings was voted Vice-President, while Martin Sheridan was made a director. Also, it was hoped that Charles Pores, a Jewish lad, would represent the Irish at the end of his unattached year. The *Times* disclosed, "The Irish club won Pores after Mel Sheppard, coach of the Millrose AA, had asserted positively that the little distance star would compete for his club. Lawson Robertson took Pores in hand after he had triumphed on Monday, and the boy definitely decided it would be for his best interests to represent the

I-AAC." Finally, as the indoor season came to a close, the Irish retained the Nationals at Madison Square Garden on March 4 with a score of 35–23 over Boston AA, with the NYAC third. The shock of the night was Kiviat, suffering from a heavy cold, being defeated in the 1000Yds by the Unicorn's Dave Caldwell, while Matt McGrath (56LB weight) and Pat McDonald (24LB shot) were the only two club winners.[38]

* * *

Still, the I-AAC couldn't escape trouble. The brief suspension of 33 athletes for failing to send in expense slips from the Paterson Elks' Games was an inconvenience which swept up Kolehmainen, Kiviat, Hugh M. Hirshon, Richard J. Egan, Gissing, and Edward Pritchard, all part of "the best collection of athletes suspended at one time in the history of the AAU," as the *New York Times* succinctly put it. Then in early April, the Met AA Registration Committee disqualified the Irish relay team from the 14th Infantry AA Games on December 5, agreeing that the referee, Ardolph L. Kline, a former acting mayor of the city, had wrongly allowed them to run the final. There was "some doubt as to the order of finish in the heat," and an "informal protest" from some of the "interested clubs" was lodged, reported the *New York Times*, suggesting, "There may be an open break between the Irish-American AC and the Metropolitan Association of the Amateur Athletic Union over the decision." Robertson told the newspaper that he was far from satisfied and threatened to involve the Military Athletic League, which provided the referee:

> We would accept the committee's verdict with grace were it not for the fact that we feel an injustice has been done General Kline.... We are confident, too, that we can prove to the satisfaction of Mr. Rubien or any other fair-minded person that we are entitled to the prize which the Registration committee, by its poor judgment, took away from us.

The club challenged the ruling through Farley and on May 17, the Irish won their appeal by a close "mail" vote of 34 to 31, with Kline's decision to include the Millrose team in the race, muddying the waters enough.[39]

With this spat resolved, 1915's summer began with Eller breaking Joe Loomis' 120Yds low hurdles world record in a time of 13 seconds at the 13th Regiment Armory's St. John's College Spring Games. Kolehmainen established a new 15Mile U.S. mark at the Monument Club Games at Celtic Park, despite "athletic experts" predicting that he wouldn't recover from blood poisoning he received in December. However, the record wasn't recognized, as the I-AAC had failed to measure the track. Another mistake at the United Affiliated Building Trades and I-AAC Joint Games on June 13—the lack of a "stable circle" to stand in—cost Ryan a new world record in the 16LB hammer. Things seemed to be rectified when on July 5, "Celtic Park's reputation for new records suffered no setback yesterday," according to the *New York Times*, as two world marks were broken by I-AAC athletes: Edward S. Fraser made a new mark for 500Yds, while Ryan broke the 35LB weight event with a throw of 62:04:00.[40]

The Mets came early on June 19, with the NYAC optimistic about taking the title for the first time since 1910. "No senior championship meeting ever had bigger fields or a higher grade of contestants than the title games at Travers Island on Saturday," previewed the *New York Times*, "The [NYAC] is in great earnest about winning the title, which year after year goes to the Irish-American AC, and has made the record entry of sixty-four men." A large number of these were college boys who were "expected to count heavily in the final result." In contrast, the Irish had 46 entries. Despite losing the 880Yds favorite, Homer Baker, on the eve of the event after a motor bike accident, the NYAC was still confident of victory, with the *Times* claiming, "New York AC Expects to Defeat Irish-American Team Today." But the predictions proved once more false with the Irish outpointing the NYAC, 92–71. "The 'Winged Fist' has the old-time punch," said the *Gaelic American*, "Last Saturday the Irish-American Athletic Club, leaning confidently on the hyphen which splices together the first part of its name, carried off the team honors in the AAU senior track and field championships of the metropolitan district." With the absence of Baker, Joe Bromilow, the I-AAC veteran, "finally came through" in the ½Mile: While Kiviat was unexpectedly beaten by NYAC's Willie Gordon in the Mile, the Irish took firsts by Meyer (100Yds, 220Yds), Eller (120Yds hur-

Hannes Kolehmainen. A three-time gold medalist in Stockholm, the Finn was snapped up by the I-AAC, according to one sarcastic Scottish newspaper report, because they were "first at the pier when the ship came in" (Library of Congress).

dles), Kolehmainen (5Miles), McDonald (16LB shot), Ryan (16LB hammer), Erickson (high jump), McGrath (56LB weight) and George Bronder (javelin). Once more, the Irish failed to make any impact on the Met Juniors, losing heavily to the Mercury Foot, 85–22. Their inability to win this title since 1912 showed both an inability to attract college men and a worrying decline in young talent.[41]

Meanwhile, the national championships, due to be held west of the Rockies for the first time since 1909, was causing concern, with the renovation of Celtic Park's grandstand and athletic field a priority: "The main object of the Winged Fist representatives this year will be to win the metropolitan senior championship," said the *New York Times* as early as April 17.

> Owing to the heavy expense necessary to send a representative to the national championships at the Panama-Pacific Exposition in San Francisco next August, the club is still undecided just what will be done regarding the "champs." If proper arrangements can be made the surest point winners of the Irish organization will make the journey across the continent. Just now it appears likely that not more than ten Winged Fistites will take part in the national meet.

As for the Junior title, Robertson confessed that the Irish could forget about that.[42]

However, as the championships approached, the I-AAC decided to send a squad. Rubien was particular impressed, writing in the *New York Times* on the eve of the competition: "At the present writing, and from the form displayed by the men in practice today, Lawson Robertson's Irish-American AC team should win the senior championship.... The points will be pretty evenly divided, and the Olympic Club of this city should closely press the New Yorkers." Sadly, his optimism proved premature: In front of 15,000 partisan fans, the Winged "O" took the Championships by 30 points to the second-place Irish's 24. "The Olympic Club of San Francisco wrested first team honors from the great field, winning by a fair margin over the Irish American Athletic Club of New York city," reported the *New York Tribune*. As for the Mercury Foot, they scored just nine points, finishing ninth. Kolehmainen, who beat Oliver Millard of the Olympic AC by a mere foot in the 5Mile run, Ryan (16LB hammer) and Bronder (javelin) were the only winners.[43]

However, there followed a foul smell of sour grapes, as Robertson vented his fury at what he called the "bad judging." The *New York Times* quoted him saying: "[I]f his men had received the treatment they deserved he felt confident they would have brought the point trophy back East with them." Meyer claimed he was robbed in the 100Yds, citing the arguing judges, who included Chicagoan Everett C. Brown, the AAU president, who finally gave the call to Joe Loomis of the CAA. Lee Talbott, now in Kansas City, was also accused of getting seven throws instead of six and taking them in succession, "in violation of the rules of competition." Robertson argued that had those crucial five points been given to the Irish, they would have got the trophy, which was untrue.[44]

Rubien hit back through the *Sun*: "IRISH CHARGE IN BAD GRACE, SAYS RUBIEN: Criticism of Judges by Club Unsportsmanlike. False and Unfortunate. BIG MEET WELL HANDLED." He was described as having "arrived yesterday from San Francisco ... very much annoyed at the criticisms that had been made on the way the Panama-Pacific games were managed," adding that the "criticisms, which have emanated from the [I-AAC]" were "very unsportsmanlike." According to Rubien, the judges' decisions were "absolutely correct," and he dismissed any criticism as "unsportsmanlike and very unfortunate." "I consider that the Irish Americans had a perfectly fair deal, as did all other organizations and athletes. The meeting was well managed and was a big success and the judges were efficient and thorough in their work."[45]

The row escalated with the I-AAC denying criticizing the competition or judges. Bannon wrote a letter to Rubien, passing along a copy to the *Sun*.

> Dear Sir: On Sunday August 22, 1915, the morning *Sun* prints what purports to be an interview from you, the substance of which, as far as the Irish American Athletic Club is concerned is that criticisms have emanated from the club reflecting on the character of two of the decisions rendered at the national championships recently held in San Francisco, namely, the 100 yard dash and 56 pound weight.... Officially the club is not acquainted with any of the facts concerning either of the events in question, and as a matter of course could not have criticized the judging of either. Personally I have not heard of any criticism from any of the club's officials. The only knowledge the club has of the entire matter has been gathered from the newspaper reports and comments. Since this interview has been given great publicity adverse to the club's interest, it is considered a matter of fairness, now that you are officially acquainted with the club's position, that it be repudiated. It might not be amiss to suggest that in the future any matter in connection with this club which might call for a confirmation or repudiation before it is rushed into public print might be submitted to the club's officials so that they at least might enjoy the opportunity and the courtesy of passing on it and thereby save the embarrassment. And inconvenience of being compelled to seek a retraction. Very truly yours. H.G. Bannon, Secretary.

The matter was left there, but it says something that within a month, Farley threw in the towel on the Registration Committee. The *New York Times* reported, "In his own words, he 'has had enough.'" He told anyone listening that if Stumpf "is so anxious to fill such an unimportant office he can step right in without any opposition from him."[46]

Other headaches included a supposed falling interest in the weight events weakening the Irish team. "Weight Men May Quit," cried the *New York Times* on August 19:

> Three of the world's greatest athletes, Pat Ryan ... Pat McDonald ... and Matt McGrath ... may be lost to competitive athletics after this year. The apparent lack of

interest in weight events on the part of promoters of track and field meetings is responsible for the contemplated retirement of these men. McDonald made the positive assertion that he was through with the game after this year, because there was not enough competition to warrant his remaining in it. The Irish-American AC "whale" indicated that Ryan and McGrath would follow him for the same reason.

Allegedly only one meeting had included weight events so far that season.[47]

Kiviat's amateur status was also questioned. The Registration Committee accused him of demanding $75 for competing at the Eastern New York Athletic League Games at Schenectady on September 18. Evidence, mostly from Roscoe C. Campbell, the official handicapper, was largely "hearsay," as letters between the pair failed to show any request for money. A week later, he was out of amateur athletics, found guilty of "demanding exorbitant expense money" at what many thought was a kangaroo court trial. One crucial witness supporting the case was the Rev. M.A. Calanti, from St. Antony's RC Church in Troy, who claimed that he paid Kiviat $25 to compete in September 1912. The I-AAC was once more enraged, although the initial reaction from Conway was that the "club's attitude as to the decision would be made known either this afternoon or to-morrow." The Irish demanded a new hearing, condemning the rushed manner in which the case was handled. The *New York Tribune* said that the I-AAC "threw down the gauntlet to the [AAU] last night," with the *Evening World* claiming that the club's athletic committee was "appealing for fair play" and asking the Metropolitan AA to correct this miscarriage of justice: "It was made plain ... last night that that club ... would fight to the last ditch to have the stigma of professionalism" removed from Kiviat:

> The Irish American Athletic Club intends to appeal to the good judgment and sense of fair play of the ... Metropolitan Association to right the grievous wrong which has been done to its track captain.... The Irish American Athletic Club does not stand for, nor does it countenance professionalism in amateur athletics. It points with pride to what it has done and is still doing to reflect glory and credit not only on the Metropolitan Association but also on the Amateur Athletic Union and the cause of amateur athletics at home and abroad.

It added that it had no objections to any "impartial, unbiased persons, and in a legal way," investigating professionalism: "If Kiviat be guilty let his guilt be proven in a satisfactory manner. And if it is established, the [I-AAC] has no more use for him than the [AAU]."[48]

A special meeting of the MAA's Board of Managers was arranged at the 71st Regiment Armory for November 9, with delegates invited from each of the body's approximately 150 clubs. But the vote went 50 to six in favor of dismissing Kiviat. John T. Dooling, Kiviat's counsel, immediately demanded that Rubien reopen proceedings, claiming "sufficient evidence to reverse" the decision. Dooling arranged a special meeting, but further bad news came when Gissing was also accused, having been a part of the I-AAC relay team that day. He denied taking "a cent" of the $125 given to the Irish team. By the end of November, Kiviat had all but abandoned clearing his name, focusing instead on plea bargaining. Perhaps all this influenced Robertson to withdraw from the Met Cross-Country Junior Championships when he heard that a water jump would be included, forcing the Senior event to be competed without the "Liverpool," which Kolehmainen won, and the Irish beat Millrose by a single point, 40–41.[49]

The Irish were starting to lose their dominance of American athletics. Kolehmainen had been the club's highest point winner in 1915 with 106 points, followed by Ryan with 99 and Jack Eller with 89, but the club struggled in the major Indoor Championships. Having already conceded the National Juniors to the Mercury Foot, 41–26, the Irish lost the 1916 National Seniors at the 22nd Corps Engineers Armory on March 18. "The Winged Fistites made a hard bid to retain their laurels, but lacked 1½ points of bettering the score of the New York AC aggregation which totaled 23½. Many things combined to upset the I-AAC men, especially the splendid showing of the out-of-town teams." With 22 points, William H. Taylor (high jump), McDonald (16LB shot), and Eller (70Yds hurdles) took firsts.[50]

At his re-election, Conway made an upbeat speech about the challenges the club had faced over the previous 12 months: "In spite of depressing conditions during 1915 our financial report shows a big decrease in expenditures, with only a slight decrease in receipts. With the exception of the [nationals] ... the club's athletes won their customary share of championships." Robertson was offered a new contract, but two months later came the news that he had agreed to succeed George W. Orton as the Quakers' athletic coach, with the *Sun* noting, "The inducement offered is one of the largest ever made to a track coach in this country, and the trainer ... immediately signed the contract."[51]

* * *

Meanwhile, New York's population was expanding, from 3.43 million in 1900 to 5.62 in 1920. As Laurel Hill became an urban district, property speculators circled like vultures to devour Celtic Park. In May 1914, the *Sun* ran a story about a failed attempt to "wipe out of existence Celtic Park." D.C. Imboden, who was representing a number of firms, including the Heiser Realty Company, the Dallton Realty Company and the Courtney Development Company, asked for more than half a dozen streets to be driven through Celtic Park. In what was an astonishing display of chutzpah, Imboden argued that his clients had spent thousands on developments, and that these couldn't be completed while the I-AAC's home stood in their way. Conway and his lawyer, John R. McMullen, countered that cutting through the stadium would "destroy a pleasure ground to which thousands of residents of New York resorted during the course of the year.... There was no similar place in the entire city." John Andrews, a Long Island civic organizer, added that "although private property, [Celtic Park] is open to the public, especially to school children ... the recreational ground of hundreds of boys and young men of the vicinity." Luckily, the Queens Public Works Commissioner, James A. Dayton, agreed and turned down the application, suspending the proposal indefinitely. However, within two years, the "real estate boomers" were back, successfully getting a street driven through the southern part of the park, cutting through the track and forcing the I-AAC to shorten it from a four-lap-a-mile circuit to four-and-a-half laps.[52]

There was indeed a certain amount of relief that the Irish were able to open the 1916 season on Memorial Day. But as the *New York Times* noted, "Small fields, reduced by scratches, and unfavorable elements took much of the zest out of the annual track and field meet of the [I-AAC]." The medley race became "rather a fizzle" when only the University of Pennsylvania and the Knights of St. Antony turned up out of seven entered, proving to be "virtually a walkover" for the Quakers. A.C. Cavagnaro of the *New York Tribune* chuckled, "The Red and Blue shirts of [the Penn athletes] frightened away all but one of its six scheduled opponents." The *Sun* was, however, scathing. Long gone were the eulogies of this being "one of the important athletic meetings of the season," with entries of "an unusually high mark." The I-AAC had had the legs of its pedestal kicked from under it: "Not only did the Irish American AC hold the meet, but it held the medals and scored the points. In most cases it was merely a matter of taking the prizes from one pocket and putting them in the other."[53]

With the championships approaching, there was pessimism that this would be the year the Irish would lose their place as the country's top athletic club. Firstly in June, they lost the Met Juniors to the New Yorkers, 97½–33, the *New York Times* remarking, "In gaining second place they did about as well as was expected, and in annexing four first places they did even better than their own trainer ... expected." Furthermore, the paper blamed a general decline in the city's athletic conveyor belt for the lack of new recruits. "The dearth of good athletic material in the metropolitan district is becoming more and more apparent each year. Were it not that the Irish-American AC and the New York AC import occasionally a college star, there would be no new blood worthy of mention in athletic competitions in this district." As for the Met Seniors, the *Times* believed that the dearth of talent on both clubs entailed "the same order of finish in the team championship is probable, with the Irish-American AC retaining its rank over the best efforts of the New York AC." Despite a stream of good high school and college youngsters at the NYAC, "the hardened and seasoned veterans of the Irish-American AC seem to have all the best of the outlook."[54]

This prediction was not shared by Robertson, who hadn't yet left the Irish, and on the eve of the competition, the *Times* changed track and conceded that the Mercury Foot were the favorites: "Fortune, it seems, will favor the New York AC.... Every indication points to a triumph for the Mercury foot organization over the team of the Irish-American AC which for some years has ruled supreme in the senior championships." Their "sturdy squad of athletes" contrasted with how the Irish hadn't looked so "weak" in years. Cavagnaro called the meeting the "much talked about duel" between the clubs for "the team supremacy" of the MA: "For the last four years the men representing the Irish-American organization have won the honors by wide margins. Many are of the opinion, however that the New Yorkers will turn the tables to-day." As predicted, the Irish were beaten by the NYAC at the PSAL Field, Brooklyn, 93–71, a virtual reversal of the previous year's score. The I-AAC winners were Eller (120Yds & 220Yds hurdles), McDonald (16LB shot), Erickson (high jump), Caldwell (pole vault) and Ryan (16LB hammer & 56LB weight). "The tide of athletic fortune, which for six years had coursed strongly in the direction of the Irish-American AC, turned yesterday and swept the Winged Fist team to a decisive defeat by the New York AC.... Upsetting tradition but not predictions."[55]

The Nationals were now two weeks away, and the Irish looked likely to lose again the title they had held for years. Although they managed to get McGrath, Tim Ahearne, and Pritchard to return, the NYAC was rumored to be taking 52 men to Weequahic Park, Newark, compared to the I-AAC's 35. Rubien told the *New York Times* that these two clubs were the only contenders for first place:

> New York is likely to again become the title-holding city. For one year both the junior and senior championships have rested with the Olympic Club of San Francisco, but this year it seems to me that both titles are coming back to this city.... The victory of the New York AC in the metropolitan championships ... has given the members of the team a world of confidence. In fact, it has given them so much courage that they might upset the prevailing opinion in certain quarters that the IAAC is a sure thing in the champs.[56]

Things were looking grim as the NYAC took the Junior title, 52–20, over the Chicago AA, with the Irish third with 16 points. Then, as the Seniors kicked off in front of the biggest crowd ever—30,000—for an athletic meet, Eller and Meyer were unable to compete, while McDonald was nowhere to be seen, detained in New York on "urgent strike duty." But despite a poor start, the Irish gradually collected crucial points to add to the firsts of Ryan (16LB hammer), McGrath (56LB weight), and Bronder, who set a new American record in the javelin of 190:6. They took their tenth Senior title since 1904 by a margin of 38–27 over the NYAC: "To top off a meeting that has never had an equal in this country, according to some of the oldest followers of the sport," gushed the *New York Times* excitedly, "the Irish-American AC once more established itself as the leading organization of its kind in the United States." It added that Robertson, seven years coaching the Irish, "will retire from its circles knowing full well that he produced the best team in the meet." The *Sun* later described the championships as "without doubt the greatest event yet held by the Amateur Athletic Union. In point of performances, attendance and a representative field the meet outdid all previous efforts of a similar character."[57]

As 1916 closed, new faces at the I-AAC were thin on the ground. Roy F. Morse, the 1915 200Yds Senior Champion, was said to have resigned from the Salem-Crescent AC and would represent the I-AAC after his unattached period. So too were Homer Baker, the former NYAC middle-distance man, and Joe Higgins, a graduate from Holy Cross. But this came with the news on October 24 that Kolehmainen was transferring his status to "unattached" at the upcoming distance championships. He gave no reason for leaving the club "whose colors he has always borne honorably in this country other than 'Maybe I join a new club soon.'" Neither Conway nor Eller, the club captain, could offer an explanation. Without him, the *New York Times* predicted that "the IAAC can entertain only little hope of winning either the senior metropolitan or national championships this season."[58]

He made good on his promise, regaining the AAU 10Mile championship unattached: "Plowing to the wire over a path lined by solid masses of persons nearly 3,000 in number ... the little Finn, with the familiar green winged fist of the Irish-American AC sheared from his white jersey." There was no Irish runner in the first 12. Kolehmainen's departure was seen as a "big loss" to the Irish, but after a meeting, the I-AAC announced that the Finn was back, with Joe Dickman entering him on the Irish team for the Met Cross-Country Championship. "Athletes of the Irish-American Athletic Club will heave a sigh of joy with the announcement that the prodigal, Hannes Kolehmainen, is again back in the fold," said the *New York Tribune*. However, another "disgruntled" athlete, Tom Barden, announced that he was entering as an individual. The *New York Times* was now dismissive of Dickman's efforts: "[He] said last night that the Finnish star would surely carry the Winged Fist emblem on Saturday, despite the fact he is still registered with the AAU as unattached.... The team named by the champions is comparatively weak, and will probably find its master in the aggregation of the Millrose AA."[59]

Dickman failed to get either runner to change his mind, and Millrose won the event with another former I-AAC import, Ville Kyronen, coming in first. Mohawk finished second, while the NYAC strolled in last. As for the Irish, Fogel (13th) was their highest place. The *New York Tribune* published a scathing critique of the I-AAC's recruitment policy, called "The Irish-American-Finn":

> We have just stumbled on what seems to us a perfectly good mystery. Early last week our veracious athletic editor informed us that Hannes Kolehmainen would run under the colors of the Irish-American Athletic Club. It looked like news to us, though we could not figure exactly which county in Ireland the Kolehmainens could have come from. It seems that the Kolehmainens did not come from any part of Ireland at all, but from Finland. So the head "Prominent Irish-American Returns" would have been erroneous. If we had written "Prominent Finn Returns to the Irish-Americans" a lot of people would have been asking us why a Finn should return to the Irish-Americans or why he should ever have been with them. It was a hyphenated problem that had us groggy and ready for the count. Just as we decided to pass it up as beyond us we learn that the prominent Finn did not return to the Irish-Americans, as was announced. He forfeited his chance to win the senior metropolitan run because he did not want to run under the colors of the Irish-American Athletic Club. So the mystery deepens. It might be well for the AAU to detail a few sleuths to learn why Hannes Kolehmainen ever was an Irish-American and why, if he ever was one, he did not remain an Irish-American. It's beyond us.[60]

Over Christmas, Kolehmainen had a change of heart and returned. "There was considerable mystery surrounding the withdrawal of Kolehmainen from the Irish club," reported the *New York Times* on January 8, 1917. "He never announced his reasons for leaving, and the club officials were reticent in speaking of his action. All of them, however, disclaimed any knowledge of a reason for his determination. His return is marked by the same degree of secrecy, except that now there is a rumor of differences having been patched up."[61]

Somehow the I-AAC had not only survived another year, but had also retaken the greatest prize in American athletics. By getting Kolehmainen back into the fold, it had increased its chances of remaining one of the country's top athletic clubs. Things looked promising when the *Gaelic American* declared at the end of March 1917: "Celtic Park will open for the season next Sunday.... This news will be more welcome than the cowslips and daffodils of springtime to the admirers of Ireland's national pastimes in New York and vicinity."[62]

But events happening a thousand miles away in Europe were getting closer, inevitably dragging America into a war it had done much to avoid. 1917 would prove a pivotal year for the United States. It would be a devastating one for the I-AAC: The once "greatest athletic club in the world" would become as doomed as the heir to the Austrian-Hungarian throne had been one June afternoon three years earlier. But unlike Archduke Franz Ferdinand, the I-AAC's mortal wounds would be self-inflicted.

16

"Service first, athletics afterward"
The I-AAC Finally Closes

Three days after news broke that Hannes Kolehmainen was returning to the Irish, the German Foreign Secretary, Arthur Zimmerman, sent a telegram to his man in Mexico City, Heinrich von Eckardt, ordering him to persuade the Mexican government to invade the southern United States should it declare war on Germany. Known as the Zimmerman Telegram incident, this correspondence is cited as the catalyst for the United States entering World War I. April 6, 1917, was the day that changed the course of the conflict into defeat for the Central powers. Five days later, the I-AAC suspended its athletic operations and offered Celtic Park to the military.

The *New York Times* ran with the headline: "IAAC DROPS SPORTS: Governors Decide to Suspend All Athletic Activities." "It was announced last night that the Board of Governors … had passed a resolution suspending all athletic activities of the club until further notice." Club secretary John F. Conway added that at an executive meeting, it was decided to urge all members, "particularly those of the athletic team, to associate themselves with some form of military preparedness." The *Times* surmised that the decision "will be a real blow to the open events in amateur athletic meets and also to the AAU metropolitan championship meets." "Daniel," writing in the *Sun*, speculated, "Just how long the suspension will last depends on the war situation." The club's "governors" had, without much debate, passed a resolution "asking every member of the club to enlist in some branch of national service," adding that those not fit or too old should "enlist in the Home Defense League." Celtic Park would be offered to the government "for use in drilling army recruits or the schoolboy contingent." "Service first, athletics afterward," Pat Conway told the *New York Times*. "Sports is a minor consideration, even to an athletic club, in a time like this."[1]

Some individual athletes continued competing, while Celtic Park officially opened on May 6 with hurling and Gaelic football and continued hosting a summer of sports, including the Mets in August. But how many athletes would remain at an inactive club? Most left; Bonhag's attempts to represent the NYAC before his unattached period was up led to censure by the AAU. Kolehmainen, whom the Irish had battled to get back, was listed as unattached when he ran in the Bronx to City Hall Marathon on May 13, while in the run-up to the Mets, both Eller and Pat O'Connor competed independently. As the *Times* conceded, this was good news for the smaller clubs; the move "will not cause stagnation in local athletic circles. The small clubs will stick by their guns and they will have the company of the New York Athletic Club."[2]

* * *

The culmination of the indoor season had already shown that the I-AAC was at best going through a period of transition. The Met Championships on March 3 at the 22nd Regiment Armory proved a success for the Irish as they beat the NYAC, 46–38, with firsts for Baker (1,000Yds), McDonald (16LB shot), Eller (70Yds hurdles), Erickson (running high jump), J. Froehlick (broad jump), Higgins (600Yds), and William Taylor (standing high jump). But at the Nationals, a fortnight later at the same venue, the Irish came in third behind the Chicago AA and the NYAC: McDonald (16LB shot) and Taylor (standing high jump) were their only firsts.[3]

New recruits were badly needed. According to the *New York Tribune*, Joe Higgins "has attracted considerable attention by his spectacular performances" and was tipped to fill Sheppard's empty shoes, as Conway enthused:

> Joe is a boy you can always depend upon to be in fine shape for any event. His two past races at the mile route have proven that he can go some distance in close to record time if he specially prepares for this event.... With the departure of Sheppard from our ranks we were sorely in need of a man to wear his shoes. For two years we were unable to find a successor to the most consistent half-miler that ever lived, but now that Higgins is in our ranks we believe we have him.[4]

But apart from him there were no other new recruits.

This couldn't hide the fact that the club was collapsing. Even a small-town newspaper, the *Watertown Daily Times*, would report:

> Slowly the [I-AAC] is dissolving. The latest to throw off the ties that bound him to Celtic Park is Pat McDonald. The big weight man has applied to compete unattached and probably will join either the Millrose AA or the New York AC when the one year period is up. Athletes feel that the Irish club would be doing only the fair thing by its men if it came out and made a definite announcement of its intentions. Since the club decided to abandon all sports during the war there have been numerous assertions that it was out of athletics for good. There have been no denials of this, and the club has not released a single athlete.[5]

In the Mets, Eller won the 220Yds low hurdles for the first time in years. According to the *Gaelic American*, the championships had aroused "the interest of all the clubs of the association.... The smaller clubs in particular feel that they will have a splendid opportunity to gain some of the laurels with the Irish-American AC disorganized and the New York AC disapproving of the holding of the championships." A record entry list was expected despite the war, and the Irish still sent a team, with Ryan and W.C. Krapowicz taking first and second in the 16LB hammer and first and third in the "Fifty-Six." Represented "by only a few of its once formidable team," according to the *New York Tribune*, the Irish came in third with 15 points as Millrose edged them for second place by a point. "One feature of the games worthy of prominent mention is that the smaller clubs of the district will have a chance to battle unmolested for supremacy on track and field ... the 'small fry' of the district will get its long sought chance." Sensationally, the championship was taken by the Salem Crescent, the first "negro organization" that ever won an AAU Championship.[6]

For the Irish, it was a worse story at the Nationals in St. Louis on September 1, where they collected all their points from Ryan's victories in the 16LB hammer and the "Fifty-Six," coming in sixth. Points came from 22 clubs, with Chicago supplying the top two point grabbers, and clearly the Big Apple was no longer the home of American athletics. "It is true that the New York Athletic Club's stand against competition in championships," said *The Sun*, "and the [I-AAC's] long hibernation had a lot to do with this city's poor showing ... there is no dodging the fact that as the athletic leader New York is in total eclipse."[7]

A little over a week after the Nationals came the news that McDonald and McGrath, "two of the best weight men in the world, will be elected to membership in the New York Athletic Club to-morrow night." It was devastating news, and no reasons were given. The *Sun* calmly noted, "With the two big Macs gone the Irish American AC is pushed nearer the brink of oblivion," adding that it was the victories of the "two big policemen athletes ... that enabled the Irish club to carry off team titles." While McGrath, unattached since April, was cleared to compete for the club, McDonald still had to wait six months. Along with Ryan, the trio were slated to take part in a special All-Around Weight contest at the closing event of the season at Celtic Park, hosted by the Irish Federation of the United States.[8]

1917 was also the first time since 1904 that a club member hadn't broken a world record, while the Irish had only one member—McDonald in the 16LB shot—picked for the AAU's All-America team. The *New York Times* highlighted Chicago AC's rise as "rendered easier of accomplishment by the withdrawal of the Irish-American AC from active competition at the first mention of hostilities." Summing up the year, the *New York Tribune* remarked succinctly, "With the decision of the [NYAC] not to be represented in any championship and the disbandment of the Irish-American Athletic Club, the local organizations were not so prominent as formerly in title competitions." The winter season was an even worse washout for the club than the summer. They were absent from the National Cross-Country Championships in Boston, the Met Indoor Championships, and the Nationals on March 16. Speaking of their absence in Boston, the *New York Times* noted, "There was a considerable upheaval in cross-country running owing to the war.... The Irish-American AC, a formidable factor in previous years, was entirely eliminated, while the New York AC only put teams in the metropolitan events which were run in the Spring and then without success."[9]

* * *

Although Celtic Park continued to be used, 1918 saw the I-AAC's activity stall completely. But if that wasn't enough to dent the Irish-Americans, at 10:55 pm on March 27 came the news that one of the greatest athletes America had known had passed away at St. Vincent's Hospital, a day short of his 37th birthday. Martin Sheridan, "the greatest amateur athlete of all time," according to the *Evening Star [Washington, D.C.]*, was one of the early casualties from the so-called Spanish Flu epidemic. "Taken ill a little more than a week ago, his condition quickly became critical, and he was in a precarious state for several days before his death," the *New York Times* reported. The *New York Tribune* claimed that recently the athlete's life "had been despaired of on several occasions by his attending physicians, but the wonderful stamina that characterized all his efforts on the athletic field made itself evident and each time he rallied and fought off death." The report continued, "Few athletes have attained the fame won by Martin Sheridan, frequently characterized by experts as the best all-round athlete of all time." Alex Sullivan, writing in the *Evening World*, recalled:

> His death is largely due to his great devotion to duty.... Last Friday he went to work feeling ill. He was told by his fellow-workers in the First Branch Bureau where he was a Detective Sergeant to go back home, but Martin insisted on working. There was never a star athlete who wasn't game, as victory often only comes to those who are most persistent—those that never give up no matter how dark their chances seem of winning. That was probably why Martin, the star of all star athletes, wouldn't return home, even though, as he said, he was "a mighty sick man."

The *Sun* revealed, "Half an hour later the athlete was on the verge of collapse. A physician was called and he was hurried to the hospital." An ambulance took him to St. Vincent's, where he was diagnosed with pleuropneumonia, a condition that most, if not all newspapers would run with. "He battled hard to throw off the grip that the Grim Reaper was trying to get on him. For the past few days he had been receiving stimulants to keep alive."

The *Evening Star* claimed that Sheridan had told a journalist a fortnight previously, "We will never have the good old times again." It was something the newspaper added melancholically, "How soon the words of the great athlete came through."[10]

Three days later, Sheridan was taken from St. Vincent Ferrer's Church, on 67th and Lexington, accompanied by a huge number of friends, colleagues, I-AAC members and leading members of the city's political establishment, to be buried at Calvary Cemetery. "Great crowds thronged about the streets over which the funeral procession passed on the way from Sheridan's late home, 722 Lexington Avenue, to the church, but the funeral itself was of inconspicuous character, in keeping with the personality of the former Olympic champion during his life." Seventy-five cops and 50 firemen "stood at the attention in the street until the casket was placed on the catafalque," as the NYPD Catholic chaplain, the Rev. Daniel Coogan, performed the service before 30 policemen escorted Sheridan to the cemetery. The honorary pall-bearers included the former New York Governor, Martin H. Glynn, and NYPD Commissioner Richard Enright, as well as Conway and Cohalan. The *Sun* added that "though the church is a large one it was barely large enough to hold the host of friends who had turned out to pay their last tribute to the hero of many a hard fought battle won." Coogan, remarking about his text for the sermon, declared, "And he did keep faith. He kept it as a policeman; he kept it as a man. He was a magnificent athlete and a fine servant of the public. He remained on duty long after any ordinary man would have given up. He kept the faith."[11]

Cigarette card image of Martin Sheridan. He was arguably the club's most famous athlete, tragically taken from this world in 1918 by "Spanish 'flu."

Immediately afterwards, plans were put forward for a suitable memorial for the Mayoman, including a hospital endowment to be given in his name. Finally, with talk of a national stadium being built in the capital and thoughts of hosting the 1920 Olympics, suggestions were made that it should be named after the Irish cop. "This, it was declared, would furnish a lasting memorial to the deeds of the once great Sheridan," the *New York Times* said. Possibly due to Sheridan's death, the I-AAC organized a Memorial Day Games, with profits estimated around $500 given over to the Sheridan Memorial Fund. Pat McDonald helped make the event a success, breaking Ryan's world record for the 35LB weight with a distance of 63:5.[12]

A proposal for a Concert and Games at Laurel Hill on July 27 "for the purpose of raising funds to erect a memorial in honor of Martin J. Sheridan," was suggested, with Police Commissioner Richard Enright requesting all policemen to support the event:

> [I]t is expected that the police force will generously respond to this appeal for the erection of a suitable monument in honor of a man who has reflected the greatest possible credit upon this department, at home and abroad. He was a man of the highest integrity and splendid type of policeman. He was a central figure in the three great international Olympian Games, and it was largely due to this athlete's pre-eminence that the honors were won by the American team.

The *New York Times* reported that the NYPD would pay its final respects to Sheridan at Celtic Park the following Saturday, "when the bluecoats will gather at an athletic meet, the proceeds of which will be devoted to erecting a suitable monument over the grave of the famous police athlete.... Every bluecoat not on active duty next Saturday afternoon will rendezvous at Celtic Park." Police athletes, like McGrath, McDonald and Erickson, were to participate. "The Police Band and Glee Club have donated their services for the occasion, and will take part in the flag raising ceremonies that will precede the athletics." Watched by 5,000 spectators, with 15,000 tickets eventually sold, Richard Enright declared:

> Athletics were the pride of the ancient Greeks because athletics were necessary to make good soldiers. The ancient Greeks brought up their men to be great soldiers, but first they taught them to be great athletes.... It is with great pride that I mention the name of Martin J. Sheridan, who through his athletic prowess brought the honors of the great Olympic Games to the Western World on two occasions.[13]

* * *

Apart from hosting the Met Juniors on July 21, which they didn't enter, the I-AAC had little further contact with athletic competition. At the Met Seniors in Elizabeth, New Jersey, on August 25, former members, like Erickson (winner in the high jump) now with Bronx Church House, and McDonald (winner of both the 16LB shot and the 56LB weight) were the only connection with the I-AAC. As for the Nationals held near Chicago, McGrath won the hammer and "Fifty-Six."[14]

Still, there was no lack of optimism and blarney emanating from Celtic

Park that a return to the big-time was imminent. As the New Year was barely hours old, the *New York Times* reported, "This was indicated yesterday when it developed that officials of the Irish-American AC are planning a return to athletic activity after voluntary idleness throughout the length of time the country was at war." The club had placed its hopes on capturing Pores and Kyronen, both former Millrose members now running unattached. The *Times* added that Conway had declared "the club would immediately commence a campaign to renew" competing:

> Every effort is to be made to regain for the club the position it enjoyed in the athletic world before this country entered the war. Many of the organization's star athletes, who in the past years have gained championship titles while wearing the Winged Fist emblem, have recently been in communication with the club officials. The majority of them have declared their intention of returning to the organization.

But instead this was the end of the road: The war had ended less than three months previously, but the peace would never bring the I-AAC a return to its heyday.[15]

The obvious question to ask after all this is why? Why would the I-AAC shut down its operations and ultimately destroy itself after almost 20 years of good work? The *New York Times* claimed, upon the club's announcement in April 1917, that the decision was taken because most members were between 19 and 25, and "the club is anxious to see these young men enroll for military service, whether conscription comes or not." It would repeat the club's line almost two months later that the club had no choice, as "all of its worth-while athletic stars of suitable age" were on duty with various regiments. One suggestion for the enthusiasm to send its young athletes to the trenches stretched back to 1898, when at one of its early meetings a resolution passed "to the effect that stockholders of the club who would volunteer for service in the coming [Spanish] war, would be exempt from any further assessments," somehow encouraged athletes to become reservists. But wasn't this the "people's club," with a large number of essential public workers—policemen unquestionably but also firemen, municipal workers, etc.—categorized by the British as "reserved occupations," who would have avoided conscription?[16]

These reasons now seem lame. Indeed one can speculate that the I-AAC hierarchy, with the exception of the unreformed "rebel" Daniel Cohalan, fell over themselves to show their patriotism, and fearing what was coming towards German-Americans, didn't want the same leveled at the Irish. Unsurprisingly, the decision to suspend competitive athletics and push young men into the military wasn't a popular choice amongst all members. As a policy, joining the war in 1914 was lukewarm at best outside a small group of anglophiles. Amongst much of Irish-America, there was a mistrustful antipathy to supporting Perfidious Albion, mirrored by the Irish state during World War II. For almost three years, Irish-America had stood firmly against American intervention, and through outlets like the *Irish World* and *The Gaelic American*, there was unashamed support for the Kaiser, and equal vitriol directed towards Irish politicians who supported the war, especially John Redmond. Unsurprisingly, the club's action "was criticized severely" by some of the members, and as the *Sun's* athletic correspondent "Daniel" noted in April 1917, they "will endeavor to show the governors the error of their decision. It is argued that the members best can keep in condition and prepare for service by continuing the usual competitions."[17]

Reflecting on this decision in June 1931 as the first housing went up on the now defunct Celtic Park, Conway was clearly downcast: "We decided to give up athletics for [the war's] duration. We wrote to President Wilson and offered Celtic Park to the nation for any purpose he saw fit. He thanked us for our patriotism but he had to decline the offer." The I-AAC could well have continued in the manner of all the other clubs, losing a limited number of athletes, while carrying on with those left behind. Ironically, the club lost more significant athletes—Ryan, McDonald, McGrath, and Kolehmainen— to rival clubs than to the trenches of France.[18]

Celtic Park remained the center of the city's top Gaelic football and hurling matches, and Irish societies' picnics for the time being at least. The Avondale AC "Big Carnival of Sports" of August 1919 hosted the U.S. Gaelic Football Championship between Galway and Cavan, while The Eccentric Firemen Games of August 17, 1919, attended by 5,000 spectators, was a day, according to the *New York Tribune*, that "reminded the old-timers of the halcyon days at the Irish grounds." A series of athletic heats were held, and the points score was won by the NYAC. Clubs like St. Cristopher, Kings County AA, Brooklyn AA, Morningside AC, Loughlin Lyceum, Jersey Harriers and Paulist AC entered athletes, although the Irish chose either not to or were unable to gather a team. For what remained of the I-AAC, there were a number of other setbacks. The ice hockey team was seriously depleted by casualties to Canadian hockey stars serving in Europe. A month after the armistice, a fire broke out in the Celtic Park dressing rooms, causing $1,000 of damage, before three manholes on East 60th Street, between Third and Lexington Avenues, suddenly exploded in January 1920 through electrical faults, causing windows to shatter along the block, including a couple at Bloomingdales. At the I-AAC clubhouse, the trophy cabinet was destroyed.[19]

* * *

These incidents were nothing compared to the damage caused by the Volstead Act of January 18, 1920. Whether illicit alcohol was a factor or not, Celtic Park suffered a major riot later that year when the New York Caledonian Club hosted its Annual Caledonian Games there. The initial belligerents weren't Scottish patrons but drunken Irishmen annoyed that their "turf" had been overtaken by foreigners in kilts. "After conducting sixty-five annual sets of games in peace, the largest Scotch organization in New York City, ran into trouble when this year it decided to hold its games in Celtic Park," reported the *Brooklyn Daily Eagle*, although the Caledonian Club had previously held events at Celtic Park without incident. The *New York Tribune*, predictably referencing that infamous Irish carnival, sighed:

> Irish patriots thirsting for Caledonian blood turned the sixty-fourth annual games of the New York Caledonian Club into a Donnybrook Fair yesterday.... Celtic Park is the field of the Irish-American Athletic Club. Patriotism blazed in every Irishman who heard the news, though it was true that the flame burned with an odor of alcohol when the patriots got to Celtic Park.[20]

Trouble began when small parties of Irishmen—"twenty-five or thirty of them and every one of them had a name that reeked of the bogs, the turf and the blue hills of Ireland.... The invaders paid for tickets without a murmur; indeed, some of them remarked afterward that it was worth double the price"—came to pick fights. "At first they swaggered about through the park," reported the *New York Tribune*, "elbowing all whom they met and mutter remarks about the Scotch." While the organizers broke up these scuffles, things escalated throughout the day. "Fights multiplied and converged until to the casual spectator, it looked as though some 600 men in kilts had assembled in a compact group for the purpose of indulging in community convulsions." By six o'clock there were scraps everywhere. Nearby Hunters Point Police station dispatched a "riot squad" of cops "whose names ranged from Cassidy to O'Hoolihan ... [who] charged through the knots of fighters in Celtic Park without regard for burr or brogue and then turned and charged again. It was a sure cure for convulsions. The mass dissolved and Scotchman and Irishman took to their heels." According to the *New York Times*, while the police "used their clubs freely ... it was some time before they got the disturbances under control." Finally, two ambulances were called, "but the physicians worked with several doctors in the crowd and broken heads were patched up without the necessity" of their use. Six men were arrested who "each loudly proclaim[ed] his Irish birth and decrying kilts and Scotch whisky." While the Games themselves were called off, the programmed dancing continued and did "not end till cock-crow."[21]

The following day, the *New York Tribune* ran with the headline "Six Freed to Nurse Hurts After Irish-Scotch Shindy: Failure to Salute Sinn Fein Colors Turned Caledonian Games Into Combat." The "[b]ruised and remorseful, participants in the fight that broke up the Caledonian Club's games at Celtic Park" were freed from the local jail with only promises to behave:

The testimony at the hearing proved one thing, the mistake made by the Scotch organization in hiring an Irish association's property for its festivities. The field is owned by the Irish-American Athletic Club. When the Caledonians, wearing kilts paraded about the field before the athletic events were scheduled to take place, they passed three flags, according to witnesses at the hearing. These were the American flag, the Scotch colors and the green, white and orange of the Sinn Fein. Witnesses told Magistrate Dale that while the marchers dipped their banners with due respect before the first two flags named, they "trailed on" past the Irish colors with never so much as a "how d'ye do." This slight aroused a group of Irishmen in the grandstand, and the exchange of polthogues came about in less time than it takes to tell it.[22]

Booze was at the center of matters two years later when the arrest of a "bootlegger," James Sullivan, for selling whiskey at the Local No. 20, International Union of Steam and Operating Engineers Picnic, ended in violence. Four people were injured by bullets, including Ruth (some reports say Rita) Curley, an 18-year-old Irishwoman shot through the abdomen, who had only been in the United States two months, and a policeman, John Bell. A number of others were injured by flying bottles and bricks. Five thousand people witnessed the carnage at an event Mayor "Red Mike" Hylan was due to address at 5:30 pm. As Sullivan was being led out of Celtic Park by police under the command of Lt. Robert McCarthy, his clients began shouting to others: "The cops have made a pinch. Come on!" This was akin to "a battle cry," commented the *Evening World*. "In an instant the pavilion was emptied of dancers. Men and women surged … demanding that [McCarthy] release Sullivan. A woman standing behind McCarthy hit him on the head with a club. He staggered but held on to his man." It seemed to be, according to the *Washington Times*, that all the "boxers, wrestlers, fighters, dancers and others forgot all about their opponents and made one universal rush" at the police. "Abusive epithets were hurled, and in an instant hundreds of men and women were running to the spot," said the *New York Times*. "Bottles started flying through the air. Then someone in the crowd fired a revolver. Bell drew his weapon and fired a shot in the air. Several other shots followed in quick succession." By the time the police arrived, the event had descended into a full-scale "40-Minute Battle." "Scores of men were fighting other men, and women were engaging in hair pulling matches," the *Evening World* continued. "The original cause of the trouble seemed to have been forgotten."[23]

By the summer of 1922, Celtic Park had acquired a reputation as a place where you could buy a drink while taking in a sporting event, carrying on a long history of clashes with the law over the sale of alcohol. In December 1901, Celtic Park's manager, Joseph McKane, was brought before the local beak charged with selling booze on the Sabbath. The *Brooklyn Daily Eagle* blared the comical sub-headline: "The Irish Athletic Association's Resort at Celtic Park Said Not to Be a Hotel," because the magistrate, seemingly without irony, commented that the stadium "does not comply with the statutory requirements as to [hotel] rooms and other necessaries" required under the Raines Law, which prevented Sunday alcohol sales in New York outside hotel guests eating or drinking in their rooms. Now, as the *New York Times* reported, "Frequent complaints that Celtic Park was being used by bootleggers as a center for their operations" prompted action from the NYPD.[24]

With a teenage girl shot and almost killed, the writing was on the wall for the Long Island stadium. The *Evening World* ran with the headline "BOOZE RIOT MAY CLOSE CELTIC PARK: Citizens Tell Prosecutor Place Is Nuisance," and divulged, "Until recently there have been no complaints against Celtic Park.... But for more than six months bootleggers have been arrested at the park every Sunday, sometimes as many as a dozen. Nearly fifty have been lined in the County Court by Judge Humphrey." The *New York*

Two agents empty barrels of liquor as NYPD Deputy Commissioner John A. Leach and police officers look on. Prohibition effectively killed off Celtic Park as a business, turning it into "a gathering place for bootleggers" (Library of Congress).

Times claimed that the riot had finally pushed Queens District Attorney Dana Wallace into investigating Celtic Park's alcohol market. "These [bootleggers] have been doing a retail business from bottles of whisky carried in their pockets, it is charged," adding that a Mister Big ran the show, "a master bootlegger ... responsible for the liquor peddling" that had to be taken out. With 90 years of hindsight, a good few films and the odd HBO series, we know that it would take more than the incarceration of one individual to knock out this business.[25]

Naturally the I-AAC was in a state of panic. Where had it all gone wrong in the past seven years? Conway belatedly issued a statement to the press: "We feel that accounts of the affair last Saturday were unfairly exaggerated and that it also is unfair to lay the blame on our club and the majority of good Irish people who attend the park weekly, instead of upon a few ruffians who get into the park and make trouble." He then turned on the messenger, criticizing press coverage that tried "to indicate that the park was a gathering place for bootleggers," adding curtly that the club had done everything in its power to prevent booze being sold.[26]

For their part, Celtic Park's management cleaned up their premises. The grounds were free from trouble for the rest of the season as a number of events took place, though bootleggers no doubt kept a discreet presence within the park. Meanwhile, the I-AAC's absence from competitive athletics was highlighted a month later when the NYAC took its fourth Met title since 1919, all won with a total in excess of a 110 points. The *New York Times* opined in its coverage, "In scoring its victory the New York AC squad retained a title ... in a similarly hollow fashion—a championship on which the club has enjoyed a monopoly since the withdrawal of the Irish-American AC from local athletics about six years ago."[27]

All the club could muster in response to this was a celebration of its 25th anniversary on Decoration Day, 1923. The *New York Times* described the event as "a revival of interest in athletics by officials and members," as 31 members, mostly retired athletes like Sheppard, McDonald, Hayes, Kiviat and Meyer, met at the office of the President of the Board of Alderman, George Hulbert, at City Hall. The proposed event would be limited to former and the few current members remaining, although it was later open to "old timers" from other clubs who had been out of competition for at least eight years. Seventeen former club Olympians were slated to compete, which in addition to those listed above included Robertson and McGrath.[28]

On the day, all the old names still living or residing in New York turned up, although how many competed is open to debate The main event was the 440Yds relay, in which the Irish combo of Kiviat, Bromilow, Schaaf and Meyer beat the NYAC team, while a "B" selection containing Robertson, Rosenberger, Archer and Sheppard came in third. The *Brooklyn Eagle* observed that the veterans, some of whom had traveled far, were there "to tell the world that they are just as young as they used to be," while the *New York Times* reminisced about the glory days of the arena, claiming it was more of a "reunion" as retired athletes met each other for the first time in years:

> It seemed as though the hands of time had been turned back almost a decade yesterday at the twenty-fifth anniversary celebration games ... when a little band of half a hundred track and field stars of yesterday, whose prowess brought fame and repeated triumphs to the Winged Fist in former years, once more appeared in their old suits and running shoes, and received a big ovation from the fifteen hundred or more present.

Nothing came from this, and the only piece of relevance that Conway performed in that year was to organize, in conjunction with the NYAC, a reception for the return of the Light-Heavyweight World Champion, Mike McTigue, who had once worked at the Mercury Foot as the assistant boxing coach.[29]

Celtic Park stuttered along, hosting Gaelic football and hurling matches until the bulk of games were moved to the GAA's own grounds at Innisfail Park on 240th Street and Broadway in 1928. Without this much-needed income, the stadium suffered the final ignominy when plans were announced at the Commodore Hotel in mid-September by the New York Greyhound Racing Association, to convert it into a dog track and to replace the 2,700-seat grandstand with one capable of accommodating 8,000 butts. Immediately, vociferous protests emerged from the "Laurel Hill Improvement Association," led by George W. Morton Jr. and the "Thompson Hill Taxpayers Association" against this "Sport of Queens." Morton claimed that the switch would be to the "detriment to the community" and would attract "a gambling and 'riff-raff' element" to the area. These efforts failed, the opening night on September 28 was postponed through legal difficulties, but from October 3, mutts ran where Olympic gold medalists had once trod. Celtic Park hosted a "forty-day schedule" with such races as the "Jimmy Walker Derby," named after the flamboyant city mayor "Beau James" Walker, and, the laughable—if it wasn't so tragic—Martin Sheridan Memorial race, "a four-dog hurdle classic" according to the *New York Times*, which was won on opening night by Mrs. Frank Adams' pooch, Peero, as police fought heroically to prevent any betting on the grounds.[30]

Dog racing—big in Britain—was a financial disaster, helped undoubtedly by the fact that betting was severely hindered. Bookies had to conjure up imaginative practices, like "selling" pictures of dogs and "buying" these pictures back later if their faces won, to overcome the betting ban. While the 1929 Gaelic football opening season began with both GAA grounds hosting matches—Celtic Park had the Tipperary versus Wexford senior game—real-estate vultures were again circling Laurel Hill. By May 1928, the *New York Times* had recorded one speculator buying up nearby land in the hope that the grounds would be bought for housing. Inevitably, what was left of the I-AAC, its Celtic Park, would sooner or later be sold off.[31]

17

"Perhaps we shall again see the day"

Little remains today to remind us of the Irish-American Athletic Club. There is the website "wingedfist.org," administered by Ian McGowan, who has accumulated a number of club trophies and artifacts, and also managed to convince the New York City Council to co-name the corner of 43rd Street and 48th Avenue "Winged Fist Way," the spot where the clubhouse once stood. "It is important that we recognize the achievements of this dynamic athletic club, which once called Sunnyside and the borough home," declared City Council member Jimmy Van Bramer at the official unveiling in March 2012. "Before its members knew it, the IAAC laid the foundation of what would become the essence of Queens, a multicultural diaspora of people who worked and lived together." Elsewhere, a small number of club items are kept by New York University's Archive of Irish America, which is also displayed online. Finally, there is what you can find in newspaper archives.[1]

One thing for sure was that the I-AAC didn't die broke. On February 22, 1930, news surfaced that the I-AAC had sold Celtic Park to the City & Suburban Homes Company for around $500,000. The *Brooklyn Daily Eagle* would later confirm that the figure was $420,000, although initially some put the price as high as $5,000,000. The *Gaelic American* reported, "The rapid building up of Long Island City made it no longer possible to retain Celtic Park. Thirty-three years ago the Celtic Park district was nearly a wilderness. Now there are few vacant lots in the neighborhood."[2]

A "limited dividend corporation," City & Suburban was founded over 30 years previously by, amongst others, Cornelius Vanderbilt, to construct low-rent homes, or "moderate-priced housing for wage-earners," as the *New York Times* described it. The newspaper would later disclose that the property was not bought "without complications," with additional "triangle gores" obtained from other owners to square out the site because the plot "was irregular in shape, having been originally acquired before the streets were laid out." Work wouldn't begin for another 18 months, constructing eight units to accommodate up to 1,000 families. Costing "several million dollars" to build, the first apartments would be leased in October 1931, with less than five months of construction.³

Speculators had been eyeing Celtic Park for years, and Conway frequently quashed rumors that it was up for sale. "I wouldn't be surprised if we held the property for the next twenty years," he optimistically told the *New York Times* in 1914. He was wrong: With the stadium lying on the edge of a swiftly expanding major city, pressure increased to sell. In 1928, the Borough decided to run streets through the grounds. "Of course, the carrying out of this scheme would make it worthless as a sports field," added the *Gaelic American*, "and the directors ... had to make arrangements to dispose of it to the highest bidder." That the club itself was on life-support made the decision easy.⁴

Meanwhile the Manhattan clubhouse hosted one of its last events in January 1930, as the city's Irish societies gathered to discuss the St. Patrick's Day parade. Nine months later, the I-AAC voted "to dissolve" the club, as state law required, before assets were sold and profits divided. The *Brooklyn Daily Eagle* reported that the move "marks almost the last step in closing up of the Celtic Park reality deal of last February." Back then, there had been "hot opposition" to the sale; now at the Hotel Astor on September 14, there was none. Richard F. Dalton, the club's representative in dealings, declared that $500 would be given for every $50 share held. The *Gaelic American* lamented:

> Until such time as a place for Irish games and sports can be secured there will no permanent grounds for holding the games of the Gael. It is certain however that no place so suitable and convenient can be found within the limits of Greater New York. The passing of Celtic Park will be regretted by many people who had enjoyed Gaelic football and hurling for more than thirty years.

The *Brooklyn Eagle* was, however, more pragmatic in its conclusion:

> The story of Celtic park strikingly illustrates the swelling of reality values in Queens, especially in easily reached sections. Incidentally, it emphasizes the importance of making other sections more accessible by improved transit conditions. As for the Irish-American Athletic Club, its name is writ large in the history of American athletics, and most of us hope that it will have a bright future in some new environment.

And a surplus would be kept in case a future park would be built further out on Long Island.⁵

As this was happening, advertisements for Gaelic football, hurling and even camogie matches at Celtic Park still appeared in the *Gaelic American*. "Those who thought that the last of the Irish games were witnessed at Celtic Park, will be pleasantly surprised to know that the [GAA] have arranged three League games to be played again in that famous arena on next Sunday, September 14"—a junior football match between Mayo and Offaly, Galway and Antrim competing in hurling, while Louth and Kildare concluded matters with a senior football match. "As usual in Celtic Park, Irish and American dancing will continue throughout the afternoon and evening." The last meeting was slated for October 12, 1930. The *Gaelic American* announced: "A great Senior Football game is scheduled for Celtic Park this Sunday, October 12, between Cork and Kildare. It sounds like old times, in the days of the famous 'Big Four' when Cork, Kildare, Kerry and Kilkenny dominated the Gaelic football field." No report of the day's events was found, and it's possible that either bad weather or the eagerness of City and Suburban to get cracking, caused this swansong to be shelved. The last event ever to grace the field of Celtic Park was probably a senior football game between Roscommon and Kerry on October 5, 1930.[6]

Still, to come away with $411,000 dollars, almost 5,000 percent profit on an investment over 32 years was impressive; to pull it off as the country was about to go into the greatest financial depression it had ever seen was very fortunate. City & Suburban found it hard to fill its homes. It didn't begin building its fifth unit until early 1937, while a sixth—completing building on three-quarters of the site—wouldn't start until 1939. But this didn't stop the bickering as arguments over the club's cadaver descended into infighting. A "$1,655,000" suit for "gross inefficiency and waste" and "diverting large sums" was brought in 1932 by Thomas Curran against former club directors, his three brothers—Peter, Frank and John—"Big Tom" Farley, George Murray Hulbert, and Cohalan.[7]

Conway had already departed earlier in the year to the great athletic club in the sky, passing away from pneumonia at his daughter Josephine Healey's Freeport home on January 16, aged 71. Having handed over the presidency of the shell club in 1925 to Tierney O'Rourke and then Harry Cunningham, the last club head, the *Gaelic American* wrote on his death: "He had been in bad health for several years past, and his old friends in New York who knew and loved him in the days of his activity missed him from their meetings and social gatherings." Interred at the New Calvary Cemetery, he joined Frawley, who had died, aged 59, in 1926 from a heart attack. Dowling would outlive Conway another two years, passing away in March 1934 from a cerebral hemorrhage, aged 68, while Daniel Cohalan would live to 81, dying in 1946.[8]

* * *

The Irish-American Athletic Club of New York, after being in existence for just over 50 years in one form or another, was now officially dead: There would be no athletic stadium built further out in the 'burbs. A letter in the

New York Times from "MJL" of New York dated June 30, 1936, spoke of the "pleasure" and the "fond memories" of Sheppard and "others of their type, who represented the Irish-American AC" that an interview by John Kieran with George Bonhag had brought him. The writer suggested that "efforts were made" in the autumn of 1935 to restart the club: "What a treat it would be to us old-timers and our present generation of athletic enthusiasts if the Irish-American AC were revived.... I hope that those active in [attempting to resurrect the club] have not given up the attempt. A club of that nature is sorely needed today."[9]

> In further correspondence the following month, Thomas Curran told the *Times*: Permit me to assure MJL that efforts to reorganize the Irish-American Athletic Club have not been abandoned. A general meeting will probably be called this fall, which all those sincerely interested should attend. Perhaps we shall again see the day when athletes of the caliber of Martin Sheridan, Mel Sheppard, Johnny Hayes, George Bonhag and others will capture Olympic trophies for Uncle Sam.

In a further letter dated September 12, he added:

> So widespread has been the response and so genuine the interest shown in the numerous letters received by me relative to the organization of the Irish-American Athletic Club, which I mentioned in my letter published August 22, that I would appreciate being accorded the privilege of space in your columns. My previous letter was followed by a veritable deluge of inquiries, with the result that efforts leading to the reorganization have received a tremendous impetus and the contemplated general meeting has been scheduled for Sept 25 at the Central Opera House, 207 East Sixty-seventh Street."[10]

There are no reports that this meeting ever took place, and the I-AAC as everyone knew it remained dead. The name, at least in the Metropolitan area, continued elsewhere: Newark had a fairly successful I-AAC unconnected with Conway, while an Irish-American football club competed in the American Soccer League in 1939. But apart from that, the I-AAC was just another defunct institution, and Celtic Park, "that well known sporting field" as the *New York Times* saluted it shortly after its sale, "has experienced the same fate which has befallen so many other celebrated athletic centers in the metropolitan area."[11]

Again the question: Why did this happen? Nobody gives a solid reason why the club suddenly collapsed, apart from "the war." A number of factors came together in the final years after April 1917. Procrastination regarding whether it would actively continue didn't help. But the "brand" and its amenities certainly would've attracted new talent. The Volstead Act probably affected profits, but Irish sports and picnics continued at the grounds, regardless.

The 1920s saw the advent of new diversions for the masses, of which the car and the movies were the most damaging, but even this can't be cited as the reason. Take baseball: In 1910, both New York franchises were runners-up in their leagues, while Brooklyn came in sixth in the NL. The average per-game attendance for the Giants was 6,478; the Yankees (earlier the Highlanders) 4,622; while Brooklyn's was 3,492. Jump forward 20 years in the first year of the Great Depression, and the Giants have an average of 11,282, the Yankees 15,385 and Brooklyn 14,251. And yet both New York teams had come in third while Brooklyn was fourth. Baseball wasn't affected by either Hollywood or the automobile.[12]

Had athletics lost its appeal? Conway, perhaps with a hint of bitterness at what had happened to his club, claimed that following the war "it was impossible to gather the old crowds together." Some suggest that track and field was solely for the "purists" who wanted to see raw athletic ability rather than aesthetic sport. The rest of us wished to be entertained, leading athletics to lose its popularity in Ireland within the GAA to Gaelic football and hurling. And yet the crowds at the elite championships failed to back up this argument. Eight thousand attended the 1930 Met AA Championships at Pershing Field, Jersey City, compared to the 1910 event at Travers Island which attracted 5,000 to 6,000 patrons. Nor can we blame the decline in ethnic identity as a factor, especially as the Swedish-American AC, a smaller, less influential, but older club than the I-AAC—founded around 1894—which changed its name, much as the GNYIAA had, in June 1908 from the Swedish Sporting Athletic Association, was able to survive until the 1930s, and come in third at the 1930 Met AA Championships. And let's not forget that Celtic Park was still busy with Irish sports virtually up to its disposal.[13]

Those who gained most out of the death of the I-AAC were undoubtedly the "staid" NYAC. With only one Spalding Trophy from 1904 to 1916, the NYAC came back to dominate the city's track and field with a vengeance. Bolstered by rich members and having the elite facilities immune to the deprivations of either wars or depressions, after returning to the 1919 Met AA Champs at Jersey City, the club went on a 36-year winning streak. While it could never impose this hegemony, as the Irish-Americans had, on the national championships—there were too many good clubs elsewhere—it was not until 1955 that any other club in the New York Metropolitan area were able to beat them in the Mets. During this time the gap between the NYAC and the rest in the city was depressing. For instance, in 1934 the club accumulated 127½ points; second-place Millrose AC gathered 25. Numerous clubs came and many went, some with names like the Grand Street Boys and the New York Curb Exchange, none of which made much impression. Two ethnic clubs—the Swedish-American and German-American—stood out, but while both made it into the top three in some years, they were nowhere near a threat to the NYAC as the I-AAC was.

Winner of the 100Yds and 220Yds titles for the triumphant Pioneer Athletic Club that day in 1955 at Downing Stadium, Randalls Island, was Andy Stanfield. A double gold medalist in Helsinki three years earlier, he was one of a line of gifted African American track athletes who emerged after World War I. Founded in Harlem by three African Americans in 1936, with Joe Yancey, Jr. its own Patrick Conway, the Pioneer AC had picked up the baton of integration left by the I-AAC's demise. Their 1955 success was achieved with a multi-racial team of not only Jewish and black athletes, but also some of Irish ancestry.[14]

By the 1996 Olympics in Atlanta, the NYAC had won 117 Olympic golds, of which 68 were in track and field. But a running gold had eluded them now for 40 years. Times changed, and as athletes became fully professional, the NYAC became even more entrenched as a club solely reliant on the "social element" that Frederick Janssen detested. As the battle for civil rights for all Americans heated up south of the Mason-Dixon Line, the NYAC became an even greater anachronism.[15]

The tumultuous year of 1968 saw black athletes take their anger out at the Mexican Olympiad. But before that, a multi-racial bunch of competitors—including a team of Soviet runners—boycotted the NYAC's Centenary showpiece, its annual indoor meeting at Madison Square Garden on February 16. In Irish-Catholic terms, a number of Catholic college teams—Manhattan, Villanova and Georgetown principally—also stayed away, but it was a *New York Times* article by Martin Arnold about Kenneth L. Woodward, *Newsweek* magazine's religion editor and spokesman for a group of 50 former Notre Dame students, Notre Dame Alumni Against Racial Discrimination, that caught the eye most. Woodward called on the Indiana university's alumni in the city, and any Catholic clergy who were club members, to resign from the NYAC "unless the club explains its membership policies with regards to nonwhites and non-Christians." He told Arnold that he had contacted the Most Reverend John J. Maguire, administrator of the Archdiocese of New York, in order to ensure that his priests didn't belong to clubs that still had a color line.[16]

What was more crucial here, as Woodward pointed out, was how the club was now closely associated with Irish-American New Yorkers:

> The New York Athletic Club has a reputation of being a Catholic club—more particularly an Irish Catholic hangout. This brings it very close to Notre Dame. We ask all Catholic clergy to resign from the club if they are convinced that the club follows racial discrimination in its membership policies. [It is] particularly scandalous for priests to support any organization that makes racism a part of its practices. We're talking about the club's general practices—not talking about a house Negro or a house Jew. It's not enough for them to say we have two or three Jewish members.

Shortly afterwards, Pete Axthelm of *Sports Illustrated* slammed the NYAC as a "crusty old Irish-dominated club."[17]

So this was where the city's Irish athletic community had arrived at 60-plus years after the I-AAC admitted John B. Taylor to a club with an already considerable non–Irish membership. The first major integrated sporting establishment had disappeared, and in its place was a club that practiced thinly disguised racial discrimination. Robert Lipsyte, writing in 1996, claimed that comparing the NYAC with both Nazi Germany and the then–South African regime were "not entirely fair," but admitted this:

> [T]he club could not be allowed to pick athletes on the basis of the comfort zone they might offer to the overwhelmingly white, disproportionately Irish Catholic membership. The protest fractured the local athletic community in one of the ways the Vietnam War fractured the larger society; if [B]lacks are good enough to compete (fight) under your colors, why aren't we good enough for total equality?[18]

However, reality was slightly different. The cost of NYAC membership, compared to the I-AAC, was always restrictive except for the rich Irish. Tammany's first-ever black leader, J. Raymond Jones, claimed in his memoirs that the NYAC "at that time was very Irish Catholic. Important Irishmen from as far away as Buffalo came to this club when in New York to pay their respects." This was 1944, and the key word here is "important." Steam baths apparently were what Irish-American politicos liked most about the NYAC, not an invitation to run the 3Mile Cross-Country event. And as Stephen Birmingham claims, while many of the city's FIFs (First Irish Families) were club members, the "notoriously anti–Semitic [club] is said to have an unwritten 'quota' for Catholic members."[19]

This combination of elitism, prejudice and expensive fees were what the I-AAC had initially fought against. In his novel, *In One Person*, set at the end of the "freewheeling seventies," John Irving describes how a bisexual wrestler—an unheard-of minority during Celtic Park's heydays—tries to get an NYAC guest pass to the club from his friend Arthur:

> "I had no knowledge of the tight-assed elements in the New York Athletic Club.... I have no idea what Arthur had to go through just to get me a guest pass...."
> "Are you crazy, Billy?" Elaine asked me. "Are you trying to get yourself killed? That place is notoriously anti-*everything*. It's anti-*Semitic*, it's anti-*black*."
> "It is?" I asked her. "How do you know?"
> "It's anti-*women*—I fucking know that!" Elaine had said. "It's an Irish Catholic boys' club, Billy—just the Catholic part ought to have you running for the hills."[20]

No one can assume that the I-AAC would have become a utopian space where all citizens were treated equally, immune to the influences of a country where racism was endemic. In fact, its fragility was clearly exposed in that it couldn't survive even two decades. But the outstanding feature that we can grab from the Irish-American Athletic Club was that it wasn't just Irish. It was primarily "American," open to all those who were born there or decided to make it their home, who could compete—regardless of their color, religion, bank balance or occupation—for the club and win it points and titles. Conway encapsulated this philosophy in 1908, telling Joe Fitzgerald: "Every man that carries the Winged Fist is made to feel at home the minute he joins our organization. He is on the same level with the judge or banker and is not patted on the back after he wins and then forgotten until his next victory. Knowing this our men get out and run their heads off to win victory for the club."[21]

Glossary of Athletic Events

Below are descriptions of the various track and field events held at club meetings and in regional and national AAU championships.

It should be noted that prior to 1932, with the exception of 1928 (when, as in 1932, the National Championship served as an Olympic qualification tournament), all AAU championship races were run to the U.S. customary system of measurement by miles or yards.

The current USA Track & Field metric equivalents are provided to demonstrate what these events compare to today in national or international Olympic competition.

Track Events

60 yards—The shortest of races, known now as the 60 meters, this sprint event was usually run in indoor meetings. An outdoor 60 yard race was held only at the 1900 and 1904 Summer Olympic Games.

100 yards—A sprint or "dash" that usually covered one side (one of the two longest) of the field, and was roughly equivalent to one-sixteenth of a mile. In indoor events this race was run over a distance of 75 yards. The modern equivalent is the 100 meters.

220 yards—Now the 200 meters, this dash covered exactly one-eighth of a mile, and normally ran one straight side of the field and a curved track at the end.

440 yards—Now the 400 meters, this was the last of the sprints. The distance was exactly one fourth of a mile and was also normally one complete circuit of the stadium field's track.

880 yards—Now the 800 meters, this was the first of the middle-distance races. It was called the half-mile in the United States and would normally entail two laps of the field. At some meetings, athletes ran in the 660 yards race, which was mainly entered by middle distance runners. The indoor version of this race was the 660 yards.

The mile (1,760 yards)—The modern equivalent of this race is the 1,500 meters. At the turn of the century the mile usually took four laps of the stadium to complete.

The indoor version was the 1,000 yards race. Various distances were run between the mile and five mile. A two mile event was common, especially at indoor events.

3 miles—The modern equivalent of this race is the 5,000 meters (3.1 miles). Three mile races were also organized as team events, with a set number of runners competing not only for first second or third positions, but also for a team trophy.

5 miles—The closest AAU Championship equivalent to the current 10,000 meters race (6.21 miles). The longest stadium race normally held, 5 miles was also included at the 1908 Olympic Games, before being discontinued in favor of the 3,000 and 5,000 meters races.

120 yard hurdles—The first set of hurdle sprints, this race was the American version of the modern-day 110m hurdles, which has runners vault over hurdles or fences. In hurdling events, races under 120 yards consisted of "high hurdles," with the step pattern consisting of three steps between hurdles. Races longer than 120 yards were considered "low hurdles" which involved a seven step pattern. The indoor version of this event was the 70 yards hurdles.

220 yard hurdles—The 220 yard hurdles race regularly held at meetings was the equivalent to the 200 meters hurdles race of today. Some meetings had a race covering 250 yards.

440 yard hurdles—Equivalent to today's 400 meter hurdles.

steeplechase—Named after the Liverpool's famous horserace at Aintree racetrack (now known as the English Grand National), the race originated as a cross-country event in Ireland. An obstacle race of varied distances, with the race at the 1908 Olympics measuring just two miles (3,200 meters). The obstacles varied, too, but usually included a total of 28 fences and seven water jumps, which translates to four fences and one water jump per lap.

broad jump—Known now as the long jump, the broad jump used to refer to two events. The first, like today's long jump, involved a runner taking a run before a jump. The second, known as the standing broad jump, was a standing jump from the plate, and was an event held at the five Olympic and Intercalated Games between 1900 and 1912.

high jump—Still known as the high jump where modern competitors take a running jump over a horizontal bar. Similar to the broad jump in that it used to refer to two events: one with a running approach to the bar, and another with a standing jump over the bar. The latter was common at indoor events.

hop, step and jump—Another jumping competition considered an "Irish event" was the hop, step (or skip) and jump, which is now known as the triple jump. The order of the movements could vary. The event could start with the athlete standing and moving off with one "hop," then a "step" or "skip" and finally a "jump." Other versions included the athlete jumping past the plate with a "hop," and continuing either with another "hop" before a final "jump."

pole vault—Same equipment as today, but there were originally two events. The first, still practiced today, was a contest for height, the second was based on the distance from pole placement to where the athlete landed.

marathon—Named after the legendary journey of Pheidippides who ran from the Greek village of Marathon, following the Athenian victory over the Persians around 490 BC, 26 miles to Athens to declare victory before suddenly dropping dead, this brutal race has always been run through streets, only using the stadium track for the finishing final half mile or so.

2 mile walk—Such short walks have been discontinued for years in favor of the 20km (12.43 miles) and the 50km (31.07 miles) walks. Rules require that walkers must always keep at least one foot on the ground and that the supporting leg should remain straight until the leg stepping passes it by.

medley or relay races—"Medley" or "relay" races were run by teams of usually four athletes. The shortest distance was the 4 × 100 yards. A mile relay would be 4 × 440 yards, a two mile relay 4 × 880 yards, while a four mile relay was four runners running a mile each. At the 1908 Olympics the Medley was run as follows: Two 200m sections by the first two runners, followed by the third running 400m and finally the last runner completing two laps with 800m. This unique event combined a team of sprinters and middle distance runners.

Field Events

discus—The throwing of a "plate" style object over a distance, with athletes swirling around to get more speed while remaining in a designated area known as a ring. There were other versions at the turn of the twentieth century performed at the Olympics. The Greek version, where the athlete threw from a podium, was featured at the 1906 Intercalated Games and at London in 1908, and a two-handed discus throw—points gained from both left-handed and right-handed throws—was part of the 1912 program.

javelin—This event involved launching a spear in the air with the furthest throw winning. In 1908 in London there were two competitions: The regular javelin event, which required that the projectile was held at the center, and the freestyle event, which permitted the athlete to hold the javelin anywhere. In Stockholm four years later, there was a "two-handed" event, identical in scoring to the discus mentioned above.

shot put—In standard AAU meetings and championships this event involved thrusting a large ball weighing 16 pounds from under the athlete's ear held close to the neck. There were other shot puts weights usually ranging from five to 21 pounds. Sixteen pound shots were used in the indoor events, although there were occasionally weight contests using eight pound balls.

hammer throw—An event from the "Highland" or "Caledonian" games of Scotland, this competition involved throwing a 16 pound large ball on a chain or bar, while gathering speed by spinning. Weights included the 16-pound stone "Sledge" which was normally a hammer with a wooden handle.

56-pound weight—Possibly the most iconic Irish athletic event that transferred from the ancient Tailteann Games to the modern Olympics. The weight was held with two hands and thrown a distance from within a metal ring. Throughout the I-AAC's existence, club athletes would perform various versions (throwing for distance or height) using different weights, including the 35-pound weight and the 42-pound stone. Throwing for height required throwing the weight over a bar. The "56" survived only two Olympic Games, the 1904 Summer Olympics in St. Louis and the 1920 Olympiad of Antwerp.

Other Events

all-around championship—Now known as the decathlon (ten events), the early "all-around championship" involved nine events (100 yards, shot put, broad jump, 100 yard hurdles, 16-pound hammer, high jump, 56-pound weight, pole vault, and the hop step/skip and jump). Points were initially accumulated by the places within each category by the athlete. But later, more elaborate scoring systems were introduced where times and distances were placed against world records to mark points. While most all-around championships included an eclectic mix of events, there were sometimes two different competitions with one consisting of track events and the other weight-oriented.

cross-country championship—This race usually covered six miles, although there were also championship runs consisting of 6.12 and 6.25 miles. The race was run through parkland or forests, to give the illusion of running "across" fields or woodland. Awards would be given to both individuals and a team.

10 mile race—The 10 mile race was usually a street or park run, competed by individual runners either alone or as part of a team. Like cross-country races, this run was usually held either in the fall or early winter and was part of the winter athletics season.

Appendix
Irish-American Athletic Club Team Honors

Amateur Athletic Union National Outdoor Champions
1904, 1906, 1907, 1908, 1909, 1910, 1911, 1912, 1913, 1914, 1916

Amateur Athletic Union National Indoor Champions
1906, 1908, 1909, 1911, 1913, 1914, 1915

Metropolitan Athletic Association (AAU) Outdoor Champions
1904, 1905, 1906, 1907, 1908, 1909, 1911, 1912, 1913, 1914, 1915

AAU National Cross-Country Team Champions
1906, 1907, 1908, 1909, 1911, 1912; 1914

Metropolitan Athletic Association (AAU) Cross-Country
1912, 1913, 1914, 1915

Chapter Notes

Chapter 1

1. *New York Post*, November 26, 2012.
2. *New York Times*, April 27, 2012; *New York Post*, May 16, 2013; *New York Post*, March 14, 2014.
3. *New York Times*, April 25, 2012.
4. http,//wallstreetjackass.typepad.com/raptureready/2012/04/ny-athletic-club-fight-.html; *New York Times*, April 24, 2012.
5. *New York Times*, April 27, 2012.
6. *New York Post*, November 26, 2012.
7. John Carlos and Dave Zirin, *The John Carlos Story* (Chicago: Haymarket Books, 2011), 15.
8. *New York Times*, June 22, 2003.
9. *New York Evening World*, January 27, 1908; *New York Tribune*, January 19, 1907; *New York Evening World*, January 7, 1911. These were Mel Sheppard nine, Jack Eller six, George Bonhag 14, Crowley six, Bobbie Cloughen two, John Flanagan seven, Martin Sheridan five, Dan Ahearne two, Bruno Brodd one, and E.A. Frey one. The club's relay teams had broken five records, while Jim Archer and William Keating jointly held the 60Yds indoor record.
10. *Gaelic American*, May 26, 1906.
11. Rebecca Jenkins, *The First London Olympics 1908* (London: Piatkus, 2008), 98.
12. John Kuo Wei Tchen, "Quimbo Appo's Fear of Fenians, Chinese-Irish-Anglo Relations in New York City," *The New York Irish*, ed. Ronald H. Bayor and Timothy J. Meagher (Baltimore: Johns Hopkins University Press, 1996), 147.
13. *Irish American Weekly*, October 11, 1879.
14. Peter Bills, *Passion in Exile* (Edinburgh, UK: Mainstream, 1998), 17–18; Patrick R. Redmond, *The Irish and the Making of American Sport, 1835–1920* (Jefferson, NC: McFarland, 2014), 49.
15. Alan S. Katchen, *Abel Kiviat* (Syracuse, NY: Syracuse University Press, 2009), 50–51, 88.
16. Rebecca Jenkins, *The First London Olympics 1908* (London: Piatkus, 2008), 98; *Irish American Weekly*, January 18, 1908.
17. *New York Evening World*, January 4, 1905; *Irish American Weekly*, January 18, 1908; *Gaelic American*, January 27, 1906.
18. *Gaelic American*, September 26, 1903.
19. *Gaelic American*, January 20, 1906; *Irish American Weekly*, January 18, 1908.
20. *New York Evening World*, January 4 and 6, 1905.
21. *Gaelic American*, October 21, 1905; *Gaelic American*, March 1, 1931.
22. *New York Tribune*, March 3, 1908; *New York Times*, January 25, 1908.
23. Gregory Bond, *Jim Crow at Play* (Madison: University of Wisconsin, 2008), n25, 478; Ian McGowan, *A Brief History of the Irish-American Athletic Club* (New York: City University of New York, 2014), 1.
24. "Olympic Medalists of the Irish-American Athletic Club," Wingedfist.org http,//www.wingedfist.org/Olympic_Medalists_of_the_I-AAC.html.

Chapter 2

1. *Irish American Weekly*, April 26, 1879.
2. *New York Times*, May 31, 1879; *New York Times*, October 5, 1879; *New York Times*, October 9, 1883; *New York Herald*, February 14, 1884.

3. *Irish American Weekly*, June 21, 1879; *Irish American Weekly*, July 5, 1879.
4. *New York Times*, September 28, 1879; *New York Sun*, September 28, 1879; *Irish American Weekly*, October 25, 1879.
5. *New York Herald*, May 25, 1880; *Wilkes Spirit of the Times*, May 29, 1880; *New York Times*, May 25, 1880.
6. *Irish American Weekly*, May 25, 1880; *New York Times*, May 25, 1880; Alan S. Katchen puts the year the original I-AAC disappeared as 1882. Alan S. Katchen, *Abel Kiviat* (Syracuse, NY: Syracuse University Press, 2009), 52; *New York Times*, January 24, 1889.
7. *New York Times*, April 12, 1890; *New York Evening World*, April 18, 1890; *Irish American Weekly*, April 12, 1890.
8. *New York Herald*, April 21, 1890; *New York Sun*, April 21, 1890.
9. *New York Times*, April 21, 1890.
10. Ibid.; *Irish World*, July 5, 1890; *New York Evening World*, July 12, 19, 29, 1890; *New York Herald*, July 30, 1890; *New York Herald-Tribune*, July 30, 1890.
11. *New York Times*, April 20, 1890; *New York Evening World*, June 10, 1890; *New York Sun*, December 22, 1890; *New York Times*, September 25, 1893; *New York Sun*, December 22, 1890; *Sporting Life*, September 6, 1890; *New York Herald*, November 10, 1890; *Sporting Life*, September 27, 1890; *Sporting Life*, October 11, 1890.
12. *New York Sun*, November 28, 1890; *Pittsburgh Dispatch*, November 23, 1890; *New York Sun*, November 28, 1890; *New York Evening World*, November 28, 1890; *New York Times*, November 28, 1890; *New York Sun*, November 28, 1890.
13. *New York Evening World*, December 20, 1890; *New York Sun*, May 11, 1891; *New York Sun*, March 12, 1893.
14. *New York Evening World*, April 21, 1891; *New York Sun*, April 21, 1891; *Sporting Life*, January 10, 1891; *Sporting Life*, November 5, 1892; *New York Evening World*, October 12, 1892; *New York Evening World*, March 11, 1891; *New York Sun*, April 11, 1891.
15. *New York Evening World*, March 9, 1891; *New York Evening World*, December 21, 1892.
16. *New York Herald*, May 31, 1894; *New York Sun*, April 10, 1894; *New York Evening World*, September 1, 1894.

Chapter 3

1. *Gaelic American*, July 25, 1908; *Gaelic American*, January 23, 1932; *New York Times*, April 12, 1897.
2. *Gaelic American*, July 25, 1908; *New York Times*, June 28, 1931.
3. *New York Sun*, January 30, 1905.
4. *New York Times*, January 31, 1898; *New York Times*, February 7, 1898. The *Gaelic American* would later write that a Dr. McAuliffe was the first president. See *Gaelic American*, March 1, 1930.
5. *New York Times*, September 15, 1895.
6. *New York Sun*, August 22, 1898; *Gaelic American*, July 25, 1908.
7. *New York Sun*, January 31, 1898; *New York Times*, January 31, 1898; *Gaelic American*, March 1, 1930; *New York Times*, December 19, 1934.
8. *New York Times*, February 7, 1898; *New York Sun*, February 28, 1898; *New York Times*, February 22, 1930; Ian McGowan, *A Brief History of the Irish-American Athletic Club* (New York: City University of New York, 2014), 3.
9. *New York Times*, February 7, 1898; *New York Sun*, January 30, 1905.
10. *New York Sun*, February 28, 1898.
11. *Brooklyn Daily Eagle*, April 12, 1898. The newspaper listed the cost at $55,000. *Brooklyn Daily Eagle*, April 21, 1898.
12. Kevin Kenny, *The American Irish* (New York: Routledge, 2000), 142; *Irish American Weekly*, July 2, 1910.
13. *New York Evening World*, January 4, 1905.
14. Robert C. Trumpbour, *The New Cathedrals* (Syracuse, NY: Syracuse University Press, 2006), 12; *New York Tribune*, July 6, 1903.
15. *Irish American Weekly*, May 28, 1898; *Irish American Weekly*, March 22, 1913.
16. *New York Times*, July 14, 1913.
17. *New York Times*, June 22, 1902; *New York Times*, July 6, 1902; *New York Times*, August 4, 1902; *New York Times*, May 31, 1903.
18. *New York Times*, July 24, 1921.
19. *New York Tribune*, April 28, 1901; *Brooklyn Daily Eagle*, February 14, 1901.
20. *New York Tribune*, May 30, 1901; *Brooklyn Daily Eagle*, May 22, 1901; *Irish American Weekly*, May 25, 1901; *Brooklyn Daily Eagle*, May 25, 1901; *New York Tribune*, May 31, 1901.

21. *New York Tribune*, May 23, 1901; *New York Evening World*, February 17, 1902; *New York Tribune*, February 17, 1902; *New York Times*, February 17, 1902.
22. *New York Sun*, February 16, 1903; *New York Tribune*, May 8, 1903.
23. *Gaelic American*, January 20, 1906; *New York Evening World*, July 26, 1904.
24. *New York Times*, July 24, 1905.
25. John T. Ridge, "Irish County Societies in New York, 1880–1914," in *The New York Irish*, ed. Ronald H. Bayor and Timothy J. Meagher (Baltimore: Johns Hopkins University Press, 1996), 291.
26. Ibid.; *New York Times*, September 29, 1902; *New York Times*, October 27, 1903.
27. It was not until 1959 that the current American Gaelic games body, the North American County Board (USA and Canada), was founded. New York remains a separate "county" covering the New York and New Jersey region. Paul Darby, *Gaelic Games, Nationalism, and the Irish Diaspora in the United States* (Dublin: University College Dublin Press, 2009), 40, 73–74, 103, 115, 118.
28. *Irish World*, October 8, 1904; *Irish American Advocate*, June 23, 1913. Cited in Paul Darby, *Gaelic Games, Nationalism, and the Irish Diaspora in the United States* (Dublin: University College Dublin Press, 2009), 72.
29. John T. Ridge, "Irish County Societies"; *New York Tribune*, October 30, 1906.
30. *Irish American Advocate*, June 26, 1909. Cited in John T. Ridge, "Irish County Societies"; Paul Darby, *Gaelic Games, Nationalism, and the Irish Diaspora in the United States* (Dublin: University College Dublin Press, 2009), 71.
31. *New York Tribune*, January 2, 1909; *New York Times*, January 2, 1909.
32. *Irish American Weekly*, March 14, 1911; *Irish American Weekly*, May 20, 1911; *Irish American Weekly*, April 2, 1910; Paul Darby, *Gaelic Games*, 72.
33. *New York Times*, July 9, 1906; *New York Tribune*, January 19, 1907.
34. *Irish American Weekly*, January 28, 1899; *New York Evening World*, May 24, 1905; *Gaelic American*, May 12, 1906; Alan S. Katchen, *Abel Kiviat* (Syracuse, NY: Syracuse University Press, 2009), 89.
35. *New York Times*, April 10, 1910; *New York Tribune*, April 10, 1910; *New York Times*, April 11, 1910.
36. *New York Times*, May 22, 1910; *New York Times*, May 29, 1910; *New York Tribune*, May 29, 1910.
37. *New York Times*, June 24, 1910; *New York Times*, June 26, 1910.
38. *New York Times*, September 18, 1910; *New York Times*, October 16, 1910; *New York Times*, October 2, 1910; *New York Times*, January 29, 1911.

Chapter 4

1. Jason Cowley, *The Last Game* (London: Simon & Schuster, 2009), 70.
2. *Irish American Weekly*, July 8, 1911.
3. Katchen makes the observation that the U.S. Olympic teams (or athletes who competed in the Olympics) contained just "five minority members" from 1900 to 1908. Along with Myer Prinstein and John B. Taylor, the others were Louis Tewanima, Frank Mt. Pleasant and George Poague. Alan S Katchen, *Abel Kiviat* (Syracuse, NY: Syracuse University Press, 2009), n19, 334.
4. Kevin McCarthy, *Gold, Silver and Green* (Cork, Ireland: Cork University Press, 2010), 83.
5. *New York Times*, May 27, 1906; *Irish American Weekly*, August 17, 1901.
6. Donald Holst and Marcia S. Popp, *American Men of Olympic Track And Field* (Jefferson, NC, McFarland, 2005), 76; Alan S. Katchen, *Abel Kiviat*, 50–51.
7. *New York Evening World*, January 7, 1911; Wingedfist.org.
8. Nancy Foner, *In a New Land* (New York: New York University Press, 2005); Peter Levine, *Ellis Island to Ebbets Field* (New York: Oxford University Press, 1992), 8, 17.
9. *American Hebrew*, January 1, 1915, 249.
10. *New York Times*, April 29, 1900; *New York Tribune*, July 18, 1920.
11. *Y Bulletin*, 1907, in *Sports and the American Jew*, ed. Steven A. Riess (Syracuse, NY: Syracuse University Press, 1998), 30.
12. *New York Times*, July 5, 1902.
13. Gil Ribak, *Gentile New York* (New Brunswick, NJ: Rutgers University Press, 2012), 69.
14. Ibid., 69–70.
15. *New York Times*, August 31, 1902.
16. *New York Sun*, May 14, 1905.
17. *New York Tribune*, April 1, 1910; *New York Sun*, February 11, 1911; *New York Times*, March 11, 1925.

18. Katchen, *Abel Kiviat*, 54, 85.
19. *New York Tribune*, May 30, 1909; Katchen, *Abel Kiviat*, 44–45.
20. Katchen, *Abel Kiviat*, 57–58; *Jersey Journal* [Jersey City, NJ], May 3, 1897; John Bryant, *Marathon Makers* (London: John Blake, 2008), 51–52.
21. *New York Tribune*, July 12, 1909; *New York Times*, August 8, 1909.
22. *New York Tribune*, September 19, 1909.
23. *New York Times*, June 4, 1911; *New York Times*, June 25, 1911; *New York Times*, July 1 1911; *New York Times*, September 17, 1911.
24. Katchen, *Abel Kiviat*, 55.
25. *Los Angeles Herald*, August 13, 1907.
26. *New York Sun*, September 19, 1916; Wingedfist.org.
27. *New York Times*, May 31, 1909; *New York Sun*, May 31, 1909.
28. Wingedfist.org; *New York Times*, June 26, 1909; *New York Times*, June 27, 1909.
29. *New York Times*, September 7, 1909; *New York Times*, September 16, 1909; *New York Times*, October 11, 1909; *New York Times*, September 28, 1925.
30. *Dundee Evening Telegraph*, September 2, 1912; *Yorkshire Post and Leeds Intelligencer*, September 3, 1912; *Nottingham Evening Post*, September 3, 1912; *Dundee Evening Telegraph*, September 13, 1912; *Dundee Courier*, September 14, 1912.
31. *New York Times*, September 29, 1912.
32. Katchen, *Abel Kiviat*, 140.
33. *New York Evening World*, August 28, 1906.
34. *New York Times*, August 24, 1906; *New York Times*, September 4, 1906.
35. *New York Evening World*, August 19, 1907.
36. John Carlos and Dave Zirin, *The John Carlos Story* (Chicago: Haymarket Books, 2011), 55; *New York Evening World*, December 2, 1908; *Washington Post*, December 3, 1908.
37. *New York Evening World*, May 16, 1903.
38. *New York Tribune*, February 5, 1905; *New York Tribune*, February 10, 1907.
39. *New York Times*, March 15, 1907.
40. *New York Times*, January 29, 1941.
41. *New York Evening World*, December 2, 1908.
42. *New York Mail*, unknown date. Cited in *Seattle Daily Times*, March 24, 1907.
43. A black officer had been employed by the Brooklyn PD before unification with New York in 1891; *New York Times*, July 11, 1915; Gregory Bond, *Jim Crow at Play* (Madison: University of Wisconsin, 2008), 424–425; *New York Times*, April 27, 1916; *New York Tribune*, March 21, 1910.
44. *Boston Journal*, July 29, 1911.
45. *New York Tribune*, June 30, 1907; *Washington Post*, September 15, 1907; *New York Sun*, September 15, 1907; *New York Evening World*, December 2, 1908; *Washington Post*, December 3, 1908.

Chapter 5

1. *Irish American Weekly*, May 14, 1898.
2. *New York Sun*, May 31, 1898; *New York Times*, May 31, 1898; *New York Herald*, May 31, 1898.
3. *New York Tribune*, July 7, 1898; *New York Sun*, July 7, 1898.
4. *New York Sun*, July 9, 1898; *New York Tribune*, July 10, 1898; *Brooklyn Daily Eagle*, July 10, 1898; *New York Times*, July 10, 1898; *Brooklyn Daily Eagle*, September 12, 1898.
5. *New York Sun*, May 30, 1899; *New York Sun*, July 5, 1899; *Brooklyn Daily Eagle*, August 11, 1899; *New York Tribune*, September 11, 1899; *New York Times*, December 1, 1899; *New York Sun*, September 19, 1898; *Brooklyn Daily Eagle*, December 23, 1898; *New York Sun*, June 9, 1899; *New York Sun*, January 14, 1900.
6. *Gaelic American*, January 5, 1907.
7. *New York Tribune*, May 31, 1900; *New York Tribune*, July 5, 1900; *New York Times*, September 4, 1900.
8. *New York Tribune*, June 6, 1900; *New York Tribune*, April 29, 1900; *New York Tribune*, June 12, 1900; *New York Tribune*, June 22, 1900.
9. *New York Tribune*, July 18, 1900; *New York Tribune*, September 7, 1900; *New York Tribune*, October 28, 1900.
10. *New York Tribune*, May 31, 1901; *New York Tribune*, June 14, 1901; *New York Sun*, June 22, 1901; *New York Tribune*, June 22, 1901.
11. *New York Tribune*, June 18, 1901; *New York Tribune*, July 5, 1901; *New York Sun*, August 5, 1901.
12. *New York Tribune*, July 28, 1901; *New York Times*, August 7, 1901; *Brooklyn Daily Eagle*, August 19, 1901; *New York Sun*, August 9, 1901.

13. *New York Evening World*, August 21, 1901; *New York Tribune*, August 26, 1901; *New York Evening World*, August 31, 1901; *Brooklyn Daily Eagle*, August 31, 1901; *New York Times*, September 3, 1901; *New York Times*, September 7, 1901.

14. *New York Tribune*, October 9, 1901; *New York Evening World*, October 11, 1901; *New York Evening World*, October 12, 1901; *New York Tribune*, October 15, 1901; *New York Evening World*, October 17, 1901; *New York Times*, October 21, 1901; *New York Tribune*, November 25, 1901; *New York Times*, November 29, 1901; *New York Sun*, November 29, 1901.

15. *New York Times*, May 2, 1902; *New York Tribune*, May 2, 1902; *New York Tribune*, May 14, 1902; *New York Evening World*, May 26, 1902; *New York Tribune*, May 26, 1902; *New York Sun*, May 31, 1902.

16. *New York Tribune*, June 7, 1902; *New York Times*, June 12, 1902; *Brooklyn Daily Eagle*, July 2, 1902.

17. *New York Tribune*, June 28, 1902; *New York Tribune*, June 24, 1902; *New York Tribune*, July 4, 1902; *New York Times*, July 4, 1902.

18. *New York Times*, July 5, 1902; *New York Evening World*, July 4, 1902; *New York Tribune*, July 5, 1902.

19. *New York Times*, May 11, 1902; *New York Times*, June 20, 1902; *New York Times*, June 22, 1902; *New York Times*, July 30, 1902; *New York Times*, August 4, 1902; *New York Times*, August 24, 1902; *New York Times*, August 13, 1902; *New York Times*, September 8, 1902.

20. *New York Times*, June 14, 1902; *New York Tribune*, June 25, 1902; *New York Times*, August 15, 1902; *New York Times*, August 25, 1902.

21. *New York Tribune*, August 27, 1902; *Brooklyn Daily Eagle*, August 30, 1902; *New York Times*, August 30, 1902; *New York Times*, August 31, 1902; *New York Tribune*, August 16, 1902; *New York Tribune*, August 31, 1902.

22. *New York Tribune*, August 27, 1902; *New York Times*, September 2, 1902; *New York Evening World*, September 2, 1902; *New York Tribune*, September 2, 1902.

23. *Brooklyn Daily Eagle*, October 14, 1902; *New York Tribune*, September 18, 1902; *New York Times*, September 20, 1902; *New York Times*, September 26, 1902; *New York Tribune*, September 29, 1902; *New York Times*, October 19, 1902.

24. *New York Tribune*, October 20, 1902; *New York Times*, October 20, 1902.

25. *New York Tribune*, September 14, 1902; *New York Sun*, September 14, 1902. There is some discrepancy between the reports of newspapers. The *New York Times* claimed that McVicar came in second instead of third and that Jerry Pierce was third, but was then disqualified after accusations of breaching his amateur status. *New York Times*, September 14, 1902.

26. *New York Times*, October 12, 1902; *New York Times*, October 13, 1902; *New York Times*, October 27, 1902; *New York Sun*, October 27, 1902; *New York Times*, November 12, 1902; *New York Times*, November 24, 1902; *New York Times*, November 28, 1902; *New York Sun*, November 28, 1902; *New York Times*, December 13, 1902.

27. *Irish World*, November 29, 1902; *New York Tribune*, December 3, 1902; *New York Tribune*, December 22, 1902; *New York Times*, December 26, 1902; *New York Times*, November 28, 1902; *Irish American Weekly*, December 13, 1902; *New York Tribune*, December 18, 1902; *New York Tribune*, December 23, 1902; *New York Times*, December 27, 1902.

28. *New York Evening World*, December 5, 1902; *New York Times*, December 5, 1902; *New York Times*, December 6, 1902; *New York Times*, December 19, 1902; *New York Evening World*, December 26, 1902.

29. *New York Times*, December 28, 1902; *New York Times*, December 6, 1902; *New York Tribune*, December 28, 1902.

30. *New York Evening World*, January 4, 1905.

31. *Gaelic American*, January 20, 1906.

32. *New York Tribune*, December 29, 1902.

33. *New York Times*, January 10, 1903; *New York Evening World*, January 10, 1903

34. *New York Tribune*, February 25, 1903

35. *New York Tribune*, February 16, 1903

36. *New York Times*, February 17, 1903; *New York Evening World*, February 18, 1903; *New York Times*, February 12, 1903; *New York Tribune*, March 12, 1903; *New York Tribune*, March 13, 1903; *New York Tribune*, March 14, 1903; *New York Times*, January 16, 1903; *New York Tribune*, January 16, 1903; *New York Times*, February 22, 1903.

37. *New York Times*, March 15, 1903; *New York Tribune*, March 15, 1903; Kevin McCarthy, *Gold, Silver and Green* (Cork,

Ireland: Cork University Press, 2010), 79; *New York Times*, July 10, 1903.

38. *New York Times*, January 16, 1903; *New York Times*, August 10, 1903; *New York Times*, July 24, 1903; *New York Times*, July 26, 1903; *New York Times*, August 24, 1903; *New York Times*, September 28, 1903; *New York Times*, October 26, 1903.

39. *Brooklyn Daily Eagle*, April 10, 1903; *Brooklyn Life*, April 11, 1903.

40. *Brooklyn Daily Eagle*, March 7, 1902; *New York Times*, April 9, 1903; *Brooklyn Daily Eagle*, April 10, 1903; *New York Tribune*, April 9, 1903; *New York Times*, April 12, 1903; *New York Tribune*, April 19, 1903; *New York Times*, May 10, 1903.

41. *New York Tribune*, May 11, 1903; *New York Tribune*, May 18, 1903; *New York Tribune*, May 31, 1903; *New York Tribune*, May 25, 1903.

42. *New York Evening World*, June 18, 1903; *Irish American Weekly*, June 20, 1903; *New York Evening World*, June 20, 1903; *New York Tribune*, July 5, 1903.

43. *New York Times*, August 23, 1903; *New York Tribune*, August 23, 1903; *New York Sun*, August 23, 1903. Bacon was listed as Barker or Baker.

44. *New York Tribune*, August 6, 1903; *New York Tribune*, September 7, 1903; *New York Times*, August 30, 1903; *New York Times*, August 24, 1903; *New York Times*, September 8, 1903; *New York Tribune*, September 8, 1903.

45. *New York Times*, September 12, 1903; *New York Tribune*, September 12, 1903; *New York Sun*, September 12, 1903; *New York Times*, September 11, 1903; *New York Times*, September 20, 1903.

Chapter 6

1. *New York Times*, July 13, 1964.
2. Margaret Mary Hennessey, "Irish Whales," in *Encyclopedia of Ethnicity and Sports In The United States*, ed. George B. Kirsch, Othello Harris, Claire Elaine Nolte (Westport, CT: Greenwood Press, 2000), 239–240; Ian McGowan, *A Brief History of the Irish-American Athletic Club* (New York: City University of New York, 2014), 7; *New York Times*, August 19, 1915; *New York Times*, February 14, 1964; Katchen, *Abel Kiviat*, 87.
3. William Dooley, *Champions of the Athletic Arena* (Dublin: General Publicity Service, 1948), 65; *New York Times*, May 18, 1954.
4. *New York Times*, July 13, 1964; *New York Evening World*, October 16, 1905.
5. *New York Times*, April 2, 1916; Mark Quinn, *The King of Spring* (Dublin: Liffey Press, 2004), 109.
6. *Freeman's Journal* [Dublin], May 4, 1896, *Morning Post* [London], May 26, 1896.
7. *New York Tribune*, October 27, 1907; *New York Evening World*, October 16, 1905.
8. Harry Greensmyth and Denis Martin, *John Flanagan* (Kilfinane, Co. Limerick, Ireland: Kilfinane (Coshlea) Historical Society, 2001), 31, cited in Kevin McCarthy, *Gold, Silver and Green* (Cork, Ireland: Cork University Press, 2010), 264.
9. *New York Times*, June 1, 1897; William Dooley, *Champions of the Athletic Arena* (Dublin: General Publicity Service, 1948), 34.
10. Katchen, *Abel Kiviat*, 55; *Philadelphia Inquirer*, June 6, 1897; William Dooley, *Champions of the Athletic Arena*, 54; *New York Evening World*, July 20, 1908; William Dooley, *Champions of the Athletic Arena*, 56.
11. *New York Evening World*, July 20, 1908; *New York Tribune*, October 27, 1907; *Gaelic American*, May 26, 1906.
12. *The Sun* August 18, 1901; *New York Times*, September 15, 1901; *New York Herald*, September 16, 1901; *New York Herald*, September 17, 1901; *New York Tribune*, August 31, 1902; *New York Times*, October 5, 1902.
13. *New York Times*, June 5, 1904. Sheridan won AAU National titles in the shot put in 1904, the pole vault for distance in 1906 and 1907, further discus titles in 1906, 1907 and 1911, and the discus Greek style in 1907. Frank Zarnowski, *All-Around Men* (Lanham, MD: Scarecrow Press, 2005), 33; William Dooley, *Champions of the Athletic Arena*, 56.
14. *New York Times*, January 29, 1941; *New York Tribune*, October 27, 1907.
15. William Dooley, *Champions of the Athletic Arena*, 65.
16. *New York Times*, May 18, 1954; "Police Athletes of the Past, Patrick McDonald," *Spring 3100* 21, no.10 (November 1950); John A. Lucas, "Pat 'Babe' McDonald," *Journal of Olympic History* 5, no.3 (Fall 1997), 8–9; John E. Findling and Kimberly Pelle, *Encyclopedia of the Modern Olympic Movement* (Westport, CT: Greenwood Press, 2004), 73; *New York Times*, August 5, 1920.

17. William Dooley, *Champions of the Athletic Arena*, 68–69.
18. Ibid., 68; *New York Times*, April 2, 1916.
19. *New York Times*, August 2, 1900; William Dooley, *Champions of the Athletic Arena*, 42; *New York Times*, September 16, 1900.
20. *New York Times*, September 30, 1900; *New York Times*, October 22, 1900; *Brooklyn Daily Eagle*, December 2, 1900.
21. *New York Sun*, August 19, 1903; *Gaelic American*, October 14, 1905; *New York Times*, September 15, 1907; *New York Times*, November 4, 1907; *New York Times*, January 9, 1908; *New York Times*, June 16, 1907; *New York Times*, June 13, 1909.
22. *New York Tribune*, August 18, 1901.
23. *New York Evening World*, August 21, 1901.
24. *New York Tribune*, September 27, 1905; William Dooley, *Champions of the Athletic Arena*, 58–59.
25. *New York Evening World*, November 8, 1904; *Gaelic American*, July 21, 1906.
26. Kevin McCarthy, *Gold, Silver and Green* (Cork, Ireland: Cork University Press, 2010), 115.
27. William Dooley, *Champions of the Athletic Arena*, 36; *New York Evening World*, June 4, 1904.
28. *New York Sun*, June 6, 1904; *New York Tribune*, June 6, 1904.
29. *New York Tribune*, September 25, 1904; *New York Evening World*, September 26, 1904; *New York Times*, May 27, 1906; *New York Times*, June 24, 1906.

Chapter 7

1. *New York Evening World*, May 25, 1904; *Washington Times*, June 5, 1904; *New York Times*, June 5, 1904; *New York Tribune*, June 5, 1904; *Irish World*, June 11, 1904; James E. Sullivan, *Spalding's Official Athletic Almanac for 1905* (New York: American Publishing, 1905), 197.
2. *New York Tribune*, November 18, 1903; *New York Times*, November 18, 1903; *Irish World*, February 6, 1904; *Gaelic American*, February 9, 1907.
3. *New York Sun*, April 8, 1904; *New York Evening World*, April 26, 1904; *New York Times*, July 26, 1904; *New York Times*, August 7, 1904.
4. *New York Times*, June 3, 1904; *St. Louis Republic*, July 4, 1908; *New York Sun*, July 5, 1904; *St. Louis Republic*, July 5, 1908.
5. Frank Zarnowski, "Thomas F Kiely—A biography," *Journal of Olympic History* 14, no. 2 (August 2006).
6. *St. Louis Republic*, July 16, 1904; *New York Tribune*, July 22, 1904.
7. *St. Louis Republic*, August 30, 1904; *New York Tribune*, September 2, 1904; *New York Times*, September 2, 1904; *New York Times*, September 4, 1904; *New York Times*, August 30, 1904; *New York Tribune*, September 6, 1904.
8. *New York Times*, April 4, 1904; *New York Evening World*, April 4, 1904; *New York Evening World*, April 15, 1904; *New York Sun*, April 17, 1904; *New York Evening World*, February 11, 1904; *New York Evening World*, April 27, 1904; *New York Times*, May 8, 1904.
9. *New York Sun*, May 31, 1904; *New York Evening World*, May 31, 1904; *New York Tribune*, May 31, 1904; *New York Times*, May 31, 1904.
10. *New York Times*, July 5, 1904; *New York Evening World*, July 4, 1904; *New York Tribune*, July 5, 1904.
11. *New York Times*, August 14, 1904; *New York Times*, August 21, 1904; *New York Tribune*, September 18, 1904.
12. *New York Evening World*, July 26, 1904; *New York Evening World*, August 1, 1904; *New York Times*, August 1, 1904; *New York Tribune*, September 11, 1904; *New York Sun*, September 11, 1904.
13. *New York Tribune*, October 24, 1904; *Gaelic American*, March 1, 1930; *New York Times*, October 31, 1904; *New York Sun*, October 31, 1904.
14. *New York Sun*, October 31, 1904; *New York Evening World*, October 31, 1904.
15. *New York Evening World*, November 8, 1904.
16. *Irish World*, November 19, 1904; *New York Evening World*, November 19, 1904.
17. *New York Evening World*, November 21, 1904.
18. Ibid.; *New York Times*, November 21, 1904; *New York Sun*, November 21, 1904.
19. *Irish World*, December 3, 1904; *New York Times*, November 25, 1904; *New York Tribune*, November 25, 1904; *New York Evening World*, November 25, 1904; *New York Evening World*, December 8, 1904; *New York Evening World*, December 10, 1904; *New York Times*, December 12, 1904.

20. *Irish World*, January 14, 1905; *New York Evening World*, January 4, 1905.
21. *New York Evening World*, February 1, 1905; *Chicago Tribune*, July 27, 1905; *The Oregonian* [Portland, OR], August 6, 1905; *New York Evening World*, January 4, 1905; *New York Evening World*, January 6, 1905.
22. *Irish World*, February 4, 1905.
23. *New York Sun*, January 30, 1905.
24. *New York Evening World*, January 28, 1905; *New York Evening World*, February 2, 1905; *New York Evening World*, February 6, 1905; *New York Tribune*, February 5, 1905.
25. *New York Evening World*, May 30, 1905; *New York Times*, May 31, 1905; *New York Tribune*, May 31, 1905.
26. *New York Times*, July 5, 1905; *New York Tribune*, July 9, 1905.
27. The *Sun* and the *New York Tribune* put the crowd at 8,000, while the *New York Times* said it was $15.000. *New York Evening World*, June 12, 1905; *New York Times*, June 12, 1905; *New York Tribune*, June 12, 1905; *New York Sun*, June 12, 1905.
28. *New York Tribune*, June 26, 1905; *New York Times*, June 26, 1905; *New York Sun*, June 26, 1905; *New York Times*, September 5, 1905.
29. *New York Times*, September 8, 1905; *New York Times*, August 27, 1905; *New York Evening World*, July 15, 1905.
30. *New York Times*, September 10, 1905; *New York Tribune*, September 10, 1905; *New York Tribune*, September 17, 1905; *New York Times*, September 17, 1905; *New York Tribune*, September 24, 1905.
31. *Gaelic American*, October 7, 1905; *New York Times*, October 16, 1905; *New York Evening World*, October 16, 1905.
32. *New York Times*, December 1, 1905; *New York Times*, December 24, 1905.
33. *Irish American Weekly*, January 13, 1906; *New York Tribune*, January 27, 1906; *New York Times*, February 4, 1906; *New York Tribune*, February 4, 1906; *New York Evening World*, February 5, 1906; *New York Evening World*, January 27, 1906.

Chapter 8

1. Patrick R. Redmond, *The Irish and the Making of American Sport, 1835–1920* (Jefferson, NC: McFarland, 2014.), 358. The Staten Island AC's website has the date as 1871. http,//www.statenislandac.org/.

2. Frederick W. Janssen, *History of American Amateur Athletics* (reprint, Whitefish, MT: Kessinger, 2010), 103; Neil L. Shumsky, *Institutional Life* (New York: Routledge, 1996), 365.
3. Kerby A. Miller, *Emigrants and Exiles* (New York: Oxford University Press, 1985), 318.
4. Richard O. Davies, *Sports in American Life* (Chichester UK: John Wiley & Sons, 2012), 58; *Irish American Weekly*, July 8, 1911; Katchen, *Abel Kiviat*, 89.
5. Joe Willis and Richard Wettan, "Social Stratification in New York City Athletic Clubs, 1865–1915," *Journal of Sport History* 3, no. 1 (Spring, 1976), 47–48.
6. http,//www.nyac.org/Default.aspx?p=DynamicModule&id=235907&vnf=1
7. *New York Times*, November 6, 1868.
8. *New York Times*, February 26, 1893; Rebecca Jenkins, *The First London Olympics 1908* (London: Piatkus, 2008), 98.
9. Frederick W. Janssen, *History of American Amateur Athletics* (reprint, Whitefish, MT: Kessinger, 2010), 75.
10. Joe Willis and Richard Wettan, "Social Stratification in New York City Athletic Clubs, 1865–1915," *Journal of Sport History* 3, no. 1 (Spring, 1976), 47.
11. *Outing*, December 1898.
12. Joe Willis & Richard Wettan. "Social Stratification," 52–54.
13. Steven A. Riess, *City Games* (Urbana: University of Illinois Press, 1991), 57; Calculated with http,//www.davemanuel.com/inflation-calculator.php?.
14. *Chicago Inter Ocean*, March 20, 1887; Steven A. Riess, *City Games*, 57.
15. Joe Willis & Richard Wettan. "Social Stratification," 54.
16. *New York Tribune*, December 23, 1902.
17. *New York Times*, September 7, 1902.
18. *New York Times*, March 23, 1891.
19. *Sporting Life*, November 29, 1890; *New York Times*, July 21, 1893.
20. *New York Times*, January 8, 1898.
21. Ian McGowan, *A Brief History of the Irish-American Athletic Club* (New York: City University of New York, 2014), 4; Kevin McCarthy, *Gold, Silver and Green* (Cork, Ireland: Cork University Press, 2010), 83. There are probably older "private" clubs in the U.S. Certainly the Olympic Athletic Club of San Francisco, founded in 1860, is older than the NYAC.

22. Richard O. Davies, *Sports in American Life* (Chichester, UK: John Wiley & Sons, 2012), 58; Ian McGowan, *A Brief History of the Irish-American Athletic Club* (New York: City University of New York, 2014), 4–5.
23. *New York Times*, February 12, 1888; *New York Times*, September 15, 1889.
24. *Brooklyn Daily Eagle*, April 24, 1898.
25. *New York Tribune*, April 10, 1910; *New York Times*, October 31, 1912; *New York Times*, January 27, 1907; *New York Times*, February 6, 1907.
26. *New York Sun*, August 22, 1898; *New York Sun*, August 28, 1898; *New York Sun*, September 25, 1898.
27. *New York Times*, September 7, 1902.
28. *New York Times*, September 7, 1902; *New York Tribune*, September 18, 1902; *New York Times*, March 7, 1903; *New York Times*, December 29, 1902.
29. *Irish American Weekly*, January 18, 1908; *Irish American Weekly*, July 8, 1911.
30. *Gaelic American*, September 29, 1906.
31. *Brooklyn Daily Eagle*, September 10, 1905.
32. *New York Evening World*, September 14, 1905.
33. *Gaelic American*, January 6, 1906.
34. *New York Times*, July 7, 1907; *New York Times*, August 25, 1907; *New York Times*, August 16, 1907.
35. *New York Times*, September 21, 1912.
36. *Montreal Gazette*, September 6, 1908
37. *New York Evening World*, September 26, 1908; *New York Tribune*, September 27, 1908; *New York Tribune*, September 25, 1910.
38. *New York Sun*, July 19, 1908.

Chapter 9

1. *New York Times*, December 30, 1907.
2. Graeme Kent, *Olympic Follies* (London: JR Books, 2008), 103; Mark Quinn, *The King of Spring* (Dublin: Liffey Press, 2004), 179–183; *Metropolitan Magazine*, July 1910, cited in Mark Quinn, *The King of Spring*, 198; Graeme Kent, *Olympic Follies*, 101.
3. *New York Times*, December 30, 1907.
4. *Gaelic American*, May 12, 1906; *New York Evening World*, March 10, 1906; *New York Tribune*, March 10, 1906.
5. *Gaelic American*, May 26, 1906; *Irish American Weekly*, March 3, 1906.
6. *New York Tribune*, April 22, 1906; *New York Evening World*, April 16, 1906; *New York Tribune*, April 17, 1906; Herbert Kerrigan, third in the high jump, was also listed as an I-AAC member, but wasn't. *New York Tribune*, May 2, 1906; *New York Tribune*, April 26, 1906.
7. *New York Tribune*, May 1, 1906.
8. *New York Evening World*, March 10, 1906.
9. *New York Evening World*, March 10, 1906; *New York Evening World*, March 23, 1906.
10. *New York Tribune*, April 2, 1906; *New York Sun*, April 2, 1906; *New York Times*, April 2, 1906.
11. *New York Sun*, April 2, 1906; *New York Times*, April 2, 1906; *New York Sun*, April 3, 1906.
12. *New York Evening World*, April 2, 1906; *New York Tribune*, April 4, 1906.
13. *New York Evening World*, May 3, 1906; *New York Evening World*, May 9, 1906; *New York Tribune*, May 10, 1906; *New York Tribune*, May 26, 1906.
14. *New York Tribune*, May 27, 1906; *New York Times*, May 27, 1906.
15. *Gaelic American*, March 31, 1906; *New York Evening World*, March 10, 1906; *Gaelic American*, May 12, 1906; *Irish American Weekly*, June 30, 1906.
16. *New York Times*, May 7, 1906; *New York Times*, May 13, 1906; *New York Times*, May 14, 1906; *New York Times*, May 27, 1906; *New York Times*, May 28, 1906.
17. *New York Times*, May 31, 1906; *New York Times*, July 2, 1906; *New York Times*, August 20, 1906; *New York Tribune*, August 20, 1906; *Gaelic American*, August 25, 1906; *New York Times*, August 26, 1906, *New York Tribune*, August 26, 1906; *New York Times*, August 27, 1906; *New York Tribune*, August 27, 1906.
18. *New York Times*, August 26, 1906; *New York Times*, September 1, 1906; *New York Times*, September 2, 1906; *New York Evening World*, September 1, 1906.
19. *New York Times*, September 2, 1906; *New York Times*, September 3, 1906; *New York Times*, September 4, 1906; *Gaelic American*, September 8, 1904.
20. *New York Sun*, September 9, 1906; *New York Times*, September 8, 1906; *New York Times*, September 9, 1906; *Gaelic American*, September 15, 1906.
21. *New York Times*, September 23, 1906; *New York Evening World*, September 20, 1906; *New York Tribune*, September 23, 1906.

22. *Gaelic American*, September 29, 1906.
23. *New York Times*, October 14, 1906; *New York Times*, October 15, 1906; *New York Tribune*, October 15, 1906; *Gaelic American*, September 8, 1906.
24. *New York Tribune*, November 5, 1906; *New York Times*, December 9, 1906; *New York Tribune*, December 9, 1906.
25. *New York Times*, December 15, 1906; *New York Times*, December 16, 1906; *New York Tribune*, December 16, 1906.
26. *New York Times*, October 7, 1906; *New York Evening World*, January 6, 1892; *New York Sun*, January 24, 1892; *New York Times*, July 25, 1892; *New York Evening World*, January 25, 1892.
27. *New York Times*, November 2, 1906; *Gaelic American*, November 17, 1906; *New York Times*, November 10, 1906. The I-AAC score was reported by the *Times* as 95. *New York Times*, November 11, 1906; *New York Tribune*, November 11, 1906; *New York Times*, November 18, 1906; *New York Tribune*, November 25, 1906.
28. *New York Tribune*, December 11, 1906; *New York Times*, November 27, 1906; *New York Times*, November 28, 1906.
29. *New York Times*, January 19, 1907.
30. *Gaelic American*, January 6, 1906.
31. *New York Times*, January 5, 1907; *New York Times*, February 2, 1907.
32. *New York Sun*, February 3, 1907; *New York Times*, February 3, 1907; *New York Tribune*, February 3, 1907; *New York Times*, February 10, 1907.
33. *New York Times*, February 14, 1907; *New York Evening World*, June 12, 1907; *New York Times*, May 30, 1907; *New York Tribune*, May 31, 1907; *New York Times*, May 31, 1907.
34. *New York Times*, June 23; *New York Tribune*, June 29, 1907; *New York Times*, July 4, 1907; *New York World*, July 5, 1907. Cited in *Gaelic American*, July 13, 1907; *New York Times*, July 1, 1907; *New York Times*, September 2, 1907; *Evening World* September 2, 1907.
35. *New York Tribune*, August 25, 1907; *New York Sun*, August 25, 1907; *New York Times*, August 25, 1907; *New York Evening World*, August 24, 1907.
36. *New York Tribune*, August 25, 1907; *New York Times*, August 25, 1907.
37. *New York Times*, September 5, 1907; *New York Times*, September 7, 1907.
38. *Gaelic American*, September 14, 1907; *New York Times*, September 8, 1907.

39. *New York Tribune*, September 8, 1907; *Irish American Weekly*, September 14, 1907; *New York Times*, September 11, 1907.
40. *New York Times*, September 29, 1907; *New York Times*, October 6, 1907; *New York Times*, December 14, 1907; *New York Times*, October 13, 1907; *New York Times*, October 14, 1907.
41. *New York Evening World*, January 27, 1908.
42. *New York Times*, November 24, 1907; *New York Tribune*, November 24, 1907; *New York Times*, October 23, 1907; *New York Times*, October 26, 1907; *New York Times*, October 27, 1907; *New York Tribune*, October 27, 1907.
43. *Irish American Weekly*, February 1, 1908; *New York Times*, January 25, 1908; *New York Tribune*, January 25, 1908.
44. *New York Times*, January 25, 1908; *New York Times*, January 26, 1908; *New York Tribune*, January 26, 1908; *New York Times*, January 27, 1908; *New York Times*, January 28, 1908; *New York Times*, February 1, 1908.
45. *New York Times*, January 28, 1908; *New York Times*, February 4, 1908; *New York Tribune*, February 6, 1908; *New York Times*, February 8, 1908; *New York Times*, February 9, 1908.
46. *New York Evening World*, February 10, 1908.
47. Ibid.
48. Ibid.; *New York Tribune*, February 16, 1908.
49. *Washington Times*, February 1, 1908; *Irish American Weekly*, March 14, 1908.
50. *New York Times*, March 5, 1908; *New York Evening World*, March 5, 1908; *New York Tribune*, March 5, 1908.

Chapter 10

1. *New York Times*, May 3, 1903; *New York Times*, June 1, 1902; *East Oregonian*, June 25, 1906.
2. *New York Times*, October 28, 1905.
3. Ibid.
4. *New York Times*, October 29, 1905; *New York Times*, October 30, 1905.
5. *New York Times*, November 2, 1905; *New York Times*, November 4, 1905; *New York Times*, November 21, 1905; *New York Times*, February 25, 1906.
6. *New York Evening World*, May 30, 1905.

7. *New York Times*, April 20, 1894.
8. Richard O. Davies, *Sports in American Life* (Chichester, UK: John Wiley & Sons, 2012), 59.
9. Katchen, *Abel Kiviat*, 89; Graeme Kent, *Olympic Follies* (London: JR Books, 2008), 100–101; *New York Times*, September 11, 1904; *New York Sun*, September 11, 1904.
10. Patrick R. Redmond, *The Irish and the Making of American Sport, 1835–1920* (Jefferson, NC: McFarland, 2014), 372.
11. *New York Times*, July 9, 1905.
12. *New York Tribune*, April 17, 1902; *New York Times*, August 21, 1904; *New York Times*, July 6, 1905.
13. *New York Sun*, February 18, 1906; *New York Times*, July 9, 1905; *New York Sun*, July 9, 1905; *New York Times*, July 6, 1905; *New York Evening World*, July 6, 1905; *New York Sun*, July 7, 1905; *New York Evening World*, July 7, 1905.
14. *New York Times*, August 27, 1905.
15. *New York Times*, September 8, 1905; *New York Sun*, September 8, 1905; *New York Times*, September 9, 1905.
16. *New York Times*, September 14, 1905.
17. *New York Times*, September 13, 1905.
18. *New York Tribune*, September 9, 1905; *New York Tribune*, September 10, 1905; *New York Tribune*, September 11, 1905.
19. *New York Times*, September 10, 1905; *New York Tribune*, September 10, 1905.
20. *New York Tribune*, September 11, 1905.
21. *New York Evening World*, September 14, 1905; *New York Evening World*, September 18, 1905; *New York Times*, September 19, 1905.
22. *Gaelic American*, January 6, 1906.
23. *Boston Evening Telegraph*, September 12, 1905; *New York Tribune*, January 13, 1906.
24. *New York Tribune*, January 13, 1906.
25. *Gaelic American*, January 20, 1906.
26. *New York Tribune*, January 13, 1906; *New York Tribune*, January 18, 1906.
27. *New York Evening World*, January 18, 1906.
28. *New York Tribune*, February 2, 1906; *New York Times*, February 2, 1906.
29. *New York Tribune*, March 16, 1906.
30. *New York Times*, May 5, 1906; *New York Tribune*, May 5, 1906.
31. *New York Evening World*, March 23, 1906; *New York Times*, May 19, 1906.
32. *Metropolitan Magazine*, July 1910; *Irish American Weekly*, May 23, 1903; *New York Tribune*, December 26, 1908; *Gaelic American*, January 6, 1906.
33. *Gaelic American*, November 4, 1905; *New York Times*, October 29, 1912; *New York Times*, July 2, 1916.
34. *Gaelic American*, November 4, 1905; *New York Times*, September 3, 1906; *New York Evening World*, February 5, 1906.
35. *New York Tribune*, January 14, 1907; *New York Tribune*, March 2, 1907.
36. *New York Times*, September 8, 1907.
37. Ibid.; *Jersey Journal* [Jersey City, NJ], May 3, 1897.
38. *New York Tribune*, December 29, 1908; *New York Times*, December 29, 1908.
39. *New York Times*, December 29, 1908.
40. Ibid.
41. *New York Times*, December 30, 1908; *New York Tribune*, January 7, 1909.
42. *New York Times*, September 5, 1909.
43. *New York Times*, December 24, 1909; *New York Tribune*, March 13, 1910; *New York Tribune*, February 1, 1910.
44. *New York Tribune*, February 3, 1910; *New York Times*, February 3, 1910; *New York Tribune*, February 5, 1910.
45. *New York Times*, February 20, 1910; *New York Sun*, February 20, 1910; *New York Tribune*, February 20, 1910.
46. *New York Tribune*, March 13, 1910; *New York Times*, March 13, 1910; *New York Times*, February 12, 1910.
47. *New York Tribune*, May 17, 1910; *New York Times*, February 1, 1911; *New York Times*, November 11, 1911.
48. *New York Times*, January 21, 1912; *New York Times*, January 3, 1913; *New York Times*, October 23, 1912.
49. *New York Sun*, November 15, 1912.
50. *New York Times*, November 15, 1912; *New York Tribune*, January 7, 1917.
51. *New York Times*, February 14, 1917; *Brooklyn Daily Eagle*, February 17, 1917; *New York Times*, February 17, 1917.
52. *New York Times*, February 14, 1917; *Brooklyn Daily Eagle*, February 14, 1917.
53. *Brooklyn Daily Eagle*, February 14, 1917.
54. Ibid.; *New York Times*, February 19, 1917; *New York Times*, February 25, 1917.
55. *New York Tribune*, January 14, 1917; *New York Sun*, January 14, 1917.

Chapter 11

1. *New York Times*, August 7, 1908.
2. John Bryant, *Marathon Makers* (Lon-

don: John Blake, 2008), 48, 135; *New York Times*, November 25, 1904; *New York Times*, November 29, 1907.

3. Kevin McCarthy, *Gold, Silver and Green* (Cork, Ireland: Cork University Press, 2010), 238; *New York Tribune*, August 3, 1908; *New York Times*, August 11, 1908.

4. *Washington Times*, December 5, 1907.

5. *Washington Evening Star*, December 6, 1907; *New York Times*, December 6, 1907; *New York Tribune*, December 6, 1907; *Washington Evening Star*, December 22, 1907; *Washington Evening Star*, December 15, 1907.

6. *Washington Evening Star*, December 6, 1907; *Washington Times*, December 7, 1907.

7. *Los Angeles Herald*, December 22, 1907.

8. *New York Evening World*, December 24, 1907; *New York Times*, December 24, 1907.

9. *New York Tribune*, December 24, 1907; *New York Times*, December 28, 1907; *New York Tribune*, December 28, 1907.

10. *New York Tribune*, December 30, 1907.

11. Ibid.

12. *New York Evening World*, January 4, 1908; *New York Times*, December 30, 1907.

13. *New York Tribune*, March 6, 1908; *Detroit Free Press*, March 15, 1908; *New York Evening World*, March 6, 1908.

14. *New York Times*, April 6, 1908; *New York Times*, April 26, 1908; *New York Tribune*, May 31, 1908.

15. Women were still not included, as James E. Sullivan was fervently against their inclusion in athletics right up to his death. Two "full-blood" Indians from Carlisle School were on the U.S. team, while Frank Le Roy Holmes, a "Brazilian"-born high jumper who once competed for the Illinois GAA, joined Taylor as the team's two "negroes." *New York Tribune*, June 7, 1908; *New York Times*, June 14, 1908; *New York Tribune*, June 14, 1908; *Irish-American Advocate*, July 18, 1908. Cited in Kevin McCarthy, *Gold, Silver and Green* (Cork, Ireland: Cork University Press, 2010), 211; *New York Evening World*, June 9, 1908.

16. They were Charles Bacon (400m hurdles), George V. Bonhag (5Mile), Joseph Bromilow (800m), George G. Cameron (cycling), Harvey Cohn (3Mile team race), John Flanagan (shot put, 16LB hammer and tug-of-war), Johnny Hayes (marathon), Bill Horr (shot put, 16LB hammer and tug-of-war), Dan Kelly (long jump), Harry Porter (high jump), Frank Riley (1500m), Lawson Robertson (100m and 200m), Mel Sheppard (800m), Martin Sheridan (discus—Greek and freestyle), James Sullivan (1500m), Lee Talbott (shot put, 16LB hammer, tug-of-war, and heavyweight wrestling), John Taylor (400m) and Robert Cloughen (100m and 200m). Ed Cook was listed as competing for Cornell. *New York Times*, June 9, 1908; *New York Tribune*, June 10, 1908; *New York Times*, June 14, 1908; *New York Evening World*, June 24, 1908; *New York Tribune*, June 21, 1908; *New York Times*, June 26, 1908; *New York Times*, June 24, 1908.

17. *New York Tribune*, June 21, 1908; *New York Times*, June 14, 1908; *New York Evening World*, June 15, 1908; *New York Times*, June 28, 1908; *New York Sun*, July 6, 1908.

18. *New York Times*, July 6, 1952; Ian McGowan, *A Brief History of the Irish-American Athletic Club* (New York: City University of New York, 2014), 14.

19. John Bryant, *Marathon Makers* (London: John Blake, 2008), 152.

20. Graeme Kent, *Olympic Follies* (London: JR Books, 2008), 108–109; John Bryant, *Marathon Makers*, 153. Bryant mentions the *New York Herald* and the *Sun*. The *New York Times* claims it was John Garrells who carried the flag, while elsewhere suggestions appeared that Sheridan was the bearer. See Kevin McCarthy, *Gold, Silver and Green* (Cork, Ireland: Cork University Press, 2010), 212.

21. Kevin McCarthy, *Gold, Silver and Green*, 214; *Irish World*, August 1, 1908.

22. *New York Times*, July 6, 1952.

23. *New York Times*, October 13, 1968; *Pittsburgh Post-Gazette*, October 15, 1908. Bryant and Graeme Kent claim that Ralph Rose was Irish-American, while Kevin McCarthy disagrees. Bryant in the same sentence wrongly claims that John J. Flanagan was also Irish-American. See John Bryant, *Marathon Makers*, 162; Graeme Kent, *Olympic Follies*, 63; Kevin McCarthy, *Gold, Silver and Green*, 212.

24. Jeremy Schaap, *Triumph* (New York: Houghton Mifflin Harcourt, 2007), 166; John Bryant, *Marathon Makers*, 157; Ian McGowan, *A Brief History of the Irish-American Athletic Club* (New York: City University of New York, 2014), 17.

25. Graeme Kent, *Olympic Follies* (Lon-

don; JR Books, 2008), 63; *New York Tribune*, August 3, 1908.
26. *New York Evening World*, July 15, 1908.
27. *New York Evening World*, July 14, 1908.
28. John Bryant, *Marathon Makers* (London: John Blake, 2008), 154–155; *Irish World*, July 25, 1908.
29. *New York Times*, July 15, 1908; *New York Evening World*, July 15, 1908; *New York Sun*, July 15, 1908; *New York Tribune*, July 15, 1908; *New York Sun*, July 16, 1908; *New York Times*, July 17, 1908; *New York Tribune*, July 17, 1908.
30. *New York Times*, July 19, 1908; *New York Evening World*, July 19, 1908; *New York Evening World*, July 20, 1908; *New York Times*, July 21, 1908.
31. *New York Evening World*, July 20, 1908; *New York Sun*, July 22, 1908; *New York Times*, July 22, 1908; *New York Evening World*, July 21, 1908; *New York Times*, July 23, 1908.
32. *New York Sun*, July 18, 1908; *New York Evening World*, July 18, 1908.
33. *Gaelic American*, July 25, 1908; *New York Evening World*, July 22, 1908.
34. *New York Times*, July 17, 1908; *New York Times*, July 19, 1908.
35. *New York Times*, July 24, 1908; *New York Evening World*, July 23, 1908; *New York Evening World*, July 24, 1908.
36. *Daily News*, July 25, 1908.
37. *New York Times*, July 26, 1908.
38. *New York Times*, July 25, 1908.
39. *New York Times*, July 27, 1908; *New York Evening World*, July 31, 1908; *New York Times*, July 31, 1908.
40. *New York Evening World*, July 31, 1908; *Chicago Tribune*, August 1, 1908; *New York Evening World*, August 13, 1908.
41. *New York Evening World*, July 31, 1908; *New York Times*, August 1, 1908; *New York Sun*, August 1, 1908; *New York Tribune*, August 1, 1908; *New York Tribune*, August 3, 1908.
42. *New York Tribune*, August 2, 1908; *New York Sun*, August 4, 1908; *New York Evening World*, August 4, 1908.
43. *New York Evening World*, August 15, 1908; *New York Times*, August 15, 1908; *New York Times*, August 17, 1908; *New York Times*, August 24, 1908; *New York Times*, August 14, 1908.
44. *Irish American Weekly*, August 1, 1908; *New York Times*, July 27, 1908; *New York Times*, July 29, 1908.
45. *New York Times*, July 28, 1908; *New York Times*, July 30, 1908; *New York Times*, August 1, 1908; *New York Evening World*, August 3, 1908; *New York Times*, August 4, 1908.
46. *New York Times*, August 14, 1908; *New York Times*, August 18, 1908; *New York Times*, August 22, 1908; *New York Times*, August 23, 1908; *New York Times*, August 25, 1908.
47. *New York Times*, July 27, 1908; *New York Times*, July 29, 1908; *New York Times*, August 4, 1908; *New York Times*, August 19, 1908.
48. *New York Evening World*, July 31, 1908.
49. *New York Evening World*, August 19, 1908; *New York Times*, August 20, 1908.
50. *New York Times*, August 24, 1908.
51. *New York Times*, August 23, 1908; *New York Times*, August 25, 1908; *New York Times*, August 29, 1908; *New York Herald*, August 29, 1908.
52. *New York Times*, August 30, 1908; *New York Sun*, August 30, 1908; *New York Sun*, August 31, 1908.
53. *New York Tribune*, August 31, 1908; *New York Times*, September 1, 1908; *New York Evening World*, August 31, 1908.
54. *New York Tribune*, August 31, 1908; *New York Evening World*, September 7, 1908; *New York Times*, September 8, 1908.
55. *New York Times*, September 22, 1908; *New York Sun*, September 22, 1908; *New York Tribune*, September 22, 1908; *New York Tribune*, November 12, 1908. They were Claude Allen, Charles Bacon, George Bonhag, Joseph Bromilow, Frank Castleman, Robert Cloughen, Harvey Cohn, Edward Cook, John Daly, John Eller, Flanagan, William Frank, Johnny Hayes, Bill Horr, John Joyce, William Keating, Sheppard, Sheridan, James Sullivan, Lee Talbott, and Ralph Young.
56. *New York Times*, July 31, 1908; *New York Times*, August 6, 1908.
57. John Schaeffer, *The Irish American Athletic Club* (New York: New York University, 2001), 11.

Chapter 12

1. *New York Tribune*, March 28, 1903; *New York Evening World*, March 28, 1903.
2. *New York Evening World*, March 28, 1903; *Irish American*, April 20, 1903.

3. *Ibid.*, Cited in Kevin McCarthy, *Gold, Silver and Green* (Cork, Ireland: Cork University Press, 2010), 81; *New York Evening World*, March 28, 1903.

4. *Gaelic American*, February 2, 1907; *New York Times*, June 14, 1909; *New York Evening World*, September 25, 1908.

5. *New York Times*, November 13, 1946; Katchen, *Abel Kiviat*, 87; http,//www.wingedfist.com/Teach_the_Young_to_Shoot.pdf; http,//www.wingedfist.com/Mauser_ad.html.

6. Terry Golway. *Irish Rebel* (New York: St. Martin's Press, 1998), 201; Matthew Pratt Guterl, *The Color of Race in America* (Cambridge, MA: Harvard University Press, 2001), 7.

7. Ian McGowan, *A Brief History of the Irish-American Athletic Club* (New York: City University of New York, 2014), 24–25; *New York Times*, November 13, 1946; James Patrick Byrne, Philip Coleman, Jason Francis King, eds., *Ireland and the Americas, Vol. 1.* (Santa Barbara, CA: ABC-CLIO, 2008), 191–192.

8. *New York Sun*, November 10, 1905; *Gaelic American*, November 18, 1905.

9. *Gaelic American*, November 18, 1905.

10. *New York Times*, February 17, 1902; *New York Evening World*, July 17, 1908; *Gaelic American*, July 25, 1908.

11. *New York Evening World*, July 22, 1908; *Gaelic American*, August 1, 1908; *Gaelic American*, September 26, 1908.

12. *Irish World*, August 8, 1908; *Gaelic American*, July 25, 1908.

13. Patrick R. Redmond, *The Irish and the Making of American Sport, 1835–1920* (Jefferson, NC: McFarland, 2014), 312.

14. Reginald Byron, *Irish America* (New York: Oxford University Press, 2000), 246–247; Michael A. Gordon, *The Orange Riots* (Ithaca, NY: Cornell University Press, 1993), 19; *New York Times*, July 6, 1853; *New York Times*, July 8, 1853. Eight died in 1870 and 62 died the following year. Michael A. Gordon, *The Orange Riots*, 42, 151; The *New York Times* noted that this was the King's County AOH 46th "annual festival and outing," meaning that the first was in 1855. *New York Times*, July 5, 1900.

15. Terence A.M. Dooley, *The Greatest of the Fenians* (Dublin: Wolfhound Press, 2003), 87–88; Tim P. Coogan, *Wherever Green is Worn* (London: Hutchison, 2001), 335; Kerby A. Miller, *Emigrants and Exiles* (New York: Oxford University Press, 1985), 458; Terry Golway, *Irish Rebel* (New York: St. Martin's Press, 1998), 168.

16. Paul Darby, *Gaelic Games, Nationalism, and the Irish Diaspora in the United States* (Dublin: University College Dublin Press, 2009), 65; *New York Herald-Tribune*, August 18, 1870; *New York Times*, August 18, 1870.

17. *New York Tribune*, July 2, 1906; *New York Tribune*, August 31, 1908; *New York Times*, July 14, 1913.

18. *New York Evening World*, June 11, 1904; *New York Evening World*, July 26, 1904; *New York Evening World*, August 1, 1904; *New York Times*, August 1, 1904.

19. *New York Evening World*, June 16, 1905; *New York Times*, July 5, 1905.

20. *Irish American Weekly*, October 4, 1902.

21. T.H. Nally, *The Aonac Tailteann* (Dublin: Talbot Press, 1922), 27; Frank Zarnowski, *All-Around Men* (Lanham, MD: Scarecrow Press, 2005), 167; *Boston Globe*, July 24, 1889.

22. *Boston Globe*, September 30, 1888.

23. Marcus De Burca, *The GAA* (Dublin: Cumann Lúthchleas Gael, 1980), 43; Séamus Ó'Riain, *Maurice Davin* (Dublin: Geography Publications, 1994), 159; *Boston Herald*, May 22, 1881; *Boston Globe*, July 24, 1889.

24. *New York Times*, July 10, 1903; *Irish American Weekly*, August 8, 1903; *Brooklyn Daily Eagle*, July 9, 1903; *New York Tribune*, August 3, 1903; *New York Times*, August 2, 1903.

25. *New York Times*, September 8, 1903; *Irish World*, August 27, 1904; *New York Times*, September 6, 1904; *Gaelic American*, September 10, 1904.

26. *New York Tribune*, September 3, 1907; *New York Sun*, September 3, 1907; *Gaelic American*, September 8, 1906.

27. *New York Times*, September 6, 1909. AAU regulations required three officials to time a record. *New York Times*, September 6 1910.

Chapter 13

1. *New York Tribune*, September 13, 1908; *New York Times*, September 13, 1908.

2. *New York Times*, September 19, 1908; *New York Tribune*, September 19, 1908; *New York Times*, September 20, 1908; *New York Tribune*, September 20, 1908; *New York Times*, September 24, 1908.

3. *New York Times*, October 5, 1908; *New York Times*, November 2, 1908; *New York Times*, October 12, 1908.

4. *New York Tribune*, November 15, 1908; *New York Times*, November 15, 1908; *New York Times*, November 27, 1908.

5. *New York Times*, December 21, 1909; *New York Evening World*, November 30, 1908; *New York Tribune*, December 2, 1908; *New York Times*, December 2, 1908; *New York Evening World*, December 2, 1908; *New York Tribune*, January 13, 1909.

6. *New York Evening World*, January 30, 1909; *New York Tribune*, February 2, 1909; *New York Times*, February 6, 1909.

7. *New York Tribune*, February 7, 1909; *New York Times*, February 7, 1909; *New York Times*, February 12, 1909; *New York Tribune*, February 12, 1909; *New York Times*, April 18, 1909; *New York Tribune*, February 24, 1909; *New York Tribune*, March 7, 1909; *New York Times*, March 14, 1909; *New York Tribune*, March 14, 1909; *New York Times*, March 21, 1909.

8. *New York Times*, June 1, 1909; *New York Tribune*, June 1, 1909.

9. *Washington Evening Star*, May 3, 1909.

10. *New York Tribune*, May 24, 1909; *New York Times*, May 31, 1909; *New York Tribune*, May 31, 1909; *New York Times*, September 5, 1909; *New York Times*, September 7, 1909; *New York Times*, September 16, 1909; *New York Tribune*, September 16, 1909.

11. *New York Times*, July 6, 1909; *New York Tribune*, July 6, 1909.

12. *New York Tribune*, June 7, 1909; *New York Times*, June 7, 1909; *New York Tribune*, June 13, 1909; *New York Times*, June 13, 1909.

13. *New York Tribune*, June 27, 1909; *New York Times*, June 27, 1909; *New York Times*, July 25, 1909; *New York Tribune*, July 25, 1909; *New York Times*, July 30, 1909.

14. Wingedfist.org; *New York Times*, January 7, 1912; *New York Times*, July 16, 1913; *New York Times*, March 2, 1910; *New York Times*, May 31, 1909; *New York Tribune*, May 31, 1909; *New York Tribune*, June 7, 1909; *New York Tribune*, June 28, 1909.

15. *New York Tribune*, July 5, 1909; *New York Times*, August 1, 1909; *New York Times*, August 2, 1909; *New York Tribune*, August 2, 1909.

16. *New York Times*, June 20, 1909; *New York Tribune*, August 30, 1909; *New York Times*, July 25, 1909; *New York Times*, July 30, 1909; *New York Tribune*, September 7, 1909; *New York Times*, September 7, 1909.

17. *Evening Statesman* [Walla Walla, WA], July 27, 1909; *New York Times*, August 8, 1909.

18. *New York Times*, September 5, 1909; *New York Times*, September 11, 1909; *New York Times*, September 18, 1909.

19. *New York Tribune*, September 19, 1909; *New York Times*, September 19, 1909; *New York Times*, September 22, 1909.

20. *New York Times*, September 16, 1909; *New York Tribune*, September 16, 1909; *New York Tribune*, September 26, 1909; *New York Tribune*, September 12, 1909.

21. *New York Times*, September 26, 1909; *New York Times*, October 3, 1909; *New York Tribune*, October 11, 1909; *New York Times*, October 11, 1909; *Washington Evening Star*, October 11, 1909. The *New York Tribune* claimed that Billy Keating partnered Charles Cassasa. *New York Times*, October 25, 1909; *New York Tribune*, October 25, 1909.

22. *New York Tribune*, October 6, 1909; *New York Times*, October 5, 1909; *New York Times*, October 6, 1909.

23. *New York Times*, November 7, 1909; *New York Times*, November 14, 1909; *New York Times*, November 21, 1909; *New York Tribune*, November 15, 1909; *New York Times*, December 27, 1909.

24. *New York Times*, February 3, 1910; *New York Times*, February 6, 1910; *New York Tribune*, February 6, 1910; *New York Times*, May 3, 1910; *New York Tribune*, May 3, 1910.

25. *Irish American Weekly*, March 19, 1910; *New York Times*, April 4, 1910; *New York Times*, May 2, 1910; *New York Times*, May 31, 1910; *New York Tribune*, May 31, 1910; *New York Times*, May 31, 1910.

26. *New York Times*, June 27, 1910; *New York Times*, July 18, 1910; *New York Times*, August 1, 1910; *New York Tribune*, August 1, 1910; *New York Tribune*, August 8, 1910; *New York Times*, August 8, 1910; *New York Tribune*, August 15, 1910; *New York Times*, August 15, 1910; *New York Times*, August 21, 1910; *New York Tribune*, August 24, 1910.

27. *New York Times*, August 24, 1910; *New York Times*, August 22, 1910.

28. *New York Tribune*, June 20, 1910; *New York Times*, June 20, 1910.

29. *New York Times*, September 6, 1909; *New York Tribune*, September 6, 1909.

30. *New York Times*, September 11, 1910; *New York Tribune*, September 11, 1910.

Bruno Brodd is listed as Bruno Brood in the *Times* and Bruno Brooder in the *Tribune*.

31. *New York Tribune*, September 12, 1910; *New York Times*, September 12, 1910; *New York Times*, October 5, 1910.

32. *New York Times*, September 21, 1910; *New York Tribune*, September 25, 1910; *New York Times*, September 25, 1910.

33. *New York Times*, September 27, 1910; *New York Times*, October 8, 1910; *New York Times*, October 9, 1910.

34. *New York Tribune*, October 9, 1910; *New York Times*, October 10, 1910.

35. *New York Times*, October 15, 1910; *Washington Evening Star*, October 16, 1910; *New York Times*, October 16, 1910; *Chicago Tribune*, October 16, 1910; *New York Tribune*, October 16, 1910; *New York Tribune*, October 25, 1910.

36. *New York Times*, October 31, 1910; *New York Tribune*, November 2, 1910; *New York Times*, November 2, 1910.

37. *New York Times*, November 6, 1910; *New York Times*, November 27, 1910; *New York Tribune*, January 9, 1911; *New York Times*, January 9, 1911; *New York Times*, January 11, 1911.

38. *New York Tribune*, December 13, 1910; *New York Times*, January 12, 1911.

39. *New York Times*, July 10, 1910; *New York Times*, November 28, 1910; *New York Evening World*, March 30, 1911; *New York Times*, September 3, 1911.

40. *New York Evening World*, January 7, 1911.

41. *New York Times*, February 5, 1911; *New York Times*, March 5, 1911; *New York Times*, May 14, 1911; *New York Times*, May 28, 1911.

42. *Irish American Weekly*, March 25, 1911; *New York Times*, May 31, 1911; *New York Times*, May 15, 1911; *New York Times*, May 29, 1911; *New York Times*, June 18, 1911.

43. *New York Times*, June 4, 1911; *New York Times*, June 5, 1911; *New York Times*, July 10, 1911; *New York Times*, July 16, 1911; *New York Times*, September 5, 1911; *New York Tribune*, September 5, 1911.

44. *New York Times*, June 25, 1911; *New York Times*, July 1, 1911; *New York Times*, July 2, 1911.

45. *New York Evening World*, September 16, 1911; *New York Times*, September 17, 1911; *New York Sun*, September 17, 1911.

46. *New York Times*, February 6, 1911; *New York Evening World*, February 6, 1911.

47. *New York Times*, February 6, 1911.
48. *New York Times*, June 26, 1911.
49. *New York Times*, April 24, 1911.
50. *New York Tribune*, September 17, 1911; *New York Times*, September 17, 1911.
51. *Ibid*.
52. *New York Times*, September 18, 1911; *New York Times*, September 19, 1911; *New York Tribune*, September 19, 1911; *New York Sun*, September 19, 1911.
53. *New York Times*, November 20, 1911; *New York Times*, November 3, 1911.
54. *New York Tribune*, November 20, 1911.
55. *New York Times*, November 21, 1911; *New York Tribune*, November 21, 1911.
56. *New York Times*, October 21, 1911; *New York Times*, October 23, 1911; *New York Tribune*, October 23, 1911; *New York Times*, November 12, 1911; *New York Times*, November 19, 1911; *New York Times*, November 23, 1911.
57. *New York Times*, December 20, 1911.

Chapter 14

1. *Calgary Herald*, January 30, 1941; *New York Times*, January 29, 1941; Patrick R. Redmond, *The Irish and the Making of American Sport, 1835–1920* (Jefferson, NC: McFarland, 2014), 250; Matt McGrath was dismissed from the force but was reinstated in August 1915. *New York Evening World*, September 11, 1916.

2. *New York Times*, May 17, 1954; *New York Times*, May 18, 1954; *New York Times*, January 29, 1941.

3. *New York Times*, July 4, 1903; *New York Tribune*, July 5, 1903; *New York Times*, February 14, 1964.

4. Hasia R. Diner, "'The Most Irish City in the Union,'" in *The New York Irish*, ed. Ronald H. Bayor and Timothy J. Meagher (Baltimore: Johns Hopkins University Press, 1996), 97; Andrew T. Darien, *Becoming New York's Finest* (New York: Palgrave Macmillan, 2013), 1.

5. Andrew T. Darien, *Becoming New York's Finest* (New York: Palgrave Macmillan, 2013), 33–34.

6. Margaret Mary Hennessy, "Irish Whales," in Kirsch, George B. Harris, Othello, Claire Elaine Nolte, *Encyclopedia of Ethnicity and Sports In The United States* (Westport, CT: Greenwood Press, 2000),

239; *New York Times*, July 17, 1916; *New York Tribune*, October 27, 1907.
   7. *New York Tribune*, April 6, 1877; *New York World*, March 23, 1878; *New York World*, June 6, 1882; *New York World*, March 24, 1887; *New York Sun*, January 25, 1903; *New York Times*, October 22, 1905; *Gaelic American*, October 13, 1906.
   8. *New York Times*, March 28, 1918; *New York Evening World*, February 5, 1906.
   9. *New York Tribune*, August 21, 1904.
   10. *Wilkes-Barre Times*, November 6, 1907.
   11. *New York Evening World*, February 1, 1905; *New York Times*, August 3, 1913; *New York Tribune*, September 27, 1905.
   12. *New York Sun*, July 13, 1907.
   13. *New York Tribune*, July 23, 1910; *New York Tribune*, August 14, 1910; *New York Times*, August 15, 1910.
   14. *New York Evening World*, July 15, 1911.
   15. Bernard Whalen and Jon Whalen, *The NYPD's First Fifty Years* (Lincoln, NE: Potomac Books, 2014), 37; Katchen, *Abel Kiviat*, 87.
   16. *New York Evening World*, September 8, 1906.
   17. *New York Times*, October 3, 1908; *New York Times*, October 9, 1910.
   18. *New York Times*, October 11, 1910.
   19. *New York Herald*, February 29, 1880; *New York Herald*, March 5, 1880; *Gaelic American*, August 10, 1907; *New York Times*, April 16, 1914; *Gaelic American*, June 9, 1906.
   20. *New York Times*, November 25, 1902; *New York Tribune*, November 26, 1902; *New York Evening World*, November 24, 1908; *New York Times*, July 27, 1914; *Gaelic American*, June 25, 1914; *Gaelic American*, August 1, 1914; Ian McGowan, *A Brief History of the Irish-American Athletic Club.* (New York: City University of New York, 2014), 28.
   21. *New York Times*, June 24, 1916; *New York Times*, July 5, 1916; *New York Sun*, July 5, 1916.
   22. *New York Sun*, October 29, 1906; *New York Times*, October 29, 1906.
   23. *New York Times*, May 20, 1909.
   24. *New York Times*, July 25, 1908; John Bryant, *Marathon Makers* (London: John Blake, 2008), 51, 52.
   25. *New York Times*, September 7, 1909; *New York Evening World*, February 27, 1908.
   26. *New York Times*, October 3, 1909; *New York Times*, July 24, 1914; *New York Evening World*, October 19, 1914.
   27. *Brooklyn Daily Eagle*, August 26, 1902; *New York Times*, March 24, 1934; William L. Riorden and Peter Quinn, *Plunkitt of Tammany Hall* (London: Signet, Penguin-Random House, 2015), 32.
   28. *New York Evening World*, January 3, 1905. With regard to the State of New York, the trial court level, not the highest court, is named the Supreme Court. In almost every other state, this court would be run by Circuit Courts.
   29. *New York Evening World*, June 5, 1911.
   30. *New York Times*, December 28, 1911; *New York Evening World*, December 28, 1911; *New York Tribune*, December 28, 1911.
   31. *New York Tribune*, October 12, 1914; *New York Times*, October 25, 1914; *New York Times*, November 5, 1910; *New York Tribune*, November 5, 1910; *Irish American Weekly*, February 22, 1902; *New York Times*, March 24, 1916; *New York Sun*, March 24, 1916; *New York Times*, September 8, 1912; *New York Times*, March 28, 1916; *New York Evening World*, May 2, 1922.
   32. *New York Times*, September 9, 1902; *New York Times*, February 5, 1902; *New York Times*, November 5, 1902; *New York Times*, September 2, 1926.
   33. *New York Times*, November 20, 1900; *New York Times*, February 27, 1907; *New York Times*, April 13, 1911; *New York Times*, June 8, 1911; *New York Times*, August 31, 1911; *New York Times*, September 29, 1911.
   34. *New York Times*, March 13, 1912; *New York Sun*, March 13, 1912.
   35. *New York Times*, November 8, 1914; *New York Times*, February 2, 1917.
   36. Bernard Whalen and Jon Whalen, *The NYPD's First Fifty Years* (Lincoln, NE: Potomac Books, 2014), 22.
   37. *New York Evening World*, December 9, 1907; Katchen, *Abel Kiviat*, 89.
   38. Scott Pitoniak, *100 Things Syracuse Fans Should Know & Do Before They Die.* (Chicago: Triumph Books, 2014), 101–102.
   39. *New York Times*, February 21, 1909; *New York Sun*, October 27, 1902; *New York Times*, October 27, 1902.
   40. *Sporting Life*, November 8, 1902.
   41. *New York Tribune*, October 30, 1902; *Sporting Life*, November 8, 1902; *New York Times*, November 3, 1902.
   42. *New York Times*, November 2, 1903; *New York Evening World*, November 2, 1903.
   43. *New York Times*, April 25, 1905; *New York Sun*, July 10, 1905; *New York Times*, July 17, 1905.

44. *New York Evening World*, April 30, 1906.
45. *New York Times*, December 6, 1907; *New York Tribune*, December 4, 1907; *New York Evening World*, December 9, 1907; *New York Times*, December 8, 1907.
46. *New York Times*, November 8, 1915; *New York Times*, November 9, 1915.
47. *New York Times*, October 5, 1908; *Brooklyn Daily Eagle*, October 5, 1908.
48. *New York Evening World*, October 5, 1908.
49. *New York Times*, July 24, 1917; *New York Times*, August 22, 1917; *New York Times*, January 15, 1919.
50. *New York Times*, September 9, 1917; *New York Times*, October 8, 1917.

Chapter 15

1. *New York Tribune*, March 3, 1912.
2. *New York Tribune*, January 26, 1912; *New York Times*, January 26, 1912; *New York Times*, December 17, 1911; *New York Times*, February 11, 1912.
3. *New York Times*, January 28, 1912; *New York Times*, January 29, 1912; *New York Tribune*, January 31, 1912.
4. *New York Times*, March 26, 1912; *New York Evening World*, March 26, 1912; *New York Times*, May 2, 1912; *New York Tribune*, March 27, 1912; *New York Sun*, April 20, 1912; *New York Times*, April 23, 1912; *New York Times*, May 14, 1912.
5. *New York Times*, May 19, 1912; *New York Times*, May 21, 1912.
6. *New York Times*, May 27, 1912; *New York Times*, June 3, 1912; *New York Times*, May 31, 1912.
7. *New York Times*, June 8, 1912; *New York Times*, June 9, 1912; *New York Times*, June 10, 1912.
8. *New York Evening World*, June 15, 1912; *New York Times*, June 24, 1912; *New York Times*, July 29, 1912.
9. *New York Evening World*, June 15, 1912; *New York Times*, June 25, 1912; *New York Times*, July 9, 1912; *New York Times*, July 14, 1912; *New York Tribune*, July 15, 1912.
10. *New York Times*, August 19, 1912; *New York Evening World*, September 3, 1912.
11. *New York Tribune*, September 7, 1912; *New York Times*, September 7, 1912; *New York Times*, September 8, 1912.
12. *New York Times*, September 21, 1912; *New York Tribune*, September 22, 1912; *New York Times*, September 22, 1912.
13. *New York Times*, September 23, 1912; *New York Times*, September 30, 1912; *New York Times*, October 21, 1912; *New York Evening World*, October 21, 1912.
14. *New York Evening World*, October 21, 1912; *New York Times*, October 22, 1912; *New York Sun*, October 22, 1912; *New York Evening World*, October 23, 1912; *New York Times*, October 23, 1912; *New York Times*, October 24, 1912.
15. *New York Times*, November 10, 1912; *New York Tribune*, November 16, 1912; *New York Times*, November 16, 1912; *New York Times*, December 1, 1912.
16. *New York Times*, November 28, 1912; *New York Tribune*, January 5, 1913; *New York Times*, January 5, 1913; *New York Tribune*, March 7, 1913; *New York Times*, March 7, 1913; *New York Tribune*, February 7, 1913; *New York Times*, February 16, 1913; *New York Tribune*, April 13, 1913.
17. *Irish American Weekly*, April 5, 1913; *New York Times*, May 31, 1913; *New York Sun*, June 20, 1913; *New York Times*, June 29, 1913; *New York Times*, July 2, 1913.
18. *New York Times*, July 5, 1913; *New York Times*, July 6, 1913; *New York Tribune*, July 6, 1913.
19. *New York Times*, August 16, 1913; *New York Sun*, August 16, 1913; *New York Times*, August 27, 1913.
20. *New York Times*, August 18, 1913; *New York Times*, September 2, 1913.
21. *New York Times*, September 21, 1913; *New York Times*, October 20, 1913; *New York Tribune*, October 20, 1913.
22. *New York Sun*, July 5, 1913; *New York Times*, September 30, 1913; *New York Times*, December 16, 1914; *New York Sun*, December 16, 1914.
23. *New York Times*, November 11, 1913; *New York Tribune*, November 13, 1913; *New York Evening World*, December 17, 1913.
24. *New York Tribune*, November 16, 1913; *New York Times*, December 7, 1913; *New York Tribune*, December 7, 1913; *New York Tribune*, January 11, 1914; *New York Times*, January 11, 1914.
25. *New York Times*, December 6, 1913; *New York Times*, February 10, 1914; *New York Sun*, February 10, 1914; *New York Tribune*, January 25, 1914; *New York Sun*, January 26, 1914; *New York Sun*, January 31, 1914.
26. *New York Times*, February 19, 1914.

27. *New York Times*, July 2, 1914; *New York Tribune*, July 6, 1914; *New York Tribune*, July 2, 1914; *New York Times*, July 3, 1914; *New York Tribune*, August 9, 1914.
28. *New York Sun*, March 25, 1914; *New York Times*, March 25, 1914.
29. *New York Tribune*, March 25, 1914; *New York Evening World*, April 22, 1914.
30. *New York Times*, April 15, 1914; *New York Times*, May 5, 1914; *New York Times*, September 25, 1914.
31. *New York Times*, March 3, 1914.
32. *Irish American Weekly*, March 28, 1914; *New York Times*, April 5, 1914; *New York Times*, May 3, 1914; *New York Times*, May 14, 1914; *New York Times*, May 31, 1914; *New York Times*, May 31, 1914; *New York Times*, July 27, 1914; *Washington Times*, July 27, 1914.
33. *New York Tribune*, September 13, 1914; *New York Times*, September 12, 1914; *New York Times*, September 13, 1914; *New York Times*, October 4, 1914; *New York Tribune*, June 21, 1914; *New York Tribune*, October 11, 1914.
34. *New York Times*, November 1, 1914; *New York Tribune*, November 1, 1914; *New York Times*, November 11, 1914; *New York Times*, November 15, 1914; *New York Times*, November 15, 1914; *New York Tribune*, November 22, 1914; *New York Times*, November 22, 1914; *New York Times*, December 12, 1914; *New York Times*, December 13, 1914.
35. *New York Evening World*, November 25, 1914; *Gaelic American*, November 7, 1914; *New York Times*, November 29, 1914; *Gaelic American*, November 21, 1914.
36. *New York Times*, October 22, 1914; *New York Times*, December 2, 1914.
37. *New York Times*, December 17, 1914.
38. *New York Tribune*, January 9, 1915; *New York Times*, February 9, 1915; *New York Times*, February 24, 1915; *New York Times*, March 5, 1915.
39. *New York Times*, March 31, 1915; *New York Tribune*, March 31, 1915; *New York Times*, December 6, 1914; *New York Times*, April 4, 1915; *New York Times*, April 5, 1915; *New York Times*, April 8, 1915; *New York Times*, May 18, 1915; *New York Sun*, May 18, 1915.
40. *New York Times*, April 10, 1915; *New York Times*, May 3, 1915; *New York Tribune*, May 3, 1915; *New York Times*, May 5, 1915; *New York Times*, June 14, 1915; *New York Times*, July 6, 1915.

41. *New York Times*, June 16, 1915; *New York Times*, June 19, 1915; *New York Times*, June 20, 1915; *Gaelic American*, June 26, 1915; *New York Times*, July 18, 1915.
42. *New York Times*, April 17, 1915; *New York Tribune*, July 18, 1915.
43. *New York Times*, August 6, 1915; *New York Tribune*, August 8, 1915; *New York Times*, August 8, 1915.
44. *New York Times*, August 19, 1915.
45. *New York Sun*, August 22, 1915.
46. *New York Sun*, August 25, 1915; *New York Times*, September 17, 1915; *New York Sun*, September 17, 1915.
47. *New York Times*, August 19, 1915.
48. *New York Tribune*, October 15, 1915; *New York Times*, October 22, 1915; *New York Tribune*, October 23, 1915; *New York Tribune*, October 26, 1915; *New York Evening World*, October 26, 1915; *New York Sun*, October 26, 1915.
49. *New York Tribune*, October 30, 1915; *New York Times*, November 10, 1915; *New York Sun*, November 11, 1915; *New York Times*, November 12, 1915; *New York Times*, November 29, 1915; *New York Times*, December 5, 1915.
50. *New York Times*, February 29, 1916; *New York Times*, January 30, 1916; *New York Times*, March 19, 1916.
51. *New York Times*, February 8, 1916; *New York Times*, April 21, 1916; *New York Sun*, June 18, 1916.
52. *New York Sun*, May 1, 1914; *New York Evening World*, May 1, 1914; *New York Times*, February 3, 1916.
53. *New York Times*, May 31, 1916; *New York Tribune*, May 31, 1916; *New York Tribune*, May 14, 1902; *New York Sun*, May 31, 1916.
54. *New York Times*, June 18, 1916; *New York Times*, July 7, 1916.
55. *New York Sun*, August 12, 1916; *New York Times*, August 26, 1916; *New York Tribune*, August 26, 1916; *New York Sun*, August 26, 1916; *New York Times*, August 27, 1916.
56. *New York Times*, September 1, 1916; *New York Times*, September 3, 1916.
57. *New York Times*, September 9, 1916; *New York Times*, September 10, 1916; *New York Sun*, September 11, 1916.
58. *New York Tribune*, October 2, 1916; *New York Times*, December 21, 1916; *New York Times*, October 24, 1916.
59. *New York Times*, October 29, 1916; *New York Tribune*, November 14, 1916; *New*

York Tribune, November 15, 1916; New York Times, November 15, 1916.
60. New York Times, November 19, 1916; New York Tribune, November 20, 1916.
61. New York Evening World, January 8, 1917; New York Times, January 8, 1917.
62. Gaelic American, March 31, 1917.

Chapter 16

1. New York Times, April 12, 1917; Duluth News-Tribune, April 18, 1917; New York Sun, April 12, 1917; Brooklyn Daily Eagle, May 5, 1898.
2. New York Times, May 6, 1917; New York Times, June 3, 1917; New York Tribune, May 13, 1917; New York Times, August 17, 1917; New York Times, August 20, 1917; New York Times, August 25, 1917; New York Times, April 12, 1917.
3. New York Times, March 4, 1917.
4. New York Times, March 18, 1917; New York Tribune, July 29, 1917.
5. Watertown Daily Times, July 9, 1917.
6. Gaelic American, August 18, 1917; New York Times, August 26, 1917; New York Sun, August 26, 1917.
7. New York Sun, September 2, 1917; New York Times, September 2, 1917; New York Sun, September 3, 1917.
8. New York Sun, September 11, 1917; New York Sun, September 14, 1917; New York Times, September 16, 1917; New York Times, October 7, 1917; New York Times, October 15, 1917.
9. New York Sun, December 30, 1917; New York Times, December 30, 1917; New York Tribune, November 25, 1917; New York Tribune, December 30, 1917.
10. New York Times, March 28, 1918; New York Tribune, March 28, 1918; New York Evening World, March 28, 1918; New York Sun, March 28, 1918; Washington Evening Star, March 31, 1918.
11. New York Times, March 31, 1918; New York Sun, March 31, 1918.
12. New York Times, April 8, 1918; New York Times, April 15, 1918; New York Times, May 31, 1918; New York Sun, May 31, 1918.
13. New York Times, July 11, 1918; New York Times, July 21, 1918; New York Sun, July 28, 1918.
14. New York Times, July 22, 1918; New York Tribune, August 26, 1918.
15. New York Times, January 1, 1919.
16. New York Times, April 12, 1917; Brooklyn Daily Eagle, May 5, 1898; New York Times, June 3, 1917.
17. New York Sun, April 12, 1917.
18. New York Times, June 28, 1931; New York Sun, August 19, 1919; New York Times, August 22, 1919. There is one article that lists Ryan as having fought in World War I for the U.S. Army. See Wingedfist.org.
19. New York Evening World, August 6, 1919; New York Tribune, August 18, 1919; New York Times, October 19, 1919; New York Evening World, December 10, 1918; New York Times, January 15, 1920.
20. Brooklyn Daily Eagle, September 7, 1920; New York Tribune, September 7, 1920.
21. New York Tribune, September 7, 1920; New York Times, September 7, 1920.
22. New York Tribune, September 8, 1920.
23. New York Evening World, July 24, 1922; New York Tribune, July 24, 1922; Washington Times, July 24, 1922.
24. Brooklyn Daily Eagle, December 11, 1901; New York Times, July 24, 1922.
25. New York Evening World, July 25, 1922; New York Times, July 25, 1922.
26. New York Tribune, July 26, 1922.
27. New York Times, August 27, 1922.
28. New York Times, May 1, 1923; New York Times, May 22, 1923; New York Times, May 30, 1923.
29. New York Times, May 31, 1923; Brooklyn Daily Eagle, May 31, 1923; New York Times, May 11, 1923.
30. New York Times, September 13, 1928; New York Times, September 21, 1928; New York Times, September 25, 1928; New York Times, September 27, 1928; New York Times, September 28, 1928; New York Times, September 29, 1928; New York Times, October 3, 1928; New York Times, October 4, 1928; Brooklyn Daily Eagle, October 4, 1928.
31. New York Times, February 3, 1929; New York Times, April 7, 1929; New York Times, May 12, 1928.

Chapter 17

1. Queens Gazette, March 14, 2012; https,//www.nyu.edu/library/bobst/research/aia/primarydocs/iaac/iaac01.htm.
2. Gaelic American, March 1, 1930.
3. New York Times, February 22, 1930; Brooklyn Daily Eagle, September 16, 1930; New York Times, June 7, 1931; New York

Times, June 28, 1931, *New York Times*, October 18, 1931.

4. *New York Times*, July 22, 1914; *Gaelic American*, March 1, 1930.

5. *New York Times*, January 30, 1930; *Gaelic American*, September 20, 1930; *Gaelic American*, March 1, 1930; *Brooklyn Daily Eagle*, September 16, 1930.

6. *Gaelic American*, September 13, 1930; *Gaelic American*, October 11, 1930; *Gaelic American*, October 4, 1930.

7. *New York Times*, March 14, 1937; *New York Times*, November 24, 1938; *New York Times*, December 24, 1932.

8. *New York Times*, January 17, 1932; *Gaelic American*, January 23, 1932; *New York Times*, September 2, 1926; *New York Times*, November 13, 1946.

9. *New York Times*, July 4, 1936.

10. *New York Times*, August 22, 1936; *New York Times*, September 19, 1936.

11. *New York Times*, June 28, 1931.

12. Baseball-reference.com.

13. *New York Times*, June 28, 1931; *New York Times*, August 10, 1930; *New York Times*, September 11, 1910; *Brooklyn Daily Eagle*, May 27, 1908.

14. http,//tedcorbitt.com/NewYorkPioneerClub.html; *New York Times*, June 26, 1955. Intriguingly, the NYAC took the National title the following month in Boulder, Colorado.

15. *New York Times*, July 1, 1996.

16. *New York Times*, February 16, 1968.

17. *Ibid.*, February 16, 1968; *Sports Illustrated*, February 26, 1968.

18. *New York Times*, July 1, 1996.

19. John C. Walter, *The Harlem Fox* (Albany: State University of New York Press, 1989), 76; Birmingham, *Real Lace* (Syracuse, NY: Syracuse University Press, 1997).

20. John Irving, *In One Person* (New York: Simon & Schuster, 2012), 312–313.

21. *Gaelic American*, July 25, 1908.

Bibliography

Newspapers and Periodicals: United States

American Hebrew, New York, NY
Boston Evening Telegraph, Boston, MA
Boston Globe, Boston, MA
Boston Herald, Boston, MA
Boston Journal, Boston, MA
Brooklyn Daily Eagle, New York, NY
Brooklyn Life, New York, NY
Chicago Inter Ocean, Chicago, IL
Chicago Tribune, Chicago, IL
Detroit Free Press, Detroit, MI
Duluth News-Tribune, Duluth, MN
East Oregonian, Pendleton, OR
Evening Star, Washington, D.C.
Evening Statesman, Walla Walla, WA
Gaelic American, New York, NY
Irish American Advocate, New York, NY
Irish American Weekly, New York, NY
Irish World, New York, NY
Jersey Journal, Jersey City, NJ
Los Angeles Herald, Los Angeles, CA
New York Evening World, New York, NY
New York Herald, New York, NY
New York Herald-Tribune, New York, NY
New York Mail, New York, NY
New York Post, New York, NY
New York Sun, New York, NY
New York Times, New York, NY
New York Tribune, New York, NY
New York World, New York, NY
Philadelphia Inquirer, Philadelphia, PA
Pittsburgh Dispatch, Pittsburgh, PA
Pittsburgh Post-Gazette, Pittsburgh, PA
Queens Gazette, New York, NY
St. Louis Republic, St. Louis, MO
Seattle Daily Times, Seattle, WA
The Oregonian, Portland, OR
Washington Post, Washington, D.C.
Washington Times, Washington, D.C.
Watertown Daily Times, Watertown, NY
Wilkes-Barre Times, Wilkes-Barre, PA

Newspapers: Britain, Canada and Ireland

Calgary Herald, Calgary, Canada
Daily News, London, UK
Dundee Courier, Dundee, UK
Dundee Evening Telegraph, Dundee, UK
Freeman's Journal, Dublin, Ireland
Montreal Gazette, Montreal, Canada
Morning Post, London, UK
Nottingham Evening Post, Nottingham, UK
Yorkshire Post and Leeds Intelligencer, Leeds, UK

Sporting Newspapers and Magazines

Outing Magazine
Sporting Life, Philadelphia, PA
Sports Illustrated
Wilkes' Spirit of the Times, New York, NY

General Magazine

Metropolitan Magazine
Spring 3100

Websites

baseball-reference.com
chroniclingamerica.loc.gov
Geneaology.com
Google
Google Books
Google News
la84.org

Library of congress.loc.gov
nyac.org
statenislandac.org
tedcorbitt.com
wallstreetjackass.typepad.com
Wikipedia
wingedfist.org

Articles, Theses and Chapters of Edited Books

Bond, Gregory. *Jim Crow at Play: Race, Manliness, and the Color Line in American Sports, 1876–1916*. Ph.D. Dissertation. University of Wisconsin, 2008.
Diner, Hasia R. "'The Most Irish City in the Union': The Era of the Great Migration 1844–1877." In *The New York Irish*, edited by Ronald H. Bayor and Timothy J. Meagher. Baltimore: Johns Hopkins University Press, 1996.
Hennessey, Margaret Mary. "Irish Whales." In *Encyclopedia of Ethnicity and Sports in the United States*, edited by George B. Kirsch, Othello Harris, and Claire Elaine. Westport, CT: Greenwood Press, 2000.
Kuo Wei Tchen, John. "Quimbo Appo's Fear of Fenians: Chinese-Irish-Anglo Relations in New York City." In *The New York Irish*, edited by Ronald H. Bayor and Timothy J. Meagher. Baltimore: Johns Hopkins University Press, 1996.
Lucas, John A. "Pat 'Babe' McDonald: Olympic Champion and Paragon of the Irish-American Whales." *Journal of Olympic History* 5, no. 3 (Fall 1997).
McGowan, Ian. *A Brief History of the Irish-American Athletic Club: The "Winged Fists" of Celtic Park*. New York: City University of New York, Academic Works, 2014.
Ridge, John T. "Irish County Societies in New York, 1880–1914." In *The New York Irish*, Ronald H. Bayor and Timothy J. Meagher. Baltimore: Johns Hopkins University Press, 1996.
Schaeffer, John. *The Irish American Athletic Club: Redefining Americanism at the 1908 Olympic Games*. New York: New York University, 2001.
Willis, Joe, and Richard Wettan. "Social Stratification in New York City Athletic Clubs, 1865–1915." *Journal of Sport History* 3, no. 1 (Spring, 1976).
Zarnowski, Frank. "Thomas F. Kiely: A Biography." *Journal of Olympic History* 14, no. 2 (August 2006).

Books (Sports)

Bills, Peter. *Passion in Exile: 100 Years of London Irish RFC*. Edinburgh, UK: Mainstream Publishing, 1998.
Bryant, John. *Marathon Makers*. London: John Blake, 2008.
Carlos, John, and Dave Zirin. *The John Carlos Story*. Chicago: Haymarket Books, 2011.
Cowley, Jason. *The Last Game: Love, Death and Football*. London: Simon & Schuster, 2009.
Darby, Paul. *Gaelic Games, Nationalism, and the Irish Diaspora in the United States*. Dublin: University College Dublin Press, 2009.
Davies, Richard O. *Sports in American Life: A History*. Chichester, UK: John Wiley & Sons, 2012.
De Búrca, Marcus. *The GAA: A History of the Gaelic Athletic Association*. Dublin: Cumann Lúthchleas Gael, 1980.
Dooley, William. *Champions of the Athletic Arena*. Dublin: General Publicity Service, 1948.
Findling, John E., and Kimberly Pelle. *Encyclopedia of the Modern Olympic Movement*. Westport, CT: Greenwood Press, 2004.
Foner, Nancy: *In a New Land: A Comparative View of Immigration*. New York: NYU Press, 2005.
Greensmyth, Harry, and Denis Martin. *John Flanagan: His Life and Times: Olympic and World*

16lbs Weight Throwing Champion. Kilfinane, Co. Limerick, Ireland: Kilfinane (Coshlea) Historical Society, 2001.
Holst, Donald, and Marcia S. Popp. *American Men of Olympic Track And Field: Interviews with Athletes and Coaches*. Jefferson, NC: McFarland, 2005.
Janssen, Frederick W. *History of American Amateur Athletics*. New York: C.R. Bourne, 1885. Reprint: Whitefish, MT: Kessinger Publishing, 2010.
Jenkins, Rebecca. *The First London Olympics 1908: The definitive story of London's most sensational Olympics to date*. London: Piatkus, 2008.
Katchen, Alan S. *Abel Kiviat*. Syracuse, NY: Syracuse University Press, 2009.
Kent, Graeme. *Olympic Follies: The Madness and Mayhem of the 1908 London Games*. London: JR Books, 2008.
Kirsch, George B., Othello Harris, and Claire Elaine Nolte. *Encyclopedia of Ethnicity and Sports in the United States*. Westport, CT: Greenwood Press, 2000.
Levine, Peter. *Ellis Island to Ebbets Field: Sport and the American Jewish Experience*. New York: Oxford University Press, 1992.
McCarthy, Kevin. *Gold, Silver and Green: The Irish Olympic Journey 1896–1924*. Cork, Ireland: Cork University Press, 2010.
Nally, T. H. *The Aonac Tailteann and the Tailteann Games: Their Origin, History, and Ancient Associations*. Dublin: Talbot Press, 1922. Reprint: Nabu Public Domain Reprints, n.d.
Ó Riain, Séamus. *Maurice Davin (1842–1927): First President of the GAA*. Dublin: Geography Publications, 1994.
Pitoniak, Scott: *100 Things Syracuse Fans Should Know & Do Before They Die*. Chicago: Triumph Books, 2014.
Quinn, Mark. *The King of Spring: The Life and Times of Peter O'Connor*. Dublin: The Liffey Press, 2004.
Redmond, Patrick R. *The Irish and the Making of American Sport: 1835–1920*. Jefferson, NC: McFarland, 2014.
Riess, Steven A., editor. *Sports and the American Jew (Sports and Entertainment)*. Syracuse, NY: Syracuse University Press, 1998.
Riess, Steven A. *City Games: The Evolution of American Urban Society and the Rise of Sports*. Urbana: University of Illinois Press, 1991.
Schaap, Jeremy. *Triumph: The Untold Story of Jesse Owens and Hitler's Olympics*. New York: Houghton Mifflin Harcourt, 2007.
Sullivan, James E. *Spalding's Official Athletic Almanac 1905*. New York: American Publishing, 1905.
Trumpbour, Robert C. *The New Cathedrals: Politics And Media in the History of Stadium Construction*. Syracuse, NY: Syracuse University Press, 2006.
Zarnowski, Frank. *All-Around Men: Heroes of a Forgotten Sport*. Lanham, MD: Scarecrow Press, 2005.

Books (American History)

Darien, Andrew T. *Becoming New York's Finest: Race, Gender, and the Integration of the NYPD, 1935–1980*. New York: Palgrave Macmillan, 2013.
Ribak, Gil: *Gentile New York: The Images of Non-Jews among Jewish Immigrants*. New Brunswick, NJ: Rutgers University Press, 2012.
Walter, John C. *The Harlem Fox: J. Raymond Jones and Tammany, 1920–1970*. Albany, NY: State University of New York Press, 1989.

Books (Irish History)

Bayor, Ronald H., and Timothy J. Meagher, editors. *The New York Irish*. Baltimore: Johns Hopkins University Press, 1996.

Birmingham, Stephen. *Real Lace: America's Irish Rich.* Syracuse, NY: Syracuse University Press, 1997.
Byrne, James Patrick, Philip Coleman, and Jason Francis King, editors. *Ireland and the Americas: Culture, Politics, and History, Vol. 1.* Santa Barbara, CA: ABC-CLIO, 2008.
Coogan, Tim Pat. *Wherever Green Is Worn: The Story Of The Irish Diaspora.* London: Hutchison, 2001.
Dooley, Terence A.M. *The Greatest of the Fenians: John Devoy and Ireland.* Dublin: Wolfhound Press, 2003.
Golway, Terry. *Irish Rebel: John Devoy and America's Fight for Ireland's Freedom.* New York: St. Martin's Press, 1998.
Gordon, Michael A. *The Orange Riots: Irish Political Violence in New York City, 1870 And 1871.* Ithaca, NY: Cornell University Press, 1993.
Kenny, Kevin: *The American Irish: A History.* New York: Routledge, 2000.
Miller, Kerby A. *Emigrants and Exiles.* New York: Oxford University Press, 1985.

Books (Other Subjects)

Whalen, Bernard,, and Jon Whalen. *The NYPD's First Fifty Years: Politicians, Police Commissioners and Patrolmen.* Lincoln, NE: Potomac Books, 2014.
Guterl, Matthew Pratt. *The Color of Race in America: 1900–1940.* Cambridge, MA: Harvard University Press, 2001.
Irving, John. *In One Person.* New York: Simon & Schuster, 2012.
Riorden, William L., and Peter Quinn. *Plunkitt of Tammany Hall: A Series of Very Plain Talks on Very Practical Politics.* London: Signet: Penguin-Random House, 2015.
Shumsky Neil L. *Institutional Life: Family, Schools, Race, and Religion.* New York: Routledge, 1996.

Reference Books

Official Athletic Rules and Official Handbook of the Amateur Athletic Union of the United States, 1908.
Official Athletic Rules and Official Handbook of the Amateur Athletic Union of the United States, 1909.
Official Athletic Rules and Official Handbook of the Amateur Athletic Union of the United States, 1910.
Official Athletic Rules and Official Handbook of the Amateur Athletic Union of the United States, 1911.
Official Athletic Rules and Official Handbook of the Amateur Athletic Union of the United States, 1912.
Official Athletic Rules and Official Handbook of the Amateur Athletic Union of the United States, 1914.
Wallechinsky, David. *The Complete Book of the Olympics.* London: Aurum Press, 1992.

Index

Acorn AA 175
Adams, Platt 173, 179
African Americans 1, 2, 8, 37, 39, 47, 49, 50, 138, 150, 189, 249, 250, 261n43
Ahearn, Daniel 132, 168, 172, 173, 174, 175, 176, 179, 181, 182, 186, 213
Ahearn, John F. 197
Ahearne, Tim 172, 212, 214, 227, 258n9
Ahlgren, Alexis 183–184
Albany, NY 57, 122, 196
Alcohol 4, 10, 18, 40, 68, 72, 133, 137, 186, 198, 237–241
Aldridge, Albert 72
Alesian Athletic Association 168
Allen, Claude 78, 85, 113, 114, 143, 168, 270n55
Alsheimer, H. 15
Amateur Athletic Association, Great Britain 66, 70
Amateur Athletic Union, United States 2, 3, 5, 6, 12, 13, 19, 20, 43, 44, 49, 53, 60, 61, 65, 82, 83, 89, 90, 95, 97, 103, 115, 117, 119, 120, 121–129, 130, 136, 138, 140, 164, 171, 172, 175, 185, 198, 201, 206, 214, 215, 216, 220, 222, 224, 228, 229, 231, 253–255, 263n13, 271n27; AAU Cross Country 5, 60, 86, 107, 114, 134–135, 169, 175, 179, 186, 211, 233, 256, 257; AAU Indoor events 108, 114, 169–170, 174, 175, 179, 180–181, 211, 217, 220, 225, 233, 257; AAU National All-Around Competition 25, 40, 55, 61, 62, 72, 73, 84, 104, 110, 122, 155, 189, 209, 256; AAU National Junior Championships 3, 5 12, 43, 63, 74, 97, 105, 106, 113, 168, 172, 177, 179 182, 210, 212, 218, 222, 225, 226, 227, 228; AAU National Senior Championships 3, 5, 6, 12, 13, 22, 40, 42, 46, 47, 52, 57, 63, 68, 70, 71, 72, 74–75, 82, 87, 94, 99, 105–106, 109, 113, 168, 173, 175, 177–179, 193, 209, 210, 212, 213, 217–218, 222, 225, 227, 228, 235, 248, 253, 257; AAU 10 Mile 5, 60–61, 83, 113–114, 175, 179, 218–219, 228, 256; All America Team 232
Amateur Hockey League 135, 136
American League Baseball Park, New York City 172
American Line 143
Ancient Order of Hibernians (AOH) 4, 30, 105, 111, 155, 158, 159, 163, 164, 171, 271n14
Andrews, John 226
Archer, J.J. "Jim" 43, 208, 241, 258n9
Arnold, Martin 249
Asbury Park Athletic Club 42
Astoria Athletic Club 88
Australia 97, 105
Austria-Hungary 216, 229; Austria 215; Hungary 215
Avondale Athletic Club 237

Bacon, Charles Joseph, Jr. 62, 63, 74, 75, 78, 87, 101, 116, 117, 131, 142, 148, 151, 169, 263n43
Badger, Roscoe 149
Bailey, W.T. 17
Baker, Homer 221, 228, 231
Baker, Wendell 170, 177
Baltimore, Homewood Field 281; 218
Banderman, J.A.C./J.D. 112
Bannon, Harry 215, 223
Barcelona Football Club 159
Barden, Tom 218, 228
Barker, Nigel 46
Barrett, Anthony J. 198
Barry, William J.M. 94
Baseball 12, 13, 19, 20, 24, 25, 27, 30, 47, 65, 89, 122, 124, 128, 160, 172, 182, 200, 203, 205, 207, 209, 248

283

Basketball 77, 122
Battenberg, Prince Louis of 161
Bawlf, Tom 135
Baxter, Irving Knot 147
Beck, F.G. 55
Bellars, Fred 112, 114, 132, 169, 170, 179
Berkeley Athletic Club 89
Berliner Sports Club, Berlin 213
Bernstein, Joe 34
Blake, Colonel John 194
Bloomingdale, Samuel 150
Bloomingdales store 33, 153, 195, 237
Bonhag, George 49, 75, 84, 87, 101, 107, 108, 110, 111, 113, 114, 116, 123, 131, 132, 146, 151, 170, 175, 177, 181, 182, 186, 190, 206, 209, 211, 231, 247, 258n9, 269n16, 270n55
Boston 30, 49, 50, 58, 70, 73, 84, 85, 100, 104, 122, 124, 135, 141, 145, 166, 172, 206, 210, 233
Boston Athletic Association 49, 115, 116, 118, 210, 212, 220
Boston Celtics 1
Bowen, A.C. 55, 57
Boxing/Prizefighting 1, 16, 17, 24, 33, 34–35, 40, 66, 70, 73, 92, 134, 198–199, 242
Boycott 8, 98, 135, 139, 159, 162, 249
Bradley, Joseph 18
Brann, Judge Henry A. 51, 198
Breen, C.M. 22
Breen, Thomas 22
Bricker, Calvin 148
Broad Jump (Long jump) 5, 39, 40, 43, 54, 56, 57, 62, 63, 71, 74, 77, 78, 85, 101, 106, 111, 118, 147, 148, 164, 168, 174, 200, 231, 254, 256, 269n16, 269n15, 269n16
Brodd, Bruno 39, 179, 180, 182, 208, 212, 218, 258n9, 273n30
Bromilow, Joseph 42, 117, 174, 175, 177, 221, 241, 261n16, 270n55
Bronder, George 222, 227
Bronx Church House Athletic Club 136, 183, 218, 235
Brooklyn, NY 15, 26, 58, 84, 108, 134, 178, 198, 200, 203–204, 218, 227; Police Department. 262n43
Brooklyn Athletic Association 237
Brooklyn Athletic Club 91
Brooklyn Dodgers 248
Brown, Everett C. 175, 222
Brown Preparatory School, Philadelphia 48, 79
Brush, John T. 205
Buffalo 12, 63, 83, 108, 110, 131, 132, 250; World's Fair 1901 (Pan-American Exposition) 54, 71

Buffalo Emmetts Gaelic Football Club 63
Burke, Thomas E. 94, 107, 176
Burns, Young 34
Bushnell, Edward 139

Cahersiveen, County Kerry 165
Cahill, George 192
Cahill, John 214
Calanti, Rev. M.A. 224
Caldwell, Dave 220
Caldwell, Kenneth S. 218, 227
Caledonian Athletic Club 90, 102
Caledonian Games 16, 102, 128, 166, 238–239, 255
Cameron, George 13, 131, 269n16
Campbell, F. 22
Campbell, Roscoe C. 224
Canada 71, 105, 134, 148, 179, 209, 210, 260n27
Canadian Athletic Championships 63, 85, 96, 106, 124, 171, 174, 193
Canadian-Irish Athletic Club 66
Carlos, John 8, 47
Carpenter, John 149
Carr, Edward Powell 62, 81, 82, 107
Carroll, Dr. William 164
Carson, Edward 10
Carter, Edward C. 170, 177
Cary, Luther 177
Cassasa, C.S. "Charlie" 174, 175, 272n21
Castleman, Frank 74, 85, 87, 122, 123, 124, 125, 127, 128, 270n55
Catholic Athletic League 184
Catholicism 8, 24, 32, 36, 126, 154, 164, 165, 198, 234, 249–250
Cavan Mens' Games 176, 237
Celtic Football Club, Glasgow 10, 36
Celtic Park, Laurel Hill, New York City 2, 13, 14, 21–33, 41, 44, 50, 52, 56, 57, 60, 61, 67, 68, 71, 73, 78, 79, 80, 81, 86, 94, 98, 104, 105, 106, 107, 110, 113, 116, 117, 122, 129, 134, 139, 142, 154, 155, 163, 164, 166, 170, 171, 172, 173, 175, 176, 179, 181, 185, 190, 191, 206–207, 208, 209, 210, 212, 213, 218, 220, 222, 229, 231, 232, 233, 235, 238, 246, 247, 250; betting 79; burglary 210–211; construction 21–25, 27–29; fans 50, 61, 62, 67, 77, 81, 84, 86, 105, 106, 107, 155, 202; fire at 237; and GAA 29–33, 57, 104, 181, 212, 237, 242, 245–246, 248; greyhound racing 242; hiring out of 3, 30 56, 105, 173, 193; and Irish identity 25–27, 29, 82, 84, 164, and Irish politics 194, 217; land developers 225, 243, 244–245; Met Championships at 25, 40, 51–52, 61, 62, 78, 142, 218; offered

to U.S. government 230, 237; prohibition 4, 239–241; riots at 202, 237–241; sale of 4, 244–246; Sunday opening 200–205
Central Athletic Association, AAU 132
Centrals Gaelic Football Club 58
Chattahoochee Tribe No. 95 of the Improved Order of Red Men 56
Chicago 52, 104, 164, 167, 205, 212, 213, 235
Chicago Athletic Association 74, 179, 212, 227, 231, 232
Chicago Irish-American Athletic Club 167, 217
Childs, Clarence 209
Christian Brothers 164
City and Suburban Homes Company 244, 246
City Athletic Club 8
Clan na Gael 4, 21, 26, 30, 105, 158, 159, 160, 163, 164, 167, 172, 176, 194
Clare, Ireland 26, 69, 144, 163, 188
Clare Men's Athletic Association 25, 61, 170, 172
Claremen's Patriotic Benevolent and Social Association 202
Clark, Ellery H. 55, 62
Clark, James 175
Clark, J.J. 17
Clarke, Tom 161
Cloughen, John 133, 197–198
Cloughen, Robert 132, 134, 149, 150, 151, 168, 170, 177, 179, 197, 208, 258n9, 269n16, 270n55
Cobb, Irvin S. 205
Cohalan, Daniel Florence 14, 37, 96, 109, 125, 128, 148, 159, 160–162, 163, 193, 197, 234, 236, 246
Cohan, George 154
Cohn, Harvey 48, 74, 77, 78, 85, 86, 87, 101, 107, 134, 143, 146, 204, 206, 269n16, 270n55
Coholan, W.T. 50
Colgate University 122, 128
College of the City of New York 60
College of the Holy Cross, Worcester, MA 228
Collins, Jerome 164
Collins, Inspector John J. 204, 205
Collins, Thomas 113, 114, 134, 170, 174, 175, 179
Colliton, J.W. 46
Columbia University 39, 60, 61, 70, 84, 87, 116, 212, 218
Condon, Edward 18
Conneff, Tom 19, 87, 94, 212

Connolly, James B. 100, 128, 138
Connolly, John D. 133
Connorton, Luke J. 201, 202
Conway, John F. 230
Conway, Patrick J. 11, 12, 21–22, 23, 25, 28, 30, 34, 36, 37, 49, 50, 51, 55, 57, 58, 60, 61, 62, 74, 75, 80, 82, 83, 84, 91, 96–97, 101, 103, 104, 106, 108, 116, 123, 124, 127, 129–130, 132, 133, 138, 139, 140, 142, 151, 152–153, 155, 156, 159, 165, 166, 178, 182, 183, 184, 185, 192, 195, 196, 199, 201, 208, 211, 212, 213, 215, 216, 219, 224, 225, 228, 230, 231, 234, 236, 237, 241, 242, 245, 246, 247, 248, 249, 251
Conway, Walter 208, 210
Coogan, Rev. Daniel 234
Cook, Edward Tiffin 43, 111, 113, 269n16, 270n55
Copeland, Al 173, 215
Corbett, Young 34
Cork, Ireland 15, 70, 71, 160, 163
Cork Men's Association 29, 111
Cornell University 60, 61, 77, 87, 97, 116, 130, 215, 269n16
Cotter, Richard 62, 63, 110
Courtney Development Company 225
Cox, W.W. 70
Craig, Ralph 209
Cregan, John Francis 94
Cregan, Michael J. 52, 75, 190
Crescent Athletic Club 62, 89, 135, 136
Croker, Richard "Boss" 92, 93, 151
Crowley, James 114, 169, 175, 258n9
Cummings, Thomas J. 219
Curran, Thomas 18, 246, 247
Curtis, Patrick 18
Curtis, William B. 90, 95, 103, 104, 139
Curtis High School, Staten Island, NY 41
Cycling 13

Daley, Arthur 64, 65, 143, 144
Dallton Realty Company 225
Dalton, John J. 110
Dalton, Richard F. 245
Daly, "Captain" James 15
Daly, John J. 23, 72, 75, 77, 79–82, 83, 107, 108, 113, 114, 174, 175, 270n55
Daming, Charles 123
Danish-American AC 167
Dargan, Andrew J. 201
Davies, John R. 198
Davin, Maurice 18
Davin, Patrick 52
Davis, R.M. 174
Davitt, Michael 165
Day, Willie 175, 181

Dayton, James A. 226
De Coubertin, Pierre 77, 167
Democratic Athletic League 196
Democratic Club 93
Denmark 215
Desborough, Lord 148
Desmarteau, Étienne 57, 77, 176
De Valera, Eamon 160, 161
Devoy, John 67, 148, 160, 164
De Witt, John R. 55, 56
Dickman, Joe 228
Dieges, Captain Charles 145
Diem, Carl 213
Dietz, John J. 198
Discus 46, 53, 55, 62, 68, 74, 77, 78, 85, 101, 105, 106, 110, 111, 113, 114, 142, 143, 145, 147, 152, 163, 168, 170, 171, 174, 177, 178, 179, 181, 182, 186, 208, 209, 210, 212, 213, 218, 255, 263n13, 269n16
Dix, John Alden 196, 197, 199
Dolan, John J. 44, 46, 132, 153
Dole, Norman 105
Dominican Lyceum Athletic Club 176, 181
Donelly, Thomas F. 198
Donohue, Charles D, State Assemblyman 203
Donovan, "Professor Mike" 94
Dooling, John T. 215, 224
Dooling, Peter J. 203
Dorland L.B. 170
Dovis, J. 22
Dowling, M.F. 31
Dowling, Victor James 30, 56, 125, 161, 162, 190, 192, 196, 197, 201, 246
Downing Stadium, Randalls Island, New York City 249
Dublin, Ireland 25, 150, 151, 152, 163, 194
Dublin Metropolitan Police 151
Duffey/Duffy, Arthur 54, 58, 59, 118–120, 164
Duffy, Colonel Edward 28
Duffy, Richard 204
Duncan, James 208
Dundalk, Ireland 152
Dungarvan, County Waterford, Ireland 152
Dunn, Jere 92
Dunn, Joe 34
Dunn/Dunne, Thomas J. 22, 198
Dunne, William 22
Dupont, Leon 101

Easter Rising, Ireland, 1916 160, 194
Eastern New York Athletic League 224
Eaton, William/W.D. 74, 100, 139, 141
Eaton Athletic Association 208

Edgren, Robert 46, 84, 122, 123, 141, 143, 145, 147, 148, 149, 182
Edward VII 143–144, 145–146, 162; Edwardian period 94
Edwards, Richard 177, 186
Edwards, W.S. 40, 56
Egan, Richard J. 98, 220
800 meter race 5, 253, 255, 269n16
880 yard (1/2 mile) race 5, 41, 45, 51, 52, 111, 113, 116, 151, 168, 170, 174, 176, 221, 253
Eisele, John L. 97
Eke, John 39, 46
Elks 53, 220
Eller, Bob 180, 181, 214
Eller, John J. 38, 43, 108, 113, 168, 173, 174, 175, 179, 181, 182, 186, 190, 192, 193, 206, 208, 209, 210, 217, 220, 221, 225, 227, 228, 231, 232, 258n9, 270n55
Elliot, Julian J. 177
Elmira, NY 128
Emeralds Hurling Club 51
Emmetts Gaelic Football Club 20
Enterprise Gaelic Football Club 51
Entre Nous Athletic Club 68
Erickson, Egon 180, 222, 227, 231, 235
Ewry, Ray C. 56, 63, 137, 141, 147

Fairbairn-Crawford, Ian 147
Fans 17, 24, 27, 29, 32–33, 51, 53, 54, 57, 60, 64, 77, 79, 81, 85, 86, 104, 105, 106, 109, 115, 122, 154, 155, 170, 171, 194–195, 202, 214, 222, 238, 248
Farley, Terence 133, 134, 184, 185, 198, 214, 220, 223
Farley, Thomas "Big Tom" 198, 246
Farrell, E.L. 171
Feber, H.C. 134
Fenton, Thomas 22
Ferdninand, Archduke Franz of Austria-Hungary 229
Ferris, Dan 65
Finland 39, 217, 229
Finn, Luke 31
Finn, Oscar 18
Fitzgerald, Joe 21, 23, 251
Fitzgibbon, James 18
Fitzpatrick, Charles 174
Five mile race 57, 62, 74, 79, 84, 108, 110, 113, 114, 170, 174, 175, 177, 179, 182, 186, 211, 212, 213, 222
5,000 meter race 206, 254
Flanagan, John 41, 51, 52, 53–54, 55, 56, 57, 62, 63, 65, 66–67, 68, 70, 71, 74, 75, 77–78, 79, 82, 83, 84, 85, 86, 87, 94, 98, 99, 105–106, 109, 110, 111, 112, 113, 116,

121, 126, 129, 131, 132, 143, 144, 145, 146, 148, 150, 151, 155, 156, 162, 163, 164, 168, 170, 171–172, 174, 175, 176–177, 178, 179, 182, 188–189, 190, 191, 192, 193, 209, 210, 212, 258n9, 269n16, 269n23
Flanagan, Tom 66
Fleming, John C. 198
Flynn, Pat 216, 218
Fogel, Arthur 218, 228
Foley, Thomas F. 196
Fordham University 60, 170
Fortescue, "Walter" 198
400 meter hurdles race 142, 148
400 meter race 5, 142, 149, 208, 253, 255, 269n16
Four mile race 84, 87, 129, 170, 175
Four mile relay race 59, 87, 175, 212
440 yard hurdles race 63, 169, 179
440 yard (quarter mile) race 5, 48, 49, 62, 84, 113, 151, 174, 177, 182, 210, 253
440 yard relay race 241
France 45, 148, 237
Frank, Dan 43, 97
Frank, William 43, 78, 84, 101, 107, 108, 113, 190, 270n55
Fraser, Edward S. 221
Frawley, James J. 22, 28, 52, 104, 164, 198–99, 246
Frawley Act 198, 199
Frey, E.A. 176, 258n9
Froehlick, J. 231
Fuji, Minoru 46

GAA "Invasion of America" 18, 19, 20, 22, 30, 52, 89, 94, 165
Gaelic Athletic Association 13, 18, 30, 32, 52, 63, 65, 66, 80, 132, 151, 152, 154, 162, 163, 164, 165, 242, 245, 248, 260n27, 269n15; GAA in New York 19, 20, 30, 32, 151, 242, 245, 260n27; GAAUS 30; Illinois GAA 132
Gaelic Football 6, 12, 19–20, 29, 30, 31, 51, 52, 53, 54, 57, 58, 60, 79, 89, 104, 110, 166, 181, 186, 200, 202, 212 231, 237, 242, 245, 246, 248; Antrim Gaelic football county team 246; Big Four Gaelic football counties (Cork, Kerry, Kildare, Kilkenny) 30, 31–32, 246; Cavan Gaelic football county team 237; Clubs replaced by counties, 30; Cork Gaelic football county team 30, 186, 194, 246; Galway Gaelic football county team 237, 246; Kerry Gaelic football county team 30, 32, 186, 246; Kildare Gaelic football county team 30, 202, 246; Kilkenny Gaelic football county team 30, 104, 110, 246; Leitrim Gaelic football county team 31; Louth Gaelic football county team 246; Mayo Gaelic football county team 246; Monaghan Gaelic football county team 197; Offaly Gaelic football county team 246; Queens County (Laois) Gaelic football county team 202; Roscommon Gaelic football county team 246; Tipperary Gaelic football county team 104, 110, 194, 243; Wexford Gaelic football county team 243
Gaelic League 30
Gaelic Park, Chicago 132
Galway, Ireland 72, 80, 82, 84, 163
Galway Athletic Club 210
Galway Mens' Association 61, 84, 104, 194
Gambling 79, 81, 92, 122, 190, 193, 198, 200, 242
Gangs 159
Garcia, Colonel William L. 133
Garretson, John J. 134
Georgantas, Nikolaos 46, 106
Georgetown University 84, 249
German-American AC 248
Germans 189, 200, 213
Germany 161, 230, 250
Gerrity, J.E. 124
Giegerich, Justice Leonard A.J. 123, 125, 127
Gifford, James H. 15
Gilbert, Alfred Carlton 105, 108
Gillis, Duncan 209
Gillis, Simon 144
Gilroy, Dennis 201
Gissing, Harry 180, 181, 182, 207, 208, 220, 225
Glarner, Andrew 176
Glasgow, Scotland 10, 36, 45
Glasgow Rangers Football Club 36
Glynn, Martin H. 196, 234
Goerwitz, George B. 201
Goff, John W. 104, 160
Goodwin, Eddie 214
Gordon, Willie 221
Gorman, Jeremiah 203
Grace Athletic Club 61
Grand Street Boys Athletic Club 248
Granger, W.Randolph 49
Grant, Alexander 164
Grant, Dick 51
Gray, C.R. 71
Greater New York Irish Athletic Association *see* Irish-American Athletic Club (I-AAC) III
Greece 46, 102–104, 105, 138, 148, 165, 166; Crown Prince of 46, 140

Greeks 45, 46, 87 90, 106, 140, 165, 166, 189, 235, 255
Green, Harry 181
Gregory, Gilbert 154
Greyhound racing 4, 242
Griffin, Merrit 147
Griffo, "Kid" 34
Gulick, Dr. Luther Halsey 127
Gulick, John C. 120
Gunn, Adam B. 55

Hallock, George 135
Halpin, Matt 3, 96, 98-99, 100-101, 102, 107, 119, 122-123, 124, 138-142, 148-149, 153, 155
Halpin, Tom 219
Halswelle, Wyndham 149
Hammer 6, 51, 52, 53, 54, 56, 57, 62, 66, 67, 68, 69, 70, 71, 77, 78, 80, 84, 85, 86, 94, 97, 98, 106, 111, 113, 114, 142, 143, 146, 151, 155, 163, 164, 165, 168, 169, 171, 172, 174, 175, 176, 177, 182, 209, 210, 211, 213, 218, 220, 220, 222, 227, 232, 235, 255, 256, 269n16
Hammerstein Case 203
Handicapping 23, 42, 59, 62, 78, 84, 105, 110, 111, 120, 129-130, 164, 170, 206, 224
Hanlon, Michael 216
Harlem Athletic Club 88
Harvard University 51, 60, 207, 208
Haskins, Guy 114-115, 117
Hayes, John 41, 131, 137, 138, 142, 149, 150-151, 153-155, 169, 195, 241, 247, 269n16, 270n55
Hayes, William 132
Hazel, Marshall 18
Hearst, William Randolph 194-195
Hearst Newspapers 9
Hedlund, Oscar F. 212
Heiser Realty Company 225
Henry, Gwynn 180, 181
Herman, Dr. George K. 132
Hibernian Football Club (Edinburgh, Scotland) 10
Higgins, Anthony 39
Higgins, Joe 228, 231
High Jump 42, 62, 63, 74, 111, 114, 116, 142, 147, 151, 168, 175, 222, 225, 227, 231, 235, 254, 256, 266n6, 269n16; Standing 101, 231, 254, 256, 266n6
Hillman, Harry L. 63, 107, 108, 113, 116, 123, 141, 148, 176
Hirshon, Hugh M. 220
Hjertberg, Ernie 39, 41, 42, 43, 58, 110, 111, 116-117, 179, 202
Hockey Club of New York 135

Hogenson, William 74
Holloway, Jack/John 72, 75, 77
Hollywood 248
Hollywood Inn Athletic Club 57
Holy Cross Lyceum, NY 203
Hop Step Jump 5, 78, 165, 172, 173, 174 175, 176, 179, 181, 182, 186, 212, 254, 256
Horgan, Denis 53, 70-71, 75, 105, 111, 162
Horr, Bill 143, 147, 148, 168, 170, 171, 269n16, 270n55
Hotel Astor 37, 104, 138, 245
Hotel Waldorf-Astoria 162, 185
Howe, Irving Tecumseh 49
Hughes, Charles E. 152
Hulbert, George Murray 198, 241, 246
Hungarian Olympic Committee 215
Hurling 6, 12, 20, 25, 29, 51, 52, 54, 57-58, 60, 62, 63, 79, 165, 201, 212, 231, 237, 242, 245, 246, 248
Hymen, Harry 43
Hynes, Tom 84, 99, 122

Illinois Athletic Club 213
Imboden, D.C. 225
Innisfail Park, New York 242
Intercollegiate Association of Amateur Athletes of America (ICAAAA) 127, 128
International cross country championship 72
Ireland 4, 26, 52, 54, 63, 66, 67-73, 75-77, 79, 80, 81-82, 86, 97, 102, 104, 105, 110, 121, 136, 142, 144, 150, 154, 160-161, 162, 165-166, 177, 189, 193, 194, 196, 212, 216, 218-219, 229, 238, 248, 254
Irish Amateur Athletic Association 63, 65, 72, 151, 152
Irish-American Athletic Club (I-AAC) I (1879 to ca. 1882-1888) 2, 10, 15-18, 25, 51, 89, 259n6
Irish-American Athletic Club (I-AAC) II (1890 to 1893) 2, 10, 18-20, 25, 51 89
Irish-American Athletic Club (I-AAC) III (1898 to 1930) aka Greater New York Irish Athletic Association 1-4, 13, 14, 15, 21-22, 53, 180, 195, 220, 225-226, 235-237, 244, 250-251; Club's membership 89, 91, 94-95, 121, 159, 250; college students and 61, 97, 110, 112, 120, 121, 130-131, 183, 226; cycling 13, 269n16; decline of 214, 216, 228, 230-233, 235, 241, 244-248; and Gaelic games 5, 6, 12, 19-20; home for Irish immigrant 9-10, 11, 12, 63, 65, 67, 72-73, 76, 90, 94, 106, 120, 165-166; ICAU and 30-33; ice hockey team 3, 5, 13, 135-136, 237; indoor

games 58–61, 97, 109, 110, 115, 125, 170, 219; lace curtain Irish, 36–37; lacrosse team 5, 13, 61–62, 77; Manhattan buildings 33–35, 245; name change from GNYIAA 1, 2, 5, 83, 85–86, 248; Olympics and 75–77, 101–104, 105, 117, 138–141, 143–157, 163, 168, 206; other ethnicities and 13, 36–50, 91, 106, 173, 228–229, 238–239, 250, 269n23; other Irish-American ACs 10, 49, 50; poaching athletes 183–186, 216; policemen and 64, 173, 188–193; politics and 109, 193–196, 198; prejudice toward the Irish and 90, 96, 106, 158–160, 162, 199–200; professionalism and 12, 41, 64, 86, 97, 99, 122–136, 214, 220, 224; prohibition and 239–241; restarting the club 247; rivalry with NYAC 73, 87, 96, 98, 122–130, 138–142, 173, 1, 77, 193, 208, 219, 221, 227, 241, 248; role in American athletics, 9, 14, 109, 113, 116, 174, 228; soccer team 5, 12, 19, 89; swimming 13; touring 113, 150; "winged fist" emblem 12, 51, 228, 236; world records 6, 9, 39, 40, 41, 42, 45, 53, 54, 55, 62, 63, 66, 70, 72, 78, 79, 85, 94, 98, 101, 105, 106, 108, 110, 111, 113, 114, 118, 142, 143, 147, 148, 151, 152, 155, 164, 167, 168, 171, 172, 173, 174, 176, 177, 179, 181–182, 206, 207, 208, 209, 210, 211, 212, 213, 217, 219, 220, 221, 232, 235
Irish-American Football (Soccer) Club 247
Irish Athletes of America 57, 201
Irish Athletic Club, Boston 49, 50, 166
Irish Counties Athletic Union (ICAU) 2, 30, 31–32, 104, 200
Irish Federation of the United States 198, 232
Irish in America 10, 89, 125–126, 143, 145, 158–159, 200, 203, 250
Irish in New York 11, 24–25, 29, 159, 164; politics 10; relations with Jews 40; sport 10, 15, 48, 72, 89, 120, 165, 229
Irish Land League 165
Irish National Volunteers 194, 202
Irish Park, Yonkers 31–32
Irish Relief Fund 193, 194
Irish Republican Brotherhood (IRB) 164, 194
The Irish Servant Girls 159
Irish Volunteers, New York 30, 105, 176
Irish Whales 3, 64–65, 69, 71, 144, 188, 189, 209
Irons, Frank 148
Irving, John 250
Italians 39, 44, 71, 89, 159, 188, 189
Ithaca, NY 53

Jackson, Arnold 209
Janssen, Frederick 88–89, 90, 249
Javelin 63, 97, 177, 179, 182, 208, 212, 218, 222, 2227, 255
Jennings, M.J. 22
Jersey Harriers Athletic Club 237
Jews 1, 2, 8, 37, 38, 39–43, 49, 89, 159, 189, 200, 214, 219, 249
Johansson, Frans 39, 186, 211
John Dalys Gaelic Football Club, Brooklyn 54, 57, 58, 60, 63, 202
Jones, J. Raymond 250
Jones, John Paul 210
Jones, William L. 132, 153, 214
Jones Wood Stadium, New York City 16, 17, 19, 164
Joseph, Irving J. 199
Journeay, Albert 215
Joyce, John J. 57, 61, 62, 72, 74, 75, 79–81, 83–85, 87, 97, 99, 108, 114, 122, 123, 124, 125, 127, 128, 169, 190, 191, 270n55
Just, Theodore 147

Kansas City, MO 104, 113, 222
Katzenstein, M. 107
Keating, William J. 111, 112, 114, 168, 175, 176, 190, 258n9, 270n55, 272n21
Keller, Sammy 34
Kelly, John W. 190–191
Kelly Dan 13, 118, 145, 148, 150, 163, 269n16
Kenny, Charles E. 138, 139
Kent, Arthur 58
Ketchel, Stanley 34
Kickhams Gaelic Football Club 30, 51, 57
Kiely, Tom 52, 63, 72–73, 75–76, 77, 104, 105, 152, 164
Kilpatrick, Charles H 170
Kings County Athletic Association 237
Kings County Athletic Club 15, 16
Kirby, Gustavus T. 127
Kiviat, Abel 1, 37–38, 41–42, 174, 175, 176, 177, 182, 208, 209, 210, 211, 212, 213, 214, 215, 216, 217, 218, 219, 220, 221, 224–225, 241
Kline, Ardolph L. 220
Knickerbocker Athletic Club 3, 35, 40, 52, 55, 56, 58, 59, 89, 92, 93, 95, 126, 193
Knickerbocker Theatre 154
Knights of Columbus 21, 26, 56, 61, 171, 172, 176, 204
Knoud, William J. 18
Kolehmainen/Kolehmainnen, Hannes 39, 45, 46, 129, 210, 211, 212, 213, 214, 215, 217, 218–219, 220 221, 222, 225, 228, 229, 230, 231, 237

Index

Kolehmainen, "William" 45, 217
Kraenzlein/Kraenzlen, Alvin/A.C. 39, 54, 72, 200
Kramer, William J. (Billy) 175, 186, 211
Krotel, Paul 203
Kyronen, Ville 217, 219, 228, 236

Lacrosse 5, 13, 61–62, 77
Langan, O.F. 112
Lanigan, Denis 106
Laurel Hill Improvement Association 242
Law and Order Society 201
League of Nations 161
Leahy, Con 63, 75, 162, 216
Leahy, Patrick 63, 75, 216
Leavitt, Robert 100, 141
Lee, Jimmy 170
Lightbody, James D. 77
Limerick, Ireland 21, 66, 69, 70, 74, 172, 177
Lipton, Thomas J. 153
Local Union No. 20 Independent United Order of Operating and Stationary Engineers 205
London, England 44, 66, 144
London Irish Rugby Football Club 10
Lonergan, Thomas 18, 19
Long Island Athletic Club 186, 218
Loomis, Joe 220, 222
Los Angeles 25, 219
Los Angeles Athletic Club 219
Loughlin Lyceum 206, 237
Louisiana Purchase Expedition 74
Lovell, Ike 208
Low, Seth 200
Lowe, W.C. 74
Lug, Clement 71
Lund, Thomas 97–98
Lunghi, Emilio 39, 44, 45, 147, 148, 167, 173, 174, 175, 176
Lynch, Thomas F. 17
Lynch, Tom 210–211

MacCabe, Joseph B. 120
Madison Square Garden 3, 11, 17, 33, 48, 58, 59, 77, 82, 87, 97, 108, 109, 125, 126, 127, 132, 152, 169, 170, 175, 179, 193, 198, 211, 220, 249
Maguire, Most Reverend John J. 249
Mahoney, Jeremiah T. 174
Mahoney, Joseph T. 63
Mahoney, Richard 18
Malcolmson, J. 181
Manhattan & Queens Traction Company 26
Manhattan Athletic Club 3, 17, 22, 23, 35, 89, 90, 92, 93, 126

Manhattan College 160, 249
Manning, John J. 197
Marathon 32, 52, 101, 104, 131, 137–138, 149–150, 151, 153–154, 155, 169, 181, 195, 207, 208, 209, 218, 231, 255
Maspeth 102, 128, 166
Matsukes, Theodore L. 171
Mayo 67, 102
Mayo Men's Association 84, 110, 134
Mayor of New York 191, 196, 200, 220; Gaynor, William J. 193; Grant, Hugh J. 198; Hylan, John Francis "Red Mike" 239; McClellan, George B. 143; Walker, James "Beau James" 242
McAvoy, Johnny 34
McCarren, Senator Patrick H. 109
McCarthy, John 80, 82
McCarthy, Robert Lt. 239
McCarthy, Tommy 135
McCarthy, William 52
McCarthyism (Joseph McCarthy) 90, 121
McCormack, John 217
McDonald, Harry P. 54
McDonald, Pat 69, 113, 116, 144, 170, 175, 177, 179, 182, 186, 188, 206, 208, 209, 210, 211, 212, 213, 214, 217, 218, 219, 220, 222, 223–224, 225, 227, 231, 232, 235, 237, 241
McDonald, Patrick Joseph 15, 16
McDonald, Young 199
McDonnell, Dr. John 50
McFadden, Bernard 118, 120
McFadden's Row of Flats 158–159
McGovern, Terry 34
McGowan, Patrick F. 154
McGrath, Matt 48, 68, 69, 94, 111, 112, 114, 121, 129, 132, 142, 143, 144, 145, 146, 151, 155, 162–163, 169, 171, 172, 182, 187, 188, 191, 193, 209, 210, 212, 214, 217, 219, 220, 222, 223, 224, 227, 232, 235, 237, 241, 273n1
McGraw, John 204–205
McGuire, Lieutenant P.J 198
McInerney, P.J. 25
McKane, Joseph T. 201, 239
McKenna, E.P. 163
McLaughlin, John J. 87
McLaughlin, Thomas 207
McLaughlin, William D. 153
McLead, William 171
McLoughlin, Jim 215
McManus, State Senator Thomas 203
McMullen, John R. 225
McNamara, J.J. 134
McQuade, Francis X. 205
McTigue, Mike 242
Melat, Young 34

Index

Mercury Athletic Club, Philadelphia 218
Mercury Athletic Club, Yonkers 169
Meredith, Ted 209, 212
Merrill, Edward S. 55
Metropolitan Athletic Association, AAU 51, 81, 86, 102, 113, 115, 117, 121, 123, 125, 126, 127–128, 141, 142, 176, 183–185, 198, 200, 211, 217, 218, 220, 221, 224, 225, 228, 257; Indoor Championships 108, 233; Junior Championships 43, 47, 62, 78, 97, 105, 182, 183, 212, 222, 226, 235; Senior Championships 6, 12, 13, 22, 29, 40, 41, 42, 43, 51–52, 53, 56, 57, 61, 62, 68, 72, 84, 85, 96, 97, 105, 107, 111, 122, 123, 125, 168, 173–174, 177, 178, 180, 182, 206, 209, 210, 213, 218, 221, 226, 230, 231, 232, 235, 241, 248, 257; Small Clubs Championship 218
Mexico 144, 230
Meyer, Alvah 1, 42, 43, 63, 78, 164, 182, 200, 206, 208, 209, 210, 213, 214, 217, 218, 219, 221, 222, 241
Middle Atlantic Athletic Association, AAU 115, 117
Middletown, NY 160
Military Athletic League 132, 133, 134, 211, 220
Millrose Athletic Association 216, 219, 220, 225, 228, 231, 232, 236, 248
Milwaukee 13, 63, 71
Milwaukee Athletic Club 63
Mitchell, James S. 18, 52, 54, 57, 63, 64, 65, 66, 67, 94, 123, 174
Mitchell, William 39
Mohawk Athletic Club 86, 142, 175, 183, 228
"Molly Maguires" 163
Montreal, Canada 12, 45, 63, 85, 90, 106, 193
Montreal Lacrosse Club 16
Monument, "Baldy" Jack 39, 179
Monument Club 175, 220
Morningside Athletic Club 237
Morrissey, John "Old Smoke" 92, 142
Morse, Roy F. 49, 228
Morton, George W., Jr. 242
Morton, T.W. 86
Mountbatten, Louis 161
Movies 248
Muldoon, Bill 189
Muller, Emil 190, 209, 210, 212, 213, 214, 218, 219
Mulligan, Dr. B.J. 57
Murphy, Charles "Silent Charlie" 109
Murphy, Charles F. 160, 196
Murphy, Edward S. 192

Murphy, Johnny 34
Murphy, Mike C. 4, 48, 94, 115, 142, 155, 206, 215
Murphy, Tommy 34
Murray, Dennis 111
Murtha, John 22
Myers, Lon 45, 58, 90, 148, 173, 176

Naismith, C.C. 74
National Association of Amateur Athletics of America 16, 88, 121
National Athletic Club 113
Nebrich, Frank 108
Negro Leagues 47
Neill, S. Colin 7
New Jersey Athletic Club 126
New Star Theater 158
New West Side Athletic Club 43, 52, 56, 62, 78
New York 39, 48, 128, 203
New York Athletic Club 1, 2, 3, 4, 7, 8, 9, 13, 15, 22, 33, 35, 36, 37, 38, 39, 40, 41, 43, 50, 52, 53, 54, 56, 57, 58, 59, 62, 63, 64, 66, 67, 71, 73, 74, 78, 83, 84, 85, 86, 87, 89, 90, 91, 92, 93, 94, 95, 96, 97, 98, 99, 104, 105, 106, 107, 108, 110, 111, 112, 113, 114, 116–117, 120, 121, 122–123, 124, 125, 127, 130, 131, 132, 135, 138, 141, 142, 146, 164, 168, 170, 172, 173, 174, 175, 177, 179, 180, 181, 182, 183, 185, 186, 193, 196, 209–210, 211, 212, 213, 214, 217, 218, 219, 220, 221, 222, 226, 227, 228, 231, 232, 233, 237, 241, 242, 248, 249, 250, 265n21, 278n14; boycotts of 8, 98, 249; and discrimination 7–8, 37, 38, 94, 96; Mercury Foot emblem 90; and religion, 8, 94, 249–250; rivalry with I-AAC 73, 87, 96, 98, 106; 122–130, 138–142, 173, 177, 193, 208, 219, 221, 227, 241, 248; rivalry with Manhattan AC 22; and snobbery 106; and violence 7–8
New York Caledonian Club 90, 238
New York City 1, 2, 3, 4, 8 10, 13, 22, 24, 25, 26, 37, 39, 43, 46, 66, 67, 68, 70, 71, 72, 77, 85, 92, 99, 104, 115, 118, 120, 132, 135, 138, 141, 142, 151, 152, 154, 157, 160, 161, 163, 164, 186, 187, 194, 196, 197, 199, 203, 205, 208, 216, 217, 222, 227, 232, 238, 240, 241, 247, 248; council 244; immigration 2, 50, 200; population 22, 24, 39, 40, 50, 200, 225
New York City Athletic Selections 58, 114, 117, 216
New York City Supreme Court 41, 104, 123, 125, 192, 196, 197, 198, 203, 215, 274n28

New York County 152; sheriff 196, 198
New York Curb Exchange 248
New York Fire Department (NYFD) 21
New York Giants 204–205, 248
New York Greyhound Racing Association 242
New York Hockey Club 135
New York Police Department (NYPD) 4, 7–8, 32, 40, 49, 57, 64, 65, 66, 67–68, 69, 73, 77, 78, 110, 112, 115, 116, 143, 154, 155, 158, 159, 172, 173, 178, 187–193, 195, 198, 199, 201, 202, 203–204, 227, 232, 234, 235, 236, 238, 239, 240, 242; and I-AAC 64, 173, 188–193; Baker, Commissioner William F. 178, 193; Bingham, Commissioner Theodore A. 143, 189, 193, 203; Enright, Commissioner Richard 234, 235; Greene, Commissioner Francis V. 202; McAdoo, Commissioner William 73, 190; NYPD Police Athletic Association 190; NYPD Police Athletic Club 189
New York Post Office Clerks' Association 23, 171, 172, 181, 208
New York State Athletic Commission 198, 199
New York State Football League 19
New York University 60
New York Yankees 248
New York Yankees Baseball Club 248
Newark 176, 227, 247; Weequahic Park 227
Newton, Arthur 52
Nichols, Captain Joseph Klapp 132
Niflot, Isidor "Jack" 85
Nonpareil Football Club 19
Norfolk, VA, Jamestown Exposition Grounds 110, 113
Northridge, SC 84, 85, 115, 170, 175
Notre Dame Alumni Against Racial Discrimination 249

Obertubessing, Herman 131
O'Connell, Daniel 165
O'Connells Gaelic Football Club 53, 57, 60
O'Connor, Charles 202
O'Connor, Pat 231
O'Connor Peter 39, 54, 71–72, 100, 101, 102
O'Gorman, James 197, 203
Olympia Athletic Club 53
Olympic Athletic Club, San Francisco 222, 227, 265n21
Olympic Committee for Human Rights (OCHR) 8
Olympics 6, 8, 13, 14, 37, 39, 40, 45, 47, 50, 61, 72, 85, 104, 106, 115, 133, 165, 166, 167, 178, 200, 204, 218, 234, 235, 242, 247, 253, 254, 255, 256, 260n3; "Anthropological Games" 47; Olympic Games, 1896, Athens 138; Olympic Games, 1900, Paris 39, 52, 67, 118, 200; Olympic Games, 1904 St. Louis 3, 40, 43 72–73, 75–77, 123, 202 "Irish Games" 77; Olympic Games, 1906 Intercalated Games 3, 40, 46, 87, 100–104, 107, 128, 131; Olympic Games, 1908, Rome (canceled) 144; Olympic Games, 1908, London 1, 2, 3–4, 9, 13, 21, 43, 44, 69, 71, 99, 117, 130, 136, 137–157, 162, 167, 172, 195; Olympic Games, 1912, Stockholm 4, 38, 41, 42, 69, 179, 205, 207, 208, 209; Olympic Games, 1916, Berlin (canceled) 213; Olympic Games, 1920, Antwerp 69; Olympic Games, 1920, Budapest (canceled) 215; Olympic Games, 1920, New York (failed bid) 235; Olympic Games, 1924, Paris 69; Olympic Games, 1968, Mexico City 144; Olympic Games, 1996, Atlanta 249
One and half mile race 78, 109, 211
100 meter race 42, 142, 206, 208, 209, 269n16, 253
100 yard race 43, 46, 54, 63, 74, 78, 109, 111, 118, 151, 168, 174, 177, 179, 182, 201, 210, 213, 218, 221, 222, 249, 253
110 meter hurdles race 100, 150, 208, 254
120 yard hurdles race 77, 85, 86, 151, 168, 173, 174, 182, 210, 220, 221, 227
One mile race 5, 17, 41, 42, 48, 55, 74, 78, 85, 86, 87, 111, 113, 168, 174, 179, 182, 210, 212, 213, 218, 221, 253
One mile relay race 84, 116, 121, 174, 181, 182
One mile steeplechase race 72
1,500 meter race 5, 44, 146, 207, 208, 209, 217
1,500 meter walk race 101, 253
Orange Athletic Club 61
Orange Playground Festival 171
Order of Scottish Clans 190
Orton George 115, 225
O'Sullivan, Michael 18
O'Sullivan, Thomas J. 18
Ozanam Athletic Club 183–184

Pacific Athletic Club, San Francisco 74
Pan-American Exposition Games, 1901 54, 71
Parsons, E.B. 114
Pastime Athletic Club 18, 48, 52, 53, 54, 55, 56, 57, 61, 62, 68, 71, 72, 75, 83, 85,

90, 106, 115, 122, 124, 126, 168, 177, 181, 208, 218
Paterson, NJ 68, 90, 181, 213, 220
Paulist Athletic Club 237
Payne, E. 171
Pearse, Padraig 193–194, 217
Pedestrian Craze 17, 22, 58, 120
Pennsylvania 111, 112, 163, 182, 190
Pennsylvania Railroad 191
Pepis, Abe 180, 210
Pershing Field, Jersey City 248
Peters, J.E. 55
Philadelphia 13, 43, 47, 53, 65, 79, 114–115, 117, 132, 133, 195, 216, 218; Baker Bowl 25; Franklin Field 39, 142
Philadelphia Phillies 193
Pickering, Captain M.J. 133
Pierce, "Jerry" 54, 262n25
Pietri, Dorando 137, 143, 149, 150
Pilgrim, Paul 183
Pioneer Athletic Club 249
Pittsburgh 43, 97, 128, 132, 135, 182, 210
Plaw, Alfred 53, 67
Plunkett, Evelyn 194
Plunkett, Joseph 194
Plunkitt, George Washington 196
Poage, George Coleman 47
Poland 39, 189
Pole Vault 46, 63, 72, 78, 85, 105, 108, 111, 113, 114, 115, 168, 180, 218, 227, 254, 256, 263n13
Polo Grounds, New York City 19, 20, 113
Polytechnic Harriers, London 181
Pores, Charles 219, 236
Porter, Harry 97, 114, 116, 130, 131, 132, 134, 142, 147, 150, 151, 168, 175, 269n16
Power, J.A. 210
Powers, Bill 129
Powers, Patrick E. 19
Prendergast, William A. 22
Prendergast, William F. 18, 22, 52, 165, 191
USS *Princess Matoika* 69
Princeton University 55, 97, 155
Prinstein, Myer 1, 39, 40, 41, 49, 54, 55, 56, 57, 62, 63, 72, 74, 75, 77, 78, 85, 100, 101, 102, 106, 164, 200, 260n3
Pritchard, Edwin 209, 220, 227
Professionalism 3, 12, 15, 27, 33, 45, 46, 58, 64, 71, 78, 82, 84, 85, 86, 95, 97, 99, 102–103, 115, 117, 118–136, 141, 185, 189, 195, 224, 249; expenses 3, 20, 30, 70, 76, 101, 118, 121, 128, 130, 131–133; and other sports 12, 86; prizes 3, 46, 57, 58, 62, 109, 120, 128, 129–130, 131–132, 133, 134, 166, 210, 214, 217, 226; "shamateurism" 118, 131, 191

Protestantism 36, 43, 94, 198
Pulitzer, Joseph 9, 21
Purcell, J.C. 55, 56
Pursell, John 18
Pushball 60

Queens, NY 2, 14, 23, 26, 41, 105, 160, 226, 241, 244, 245
Quinilin, M. 22

Raines Law 240
Ravenall, Jimmie 49
Real, William 211
Red Men 26, 56, 61
Redmond, John 52, 237
Redmond, William 10
Reilly Joseph 195
Reiner, Richard 217
Reynolds, John J. 38
Reynolds F.J. 43, 208, 209
Riley, Frank 125, 174, 177, 179, 180, 269n16
Riots 4, 109–110, 133, 198, 202, 214, 237–238, 240–241, Orange Day riots (1870s) 40, 163
Robbins, William 149, 170, 174, 175, 179
Robertson, Lawson 39, 41, 42, 49, 63, 70, 74, 78, 84, 98, 101, 103, 108, 121, 134, 135, 139, 142, 150, 151, 152, 153, 170, 179, 180, 181, 192, 202, 206, 207, 214, 215, 216, 219, 220, 222, 223, 225, 227, 228, 241, 269n16
Robertson, William "Sparrow" 215
Romary, Janice Lee 144
Roosevelt, Alice 74
Rose, Kid 34
Rose, Ralph 69, 71, 77, 143–146, 155, 186, 206, 209, 210, 217, 269n23
Rosebault, Charles J. 26, 27
Rosenberger, James 43, 170, 174, 179, 180, 181, 208, 209, 241
Rothstein, Arnold 40
Rovers Gaelic Football Club, Washington D.C. 54
Royal Arcanum Wheelmen of Manhattan 53
Rubien, Frederick W. 206, 220, 222, 223, 224, 227
Rugby football 10, 52, 149
Russia 39, 46; Russian Army 217
Ryan, Pat 64, 65, 69–70, 182, 188, 192, 209, 210, 211, 212, 213, 214, 216, 217, 218, 219, 220, 221, 222, 223, 224, 225, 227, 232, 235, 237, 277n18
Ryan, Schemer" 198
Ryan Mike 181

Sabbatarianism 2, 4, 200–203, 205; Sabbath Observance Society 202

St. Bartholomew's Athletic Club 53, 56, 61, 71, 129, 138, 195, 214
St. Enda's College, Dublin, Ireland 194, 217
St. Francis Xavier College, NY 53, 77
St. George's Athletic Club 53
St. John's Hospital, New York City 177
St. Louis 3, 12, 74–76, 82, 96, 232; Francis Field, St. Louis 74
St. Mary's Athletic Club 176
St. Nicholas Ice Rink 135
Salem Crescent Athletic Club 47, 228, 232
San Francisco 69, 74, 163, 167; earthquake, 1906 202, 222–223, 227, 265n21; Panama-Pacific Exposition, 1915 222, 223
Sarsfield Gaelic Football Club, Portchester 19
Schaff 175, 181
Schwegler, George 181
Scott, Louis 182
Scottish-American Athletic Club 88, 193
Seabury Investigations 198
Seattle 42, 173; Alaska-Yukon-Pacific Exposition, 1909 173
Seattle Athletic Club 181
Second Naval Battalion 216
Senate Foreign Relations Committee 161
Sequin, Patsy 135
Settlement Athletic Club 53, 57
Seven Mile race 170
Shanahan, Dan 172, 176
Shaw, Arthur 150, 182
Sheehy, Edward 198
Sheldon, Richard 55, 70, 78
Sheppard, Mel 3, 29, 34, 43–44, 79, 87, 102, 103, 105, 106, 107, 108, 111, 113, 114, 115, 117, 128, 129, 131, 132, 133, 134, 138, 142, 146, 147, 150, 151, 155, 156, 163, 168, 170, 173, 174, 175, 176, 177–179, 181, 180, 182, 186, 207, 208, 209, 210, 211, 213, 214, 216, 217, 219, 231, 241, 247, 258n9, 269n16, 270n55
Sheridan, Dick 57, 62, 67
Sheridan, Martin 4, 34, 46, 50, 55, 62, 65, 67–68, 74, 75, 77, 78, 79, 82, 84, 85, 96, 101, 103, 104, 105, 106, 108, 109, 110, 111, 113, 114, 115, 116, 122–123, 124, 126, 132, 139, 140, 141, 142, 143, 144, 145, 146, 147, 148, 150, 152, 155, 162–163, 168, 170, 171, 172, 174, 177, 178, 179, 181, 182, 186, 188, 190, 191, 192, 193, 207, 208, 209, 212, 219, 233–235, 242, 247, 258n9, 263n13, 269n16, 269n20, 270n55
Sherrill, Charles H. 98, 140, 181
Short Hills Athletic Club 88

Shot put (16 pounds) 6, 53, 60, 65, 70–71, 74, 77, 80, 101, 111, 155, 164, 168, 177, 182, 208, 212, 213, 218, 222, 225, 227, 231, 232, 235, 255, 256, 263n13, 269n16; eight pounds 108; twelve pounds 209; fourteen pounds 213, eighteen pounds: 206, 217; twenty-one pounds 210; twenty-four pounds 108, 114, 175, 179, 186, 211, 217, 220, 255, 256, 263n13, 269n16
Shrubb, Alfred 72, 213, 218
660 yard race 42, 116, 117, 176
Six mile race 107
60 yard hurdles race 115
60 yard race 59, 179, 253, 258n9
Slade, William 176
Smart Set Athletic Club 47
Smith, C.E. 24
Smith, Frank W. 56
Smithson, Forrest 115
Snedigar, Ole 74
Soccer 36, 57, 89, 149, 247
Soderstrom, Bruno 115
South Africa 250
South Africa 250; Boer War 194
South Boston Athletic Club 50, 171
South London Harriers 86
South Paterson, NJ 182
Spain 22
Spalding, Albert 104, 119
Spanish-American War 22, 236
Spanish Flu 233
Spanish War Veterans' Games 133
Spelissy, Dennis A. 194
Stadium construction 24–25
Stagg, Amos Alonzo 146
Stamford Bridge Stadium, London 70, 181
Stanfield, Andy 249
Star Athletic Club 52, 53, 61
Staten Island 16, 20, 41, 174
Staten Island Athletic Club 88, 265n1
Steeplechase race 23, 77, 114, 216, 254
Steers, Alfred E. 204
Steil, John 53
Stein, Jock 36
Steinberg, Charles 196
Stimson, E.C. 16
Stoddard, E. 16
Stoneham, Charles A. 205
Stumpf, Jacob 129, 185, 210, 223
Sullivan, D.A. 141
Sullivan, Father Francis 184
Sullivan, Jack "Montana Jack" 141
Sullivan, James E. 2, 9, 12, 47, 58, 60, 61, 65, 68, 75, 77, 95, 97–98, 101, 102, 108, 109, 111, 115, 117, 119, 121, 122, 123, 124, 125, 126–127, 130, 132, 138, 143, 149, 156,

Index 295

174, 175, 182, 183, 186, 193, 215, 218, 269n15
Sullivan, James P. 85, 86, 87, 113, 155, 269n16, 270n55
Sullivan, John L. 70
Sullivan, Joseph P. 122
Sullivan, Michael 30, 109
Sullivan, Timothy, "Big"/"Dry Dollar" 40, 92, 109, 155, 195
Sullivan, William 164
Surrey Athletic Club 181
Svanberg, John 181
Sweden 150, 208
Swedish-American Athletic Club 248
Sweeney, Michael 116, 147
Syracuse University 39, 84, 200

Tailteann Games 4, 45, 61, 63, 67, 77, 85, 148, 165–166, 167, 173, 177, 255
Talbott, Lee 142, 148, 151, 175, 222, 269n16, 270n55
Tammany Hall 14, 37, 40, 109, 151, 159, 160, 161, 192, 193, 195, 196, 197, 198, 199, 200, 250
Taylor, Allen 13
Taylor, John Baxter 47–50, 84, 97, 110, 111, 113, 116, 138, 142, 149, 150, 151, 168, 250
Taylor, William H. 225, 231
Teeven, J.H. 46
Telltown, near Kells, Meath 165
Ten mile race 109, 113, 218
Ten mile relay race 61
10,000 meter race 254
Tener, John K. 182
Thomas F. Meaghers Hurling Club 51, 54, 57, 62, 202
Thompson Hill Taxpayers Association 242
Thorpe, James 207, 209
Three-fourths mile race 212
Three mile cross country race 250
Three mile race 16, 44, 52, 54, 55, 78, 81, 84, 85, 108, 110, 111, 122, 147, 181, 206, 213, 214, 254
Three mile walk race 114
Tipperary 20, 22, 48, 68, 72, 138, 187; County Tipperary Men's Association 61, 129, 210
Tolan, Eddie 118
Toronto, Canada 90, 191, 208
Towne, Charles A. 161
Trade unions 13, 21; Brewery Employees Association 54; Bricklayers and Masons' Union 171, 181; Central Labor Union 61; Eccentric and Standard Engineers' Association 54, 77, 105, 129, 154, 176,
209, 213, 237; Grocery Clerks' Union 56; International Union of Steam and Operating Engineers 239; Journeymen Horseshoers' Union 61
Travers Island, New York City 50, 67, 78, 93, 96, 105, 106, 107, 108, 111, 143, 163, 171, 177, 210, 221, 248
Trinity Athletic Club 204
Troy 90, 224
Tsiklitiras, Konstantinos 147
Tug of War 16, 54, 75, 77, 148, 162, 269n16
Turn Verein 18
Turner, George Kibbe 159
200 meters hurdles race 254
200 meters race 5, 149
220 yards hurdles race 105, 108, 113, 168, 169, 174, 179, 182, 210, 227, 232
220 yards race 5, 43, 52, 63, 74, 78, 85, 106, 111, 132, 168, 174, 177, 180, 181, 182, 186, 210, 213, 218, 221, 249, 253
Two mile race 5, 17, 55, 114, 179, 208, 215
Two mile relay race 60, 110, 116, 177
Two mile steeplechase race 107
Two mile walk race 217
Two-thirds mile race 174, 176

Union Bicycle Club 18
Union Boat Club 193
Union Settlement Athletic Club 53, 68
United Affiliated Building Trades 220
United Irish-American Societies of New York (UIAS) 78, 108, 159
United Kingdom (Great Britain) 58, 71, 75, 91, 97, 137, 143, 144, 160, 161, 162, 172, 242; British Army 216; England 17, 80, 161, 162, 180, 181; Scotland 36, 39, 72, 217, 255
United Scottish Clans 171
United States, President of: Cleveland, Grover 143; McKinley, William 54; Roosevelt, Teddy 74, 101, 152, 155, 156, Wilson, Woodrow 160, 161, 237
United States Army 4, 13, 17, 28, 131, 132, 134, 152, 230, 236, 277n18; Battery D Regiment 212; 1st Regiment, Pennsylvania National Guards 114, 117; 5th U.S. Artillery 58; 7th Regiment 181, 206; 8th Regiment Company G. 71; 13th Regiment 103, 108, 211, 215, 217, 220; 14th Infantry Regiment 134, 220; 22nd Corps Engineers 225; 22nd Regiment 115, 170, 134, 181, 211, 231; 23rd Regiment 108; 47th Regiment 170; 69th Regiment 28, 53, 194; 71st Regiment 133, 224; 74th Regiment 110, 131
United States Marshal 196

University Athletic Club 92
University of Chicago 63
University of Michigan 13, 175
University of Notre Dame 1, 249
University of Pennsylvania 43, 47, 48, 55, 58, 60, 84, 110, 113, 115, 116, 117, 200, 215, 225, 226
Utica, NY 83

Valentine, Drew 208
Valentine, Howard/HV 111, 141
Vanderbilt, Cornelius 244
Van Duyn, Cornelius 105, 123
Victorians 10, 94
Vietnam War 250
Villanova University 249
Volstead Act (Prohibition) 4, 14, 200, 237, 240, 247
von Eckardt, Heinrich 230
von Reichman, Walter 213

Wallace, Dana 241
Walsh, Andy 87
Walsh, Con 70, 71, 111, 132, 162, 174, 212
Walsh, John J. 113
Walsh, Patrick J. 58, 94, 127, 184, 185
Wanamaker's New York Department Store 216
Washington, George 144, 146
Washington, D.C. 47, 54, 139
Weeks, Bartow Sumter 104, 128, 140, 196
Wefers, Bernie 110, 111, 117
Weights: 28LB 83; 35LB 212, 213, 221, 235, 256; 42LB Stone 213; 56LB 5, 15, 52, 53, 54, 57, 62, 63, 69, 74, 77, 78, 79, 85, 86, 101, 105, 106, 108, 111, 113, 116, 168, 170, 172, 174, 176, 177, 182, 186, 190, 210, 211, 212, 213, 217, 218, 220, 222, 223, 227, 232, 235, 255
Wellington, Aleck 135
Wells, Mat 34

West Side YMCA Athletic Club 53, 171
White Star Line 44, 75, 104, 153
Whitman, Charles S. 199
Whitney, Casper 130
Whitney, Lawrence 209
Whitten, Dick 135
Wilson, Harold Allan 39, 44, 45, 146, 173, 174, 175, 208
Wolf, Major Charles J. 131
Wolfe Tones Gaelic Football Club 58
Wolff, Daniel, Yonkers Police Department 32
Woodward, Kenneth L. 249
Worcester Shamrocks Gaelic Football Club, Worcester, MA 53
World Series 40, 205
World War I 4, 160, 205, 215, 230, 249, 277n18
World War II 237
World's Fair Exposition 54, 75, 76, 82, 173

Xavier Athletic Association/Xavier Athletic Club 52, 53, 62, 83, 87, 105, 107, 175

Yale 48, 50, 54, 60, 84, 105, 128
Yancey, Joe, Jr. 249
Yankee Prince 154
YMCA 42, 152; Central YMCA 124; Paterson 213; Syracuse 40; Yonkers 218
Yonkers, NY 31–32, 60, 138, 169, 195, 200, 212, 214, 218
Young, Ralph 43, 105, 106, 270n55
Young Irelands Gaelic Football Club, Worcester 57
Young Irelands Gaelic Football Club, NY 54, 58, 60
Young Mens' Hebrew Association 39

Zimmerman, Arthur 230
Zink, A. 112
Zuna, Frank 218